THE COLLECTED COURSES OF
THE ACADEMY OF EUROPEAN LAW

VOLUME XXXIII/1

The Legitimacy of EU Environmental Governance and the Role of the European Courts

THE COLLECTED COURSES OF THE ACADEMY OF EUROPEAN LAW

Edited by: Professor Arnulf Becker Lorca, Professor Gráinne de Búrca, Professor Sarah Nouwen, and Professor Joanne Scott

Assistant Editor: Joyce Davies

The Academy of European Law is housed at the European University Institute in Florence, Italy. The Academy holds annual advanced-level summer courses focusing on topical, cutting-edge issues in Human Rights Law and The Law of the European Union. The courses are taught by highly qualified scholars and practitioners in a highly interactive environment. General courses involve the examination of the field as a whole through a particular thematic, conceptual, or philosophical lens or look at a theme in the context of the overall body of law. Specialized courses bring together a number of speakers exploring a specific theme in depth. Together, they are published as monographs and edited volumes in the Collected Courses of the Academy of European Law series. The Collected Courses series has been published by Oxford University Press since 2000. The series contains publications on both foundational and pressing issues in human rights law and the law of the European Union.

OTHER TITLES IN THE SERIES INCLUDE:

Global Rights?
Human Rights in Complex Governance
Edited by Nehal Bhuta and Rodrigo Vallejo

New Frontiers of EU Funding
Law, Policy, Politics
Edited by Claire Kilpatrick and Joanne Scott

Human Rights in Transition
Edited by Nehal Bhuta

The Emergence of European Society through Public Law
A Hegelian and Anti-Schmittian Approach
Armin von Bogdandy

Revisiting the Fundamentals of the Free Movement of Persons in EU Law
Edited by Niamh Nic Shuibhne

Data at the Boundaries of European Law
Edited by Deirdre Curtin and Mariavittoria Catanzariti

Legal Mobilization for Human Rights
Edited by Gráinne de Búrca

The UK's Withdrawal from the EU
A Legal Analysis
Michael Dougan

Justifying Contract in Europe
Political Philosophies of European Contract Law
Martijn W. Hesselink

Contemporary Challenges to EU Legality
Edited by Claire Kilpatrick and Joanne Scott

The Legitimacy of EU Environmental Governance and the Role of the European Courts

Edited by

MARIOLINA ELIANTONIO
EMMA LEES

OXFORD
UNIVERSITY PRESS

OXFORD
UNIVERSITY PRESS

Great Clarendon Street, Oxford, OX2 6DP,
United Kingdom

Oxford University Press is a department of the University of Oxford. It furthers the University's objective of excellence in research, scholarship, and education by publishing worldwide. Oxford is a registered trade mark of Oxford University Press in the UK and in certain other countries.

Published in the United States of America by Oxford University Press
198 Madison Avenue, New York, NY 10016, United States of America.

British Library Cataloguing in Publication Data
Data available

Library of Congress Control Number: 2025933449

ISBN 978–0–19–897280–8

DOI: 10.1093/oso/9780198972808.001.0001

Printed and bound by
CPI Group (UK) Ltd., Croydon, CR0 4YY

MIX
Paper | Supporting responsible forestry
FSC® C013604
FSC www.fsc.org

The manufacturer's authorised representative in the EU for product safety is Oxford University Press España S.A., Parque Empresarial San Fernando de Henares, Avenida de Castilla, 2 – 28830 Madrid (www.oup.es/en or product.safety@oup.com). OUP España S.A. also acts as importer into Spain of products made by the manufacturer.

Contents

Notes on Contributors

Nicolas de Sadeleer is full professor in UCLouvain, Saint-Louis and holds a Jean Monnet Chair on deforestation and forest degradation. He is a specialist of EU law (institutions, internal market), environmental law (international and domestic), and comparative law. He is an active commentator on EU legal and political issues in the areas of trade, investment, and sustainable development. In addition to holding guest academic positions at over forty universities around the world, he has been the recipient of six international university chairs. His research has been published with leading scholarly publishing houses and journals around the globe.

Mariolina Eliantonio is Professor of European and Comparative Administrative Law and Procedure at Maastricht University. Her research focuses on the role of EU and national courts in the process of European integration. She particularly studies soft law, technical standardization, and multi-level administrative cooperation in the European Union, as well as access to justice and procedural rights in environmental governance. She was the organizer of the 2022 edition of the Academy of European Law Summer School of The Law of the European Union at the European University Institute, and she has held visiting positions in several universities. She teaches courses in European and comparative administrative law.

George Iordachescu is a senior researcher working in the Forest and Nature Conservation Policy Group at Wageningen University, where he leads the ERC-funded project 'GreenFrontier: Politics of Conservation and Unequal Ecological Exchange in the European Peripheries'. He has a background in social anthropology, and his work spans across political ecology, human geography, and green criminology. His research interests include the governance of nature protection, environmental crime, and environmental politics in the EU. His previous research at the University of Sheffield looked at the hidden dynamics of illegal wildlife trade in European species as part of the ESRC-funded 'Beastly Business' project, and at the impact of EU regulations on the criminalization and securitization of illegal logging in the Carpathian Mountains as part of the ERC-funded 'BIOSEC' project.

Michał Krajewski is an inquiries officer at the Office of the European Ombudsman in Brussels. Previously, he worked as an Assistant Professor at Maastricht University and as a Postdoctoral Research Fellow at the University of Copenhagen. He holds a doctoral degree in law from the European University Institute. His academic research concerns the institutional, procedural, and epistemic assets and limitations of courts in reviewing the legality of EU administrative action, especially when administrative action is underpinned by complex and uncertain knowledge, and the added value of extra-judicial bodies, such as boards of appeal and the European Ombudsman.

Emma Lees is Professor of Environmental and Property Law, University of Cambridge and a Fellow of Downing College. From 2021 to 2024, she was on special leave at the European University Institute as Professor of Transnational Law. Professor Lees' research focuses on all aspects of national and European environmental law, but has a particular focus on land use controls and biodiversity protection rules. She also has a broad research interest in land law and landlord and tenant law.

Danai Petropoulou Ionescu is a PhD Candidate in EU Administrative Law and Governance based at the Department of Public Law and the Department of Political Science at Maastricht University. Her research addresses questions of democracy, legitimacy, and administrative governance at the EU level. Her work particularly focuses on soft governance practices and mechanisms at the EU level—for instance, in terms of participation and transparency.

Luca Prete is référendaire in the chambers of Advocate General Emiliou at the European Court of Justice, after also serving in the chambers of Advocates General Bobek and Wahl, and Judge Tizzano. Previously, he worked in the European Commission, in the Legal Service, and in DG Competition. Prior to this, he was an associate in the Brussels office of Skadden Arps. Mr Prete regularly publishes and lectures on various aspects of EU law, with an emphasis on institutional matters, legal remedies, competition law, the internal market, and external relations. Mr Prete is a qualified Italian lawyer. He holds a law degree from the University of Bologna, an LLM from the College of Europe in Bruges, and a PhD from the Vrije Universitetit Brussel.

Gerd Winter is Professor Emeritus of Public Law at the Law Department of the University of Bremen. He studied law and legal sociology. He has held a visiting position at Yale University. His teaching and research focus on administrative law, EU institutional law, environmental law in a comparative and multi-level perspective, and the sociology of public law. He has frequently acted as counsel in environmental law litigation at the national and EU levels. He has been a consultant in administrative and environmental law reforms in a number of transition states, with a focus on Georgia.

1

Legitimacy

What's in a Name?

Mariolina Eliantonio, Michał Krajewski, and Emma Lees*

1. Introduction

While, intuitively, the notion of legitimacy is linked to those of 'power', 'rule', and 'authority', understandings of the concept change depending on the 'vantage points' from which it is observed. Certainly, it cannot be (usefully) defined in the abstract. Instead, in this introductory chapter we pursue a less ambitious, although still challenging, goal: to explain the different ways in which the operation of the European and national courts, along with some EU quasi-judicial bodies,[1] might contribute to the legitimacy of EU environmental governance as a whole. We argue that such courts can do so to the extent that they move towards the following aspects, explained in more detail in the sections which follow: first, they operate in a way that enables them to hold other actors in the governance system to account; second, the courts have the capacity or skills to perform this function successfully both in procedural terms and in the way they approach their reasoning; third, they comply with certain process values in making their decisions; and, finally, the outcomes of their decisions achieve certain substantive goals. In the latter case, these substantive goals include both goals of certainty and predictability in the law as well as environmental protection. Each of these aspects exists on a spectrum so that the more one is fulfilled, the more a court is enabled to contribute to the legitimacy of the system on which it adjudicates. In creating this framework, however, we acknowledge that it must be sensitive to the context within which the courts

* This chapters reflects my personal views only and cannot be attributed to the European Ombudsman.

[1] That is, the Court of Justice and the General Court of the EU (the EU Courts) and also national courts in the EU and the European Court of Human Rights, as well as some quasi-judicial EU bodies, such as boards of appeal set up in certain EU agencies.

Mariolina Eliantonio, Michał Krajewski, and Emma Lees, *Legitimacy* In: *The Legitimacy of EU Environmental Governance and the Role of the European Courts*. Edited by: Mariolina Eliantonio and Emma Lees, Oxford University Press.
DOI: 10.1093/oso/9780198972808.003.0001

operate. In some cases, the aspects within the framework may pull in opposing directions.

Legitimacy is, as a starting point, a political concept. It refers to the reasons for which the exercises of authority in a given political structure are rationally justifiable towards those subjected to this authority. However, legitimacy can be judged only within the context of specific political actions and processes and not in the abstract. These arenas are shaped by exogenous factors and, as such, the precise content of the concept will flex according to the context within which power is exercised. The goal of this chapter, therefore, is to present a framework for legitimacy in a zoomed-out form, before focusing on the specific arena of EU environmental law, to emphasize both the concept's malleability and the ways in which it is rendered specific in the particular context of environmental law and adjudication. Our contribution can be read, then, not as a *definition* of legitimacy as a political concept but as a framework to organize and operationalize the different aspects of legitimacy and how they play out in respect of environmental litigation.

In the sections which follow, we explain this framework further and note where the different chapters of this volume find themselves within it. First, we consider the function of the courts within governance processes as a whole. The political dimensions of legitimacy are intimately connected with the democratic state and its operation and, as such, we explain how courts—somewhat divorced as they are from direct political accountability in the form of electoral processes—can nevertheless contribute to the legitimacy of the governance system as a whole by holding others to account.

Second, we explain that the capacity of any institution, the courts included, to increase or to undermine the legitimacy of the governance processes to which they contribute is dependent upon its capacity to discharge the function attributed to it. Courts will therefore contribute more fully to the legitimacy of the system to the extent that they are able to perform the judicial function, thanks to their institutional and procedural features, such as independence, adequate expertise, appropriate procedural framework involving affected parties, and allowing for fact-finding and exchanges of legal arguments, among other things. This is not only a question of formal or procedural 'assets' within the court system but also concerns the ways in which the courts reason and express themselves. In environmental law, as we shall see, this can be particularly challenging thanks to the specific features of the environment as an object of law which push the boundaries of what courts are typically well-equipped to do.

Third, we consider the processes that must be followed by courts to enhance the legitimacy of the system as a whole. This third aspect is linked to the main process values of judicial decision-making. In cases where courts do not meet these process values, their decisions will contribute less successfully to the legitimacy of the governance system on which they are called to adjudicate. These values include equality of access, fair hearings, and matters such as standing and costs rules.

Fourth, considering the courts' ability to make legally and factually 'correct' decisions, we consider the outcomes of judicial decisions and how these outcomes can contribute to the legitimacy of the governance system. In particular, we examine the consequences of such decisions for the environment and how those consequences form part of our legitimacy assessment as well as looking at the other systemic consequences of outcomes of litigation, including increased certainty and predictability in the law.

2. Two Preliminary Remarks: Legitimacy as a Spectrum and the Role of Courts as 'Legitimacy-Enhancing' Actors

In the following sections, we explain the four aspects of legitimacy that we explore in this volume. Before doing so, however, it is first necessary to emphasize that while discussions around legitimacy are sometimes premised on a distinction between the legitimate and the illegitimate, in reality this is more often a question of the spectrum between the *more* and *less* legitimate. When we consider the interplay between the various aspects of legitimacy, to reach a definitive conclusion that a specific act or actor is or is not legitimate is unlikely to account for the complexity of the relationships between actors in the modern administrative state, especially in the context of polycentric environmental problems. What we say in this chapter is, as a result, designed to be a way of situating discussions of particular aspects of EU environmental governance within the broad conceptual frame that is 'legitimacy'. We do not mean to imply by it that assessments of legitimacy are a 'tick-box' exercise, far from it. Rather, we use these aspects, as explained earlier, as an organizational tool to situate specific arguments about the role of the courts in EU environmental governance within a framework that gives some concrete meaning to the concept of legitimacy.

It is also important to note here that, at its most basic level, the notion of legitimacy stems from the Weberian conception that 'the basis of every system of authority, and correspondingly of every kind of willingness to obey, is a belief, a belief by virtue of which persons exercising authority are lent prestige'.[2] In other words, legitimacy is ultimately a factor of the degree to which citizens believe that political authority deserves to be obeyed. If we move from a descriptive to a more normative notion of legitimacy (when is political authority being appropriately exercised so that it *deserves* to be obeyed?),[3] the need for benchmarks of acceptability or justification of political power or authority become relevant. This is because legitimacy stems from the manner in which political power is exercised and grounds political authority and, as such, legitimacy standards both justify, and in some cases can constrain, the exercise of political power.[4]

In contemporary political philosophy, these benchmarks are typically associated with the democratic processes through which political authority is exercised. From this perspective, democratic forms of political organization, and in particular democratic processes, are deemed necessary for political legitimacy.[5] Habermas in particular argued that people's participation in the deliberations is necessary for political legitimacy. However, in his view, democratic decisions gain legitimacy thanks to both the deliberative quality of the procedures in which they have been made and their substantive quality[6] and this is where courts can enter the picture as *part of* the democratic process. In considering normative explanations of when authority deserves to be respected, therefore, courts play an important role in modern governance systems even though their authority is not directly a result of the electoral process at play. This means that we must develop an approach to legitimacy that is specifically related to the courts' actions.

With these two points in mind—first, that the aspects of legitimacy discussed here exist on a spectrum and, second that the 'tests' for the contribution of courts to the legitimacy of governance systems will be distinctively different from other players within the political arena—we can proceed to explore our framework in more detail.

[2] M. Weber, *The Theory of Social and Economic Organization*, trs A. M. Henderson and T. Parsons (1964) 382.

[3] D. Beetham, *The Legitimation of Power* (2nd edn, 2013).

[4] Buchanan, 'Political Legitimacy and Democracy', 112 *Ethics* (2002) 689.

[5] Ibid.

[6] J. Habermas, *Between Facts and Norms*, tr. W. Rehg (1996) 304.

3. First Aspect: The Function of the Judiciary in Governance Processes as a Whole

The first aspect within our organizing framework emerges from the fact that governance is an expression of the exercise of political power. The fact that power is exercised *through* governance processes makes the function of those processes critical to the legitimacy of the system as a whole. Different governance processes—voting in parliament, deliberating in court—have different functions and those subject to power participate in these in different ways. Scharpf and, later on, Schmidt have characterized this as the 'input', 'throughput', and 'output' sides of political legitimacy.[7] This conception of legitimacy (and its link to the democratic process) brings together the notion of liberal democracy, which attaches importance to principles such as accountability or rule of law,[8] and the deliberative conception of democracy, which instead sees legitimacy as being more related to principles such as transparency and the deliberative quality of the rules that govern a society by recognizing that processes can contribute in different ways to the legitimacy of the system as a whole.[9]

Scharpf identifies two interdependent strands of democratic thinking in the history of political thought—one focused on 'governing *by* the people' and the other 'governing *for* the people'.[10] With 'input' legitimacy, Scharf refers to the need for mechanisms binding political decisions with citizens' preferences. The function of these mechanisms is to ensure that citizens' preferences are inputted into exercises of power. These mechanisms usually take the form of representative institutions enabling the democratic accountability of political decision-makers by the means of elections or other moments of interest expression, as well the accountability of decisions through (quasi-)judicial control. On the other hand, Scharpf argues, 'democracy would be an empty ritual' if the democratic mechanisms were not able to produce 'a high degree of effectiveness in achieving the goals, and avoiding the dangers, that the citizens collectively care about'.[11] Output

[7] F. Scharpf, *Governing in Europe, Effective and Democratic?* (1999); Schmidt, 'Democracy and Legitimacy in the European Union Revisited: Input, Output and "Throughput"', 61 *Political Studies* (2013) 2.

[8] For an analysis of the liberal conception of democracy and democratic legitimacy, see H. Addink, *Good Governance: Concept and Context* (2019) and K. Goldmann, *Transforming the European Nation-State: Dynamics of Internationalization* (2001).

[9] Further on the deliberative conception of democratic legitimacy, see J. Parkinson, *Deliberating in the Real World: Problems of Legitimacy in Deliberative Democracy* (2006).

[10] Scharpf (n. 7) 6.

[11] Scharpf, 'Economic Integration, Democracy and the Welfare State', 4 *Journal of European Public Policy* (1997) 18, at 19.

legitimacy refers thus to the capacity of governance structures to efficiently and effectively 'solve problems requiring collective solutions'.[12]

Going beyond this input/output dichotomy, however, Schmidt later added a third dimension to assess legitimacy, that of 'throughput'.[13] This focuses on the *governance process* in itself and specifically on its accountability and transparency credentials.

Because the focus of this volume is environmental adjudication (and, therefore, an accountability mechanism in the broader governance frame), it is the aspect of throughput legitimacy that takes us one step further on our journey. We are looking at one actor within the governance processes—courts—to see how their contribution operates as part of the wider whole. In the next section, we therefore focus on how courts, in performing this accountability function, contribute to the legitimacy of the governance structures as a whole. Courts, as governance actors, (can) vest governance structures with legitimacy. In short, the governance system as a whole will be rendered more or less legitimate to the extent to which courts are able and willing to perform their function of holding those who exercise power to account.

Before moving on to the second aspect, however, it is useful to pause here to reflect on how and why this function of holding to account can be difficult in the context of environmental problems. As is well known, the role of courts is both to allocate winners and losers in any particular situation and to generate rules of general application.[14] But the role of the court in relation to the environment also tends to achieve more than these two outcomes in ways relevant to their function of holding to account. First, they allocate power. The judge has the ability to permanently shift the locus of power for decision-making within the political system. For example, when a judge determines the relationship between a central authority and a local decision-maker (holding one or the other to account), they also shift the relationship between the citizenry and the decision which is made. In environmental cases, this dislocation can be particularly acute.

Second, courts determine the kinds of reasons that are 'accepted' within the system as being reasons for a particular outcome. Here, we could consider the example of cultural reasons specific to a local group which are not shared by the citizenry as a whole. If these reasons are deemed irrelevant, the outcome of

[12] Scharpf (n. 7) 11.
[13] Schmidt (n. 7).
[14] E. Lees and O. W. Pedersen, *Environmental Adjudication* (2020) ch. 1.

the litigation is important not only for the substantive outcome but also for the place of the marginalized group in the system.

Finally, through remedial discretion, courts also determine how a breach of the rules of the system is translated into remedial action. Strong, action-orientated remedies in relation to the environment may be more powerful than a large fine and very minimal remedies may render a 'victory' illusory. Each of these functions may be judged differently when thinking about what is or is not a legitimate use of political power.[15] As a result, in the 'holding-to-account' function of courts, these may hold to account both by removing or according power over certain questions, and by constraining the kinds of reasons which can be relied upon in reaching a particular decision.

Winter's contribution in this volume emphasizes the holding to account aspects of the judicial function in European courts by focusing on the question of fundamental rights and how such rights constrain administrative and legislative action in relation to the environment. In this case, the mechanics of fundamental rights adjudication become the means by which the courts can strengthen their ability to 'police' environmental protection where their ability to do so might have otherwise been limited. Similarly, by examining remedial approaches and the question of standing, Prete reveals the ways in which the courts can limit who is able to access the courts to hold other actors to account and, indirectly, what the 'end result' of such an accountability process might be. These two chapters therefore reveal the contours of this 'holding-to-account' function.

4. Second Aspect: Exercise of Capacity

The second aspect of legitimacy lies in the 'capacity' of the adjudicator. For an institutional exercise of power to contribute to the legitimacy of a governance system, the institution making decisions must exercise its capacity to make appropriate decisions based on sound reasoning (rather than blind luck, for example). When a court performs its function of holding to account, it must have the tools to do this successfully if it is to contribute to the legitimacy of the system on which it adjudicates. In relation to environmental problems, the tools needed are different from those needed to adjudicate successfully in relation to, for example, immigration or competition law.

[15] Ibid. chs 5–7.

Warnock argues that for an institution such as a court to be a legitimate decision-maker (and, in our framework, to consequently contribute to the legitimacy of the environmental governance system) in the context of environmental law, it must first be capable of understanding and reasoning about the problem it faces.[16] Courts which rely on guessing are not contributing to the legitimacy of the system, even if the outcome is 'correct'. A court has to be more than a successful decision-maker in terms of reaching the 'right' outcome: it needs to do so, as it were, for the right reasons.[17] To discover those reasons, it must have the institutional capacity to deal with the complexity of the problem before it. When we consider environmental problems, we can see that they share (in many cases) a number of important features that can create distinct challenges for courts. They are polycentric; often there is incomplete and complex information; and the stakes can also be very high.

How to operationalize this notion of 'capacity' in our context? Warnock posits that legitimacy in such a process emerges from the interaction between four factors:

> (1) identifying the distinct characteristics of environmental problems; (2) acknowledging the commensurate challenges for law and dispute resolution that this nature poses; (3) developing environmental law principles, procedures and remedies that respond to rather than ignoring that nature; and (4) understanding how each of the preceding developments will be facilitated by particular adjudicative forms, functions and powers.[18]

The more a court is able to achieve these four objectives—that is, the more fully it exercises its capacity—the more it is able to perform its function of holding to account and, therefore, to contribute to the legitimacy of the governance system. This recognition of the importance of capacity requires a clear-sighted view of the specific nature of environmental problems and existing governance networks.

As a starting point, EU environmental judicial processes contribute more or less to the legitimacy of EU environmental governance if the courts are well-equipped to handle the challenges which emerge from the distinct characteristics of environmental problems. We can see attempts to find 'tools' to deal with these distinct problems in the chapters that follow. However, it seems that the

[16] C. Warnock, *Environmental Courts and Tribunals* (2020) 93 and 115.

[17] Fuller and Winston, 'The Forms and Limits of Adjudication', 92 *Harvard Law Review* (1789) 353, at 366–367. See also Lees and Pedersen (n. 14) 14–16.

[18] Warnock (n. 16) 200.

most obvious aspect of legitimacy as capacity, apart from judicial independence, is that courts possess or have access to adequate legal and extra-legal knowledge, including possibly specialist knowledge to some degree, to conceive of different ways in which law can engage with contemporary environmental issues. A legitimacy-producing capacity is largely based on epistemic capacity, which implies the need for knowledge about law and science alike.

Achieving such capacity is problematic. Science, especially regulatory science, rarely provides the 'single right answer' to a complex question. The uncertainty and inconclusiveness of empirical data may be so acute that courts will have great difficulties in achieving the usually required standard of 'rationality' in their decision-making.[19] For example, the complexity and uncertainty of scientific information involved in environmental litigation affects the ways in which courts must reason about that evidence and the ways in which they can rely on external experts.

Courts may try to handle scientific complexity and uncertainty by applying several strategies. They may verify the qualifications of experts involved in producing a scientific opinion; the predominant view in the scientific community; the methodological soundness of the scientific opinion; or whether it has been published in a peer review outlet.[20] They may also scrutinize at least the intelligibility of scientific opinions[21] or even engage in verifying certain aspects of substantive scientific assessments.[22] However, by engaging with the substance of scientific assertions, even in a limited fashion, at the least judicial review courts risk imposing their own standards of causality, probability, and proof on the expert administration or policymakers, thereby questioning the precautionary approach to the management of uncertain risks.[23] Their judicial capacity to handle these issues is critical to the legitimacy of the governance system as a whole.

[19] N. De Sadeleer, *Environmental Principles—From Political Slogans to Legal Rules* (2002).

[20] Ky, 'Qualifications, Weight of Opinion, Peer Review and Methodology: A Framework for Understanding the Evaluation of Science in Merits Review', 24 *Journal of Environmental Law* (2012) 207.

[21] Eliantonio and Krajewski, 'Scientific Uncertainty before the Court of Justice and the General Court: Is the Judicial Toolbox Sufficient?', in M. Eliantonio, E. Lees, and T. Paloniitty (eds), *EU Environmental Principles and Scientific Uncertainty before National Courts—The Case of the Habitats Directive* (2023) 327.

[22] K. Sulyok, *Science and Judicial Reasoning: The Legitimacy of International Environmental Adjudication* (2020).

[23] Vos, 'The European Court of Justice in the Face of Scientific Uncertainty and Complexity', in M. Dawson, B. de Witte, and E. Muir (eds), *Judicial Activism at the European Court of Justice* (2013) 161. See also Janssen and Rosenstock, 'Handling Uncertain Risks: An Inconsistent Application of Standards?', 7 *European Journal of Risk Regulation* (2016) 144.

Similarly, the often vague and discretionary terms in which environmental regulations are couched will mean that the process of interpretation is perhaps more challenging than in other spheres, shining a light on ways in which the judiciary approach this task. The 'capacity' of the judiciary to perform this difficult interpretation role depends upon the 'assets'[24] of courts, that is, their specific institutional and procedural features and their functioning in practice. Apart from the basic standards of judicial independence, these assets encompass whether the judges possess or can gain access to relevant expertise (through judicial specialization or the ability to engage with opinions delivered by partisan or court-appointed experts); whether the judicial proceedings are accessible to representatives of the relevant private and public interests resulting in judicial sensitivity to various perspectives on the matter; whether the judicial proceedings provide for participation rights for interested parties within the judicial process resulting in a meaningful exchange of reasoned arguments; whether the judicial proceedings are not overly formalistic allowing the judges to proactively determine the applicable law and seek the empirical truth; as well as whether the judicial remedies are adequate.

From this, we can conclude that capacity is not only a technical question about an individual judge's ability to read and handle scientific information. It is a more systemic question about the tools available to courts to perform their roles relating to evidence, interpretation, and remedies in a way which properly accounts for the nature of the problem before them and then, crucially, when and whether the courts take advantage of these assets in order to properly address the problem before them.

A number of the chapters in this volume are concerned with capacity and the judicial techniques employed to overcome the challenges of environmental adjudication. For example, Iordachescu and Krajewski analyse how generalist courts, not possessing direct access to specialist scientific knowledge, handle cases involving scientific complexity and uncertainty, and how they delineate their engagement with scientific issues in their rulings. Similarly, Lees as well as Eliantonio and Petropoulou Ionescu, argue that one important function of the environmental principles and of soft law measures in the European courts is to overcome capacity limitations by providing the courts with the tools to overcome their lack of specialist knowledge. These chapters examine whether and to what extent courts fully exercise the capacity they have in ways which enhance the overall legitimacy of the EU governance framework.

[24] Mendes and Venzke, 'The Idea of Relative Authority in European and International Law', 16 *International Journal of Constitutional Law* (2018) 75.

5. Third Aspect: Process Values

Our third aspect relates to the procedural approach followed by a court in performing its accountability function. First, as noted by Hovell, regardless of the specific formulation of the notion of legitimacy,[25] it 'envisages a connection between decision-making authority and community values sufficient to ground acceptance of that authority in the relevant community'.[26] Legal processes can forge this connection.[27] They will do so when the process which the court follows is a robust one. Of course, it is not possible to entirely separate process from outcome. Different visions of the legal process presuppose different visions of substantive law and its ability to constrain and orient the exercise of public power.[28] However, because of the accountability function of courts, particularly salient questions about legitimacy concern the judicial process and especially that of the judicial review of decisions adopted by political or administrative bodies. Before we consider how the outcomes of those processes contribute to the legitimacy of the environmental governance system as a whole, therefore, it is important to pause to consider the process itself.

As a starting point, it should be noted that different values may be the centre of attention when we consider judicial processes. Some emphasize individual dignity within those processes,[29] whereas others focus on the importance of public deliberation which includes deliberation in the judicial fora.[30] What unites such process-focused accounts, however, is the need to follow the 'right' process, emphasizing such elements as its inclusivity, the possibility for open and reasoned exchanges (albeit modulated by the particularities of judicial hearings), and the equality of voice of all participants. These accounts can presuppose a vision of law as a deliberative undertaking, bereft of predetermined content, only providing arguments and means through which the participants in the public deliberation may advance and justify their normative

[25] Take, e.g., Beetham's requirement that decision-making authority should find its foundation in 'beliefs shared by both dominant and subordinate'. Beetham (n. 3).

[26] D. Hovell, *The Power of Process: The Value of Due Process in Security Council Sanctions Decision-Making* (2016) 6.

[27] Ibid. 62.

[28] Ibid. 63.

[29] Mashaw, 'Administrative Due Process: The Quest for a Dignitary Theory', 61 *Boston University Law Review* (1981) 885; Saphire, 'Specifying Due Process Values: Towards a More Responsive Approach to Procedural Protection', 127 *University of Pennsylvania Law Review* (1978) 111.

[30] Steele, 'Participation and Deliberation in Environmental Law: Exploring a Problem-Solving Approach', 21 *Oxford Journal of Legal Studies* (2001) 415.

propositions.[31] This model corresponds to the Rawlsian idea of *pure* procedural justice which presupposes no substantive criteria for the correctness of outcomes and conceives of procedural justice as a value in and of itself. Following the 'right' procedure, in this view, is sufficient for legitimacy.[32] However, it is not necessary to subscribe to a purely 'process-oriented' account to see the value in robust processes. Thus, we can also emphasize the need for access to the legal process to voice a grievance, engage in reasoned exchange of arguments, induce a genuine consideration of these arguments,[33] as well as the transformation of preferences of the parties during the process.[34]

Importantly, when we turn to look at environmental governance specifically, the value of process may shift somewhat from pure procedural accounts to ones in which procedure is, first and foremost, an instrument maximizing the chances for a correct outcome. Purely procedural thinking about judicial process tends to emerge in writings concerned with constitutional review of legislation, a very specific form of legal process, which is evidently based on particularly open-ended and controversial constitutional standards, in which it is difficult to even conceive of substantive benchmarks of 'correct' outcomes.[35] Nonetheless, these lessons from pure procedural thinking, for instance the one emphasizing the legitimizing potential of democratic deliberation, can also be employed when we turn to think about the environment. The insights offered within these deliberative constitutional accounts could be employed to justify the increasing judicial engagement with human rights to a healthy natural environment (see Winter's chapter) and also complex data about the state of the environment and climate catastrophe and the ensuing judicial scrutiny of laws and policies in this light.[36] In cases where the stakes are high and the substantive law is particularly open-ended, the deliberation-enhancing process becomes even more significant, as with environmental rights jurisprudence. This pushes towards, for example, flexible rules of evidence affecting who is able to speak in court to encourage deliberation.

[31] Habermas (n. 6) 209. With regard to EU environmental law, Fisher, 'Unpacking the Toolbox: Or Why the Public/Private Divide is Important in EC Environmental Law', in M. Freedland and J. Auby (eds), *The Public Law/Private Law Divide: Une entente assez cordiale?* (2006) 215.

[32] Solum, 'Procedural Justice', 78 *Southern California Law Review* (2004) 181.

[33] Harel and Shinar, 'Between Judicial and Legislative Supremacy: A Cautious Defense of Constrained Judicial Review', 10 *International Journal of Constitutional Law* (2012) 950.

[34] C. H. Mendes, *Constitutional Courts and Deliberative Democracy* (2013).

[35] C. Zurn, *Deliberative Democracy and the Institutions of Judicial Review* (2007).

[36] See the argument about the disruption of judicial process by climate change disputes, Fisher, Scotford, and Barritt, 'The Legally Disruptive Nature of Climate Change', 80 *Modern Law Review* (2017) 173.

Furthermore, thinking about legal processes in deliberative terms is also present in the literature about risk regulation, and environmental law in general. A deliberative account of the regulation of risks to the natural environment emphasizes 'complex socio-political disputes involving values and epistemological problems'[37] and underscores the role of public deliberation in tackling these challenges. In this account, the role of judicial processes cannot be reduced to the collection and objective analysis of data followed by the accommodation of clashing normative preferences. A genuine deliberation and transformation of preferences is necessary for generating legitimate outcomes.

The analysis of process-related values that courts pursue may be useful in appraising how different procedural arrangements contribute to the legitimacy of the governance system. In this volume, Prete's chapter concerning the narrow access of potential litigants to the EU courts focuses on this aspect of procedure and its relationship with the legitimacy of EU environmental governance. Depending on how one conceives of the value of the judicial process, it could be argued either that narrow access decreases the chances that courts will be able to control the legality of EU acts and other instances of incorrect implementation of higher order law or those based on an inaccurate empirical basis (since there will be no litigant both entitled and interested in bringing such issues to courts) or that, because of this narrow access, courts will miss important opportunities to engage in more open deliberation on controversial legal issues during such judicial proceedings.

6. Fourth Aspect: Outcomes

Finally, we consider that the legitimacy of a given environmental governance system may be enhanced (or undermined, as the case may be) by the courts' meeting of certain values in terms of outcome. This not only refers to the outcome in terms of the protection of the environment but also in terms of legal certainty, clarity, and consistency. For example, the decision a court makes may itself 'muddy' previously clear rules or generate unexpected outcomes. Such a decision may enhance environmental protection but it will not enhance the rule of law. From this perspective, the judicial process contributes to the legitimacy of the governance system to the extent to which it (amongst other things) reduces the risk of substantive error in administrative decision-making

[37] E. Fisher, *Risk Regulation and Administrative Constitutionalism* (2007) 33.

and, accordingly, maximizes the chances for the 'correct' substantive outcome.[38] This idea corresponds to the Rawlsian model of *imperfect* procedural justice. This model presupposes the existence of a distinct substantive criterion of correctness that can be materialized (at least to an extent),[39] although it also considers that *perfect* procedural justice, in which the legal process would always vouch for the correct outcome, is unattainable (as the resources necessary for carrying out the legal process are always limited). This model itself appears in different forms and the challenging task is, of course, to determine what is meant by the 'correct' 'outcome'. These two notions are examined in turn.

A. Outcome

To unpack this discussion we, first, consider how the notion of 'outcome' is understood in our organizational scheme. In this respect, whilst a traditional approach might see the outcome of the judicial process as the application of substantive law to concrete facts, in relation to modern law it is more appropriate, in our view, to see the outcome as extending beyond this narrow view.

Thus, in the most classical version, the judicial process is the 'transmission belt' of the lawmaker. It has a narrow role of increasing the accuracy in the application of substantive law to concrete facts without ascribing to it a more ambitious goal of achieving the objectively or universally correct or just outcome and without taking account of the 'offshoots' of this application of the law to the facts. Hovell links this classical idea of 'outcome' to legal positivism. It presupposes the existence of precise and unambiguous substantive legal standards apt for application and does not take account of the iterative nature of much judicial reasoning.[40]

This classical conception of 'outcome' does not correspond to the reality of the various branches of contemporary law, including environmental law. Because law is characterized by underdetermined or indeterminate concepts, which imply significant political and technical discretion in their concretization, the outcome is more than simply the application of the law to the facts. We face an increasing transfer of power to specialized executive bodies and administration, as well as private parties, but the choices to be made remain complex and uncertain. Courts visibly struggle to constrain and orient such choices

[38] Hovell (n. 26) 63–69.
[39] Solum, 'Procedural Justice', 78 *Southern California Law Review* (2004) 181, at 239–240.
[40] Hovell (n. 26) 63–69.

by legal means. The vision of the judicial process as merely applying the pre-established precise legal standards in individual and concrete cases becomes unconvincing. As such, our account of the 'outcome' of a judicial process goes beyond what we might term 'the result'. Rather, it also includes the ways in which power is later divided, the reasons given credence in the decision, and the wider and more systemic consequences in terms of the way the legal rules are understood in future litigation and more generally.

In an alternative view of the notion of 'outcome', the judicial process contributes to the legitimacy of the governance system as a whole by creatively *crafting* the best solution rather than *decoding* it from a legal act that lawmakers have passed[41] so that the outcome encompasses the integration of their approach into future cases. Creating this solution still occurs through an engagement with legal rules and principles but their open-ended character is acknowledged. Such as an engagement with legal rules and principles within the legal process consists in the aggregation and consideration of private and public interests affected by the decision-making.[42] From this perspective, the judicial process has a broader goal of producing the best possible decision by considering all the relevant interests without assuming that such a decision is only discovered by dint of pre-established legal standards.

Hence, it is especially important to provide access and opportunities for active participation in litigation to the representatives of the affected public and private interests, especially considering the polycentricity of environmental law issues as explained earlier in relation to process.[43] Accessibility and participation are believed to increase the problem-solving capacity of the legal process.[44] In the context of risk regulation and environmental law, those handling the judicial process, according to this model, are tasked with the collection of empirical data and their objective expert assessment. Subsequently, they must identify the relevant value preferences through engaging with interest representatives. For this reason, as we explained previously, there is a strong relationship between process values and outcome values but the moment of 'assessment' of the degree to which legitimacy is enhanced overall is different.

[41] Barnes, 'Towards a Third Generation of Administrative Procedure', in S. Ackerman, P. Lindseth, and B. Emerson (eds), *Comparative Administrative Law* (2017) 308.

[42] Stewart, 'The Reformation of American Administrative Law', 88 *Harvard Law Review* (1975) 1667.

[43] Lees and Pedersen (n. 14) 30.

[44] Steele, 'Participation and Deliberation in Environmental Law: Exploring a Problem-Solving Approach', 21 *Oxford Journal of Legal Studies* (2001) 415.

B. Correctness

Even recognizing that the outcome of a judicial decision is more than the simple result in the case (party x won or party y won) does not tell us when that outcome is 'correct'. There are a number of different factors which emerge in the literature which allow us to assess the correctness of a decision. In the section which follows, we explain what some of these may be. We do not argue that one or the other is the 'best' account of a correct outcome. Again, since the goal of this chapter is to provide an organizational frame, the purpose behind this discussion is to reveal where, if authors disagree on whether decision A or B contributes to the legitimacy of the system, that disagreement is situated within the framework of legitimacy as a whole. To this end, we discuss internal and external factors, or sub-criteria, relating to 'correctness'. Internal sub-criteria refer to factors such as the consequences which a judicial decision has for the clarity of the law, the consistency of the law, or the degree to which those subject to the rules as interpreted are equal before the law. These internal sub-criteria for legitimacy are all characterized by compliance with 'rule of law'-related values. The external sub-criteria, which we discuss here, relate instead to the impact of a decision in 'the real world': does the decision enhance protection of the environment, does it produce efficient governance, and the like?

These sub-criteria form part of a 'correct' assessment for different reasons. The rule-of-law values are relevant precisely because we are looking at the role of courts. Being 'a judge' within the democratic state brings with it norms of political behaviour which are characteristic of how the judicial role is primarily conceived in terms of enforcing the rule of law. Members of the judiciary are held to different standards than members of the executive branch. These standards are, in our language, 'internal' to that role. They include, at least, clarity and fairness in outcome and equality before the law and are underpinned by the substantive notion of the rule of law. It is not necessary here to give a detailed assessment of the various models of rule of law but it is important to acknowledge that these internal standards are complex and themselves disputed. To take an example of legal certainty, such certainty can come in at least two forms. First, it might refer to linguistic or normative certainty: the rule is clear (even if it produces absurd results). But it may also refer to a kind of moral certainty, that is, where the closer the rule is to our moral or societal intuition of what is 'right', the more certain the law will be since there will be less challenge or pressure within the system for change to that norm.

The 'real world' sub-criteria emerge not internally by virtue of the nature of the decision-maker's role but externally from the factual and practical context within which they are exercising that role. In other words, the outcomes of the judicial process will contribute to the legitimacy of the overall system of governance to the extent that they contribute to fostering the overarching goals of this system such as efficiency, environmental protection, upholding fundamental rights, etc. These, of course, vary according to context. Thus, in the context of the environment, the environmental consequences of a judicial decision are relevant. In the context of consumer protection, the consequences on the market are important too, etc.

In the following two subsections, we explain how these play out in the context of environmental litigation.

1. Internal Correctness: Legal Standards in EU Environmental Litigation

As mentioned earlier, in considering internal correctness, we mean, in essence, compliance with rule of law 'ideals'. Judicial action contributes to the legitimacy of the governance system to the extent to which it is carried out in compliance with the substantive requirements of the rule of law relating to equality before the law, consistency, and fairness. These go beyond process values and pertain to substantive equality in outcome, rather than equality *within* the process itself. When we zoom in to consider environmental law in the EU, we are asking to what extent the EU courts are following these rule of law principles in addressing the specific challenges raised by environmental litigation.

Legal clarity here is particularly important given the criminal or civil sanctions raised through many environmental law regimes. Such clarity, from a purely practical perspective, makes compliance more likely. Furthermore, the challenge of indeterminacy in environmental law standards makes the task of the court especially challenging. As Diver notes, '[t]he degree of precision appropriate to any particular rules depends on a series of variables peculiar to the rule's author, enforcer, and addressee'[45] but decisions which tend towards enhancing legal clarity will, all else being equal, contribute more to the legitimacy of the system. In this respect, clarity is intimately connected with consistency. Inconsistent law is, by definition, unclear in the sense that it cannot be predicted nor can it be followed, which will itself generate future uncertainty. The more clear the rules, the easier it is to apply them in a consistent manner. Thus, when we judge the interpretation of environmental norms, we must also look at the systemic consistency of that interpretation as well as its clarity, in our legitimacy assessment.

[45] Diver, 'The Optimal Precision of Administrative Rules', 93 *Yale Law Journal* (1983) 65, at 76.

In order to contribute to the legitimacy of the governance system in this 'internal sense', the judicial process in question must also comply with a deeper conception of the rule of law, considering equality before the law and the substantive principles of justice (such as the non-retroactivity of rules imposing punishments). In the context of the environment, these may generate specific challenges. Equality before the law is made more complex by the polycentricity and 'diffuseness' of environmental interests. The playing field is not level. Similarly, the grave threat of environmental degradation may represent an incentive to impose retroactive sanctions or remedies for such harm. This renders the courts' challenge harder, and thereby their contribution to the legitimacy of the system more difficult to achieve.

2. External Correctness: Judicial Contribution to Environmental Governance

External correctness, as discussed earlier, concerns the 'correctness' of the 'outcome' of the judicial process in relation to the values and goals of the governance system pertaining to the 'real world' as opposed to judging it from the perspective of the appropriate judicial role. When applied to environmental litigation, this means that the judicial process will contribute more or less to the legitimacy of the system as a whole to the extent to which it is capable of achieving a high(er) level of environmental protection. Of course, this argument can apply to other outcomes, such as economically efficient policies, etc. However, the principle that the environmental outcome is relevant to the legitimacy generated by courts comes from the nature of the EU as a governance system and its Treaty framework which renders this goal one of the underpinning goals of the 'state'.

In an influential exploration of the different conceptions of justice delivered by courts, Damaška conceptualized two basic understandings of the judicial function, each having different consequences for the institutional and procedural set-up of courts.[46] In a traditionally liberal state, the role of the law and the judges is to protect individual liberty against unlawful encroachments by other parties and public authorities. If legal violations occur, the affected parties themselves have to bring and advance their case before a 'silent' judge who decides which version of the law and empirical truth is more convincing. In an interventionist state—which the EU arguably resembles in the area we are interested in due to the developing positive harmonization of environmental

[46] M. Damaska, *The Faces of Justice and State Authority: A Comparative Approach to the Legal Process* (1991).

protection—the role of the law and the judges is to shape society, that is, enforce policies that are to transform society. Hence, the role of courts is to (help) materialize this vision as expressed in the fundamental documents of the governance system, the Treaties. Judges should be proactive rather than only passively deciding between the competing visions of the law and empirical truth as presented by the parties. Judges share the responsibility for determining the law and the empirical truth and achieving the normative goals of the legal order. The judiciary has a policy-enforcement function.

From this perspective, the relevant question is to what extent courts enhance the environmental protection within the Union by effectively solving complex environmental disputes involving uncertain empirical data and concretizing environmental law principles. This final piece of our legitimacy assessment is the external consideration of how the judicial response to environmental problems affects 'the wider world'.

However, the degree to which the environment is protected is not the only sub-criterion relevant here. Other policy goals, such as the pursuit of efficiency[47] or the enhancement of fundamental rights, might be regarded as equally relevant. The same could be argued for the goal of a sustainable industrial policy or a successful trade strategy.

This last point is the focus of De Sadeleer's work in this volume. The ways in which courts reason not only about environmental protection but how such consideration relates to other goals pursued by the system, including the aspiration of a free and open market, will be critical to the legitimacy of the system as a whole. Critically, whilst the balance struck could be justified in many different ways, the approach that the courts take to their task of balancing such values reveals much about their role. Iordachescu and Krajewski's chapter also examines the ways in which judicial decision-making has substantive consequences for the environment by considering how scientific complexity impacts the sorts of activities that are, and are not, permitted to continue once the courts have reviewed such administrative decisions.

7. Conclusion

In this introductory chapter, we have presented a general but, hopefully, practicable blueprint for examining how courts may contribute to the legitimacy of the EU environmental governance structure. This sketch does not aim to

47 Hovell (n. 26) 63–64.

provide a comprehensive assessment of the notion of judicial legitimacy as an abstract concept or the judiciary's contribution to the legitimacy of the broader governance system in environmental matters. Instead, we have essentially proposed a series of questions that help analyse in a structured way the role of judicial decision-making in a broader environmental governance framework.

In summary, our blueprint is based on the assumption that courts in the EU provide primarily 'throughput' legitimacy by holding public authorities to account for their decisions. It starts from the assessment of the capacity of courts to act as accountability fora with regard to decisions affecting the environment. This capacity depends on their institutional features, whether they have access to expertise, the procedural tools at their disposal that enable fact-finding, the remedies they are empowered to grant, and any other practical arrangements thanks to which courts can exercise their powers in environmental cases. Subsequently, the analysis becomes more focused on the features and the conduct of the judicial process itself in view of assessing whether it enables informed and reasoned deliberation between the relevant actors. The final question relates to the outcomes of the judicial process, both the immediate outcomes (such as who won and on what grounds) and long-term ones (how the interpretation of law favoured by the court will affect future cases and whether it will improve the state of environmental protection). It also relates to the criteria for assessing these outcomes, covering both the 'internal' legal criteria (such as legal certainty and consistency of law) and the judiciary's 'external' contribution to environmental governance (whether court rulings contribute to achieving the environmental goals of the polity).

The following chapters of this volume will put this blueprint into practice by focusing on the above elements. Individual chapters do not focus on specific elements. Rather, they should be read with the blueprint in mind as they offer conclusions pertaining to several, if not all, the elements of the blueprint. Some interpretation of the individual chapters in light of the blueprint presented here will be offered in the conclusions of this volume.

2

Walking the Tightrope

Legitimacy and the Use of Environmental Soft Law in the European Courts

Mariolina Eliantonio and Danai Petropoulou Ionescu

1. Introduction

This volume is dedicated to an analysis of the role of the EU Courts in the legitimacy of environmental governance at large. Much like environmental problems themselves, there are many facets to this discussion. The complexity of such problems and the clear need for specialized knowledge of the field pose a significant challenge for courts when dealing with uncertainty, identifying the appropriate remedies, or applying environmental principles. This chapter adds another piece to this puzzle by exploring the utilization of soft law instruments by the EU Courts in adjudicating environmental matters. As the introduction of this volume rightly points out, for a court to successfully carry out its function of holding to account, it must be equipped with the appropriate tools. The traditional understanding of the role of courts posits that these institutions bear the responsibility of applying legal norms to the facts of the cases on which they adjudicate.[1] This task is of a particular nature in the context of environmental problems as the necessary tools are quite different from those needed to adjudicate in areas where techno-scientific expertise is not a factor—for instance in areas such as migration or fundamental rights. This is especially true of generalist courts, such as the Court of Justice of the European Union (CJEU), which unlike specialist environmental courts, are not based on the premise that the necessary expertise is available and accessible in-house.[2] In this sense, we argue, they may require an extra 'crutch' when adjudicating matters of environmental concern.

[1] Scott and Sturm, 'Courts as Catalysts: Rethinking the Judicial Role in New Governance', 13 *Columbia Journal of European Law* (2007) 565, at 568.

[2] For a compelling analysis of common law environmental courts and tribunals, see C. Warnock, *Environmental Courts and Tribunals: Powers, Integrity, and the Search for Legitimacy* (2020).

Mariolina Eliantonio and Danai Petropoulou Ionescu, *Walking the Tightrope* In: *The Legitimacy of EU Environmental Governance and the Role of the European Courts*. Edited by: Mariolina Eliantonio and Emma Lees, Oxford University Press.
DOI: 10.1093/oso/9780198972808.003.0002

When dealing with matters relating to the environment, courts are required to confront complexity, uncertainty, and an array of scientific information in order to reach legally correct and scientifically sound decisions.[3] There is, due to this, a need for a different kind of institutional capacity when compared to other policy areas. It follows that a lack of such capacity has the potential to undermine a court's ability to fully engage with the facts of environmental cases. This density and complexity of environmental law—both from a substantive and procedural perspective—is a known fact. In the EU landscape, environmental law is notoriously complex, fragmented, and difficult to systematize.[4] This can be partly attributed to the fast pace of scientific developments, their highly technical nature, and an uncontrolled infiltration of environmental aspects into other Union regulatory areas. In recognition of this burden that regulating environmental matters poses, and in an effort to alleviate it, the European Commission has often engaged with alternative regulatory practices such as soft law. In fact, based on calculations from the EUR-Lex database, the Commission has adopted over 200 such instruments to aid the transposition, interpretation, and application of EU environmental law provisions. These instruments, inter alia, provide technical or methodological guidance, scientific definitions, procedural recommendations, and scientific information to the national competent authorities in charge of the implementation of EU environmental law. In this way, they are meant to increase the administrative and technical capacity of national authorities to assess environmental questions while implementing EU law.

In turn, the role of the courts in this—and, in fact, the stage at which they may engage with such soft law instruments—comes at the point of adjudication. In this chapter, we argue that soft law instruments may also contribute to the establishment of such capacity for the courts by complementing their existing toolbox—although this contribution may, at the same time, also pose a challenge. On the one hand, these tools can allow the court to correctly identify the problem at hand, analyse the relevant facts, and reach sound decisions based on up-to-date scientific knowledge. While, indeed, the CJEU must ultimately deliver its judgment on the basis of legal rules, in environmental law these rules frequently rely on non-legal notions such as 'good environmental status' or 'endangered species'.[5] Soft law instruments are of special importance

[3] See also Chapter 6 in this volume.

[4] J. Holder and M. Lee, *Environmental Protection, Law and Policy: Text and Materials* (2007) 145; M. Peeters and M. Eliantonio (eds), *Research Handbook on EU Environmental Law* (2020) 1; J. Peterson and E. Bomberg, *Decision-Making in the European Union* (1999) 173.

[5] For an in-depth discussion of the interpretation of such terms by the CJEU in EU biodiversity law, see Garcia-Ureta, 'The European Court of Justice's Approach to Scientific and Factual Matters in the

here, as they often provide explanations, information, and criteria related to these notions. This can, then, contribute to a better understanding of environmental problems by national authorities and courts alike, thereby ultimately leading to more legitimate environmental governance. On the other hand, soft law instruments as such are also the product of executive rule-making practices, which are not endowed with the same legitimacy credentials as legislative rules. Consequently, therefore, the use of such instruments by the CJEU to adjudicate on environmental disputes may pose a threat to the legitimacy of the governance system as a whole. Our goal here is to explore how the EU Courts use soft law 'tools' to carry out their task of ensuring that the interpretation and application of the Treaties and EU law are observed, as set out in Article 19(1) of the Treaty on the European Union and, in turn, how this engagement contributes to the overall legitimacy of EU environmental governance.

Of course, there are many questions to be asked about the interplay between soft law instruments, courts, and legitimacy. Some relate to matters of judicial control and soft law's characteristic lack of legal bindingness. Some pertain to the question of effective judicial protection and the vast array of practical and legal effects that soft law produces. Other questions relate to the somewhat ambiguous input legitimacy of soft law instruments and their use by courts or quasi-judicial authorities. There are, similarly, many different answers to all of these questions. Much of the literature on this topic is dedicated to making an argument for or against soft law. Whether it should or should not be used by courts, whether soft law as a means of governance should be used and to what extent, or whether soft law instruments should be subject to judicial review.[6] Put simply, consensus on this interplay is far from settled—still, the general opinion seems to tend towards the more sceptical side. The relationship between soft law, courts, and legitimacy becomes all the more complicated when we add the layer of techno-scientific expertise, a layer that is ever present in the litigation and adjudication of environmental matters.

A lot of these questions have been broadly addressed in the literature at different levels, mostly focusing on the general role of courts in the context of soft law and soft governance. This has largely been done both on a general and a

Habitats Directive—Between Uncertainty and Precaution', in M. Eliantonio, E. Lees, and T. Paloniitty (eds), *EU Environmental Principles and Scientific Uncertainty Before National Courts: The Case of the Habitats Directive* (2023) 31.

6 For an overview of this debate and reference to the scholars who have, over the course of the years, engaged in this debate, see Eliantonio and Korkea-aho, 'Soft Law and Courts: Saviours or Saboteurs of the Rule of (Soft) Law?', in M. Eliantonio, E. Korkea-aho, and U. Mörth (eds), *Research Handbook on Soft Law* (2023) 190.

more conceptual level,[7] addressing questions such as the ones posed earlier. The empirical exploration of the use and status of soft law instruments in courts has been much more limited and has taken place in the context of several Member State jurisdictions[8] or in the EU Courts across policy areas.[9] This chapter aims to contribute to the empirical understanding of the interaction of the EU Courts with soft law instruments and to explore in what way and with what aim the CJEU uses soft law in adjudicating environmental matters. In doing so, we seek to deepen our understanding of the capacity-building capabilities of soft law instruments in the context of environmental adjudication in the EU Courts.

This exploration will provide valuable insight into two key matters. First, whether soft law, as a tool in the 'hands' of the Court, can be valuable in increasing its capacity to adjudicate environmental matters. Second, whether and in what ways courts take advantage of the tools available to them to address the problems before them. The latter is especially interesting as, contrary to domestic courts which have an obligation stemming from the *Grimaldi* case law[10] to take relevant soft law into account,[11] the EU Courts can engage with these instruments at their own discretion. Delving into these two aspects will allow us to draw broader conclusions about the role of the CJEU as a 'contributor' to the greater legitimacy of the Union's environmental governance system and also about the 'usefulness' of soft law as a tool in environmental regulation and adjudication at large.

[7] Scott and Sturm (n. 1); Korkea-aho, 'National Courts and European Soft Law: Is *Grimaldi* Still Good Law?', 37 *Yearbook of European Law* (2018) 470; Kovács, Tóth, and Forgács, 'The Legal Effects of European Soft Law and Their Recognition at National Administrative Courts', 2 *ELTE Law Journal* (2016) 53; Liguori, 'Taking Soft Law into Account … of Course! But What Does That Concretely Mean?', 16 *Review of European Administrative Law* (2023) 37.

[8] M. Eliantonio, E. Korkea-aho, and O. Stefan (eds), *EU Soft Law in the Member States: Theoretical Findings and Empirical Evidence* (2020); Fredriksson, Blomqvist, and Winblad, 'Conflict and Compliance in Swedish Health Care Governance: Soft Law in the "Shadow of Hierarchy"', 35 *Scandinavian Political Studies* (2012) 48; Hofmann, 'Types of EU Soft Law and Their National Impact', in M. Eliantonio, E. Korkea-aho, and O. Stefan (eds), *EU Soft Law in the Member States: Theoretical Findings and Empirical Evidence* (2021) 39; E. Korkea-aho *et al.*, *EU Environmental Soft Law in the Member States: A Comparative Overview of Finland, France, Germany, Italy, the Netherlands, Slovenia and the UK* (2020), https://papers.ssrn.com/sol3/papers.cfm?abstract_id=3656418 (last visited 2 October 2024).

[9] Eliantonio and Stefan, 'Soft Law Before the European Courts: Discovering a "Common Pattern"?', 37 *Yearbook of European Law* (2018) 457.

[10] Case C-322/88, *Grimaldi v. Fonds des maladies professionnelles* (EU:C:1989:646).

[11] A legal duty to take soft law 'into consideration' remains rather vague and the evolution of the doctrine does not seem to be particularly stable. For a broader discussion on the matter, see Korkea-aho (n. 7) and Liguori (n. 7).

A. Methodological Design and Approach of the Study

From a practical standpoint, and given the vastness of EU environmental law, we focus on soft law adopted in three key areas of environmental regulation: biodiversity, impact assessment, and water management. Specifically, we focus on guidance documents adopted under specific legal acts in these areas: namely, the Habitats[12] and Birds[13] Directives as well as the Wildlife Trade Regulation[14] and the Invasive Alien Species Regulation[15] relating to *biodiversity*, the Environmental Impact Assessment[16] (EIA) and Strategic Environmental Assessment[17] (SEA) Directives relating to *impact assessment*, and the Water Framework[18] and Marine Strategy Framework[19] Directives relating to *water management*. It should be noted that this selection only includes soft law instruments fulfilling the so-called 'post-law' function, that is, instruments whose aim is to interpret and help the transposition and application of the hard law instrument to which they pertain.[20] The nature of these instruments is an important point to note in this discussion as they have been adopted for the very purpose of dissipating (or at least reducing) uncertainty at the level of the national legislators and competent administrative authorities because of the vagueness of several key concepts and procedures contained in these hard law instruments.

The list of legislative acts and the sum of identified guidance documents is summarized in Table 2.1. Addressing such a broad spectrum of cases, including acts of both a substantive and procedural nature—such as the Nature Directives or the Environmental Assessment Directives, respectively—allows us to do justice to the inherent heterogeneity of the field of EU environmental law and to draw cross-cutting conclusions. This will, in turn, give us the opportunity to reflect on the many different aspects of regulating environmental matters[21] as well as how the EU Courts interact with soft law instruments in different scenarios and in response to different types of legal issues. It should be

[12] Council Directive 92/43/EEC, OJ 1992 L 206/7 (Habitats Directive).
[13] Directive 2009/147/EC, OJ 2009 L 20/7 (Birds Directive).
[14] Council Regulation (EC) No 338/97, OJ 1997 L 61/1 (Wildlife Trade Regulation).
[15] Regulation (EU) No 1143/2014, OJ 2014 L 317/35 (Invasive Alien Species Regulation).
[16] Directive 2014/52/EU, OJ 2014 L 124/1 (EIA Directive).
[17] Directive 2001/42/EC, OJ 2001 L197/30 (SEA Directive).
[18] Directive 2000/60/EC, OJ 2000 L327/1 (Water Framework Directive).
[19] Directive 2008/56/EC, OJ 2008 L164/19 (Marine Strategy Framework Directive).
[20] This categorization was proposed by L. Senden, *Soft Law in European Community Law* (2004).
[21] For an interesting discussion on the heterogeneity of EU environmental law and the value of specificity, see Lees and Paloniitty, 'Science in Court—The Importance of Specificity', in M. Eliantonio, E. Lees, and T. Paloniitty (eds), *EU Environmental Principles and Scientific Uncertainty Before National Courts: The Case of the Habitats Directive* (2023) 9.

Table 2.1 Overview of guidance documents in selected areas

Policy field	Legal act	Year	Number of guidance documents
Biodiversity	Habitats Directive 92/43/EEC	1992	5
	Birds Directive 2009/147/EC	1979	4
	Natura 2000 Network	1992	13
	Wildlife Trade Regulation 338/97/EC	1996	8
	Invasive Alien Species Regulation 1143/2014	2014	9
Impact assessment	EIA Directive 2014/52/EU	1985	15
	SEA Directive 2001/42/EC	2001	3
Water management	Water Framework Directive 2000/60/EC	2000	40
	Marine Strategy Framework Directive 2008/56/EC	2008	26
		Total:	**123**

noted at the outset that in this chapter we will not address how the EU Courts have *directly* interacted with soft law measures in the process of, for example, reviewing their validity.[22] Instead, the question central to this study is how the EU Courts have, in the cases before them in the area of environmental matters, treated and used soft law instruments as a tool in their adjudication.

In order to identify the cases where the EU Courts have relied on soft law measures in their adjudication, we followed a series of precise steps. First, we compiled a dataset of all guidance documents adopted by the European Commission under each legal act examined here.[23] The second step was to use the CJEU's CURIA case law database to search for cases stemming from the field of environmental law in which the title or code of each guidance document was referenced in the Court's judgment or the Advocate General's (AG) opinions. On the basis of the data retrieved from the CURIA database, we took stock of all cases—including judgments and opinions—in which the guidance

[22] This is because the dataset, compiled according to the method presented in the next section, did not return any annulment cases concerning the selected soft law measures. This is not surprising, at least when it comes to direct actions according to Art. 263 TFEU, given the negligible chances of success of the admissibility of such actions. On this, see Eliantonio, 'Soft Law in Environmental Matters and the Role of the European Courts: Too Much or Too Little of It?', 37 *Yearbook of European Law* (2018) 496.

[23] The full dataset can be shared upon request to the authors.

Table 2.2 Overview of references to environmental guidance documents in CJEU case law

Policy Field	Legal act	Referenced guidance documents
Biodiversity	Habitats Directive	5 (out of 5)
	Birds Directive	1 (out of 4)
	Natura 2000*	3 (out of 13)
Environmental assessment	EIA Directive	1 (out of 15)
	SEA Directive	1 (out of 3)
Water management	Water Framework Directive	6 (out of 40)
	Total references	**17 (out of 80)**

* Natura 2000 is a network of nature protection areas in the territory of the European Union based on the territories covered by the Habitats and Birds Directives. Natura finds its legal basis in Article 3 of the Habitats Directive but is in itself not a legal act and therefore not the direct subject of case law. Nonetheless, guidance documents that have been adopted under the Natura 2000 scheme have been referenced by the Court in cases brought under the two Nature Directives.

documents were referenced. This stock-taking exercise resulted in the set of cases presented in Table 2.2, which only includes the legal acts and corresponding guidance documents which were referenced by the Courts. The cases in which guidance documents were adopted by the Commission but were not referenced in the Court's case law were excluded from the analysis.[24]

The following step was to conduct an in-depth review of the cases in order to understand how the Courts interacted with the soft law instruments—for instance, whether they engaged with the instruments substantively or whether they were simply referred to. This included understanding the facts of the cases, the legal issues at hand, as well as the Court's rationale. In doing so, we took an inductive approach and aimed to identify potential 'trends' in the ways in which the Court engages with soft law. For instance, whether soft law was used to better understand the intricacies of the problems before them or whether it was simply used as a scientific reference. We recognize that, since the EU Courts do not have an obligation to engage with these instruments, the interaction between the two is more or less dynamic and bottom-up. This, on the one hand, makes the interactive process an interesting topic of study. On the other hand, it also makes it somewhat difficult to track. This becomes

[24] This is the case for guidance documents under the Wildlife Trade Regulation, the Invasive Alien Species Regulation, and the Marine Strategy Framework Directive.

all the more complicated when we take into account the particular features of environmental problems and the issues they are known to pose to courts and decision-makers. This interaction is what we will untangle here.

The chapter is organized in the following manner. The next section will delve into the status quo of EU environmental soft law by taking stock of how the Commission uses such instruments or larger regulatory structures to address environmental matters. This will, then, help us gain a better understanding of how far-reaching soft law is in this area. Section 4 will turn our attention to the debate about the challenges of environmental adjudication by generalist courts and will specifically focus on the potential role of soft law as a tool to deal with questions requiring scientific expertise. This section will also address questions regarding the—oft-troubled—relationship between soft law and courts. Section 5 will then present the findings of our empirical analysis, using both quantitative and qualitative methods. In this section, we will outline in what ways and for what aims the EU Courts engage with soft law when adjudicating environmental matters. Section 6 will then address the core issue of this chapter by contextualizing our empirical findings within the greater question of the legitimacy of EU environmental governance, and particularly whether soft law instruments contribute to or endanger the legitimacy of the Union's environmental action. The final section of the chapter will offer some concluding remarks about the use of soft law instruments as tools in environmental adjudication and beyond and put forth some—somewhat preliminary—thoughts about the difficulty of striking a balance between expertise and legitimacy in environmental matters.

2. Status Quo: Science, Soft Law, and the EU Environmental Field

Let us start from the basics. The relationship between law and scientific knowledge is intricate and has many ups and downs. It is relevant in all stages of the 'law'—in legislative processes, in interpreting, applying, and enforcing legislative provisions.[25] Deciding what needs to be regulated, how it is to be regulated, and how the law is to be applied in individual cases often requires the involvement of scientific expertise. Environmental law is one of the foremost fields where this relationship is vital. The complexity and techno-scientific

[25] Thorén, Soininen, and Kotamaki, 'Scientific Models in Legal Judgements: The Relationship Between Law and Environmental Science as Problem-Feeding', 124 *Environmental Science and Policy* (2021) 478.

uncertainties that are characteristic of environmental problems often necessitate both that the EU legislators rely on scientific input to identify issues in need of regulation and come up with suitable solutions and that the national and Union-level judicial authorities depend on scientific assessments—in part or in whole—to issue appropriate judgments.[26] This creates a capacity misalignment between environmental problems which need to be regulated and decision-makers who may not have the necessary expertise to do so. In response to this, an array of complementary regulatory structures have been established at all governance levels—local, regional, European, global—such as networks, expert groups, consortia, and industry partnerships to alleviate the complexity and fulfil the need for expertise. Many such structures operate informally and are void of binding decision-making power—usually taking the form of soft law instruments, statements, plans, etc. In essence, this makes the EU environmental field particularly prone to the new governance and soft law phenomena. Still, in order to grasp the full extent of the role of soft law in this field, we must first take a step back and understand why and how these instruments emerge in the EU.

The need for a common environmental policy—or at least, a policy direction—within the Union made its official debut in a Council Declaration in 1973 calling for a first environmental action plan in its Preamble.[27] While at that point it remained, for the most part, a declaration of political will, the 1980s brought about significant developments in the field of EU environmental action. In fact, in 1985, the CJEU established that environmental protection is an essential objective of the European Community in its *ADBHU* ruling.[28] This sentiment culminated in the Single European Act of 1987 which, among others, highlighted throughout the salience of coordinated Community action on environmental matters and established an explicit basis for Union environmental legislation.[29] This was the first instance where environmental protection was introduced into the EU legal system.[30] Currently, the body of EU environmental law is rather immense; in fact, over 200 pieces of legislation in the field of environmental law are currently in force, dealing with matters

[26] Thorén, Soininen, and Kotamaki (n. 25); Rose, 'Environmental Law Grows Up (More or Less), and What Science Can Do to Help', 9 *Lewis & Clark Law Review* (2005) 273; Fisher, Scotford, and Barritt, 'The Legally Disruptive Nature of Climate Change', 80 *Modern Law Review* (2017) 173.

[27] Council Declaration of 22 November 1973, OJ C112/1.

[28] Case C-240/83, *Procureur de la République v. ADBHU* (EU:C:1985:59), para. 13.

[29] Single European Act, OJ 1987 L 169/1, Arts 130r, 130s, 130t. The provisions of the SEA pertaining to the environment are now reflected in Arts 191–193 TFEU.

[30] Holder (n. 4) 1.

spanning from climate change to industrial emissions to biodiversity loss.[31] Given the current focus on environmental matters—a focus that extends well beyond the bounds of the EU—the volume of EU legislation is only expected to rise in the near future.

As mentioned in the introduction, while a staple of EU legal and political action, environmental policy is still rather complex, fragmented, and difficult to systematize.[32] In attempting to implement EU and international obligations relating to the environment, the EU has developed an extensive *acquis* in the form of directives, regulations, decisions, and a series of additional soft law measures.[33] Perhaps precisely due to the rather uncontrolled infiltration of environmental aspects in other Union policy fields,[34] the competences of the EU to legislate on environmental matters remain rather 'blurry'.[35] This situation poses a challenge to scholarship, as gaining a comprehensive insight into the state of play of EU environmental law—for instance, in terms of compliance or effects—is a rather complicated endeavour.[36] What is the place of soft law in all this?

However, regulating issues that rely on scientific expertise, for instance setting out technical provisions relating to installations producing titanium dioxide in the Industrial Emissions Directive,[37] is no easy task. The high complexity and technical nature of the field may pose difficulties for national administrations and courts to interpret or apply specific EU law provisions.[38]

[31] European Commission, 'Environment: Law and governance' (n.d.), https://environment.ec.europa.eu/law-and-governance_en (last visited May 2024); S. Happaerts and T. Delreux, *Environmental Policy and Politics in the European Union* (2016) 13.

[32] Holder (n. 4) 145; Peeters and Eliantonio (n. 4) 1; Peterson and Bomberg (n. 4) 145.

[33] Holder (n. 4) 145; Born and Schoukens, 'Biodiversity Litigation Before the Court of Justice of the European Union: A Promising Pathway for Better Enforcement of International Biodiversity Law?', in G. Futhazar, S. Maljean-Dubois, and J. Razzaque (eds), *Biodiversity Litigation* (2023) 293, 306.

[34] The phenomenon of incorporating references to and objectives of environmental matters in Union legislation is commonly referred to as 'greening'. This approach was exemplified in the commitment put forth in Art. 2 of the 1997 Amsterdam Treaty which recognizes the protection and improvement of the quality of the environment as a task of the Community. This is further substantiated in Art. 6 of the EC Treaty of 2002 which sets out that environmental protection must be integrated into the definition and implementation of Community policies. This direction is also reflected in Art. 3(3) of the Treaty on European Union (TEU) which stipulates that the Union shall work for the sustainable development of Europe based on a high level of protection and improvement of the quality of the environment and in Art. 11 TFEU which calls for environmental protection to be integrated into Union policies and activities. This integration of environmental protection clauses in policy objectives that do not pertain specifically to environmental matters is reflected in the rhetoric used, e.g., in mentions of 'sustainable development', 'green jobs', etc.

[35] Anker, 'Competences for EU Environmental Legislation: About Blurry Boundaries and Potential Opportunities', in M. Peeters and M. Eliantonio (eds), *Research Handbook on EU Environmental Law* (2020) 7.

[36] Peeters and Eliantonio (n. 4) 2.

[37] Directive 2010/75/EU, OJ 2010 L 334/17.

[38] Eliantonio and Lisi (n. 8).

To aid with the application, transposition, and interpretation of EU environmental legislation at the Member State level, the Commission has adopted a considerable number of soft law instruments in an effort to increase the capacity of the relevant authorities to deal with environmental matters. So much so that already in the early 2000s soft law measures were considered a substantial part of the body of EU environmental law.[39] These instruments come in various forms, such as Commission notes, guidance documents, or interpretative aids. The highly technical nature of the field and its dependency on scientific developments, which may result in rapid changes in terms of what is needed, mean that these instruments are almost indispensable for the national authorities. In short, soft law and soft governance mechanisms are by no means a rare phenomenon in the field of EU environmental policy.

In fact, several informal 'soft' governance structures have been established and over 200 soft law instruments authored or commissioned by the European Commission in the major areas of environmental policy have been adopted.[40] Unfortunately, a comprehensive overview of soft law measures and structures in EU environmental regulation does not exist and cannot be calculated due to the inconsistency of the publication of soft law measures and the inherent informality of such governance approaches.[41] A preliminary look at the available information on the volume of EU soft law confirms that these measures represent a large proportion of EU environmental action. As Table 2.1 summarizes, in the areas of biodiversity, impact assessment, and water management policy more specifically, a total of 123 guidance documents have been adopted by the European Commission in cooperation with different actors such as external consultants, national authorities, or research institutions.[42] Further, and as shown in Figure 2.1, the adoption of soft law measures as such is a steady trend in the area, starting from the year of adoption of the respective legal act.

[39] Papadopoulos, 'Accountability and Multi-Level Governance: More Accountability, Less Democracy?', 33 *West European Politics* (2010) 1030; Jordan, Wurzel, and Zito, 'The Rise of "New" Policy Instruments in Comparative Perspective: Has Governance Eclipsed Government?', 53 *Political Studies* (2005) 477, 481.

[40] The body of *all* soft law in the field of EU environmental policy is expected to be much higher considering the instruments adopted under the ambit of non-major environmental legal acts, those adopted stand-alone without reference to a binding legal act, or those produced by actors other than the Commission, such as agencies, the European Parliament, or the Council. Unfortunately, there is no reliable way to calculate the exact number of soft law measures in EU environmental regulation so we must rely on this indication.

[41] See e.g. Eliantonio (n. 22).

[42] For an in-depth analysis of the adoption of instruments in the area of climate change, see Petropoulou Ionescu and Eliantonio, 'Soft Law Behind the Scenes: Transparency, Participation and the European Union's Soft Law Making Process in the Field of Climate Change', 14 *European Journal of Risk Regulation* (2023) 292.

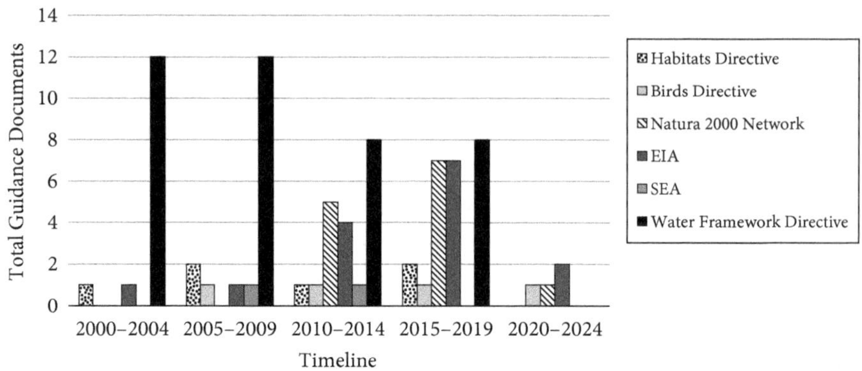

Figure 2.1 Timeline of adoption of guidance documents in selected areas

However, though the body of guidance documents alone is rather impressive, in the wider area of the environment, soft modes of governance are utilized to an even greater extent. For instance, in the area of wildlife trafficking and in addition to the Wildlife Trade Regulation, the Commission has also adopted two EU Action Plans, covering the periods of 2016–2020[43] and 2020–2027.[44] The Action Plans build on existing EU regulations relating to wildlife trade and trafficking and aim to set priorities, respond to current challenges—for example, climate change or environmental degradation—and build links with related policy areas. In addition to such, more concrete, measures, one can identify an array of expert groups, networks, or informal bodies aimed at producing and disseminating scientific or technical information (often in the form of soft law instruments) for the purpose of creating, planning, and implementing policy goals relating to the environment. The body of soft law is, in simple terms, far-reaching but ill-structured.

The reception of the Commission's environmental soft law by national authorities and national courts is also far from settled. Recent literature on EU soft law in the Union's Member States suggests that the use of these instruments at the Member State level differs from one case to another and that little to no consistency across legal systems can be identified.[45] For instance,

[43] European Commission, 'Communication from the Commission to the European Parliament, the Council, the European Economic and Social Committee and the Committee of the Regions: EU Action Plan against Wildlife Trafficking' (2016) COM(2016) 87 final.

[44] European Commission, 'Communication from the Commission to the European Parliament, the Council, the European Economic and Social Committee and the Committee of the Regions: Revision of the EU Action Plan Against Wildlife Trafficking' (2022) COM(2022) 581 final.

[45] This is extensively researched in several contributions to Eliantonio, Korkea-aho, and Stefan (n. 8) as well as in the comparative overview and listed country reports of the SoLaR project, Eliantonio and Lisi (n. 8).

while overarchingly soft law instruments have not been transposed into the national legal systems in the form of binding acts, some Member States have given binding effect to soft law instruments at the national and regional levels, others have transposed soft law into their national legal systems in a non-binding form such as circulars, and yet others have limited themselves to referring to the original EU level instruments without adopting any state-level measures.[46] Just like the overall field of environmental law in its entirety, its soft law counterpart is equally complex, fragmented, and difficult to systematize. What is more, this trend extends to the use of environmental soft law by national courts. For instance, when it comes to the judicial response to the status and the effects of environmental soft law—that is, whether the instruments are taken into account in environmental litigation—there is considerable variation in relation to the relevant legal acts and the national authorities.[47] In essence, the use of environmental soft law in courts may depend on the judicial system and/or on the relevant legislative act from which the instrument stems.

For example, references to EU soft law stemming from the Water Framework Directive are almost non-existent in the national case law, while soft law related to the Habitats Directive or the EIA Directive are more frequent.[48] Variation is also evident in relation to the judicial systems of the Member States. In fact, research reveals that there is a high degree of heterogeneity in terms of recognizing and utilizing soft law instruments in environmental litigation across the Member States, where some Member States like France make almost no reference to environmental soft law irrespective of the preceding legal act,[49] while Italian and Finnish courts make use of soft law instruments to support the reasoning and arguments of the court.[50] A similar picture seems to emerge in the use of environmental soft law instruments by the CJEU. While the Court does employ soft law instruments as a means of interpretation and makes reference to it explicitly, this occurs in a somewhat ad hoc manner.[51] However, as mentioned previously, while national courts have an obligation to take soft law into account, stemming from the *Grimaldi* doctrine,[52] the CJEU does not. Still, in the environmental field, both national and EU Courts seem to make use of soft law instruments—although in a seemingly random manner—to interpret

[46] Ibid., including the corresponding country reports.
[47] Ibid.
[48] Ibid. 10.
[49] Ibid., country report on France by G. Lisi *et al.*, 35.
[50] Ibid., country reports, Italy by G. Lisi and M. Eliantonio, 61; Finland by E. Korkea-aho, 24.
[51] Eliantonio (n. 22) 512.
[52] Case C-322/88, *Grimaldi v. Fonds des maladies professionnelles* (EU:C:1989:646).

relevant EU environmental law provisions or take into account as a source of information. That being said, the manner in which courts substantively engage with soft law remains unclear. Shedding light on this aspect is, in fact, one of the core objectives of this chapter. What *is* clear is that, notwithstanding its inherent inconsistencies, soft law has become an intrinsic aspect of environmental policy at the national and Union levels—albeit rather erratically—thus highlighting the need for further research and discussion on the matter.

3. Damned if You Do, Damned if You Don't: Environmental Science in the Courtroom and the Issue of Soft Law

In the last two decades, research on soft law—as a general phenomenon—has reached a moderate consensus on its definition, its capacity to produce effects, and its somewhat ambivalent relationship with questions of legitimacy and democracy. It is widely accepted that soft law norms are those which are laid out in instruments that are not legally binding but have the capacity to produce certain practical and legal effects.[53] It is also widely accepted that soft law measures, through several means, such as peer-pressure tactics or norm-setting, may produce a wide variety of practical and legal effects,[54] spanning from framing of national or EU-level policies to providing authoritative interpretations of EU law provisions. Still, the issue of soft law's relationship to legitimacy is a little more complicated. While there is general agreement that soft law instruments have many advantages—for instance, in terms of their cost-effective adoption process, their ability to facilitate administrative processes and increase administrative and technical capacity, or their flexibility and adaptability—scholarship also agrees that soft law comes with several disadvantages[55]—often stemming from the same characteristics that render it beneficial. The quick adoption of soft law entails that such a process is not

[53] This definition was originally provided by L. Senden and has gradually become the 'golden standard' of our understanding of EU soft law. See L. Senden, *Soft Law in European Community Law* (2004) 112.

[54] See e.g. Eliantonio (n. 22); Arroyo Jiménez, 'Beyond Bindingness: A Typology of EU Soft Law Legal Effects' in P. L. Láncos, N. Xanthoulis, and L. Arroyo Jiménez (eds), *The Legal Effects of EU Soft Law: Theory, Language and Sectoral Insights* (2023) 9; Stefan, 'European Union Soft Law: New Developments Concerning the Divide Between Legally Binding Force and Legal Effects: European Union Soft Law', 75 *The Modern Law Review* (2012) 879; as well as several contributions in M. Eliantonio, E. Korkea-aho, and U. Mörth (eds), *Research Handbook on Soft Law* (2023).

[55] Petropoulou Ionescu and Eliantonio (n. 42); Petropoulou Ionescu and Eliantonio, 'Democratic Legitimacy and Soft Law in the EU Legal Order: A Theoretical Perspective', 17 *Journal of Contemporary European Research* (2021) 45; Ulrika Mörth, *Soft Law and New Modes of EU Governance—A*

highly systematized and does not account for the participation of concerned actors.[56] Its flexibility and adaptability, which makes soft law a strong 'ally' in times of crisis or uncertainty and in matters requiring expertise, also makes it difficult to control. Its capacity to accommodate varying normative preferences likewise becomes fertile ground for imbalances in implementation. These are all opposite sides of the same coin. In many ways, engaging with soft law requires an intricate balancing act—much like walking a tightrope.

This ambiguity in the use of soft law as an instrument, be it by the executive as a means of complementing legislative acts and outlining policy objectives or by courts as an interpretation aid, raises many questions regarding the impact of such measures on the quality and legitimacy of EU public action. On the one hand, soft law measures can increase the decision-making capacity of public authorities and courts by acting as an interlocutor between dense scientific information and public action. By extension, the increased capacity of authorities to make well-informed decisions based on scientific information can have a positive impact on the legitimacy of said decisions, eventually benefiting the overarching system of governance as a whole. This is a basic tenet of evidence-based policymaking. It rests on the underlying assumption that knowledge and information can help public authorities understand problems more accurately, eventually allowing them to identify and assess solutions more effectively.[57] This assumption is, in fact, at the core of the Union's efforts towards better regulation.[58]

Democratic Problem (2005), https://www.mzes.uni-mannheim.de/projekte/typo3/site/fileadmin/research%20groups/6/Papers_Soft%20Mode/Moerth.pdf, 25 (last visited 2 October 2024); Rocca and Eliantonio, 'European Union Soft Law by Agencies: An Analysis of the Legitimacy of Their Procedural Frameworks', in M. Conticelli, M. de Bellis, and G. della Cananea (eds), *EU Executive Governance: Agencies and Procedures* (2020) 177; Scott, 'In Legal Limbo: Post-Legislative Guidance as a Challenge for European Administrative Law', 48(2) *Common Market Law Review* (2011) 329.

[56] Petropoulou Ionescu and Eliantonio (n. 42); Vaughan, 'Differentiation and Dysfunction: An Exploration of Post-Legislative Guidance Practices in 14 EU Agencies', 17 *Cambridge Yearbook of European Legal Studies* (2015) 66; Stefan, 'Soft Law Making at the European Commission: Not Much of a One-Institution Show', in M. Eliantonio, E. Korkea-aho, and U. Mörth (eds), *Research Handbook on Soft Law* (2023) 252; Vaughan, 'Fictions and Fuzziness: Soft Law Rule-Making Among the EU's Decentralized Agencies', in M. Eliantonio, E. Korkea-aho, and U. Mörth (eds), *Research Handbook on Soft Law* (2023) 223.

[57] This is well recognized within the Union policymaking arena, e.g. by the Commission in its Commission Staff Working Document, 'Supporting and connecting policymaking in the Member States with scientific research' (2022) SWD(2022) 346 final.

[58] Communication from the Commission to the European Parliament, the Council, the European Economic and Social Committee and the Committee of the Regions Empty, 'Better regulation: Joining forces to make better laws' (2021) COM(2021) 219 final, 3.

On the other hand, the same tenets of evidence-based governance place certain requirements on what actually counts as 'evidence'. Rigour, independence, and scientific consensus are some of the applicable qualifiers.[59] These hardly apply to soft law instruments, which are, ultimately, more legal and political than scientific in character. They are adopted by the Commission as a means to complement the environmental policy process and though often including expert input—for example, via the consultation of environmental science experts or academic institutions in the adoption process—they are far from the standard of scientific inquiry. After all, their purpose is not to advance scientific understanding but to ease administrative and judicial decision-making. What is more, soft law tends to be somewhat of a controversial player in terms of the legitimacy of its authority, which often comes into question due to its tendency to escape most forms of control[60] and the relative uncertainty of its legal effects.[61]

This leaves courts in an almost impossible situation. When they do use soft law as an interpretative aid, courts become open to criticism for endowing such instruments with authority—and subsequent legal or practical effects—that they are not meant to have.[62] When courts do not use soft law in their adjudication, they may be perceived as having too strict an interpretation of the divide between hard and soft law or as not utilizing the expertise at their disposal. In short, as per the idiom, they are damned if they do and they are damned if they don't. The EU Courts themselves seem to be aware of this tension relating to the use of soft law.[63] The literature puts forth a number of cautionary tales regarding this use of soft law by the Courts and the potential impact that

[59] For a broader discussion on what constitutes 'evidence' in evidence-based policymaking, see Gade, 'When is it Justified to Claim that a Practice or Policy is Evidence-Based? Reflections on Evidence and Preferences', 20 *Evidence & Policy* (2024) 244.

[60] See e.g. several contributions in M. Eliantonio, E. Korkea-aho, and U. Mörth (eds), *Research Handbook on Soft Law* (2023); Eliantonio and Stefan (n. 9); Petropoulou Ionescu and Eliantonio (n. 55); Petropoulou Ionescu and Eliantonio (n. 42); Tsakatika, 'A Parliamentary Dimension for EU Soft Governance', 29 *Journal of European Integration* (2007) 549; Senden and van den Brink, 'Checks & Balances in EU Soft Rule-Making', Study for the European Parliament Directorate-General for Internal Policies, Policy Department Citizens' Rights and Constitutional Affairs (2012), <https://www.europarl.europa.eu/RegData/etudes/etudes/join/2012/462433/IPOL-JURI_ET(2012)462433_EN.pdf> (last visited 1 June 2024).

[61] Chinkin, 'The Challenge of Soft Law: Development and Change in International Law', 38 *The International and Comparative Law Quarterly* (1989) 850.

[62] Eliantonio and Korkea-aho (n. 6).

[63] Ibid. 192.

it may have on legitimacy, democracy, and the rule of law.[64] Nonetheless, the EU Courts and national courts do make use of soft law and they do so rather frequently—especially in the environmental field.[65] This raises the question why, given the uncertainty and potential criticism of using soft law, the EU Courts decide to use it regardless.

The environmental field is of special importance here. As we have argued throughout this chapter, environmental problems are of a very particular character and create a distinct set of challenges for adjudication and policy. In turn, legal and administrative reasoning, as well as the toolbox needed to effectively reason, must be adapted to respond to these challenges.[66] This is especially true of generalist courts, which find themselves in the position of having to 'square the circle' and accommodate scientific facts and legal interpretations without possessing the necessary expertise to do so.[67] This may apply to several stages of the adjudication process, from understanding the problem at hand to reaching or justifying a decision.[68] The lack of readily available expertise on environmental matters may, then, create issues in adjudication due to the impermeability of scientific terms, gaps in available data, or unsettled scientific interpretations.[69] We posit that this is the point where soft law may become useful in the Courts' hands. It is well known that soft law instruments can be—and to an extent, are even *meant* to be—utilized as interpretative tools to 'flesh out' or provide context for hard law obligations.[70] What is not as well known are the ways in which courts substantively engage with these instruments. This is precisely what we aim to address in this chapter.

[64] Klabbers, 'The Redundancy of Soft Law', 65 *Nordic Journal of International Law* (1998) 167; Österdahl, 'The ECJ and Soft Law: Who's Afraid of the EU Fundamental Rights Charter?', in U. Mörth (ed.), *Soft Law in Governance and Regulation: An Interdisciplinary Analysis* (2004).

[65] Eliantonio and Korkea-aho (n. 6) 192.

[66] Warnock (n. 2) 161; Eliantonio and Krajewski, 'Scientific Uncertainty before the Court of Justice and the General Court: Is the Judicial Toolbox Sufficient?', in M. Eliantonio, E. Lees, and T. Paloniitty (eds), *EU Environmental Principles and Scientific Uncertainty Before National Courts: The Case of the Habitats Directive* (2023) 327.

[67] Eliantonio and Krajewski (n. 66) 328.

[68] On the broader discussion of the challenges posed on courts by environmental issues, see K. Sulyok, *Science and Judicial Reasoning: The Legitimacy of International Environmental Adjudication* (2021).

[69] García-Ureta (n. 5) 31; Eliantonio and Krajewski (n. 66) 328; Preston, 'Biodiversity in the Court: The Certainty of Contests about Uncertainty', in M. Eliantonio, E. Lees, and T. Paloniitty (eds), *EU Environmental Principles and Scientific Uncertainty Before National Courts: The Case of the Habitats Directive* (2023) 297; Stuart-Smith *et al.*, 'Filling the Evidentiary Gap in Climate Litigation', 11 *Nature Climate Change* (2021) 651.

[70] Eliantonio (n. 22).

4. Environmental Matters in the CJEU: What Room for Soft Law?

The resolution of environmental disputes requires a complex consideration and balancing of environmental, social, and economic factors.[71] This process requires the identification of relevant facts, the determination of the merit of each of these facts, and, eventually, the evaluation of their merit in relation to each case at hand.[72] In the case of the CJEU, we have argued throughout this chapter that the necessary expertise to effectively carry out these steps in adjudication is often lacking. It is, ultimately, an issue of technical, scientific, and administrative capacity. We argue that soft law instruments have the potential to alleviate this issue—although that may come with its own setbacks. This section sets out to explore the dynamic relationship between the EU Courts and the use of soft law as an interpretative aid. As explained in Section 2, the empirical part of this study was conducted by closely examining the environmental case law of the CJEU in cases where either the judges or AGs) utilized soft law in their argumentation. Our aim is to find out how this utilization takes place and how the Court makes use of this particular 'tool' to increase its decision-making capacity when adjudicating environmental matters. We proceed by first offering a few quantitative impressions on how the Court engages with soft law, before moving on to a qualitative analysis. In the latter step, our goal was to identify potential themes in the CJEU's engagement with soft law instruments, especially in light of the known challenges that environmental matters pose for (generalist) courts such as the CJEU.

A. Quantitative Insights: The Who, the What, and the When

Let us start our empirical exploration by looking at the broader status quo of the Court's engagement with environmental soft law. In this section, we provide an overview of the use of soft law in the process of adjudicating environmental matters stemming from the areas of biodiversity, environmental assessment, and water management, in terms of who uses it, how often, and in the context of what procedure. We address these three aspects in turn.

Who uses soft law? Our analysis showed that out of the 80 total guidance documents adopted by the European Commission in the areas of biodiversity,

[71] Warnock (n. 2) 162.
[72] Ibid. 162.

environmental assessment, and water management, 17 documents have been explicitly utilized by the EU Courts in their adjudication. Table 2.3 provides an overview, per field and legal act, of the references the Court (including the AGs) has made to guidance documents in its case law stemming from the legal act in question. In total, we identified 42 references to environmental soft law within a total of 34 cases.[73] By and large, these references occur in the AG Opinions, and more often than not they are not taken up in the rulings. Specifically, 33 out of 42 references come up in Opinions, while only nine come up in the Court's rulings. More or less, using soft law seems primarily to be an AG business. This occurrence does not cause much surprise. In contrast to the Court's rulings, the AGs enjoy more discretion in drafting their opinions and have the freedom to offer much more discursive reflections than judges

Table 2.3 Overview of references to guidance documents in CJEU environmental case law

Field	Legal act	Referenced guidance documents	References to guidance documents in case law
Biodiversity	Habitats Directive	5 (out of 5)	24 (19 in AG Opinions and 5 in rulings)
	Birds Directive	1 (out of 4)	4 (2 in AG Opinions and 2 in rulings)
	Natura 2000*	3 (out of 13)	3 (2 in AG Opinions and 1 in ruling)
Environmental assessment	EIA Directive	1 (out of 15)	1 (in AG Opinion)
	SEA Directive	1 (out of 3)	2 (in AG Opinions)
Water management	Water Framework Directive	6 (out of 40)	8 (7 in AG Opinions and 1 in ruling)
	Total references	**17 (out of 80)**	**42 (33 in AG Opinions and 9 in rulings)**

* Natura 2000 is a network of nature protection areas in the territory of the European Union based on the territories covered by the Habitats and Birds Directives. Natura finds its legal basis in Article 3 of the Habitats Directive but is in itself not a legal act and therefore not the direct subject of case law. Nonetheless, guidance documents that have been adopted under the Natura 2000 scheme have been referenced by the Court in cases brought under the two Nature Directives.

[73] The difference in the number of cases versus the number of references stems from the fact that some cases make reference to several instruments in their argumentation.

as, ultimately, they are not the ones actually delivering the rulings.[74] That, of course, does not mean that judges do not use soft law in rulings—as Table 2.3 clearly shows—but instead that, perhaps, there might be some further limitations to their engagement.

What soft law is used by the EU Courts? Going back to Table 2.3, we can see that there is some variation regarding which instruments are referenced and to what extent. For instance, in the case of the Water Framework Directive, we see that out of the total 40 guidance documents adopted by the European Commission only six are referenced by the CJEU, while all five instruments adopted under the Habitats Directive are referenced. What is more, some instruments seem to be referenced again and again by the Court in both rulings and AG Opinions. This is most evident in the case of the Habitats guidance documents, where five instruments have accrued 24 references. For example, the Commission's guidance on the strict protection of animal species seems to be of particular importance[75] as it appears in four rulings and six AG Opinions across eight cases. A similar picture can be observed in the guidance document on the provisions of Article 6 of the Habitats Directive,[76] which is referenced in seven AG Opinions and one ruling across seven cases. This particular 'popularity' of specific soft law instruments is mostly observed in the area of biodiversity and particularly in the guidance documents stemming from the Habitats Directive. Only a few instances of repeated use can be observed in the other two areas, specifically once in the guidance on the implementation of the SEA Directive which is referenced in two different cases[77] and once in the guidance on the application of exemptions to the Water Framework Directive's environmental objectives which is similarly referenced twice.[78]

[74] Reflecting on the role of AGs in the EU judicial system, former AG Léger, e.g., stated that Opinions '[place] the judgment in a more profound and coherent legal perspective. Depending on the importance of the questions asked, an Opinion can resemble a mini-thesis that exposes the legal and factual aspects of a case, any relevant comparative law from the national jurisdictions as well as academic commentaries. Finally, the Opinion serves a vital function in assuring the parties that their case has been heard and their arguments considered.' Léger, 'Law in the European Union: The Role of the Advocate General', 10 *The Journal of Legislative Studies* (2004) 1, at 5.

[75] European Commission, 'Guidance document on the strict protection of animal species of Community interest under the Habitats Directive 92/43/EEC' (2007), https://op.europa.eu/en/publication-detail/-/publication/1059d053-7082-421a-9bdc-54b2749c16c7 (last visited June 2024).

[76] European Commission, 'Managing Natura 2000 sites: The provisions of Article 6 of the 'Habitats' Directive 92/43/EEC' (2000), https://op.europa.eu/en/publication-detail/-/publication/2c9f4a14-8f97-43ac-a274-4946c142b541 (last visited June 2024).

[77] European Commission, 'Implementation of directive 2001/42/EC on the assessment of the effects of certain plans and programmes on the environment' (2003), https://op.europa.eu/en/publication-detail/-/publication/7c2796c8-2786-4faf-bafd-e7bb93082b16 (last visited June 2024).

[78] European Commission, 'Guidance Document No 20. Guidance document on exemptions to the environmental objectives' (2009), https://op.europa.eu/en/publication-detail/-/publication/a6f63214-46fb-4ab3-bdd5-3117011d51d4/language-en (last visited June 2024).

What does this tell us? While soft law itself, as a phenomenon, puts forth a façade of non-hierarchical norms, it is clear that institutional practice may give rise to some semblance of hierarchy between different soft law instruments or specific soft law measures. By utilizing some guidance documents more than others, and even more so when this is done repeatedly, the Court has the capacity to contribute to the building of authority for soft law. Certainly, this may happen for a myriad of reasons—for example, a guidance document might be more relevant in light of the cases that reach the CJEU or it may simply be more useful in terms of its content. After all, not all soft law instruments are made the same, far from it. Still, this occurrence is in line with the process of what is known in the literature as 'hardening', where through the gaining of a positive reputation—for example, through the reliance of the EU Courts on specific instruments—soft law gains power,[79] often beyond what it is meant to have. What also emerges is that it seems that there are areas where the CJEU has a higher need for the expertise—either technical, methodological, or scientific—contained in soft law. We come back to this in the next section.

Lastly, when do the EU Courts resort to soft law? Table 2.4 provides an overview of the proceedings in which the identified references to soft law have occurred. As shown, primarily these references emerge in preliminary ruling proceedings, followed by infringement proceedings to a lesser extent which are only present in the case of biodiversity law. This is, once more, to be expected for two reasons. First, due to the nature of EU environmental law at large, and more specifically the nature of these four Directives, the transposition, implementation, and enforcement takes place almost entirely at the national level

Table 2.4 Overview of the types of proceedings where environmental soft law is referenced

Field	Total cases	Infringement proceedings	Preliminary rulings	Action for annulment
Biodiversity	27	8	18	1
Environmental assessment	3		3	
Water management	4		4	

[79] Österdahl (n. 64) 51.

according to the model of indirect administration.[80] It is therefore only logical that the CJEU has engaged with the selected soft law instruments in the context of litigation concerning compliance of national law and administrative measures and practices with EU requirements. Second, the role of soft law instruments as interpretation aids and the very purpose of preliminary rulings to provide final interpretations of EU law provisions is a rather fitting match. In these instances, the guidance documents seem to be used to fulfil their purpose, since part of their objective is to provide clarification of ambiguous or unclear terms contained in EU law. In addition to the references to soft law in preliminary rulings and infringement proceedings, we have also identified a single instance where soft law was brought up in an action for annulment. This occurred in the *Sahlstedt* case,[81] concerning the procedure under the Habitats Directive for the designation of special areas of conservation. This case is of particular interest in light of *how* the Court engages with soft law—but this will be discussed later. In terms of the proceedings where soft law has been at stake, this case remains an outlier.

B. Qualitative Insights: The How and the Why

Having gained some general insights into the engagement of the CJEU with soft law instruments in the preceding section, this section zooms in and explores how and why soft law is used by the Court in its adjudication. Our aim here is to 'decipher' the Court's use of soft law and identify potential themes in how and why these instruments are used. In turn, this will help us gain a clearer picture of the motivation and approach of the Court when it comes to soft law, which will subsequently help us draw some broader conclusions about how this approach affects questions of legitimacy in environmental governance.

In carrying out this analysis, we conducted a close and in-depth review of the Court's case law in which each respective guidance document was referenced. This review included understanding the facts of each case, the legal issue at hand, and the arguments brought forth by the parties as well as those of the Court. In doing so, we identified five interconnected themes in the engagement with soft law, based on the function that soft law instruments were used to fulfil. First, we identified a number of instances in which soft law was merely used as a reference without any substantive engagement. Second, in a

[80] On this notion, see J. H. Jans, S. Prechal, and R. Widdershoven, *Europeanisation of Public Law* (2015).

[81] Case C-362/06 P, *Sahlstedt and Others v. Commission* (EU:C:2009:243).

number of cases, soft law was used by the Court as a scientific reference. Third, and possibly reflecting the complexity of environmental problems, we found that in several cases the Court uses soft law as a tool to understand the problem at hand. In the fourth theme we identified, the Court relies on soft law as a tool to justify a certain decision or a certain interpretation of an EU law provision. The fifth and final theme relates to cases where the Court referenced soft law as an argument to make a specific decision. In all of these themes, in one way or another, the Court uses soft law to increase its decision-making capacity—albeit at different levels. We discuss these in turn.

1. Soft Law *En Passant*

The first theme that we identified is in cases where soft law is referenced *en passant*—for example, in a footnote—without any substantive engagement with the content or arguments of the respective guidance document. Let us look at some examples.

In the Opinion of AG Kokott in *Föreningen Skydda Skogen*,[82] a case concerning a request for a preliminary ruling under the Habitats Directive, the Commission's guidance on the strict protection of animal species of Community interest[83] is referenced twice.[84] In both instances, AG Kokott acknowledges the relevance of the guidance document for the question of the referring court but points out that the Court has not taken the guidance into account even though, she posits, it appears that the substantive interpretation provided for in the guidance document has been implicitly adopted by the Court. In the same manner, in her Opinion in *Commission v. Ireland*,[85] a case relating to the failure of Ireland to designate sites as special areas of conservation, AG Ćapeta makes reference to the guidance document on the provisions of Article 6 of the Habitats Directive at two points through the use of footnotes.[86] Both of these references are provided entirely as contextual information and are, in fact, not explicitly mentioned in the text of the Opinion. The same level of engagement is also observed in the Opinion of AG Campos

[82] Opinion of AG Kokott in Joined Cases C-473/19 and C-474/19, *Föreningen Skydda Skogen* (EU:C:2020:699).

[83] European Commission, 'Guidance document on the strict protection of animal species of Community interest under the Habitats Directive 92/43/EEC' (2007), https://op.europa.eu/en/publication-detail/-/publication/1059d053-7082-421a-9bdc-54b2749c16c7 (last visited June 2024).

[84] Opinion of AG Kokott in Joined Cases C-473/19 and C-474/19, *Föreningen Skydda Skogen* (EU:C:2020:699), paras 48 and 103.

[85] Opinion of AG Ćapeta in Case C-444/21, *Commission v. Ireland (Protection des zones spéciales de conservation)* (EU:C:2023:90).

[86] Ibid. paras 23 and 38.

Sánchez-Bordona in *A and Others*.[87] In this case, brought under the SEA Directive, the Belgian court had submitted a request for a preliminary ruling to determine whether national courts are entitled to temporarily maintain the effects of national legislation in a dispute in the event that it is not compatible with EU law.[88] In his Opinion, AG Campos Sánchez-Bordona makes reference to the guidance document on the implementation of the SEA Directive on the assessment of the effects of certain plans and programmes on the environment through a footnote.[89] While not engaging with the arguments of the guidance, AG Campos Sánchez-Bordona points out that the Commission's guidance is meant to alleviate the difficulties posed by the SEA Directive on national authorities by providing an explanation of the terms 'plans and programmes' to aid in the identification of significant environmental effects.

The above examples indicate the most incidental and cursory use of soft law in environmental adjudication. So much so that this use begs the question of why it is even included in the first place. While the Opinions of AG Kokott and AG Campos Sánchez-Bordona demonstrate an acknowledgement of the content of the respective soft law instruments and their overall relevance in each case, the Opinion of AG Ćapeta simply gives a very subtle 'tip of the hat' that can easily be missed. With this in mind, there is little that can be said about the CJEU's *en passant* engagement with guidance documents without falling into the trap of conjecture or speculation. Still, although faintly, we can see that even in cases like this, soft law instruments seem to be a useful 'crutch' for the Court. A further consideration in this regard is that *en passant* does not necessarily mean uncritical. While it is true that in these cases soft law exists at the margins, it also could indicate the full acceptance of the content of the respective soft law instruments by the Court, without the need for an in-depth critical analysis. However, further empirical research that reaches beyond the scope of this chapter would be needed to examine this point in more depth.

2. Soft Law as Scientific Reference

The second theme we observed was in reference to soft law instruments as sources of scientific information—at times, more or less authoritative. This type of engagement hints at one of the more recognized issues brought about by environmental matters in the generalist courtroom: the lack of specialist knowledge. As we have argued throughout this chapter, environmental

[87] Opinion of AG Campos Sánchez-Bordona in Case C-24/19, *A and Others (Wind turbines at Aalter and Nevele)* (EU:C:2020:143).
[88] Ibid. para. 4.
[89] Ibid. para. 39.

problems come with a particular type of baggage which requires the consideration of scientific fact and scientific knowledge in the process of adjudication. Such consideration can occur in many ways and at different levels, and with varying degrees of substantive engagement. The first step, however, is the acknowledgement of the scientific knowledge contained in soft law as a resource. Let us take a closer look.

In the case *Waddenvereniging and Vogelsbeschermingvereniging (Waddenzee)* on whether the annual authorization of cockle fishing was to be regarded as approval of a plan or project and, subsequently, on the identification of the requirements for an 'appropriate assessment' under the Habitats Directive,[90] AG Kokott in her Opinion stated that the Directive does not lay down any methods for carrying out an appropriate assessment[91] thus recognizing a methodological knowledge-gap stemming from the application of the Habitats Directive. On this basis, the AG made reference to two of the Commission's guidance documents, specifically to the methodological guidance on the provisions of Article 6(3) and (4) of the Habitats Directive[92] and the guidance on the provisions of Article 6 of the Habitats Directive.[93] While recognizing that the instruments in question do not have legally binding force, the AG pointed out that both might be 'helpful' as sources of expertise on the matter. AG Kokott followed the same line in *Commission v. France*[94] on appropriate measures to protect the European hamster under the Habitats Directive. In this case, the Court was tasked with determining whether France was taking sufficient measures to that effect. The first step of this was to consider which measures are required by Article 12(1)(d) of the Habitats Directive for the European hamster, before assessing whether France was acting appropriately. In doing so, the AG explicitly stated that she took into account the guidance document on the protection of species under the Habitats Directive[95] as a source of useful guidance on the interpretation of the relevant

[90] Case C-127/02, *Waddenvereniging and Vogelsbeschermingvereniging* (EU:C:2004:482).

[91] Opinion of AG Kokott in Case C-127/02, *Waddenvereniging and Vogelsbeschermingvereniging* (EU:C:2004:60), paras 21 and 95.

[92] European Commission, 'Methodological guidance on the provisions of Article 6(3) and (4) of the Habitats Directive 92/43/EEC' (2021) OJ C 437/1. *NB: The AG makes reference to an earlier version of this instrument.*

[93] European Commission, 'Managing Natura 2000 sites: The provisions of Article 6 of the 'Habitats' Directive 92/43/EEC' (2000), https://op.europa.eu/en/publication-detail/-/publication/2c9f4a14-8f97-43ac-a274-4946c142b541 (last visited June 2024).

[94] Opinion of AG Kokott in Case C-383/09, *Commission v. France* (EU:C:2011:23).

[95] European Commission, 'Guidance document on the strict protection of animal species of Community interest under the Habitats Directive 92/43/EEC' (2007), https://op.europa.eu/en/publication-detail/-/publication/1059d053-7082-421a-9bdc-54b2749c16c7 (last visited June 2024).

provisions.[96] Interestingly, the AG also pointed towards the administrative expertise that the guidance document contains by hinting at the involvement of the Commission's DG Environment and the Member States in its drafting. AG Kokott then proceeded to reference the guidance at several points in her Opinion, recognizing it as a source of specialist knowledge while also acknowledging its non-binding character.[97]

In *Commission v. Malta*,[98] the Commission claimed that Maltese legislation, which permits the capture of seven species of wild finches, was in breach of the Birds Directive. In her Opinion, AG Sharpston addresses the condition of 'no other satisfactory solution', the fulfilment of which would allow Malta to derogate from certain provisions of the Birds Directive. The AG argues that the Member State must have genuinely explored and assessed whether there was 'no other satisfactory solution' to address the activity in question. In that context, she stated 'I draw here attention to the helpful methodology that the Commission has developed with regard to hunting derogations in its (non-binding) Guide to Sustainable Hunting—a methodology to which Malta subscribes, as it expressly stated in its defence.'[99] While the AG did not make any other direct references to this instrument, it seems that the guidance was (mutually) recognized by both the AG and Malta as a source of authoritative methodological expertise on the matter. Similarly, in the Opinion of AG Kokott in *Commission v. Austria*,[100] where the Court was inter alia tasked with establishing whether non-ecological interests are to be taken in to account within the scope of Article 6(1) of the Habitats Directive, the AG makes reference to both the previous case law of the Court in connection with the selection of protection areas under the Birds Directive and scientific sources including an academic article and the Commission's guidance entitled 'Managing Natura 2000 sites'.[101] While the latter two sources are, certainly, not of equal scientific standing, AG Kokott seems to recognize the guidance as an important source of specialist knowledge.

That being said, one must also point out that not all such engagement with soft law is in positive recognition of the expertise contained therein

[96] Opinion of AG Kokott in Case C-383/09, *Commission v. France* (EU:C:2011:23), para. 28.
[97] Ibid. para. 28.
[98] Case C-557/15, *Commission v. Malta* (EU:C:2018:477).
[99] Opinion of AG Sharpston in Case C-557/15, *Commission v. Malta* (EU:C:2017:613), para. 67.
[100] Opinion of AG Kokott in Case C-508/04, *Commission v. Austria* (EU:C:2007:9).
[101] European Commission, 'Managing Natura 2000 sites: The provisions of Article 6 of the "Habitats" Directive 92/43/EEC' (2000), https://op.europa.eu/en/publication-detail/-/publication/2c9f4a14-8f97-43ac-a274-4946c142b541 (last visited June 2024).

nor its relevance. This does not necessarily take away from the 'usefulness' of the expertise of soft law but it does raise questions pertaining to the—arguably, normative—choice to accept or reject it. For example, in its ruling in *Commission v. Finland*,[102] the Court asserted that decisions on derogating from the system of protection established by the Birds Directive must be based on well-established scientific knowledge, which must also be available to the national authorities at the time they grant the authorization.[103] This case pertains to an infringement procedure on granting authorization to hunt protected birds. In its argumentation, the Court took a critical stance towards the Commission's guidance document on the sustainable hunting of birds,[104] guidance which was previously found to be helpful by AG Sharpston in *Commission v. Malta* (see above). The Court asserted, repeatedly, that it was not clear whether or not the guidance document, adopted 12 years prior to the ruling in 2008, was out of date and, subsequently, whether Finland was right to rely on it. Specifically, the guidance document established that the common eider is a huntable bird species and therefore an authorization to derogate from the Directive could be granted, although at the time of adoption of the guidance the species was designated with an unfavourable conservation status. Ultimately, the Court did not accept the argumentation of the Finnish authorities which had, allegedly, relied on the guidance to grant authorization to hunt common eiders.

Is this case a rejection of soft law? Not really. Just as all the cases explored earlier are not decisive and overarching acceptance. Yet, it does indicate that there are certain qualifications—in this case relating to the temporal scope of scientific information—and that there are some unspoken standards for the expertise of soft law to be deemed appropriate and suitable. This is something that we would expect of a typical scientific inquiry. As we argued earlier, however, soft law does not fall within this category. This does raise a question about who decides (and on the basis of which standards) the quality and applicability of soft law measures as scientific references or sources of expertise, in either accepting or rejecting those measures.

[102] Case C-217/19, *Commission v. Finland (Spring hunting of male common eiders)* (EU:C:2020:291).
[103] Ibid. para. 70.
[104] European Commission, 'Guide to Sustainable Hunting Under the Birds Directive Council Directive 79/409/EEC on the conservation of wild birds' (2008), https://circabc.europa.eu/ui/group/3f466d71-92a7-49eb-9c63-6cb0fadf29dc/library/4b5dffd4-369c-4c4b-a249-625adc2a7545 (last visited June 2024).

3. Soft law as a Tool to Understand the Problem

Let us take a step further. The next theme we identified, signifying a deeper engagement with soft law, is in cases where the Court uses soft law instruments to understand the problem at hand. As previously argued, environmental problems require a wide set of skills from courts. One of the biggest challenges of these problems is comprehending the full extent of the issue so that a well-founded and well-reasoned decision can be made. In this process, the Court often needs to rely on non-legal expertise in order to achieve this understanding. We examine this in more detail.

In *Commission v. Finland*,[105] a case relating to the granting of derogations for wolf hunting under the Habitats Directive, the Court was asked to determine the existence of 'no other satisfactory solution' and to establish whether granting authorization for (controlled) wolf hunting would worsen the unfavourable conservation status of the species in question. In its reasoning, the Court referred to the Commission's guidance on the strict protection of animal species[106] to argue that it was possible that the killing of a limited number of wolves may have had no effect on the objective envisaged in Article 16(1) of the Habitats Directive, which consists in maintaining the wolf population at a favourable conservation status in its natural range.[107] Such a derogation, the Court argued, would be neutral for the species concerned.[108] In this instance, contrary to the cases examined in the preceding section, the Court did not simply accept the expertise of the guidance document but took a further step in utilizing said expertise to understand whether or not derogations could be deemed positive, negative, or neutral. In a similar case, stemming from a request from a preliminary ruling in *Naturschutzbund Deutschland-Landesverband Schleswig-Holstein*,[109] the Court used the Commission's 'Guidance on Aquaculture and Natura 2000'[110] to interpret the concepts of 'habitat records' and 'target documents'.[111] This was specifically done in

[105] Case C-342/05, *Commission v. Finland* (EU:C:2007:341).

[106] European Commission, 'Guidance document on the strict protection of animal species of Community interest under the Habitats Directive 92/43/EEC' (2007), https://op.europa.eu/en/publication-detail/-/publication/1059d053-7082-421a-9bdc-54b2749c16c7 (last visited June 2024).

[107] Case C-342/05, *Commission v. Finland* (EU:C:2020:291), para. 29.

[108] Ibid. para. 29.

[109] Case C-297/19, *Naturschutzbund Deutschland-Landesverband Schleswig-Holstein* (EU:C:2020:533).

[110] European Commission, 'Guidance on Aquaculture and Natura 2000 Sustainable aquaculture activities in the context of the Natura 2000 Network' (2019), https://op.europa.eu/en/publication-detail/-/publication/3c04edd0-8e4e-11e9-9369-01aa75ed71a1 (last visited June 2024).

[111] Case C-297/19, *Naturschutzbund Deutschland-Landesverband Schleswig-Holstein* (EU:C:2020:533), paras 59–60.

reference to Annex I to Directive 2004/35, and particularly the notion of significant damage, in order to reach a decision.

In his Opinion in *Grace and Sweetman*,[112] AG Tanchev made use of the Commission's soft law to understand the problem but not only from a scientific perspective. The case concerned a request from the Irish courts for a preliminary ruling stemming from the decision of the Irish Planning Appeals Board (An Bord Pleanála) to grant ESB Wind Developments Ltd and Coillte permission for a wind farm project in a special protection area which was classified as it hosted the natural habitat of the protected hen harrier. The AG made use of the Commission's guidance on wind energy development and Nature 2000 sites in two ways.[113] The first pertains to understanding the special protection requirements of the hen harrier as a species, including the natural habitats of the bird, and its relationship with human intervention. This type of engagement is more akin to a scientific resource—as we discussed previously—but it is not used simply as an external reference. Instead, the AG took the content and arguments of the guidance into account in the process of understanding the problem relating to the species.[114] The second relates to understanding the role of the precautionary principle in the context of the implementation of Article 6(3) of the Habitats Directive as a means to interpret the distinction between protective measures forming part of a plan or project and compensatory measures.[115] In this way, the AG engaged substantively with the content of the guidance and used it as a tool to comprehend the intricacies of the issues in areas which his expertise might not have covered.

This type of engagement is particularly evident in the Opinion of AG Jääskinen in *Bund für Umwelt und Naturschutz Deutschland*.[116] The case concerned a request for a preliminary ruling stemming from the Water Framework Directive regarding the scope of the concepts of 'environmental objectives' and of 'deterioration' of the status of bodies of water.[117] When tackling the notion of 'deterioration', the AG referred to the debate in the legal literature on the meaning of this concept. In his Opinion, because of the need for further information to understand the meaning and scope of the concept for 'a more

[112] Case C-164/17, *Grace and Sweetman* (EU:C:2018:593).

[113] European Commission, 'Guidance document on wind energy developments and EU nature legislation' (2020), https://op.europa.eu/en/publication-detail/-/publication/2b08de80-5ad4-11eb-b59f-01aa75ed71a1 (last visited June 2024).

[114] Opinion of AG Tanchev in Case C-164/17, *Grace and Sweetman* (EU:C:2018:274).

[115] Ibid. paras 58 and 79.

[116] Opinion of AG Jääskinen in Case C-461/13, *Bund für Umwelt und Naturschutz Deutschland* (EU:C:2014:2324).

[117] Ibid. para. 2.

in-depth study of the technical aspects arising from the WFD',[118] the AG referred to the relevant guidance document on the classification of ecological status and ecological potential.[119] In the same opinion, the AG also made a point regarding the authority of the guidance by highlighting that several parties referred to the same Commission guidance document but drew contradictory conclusions from it.[120] In that regard, the AG argued, there seemed to be some confusion between the concept of deterioration and a failure to comply with the provisions of the WFD itself.[121] The AG considered that the guidance document in question established that the Member States are required to adopt all the measures which enable the good status of bodies of water to be attained, in particular by implementing the environmental objectives referred to in Article 4 of the Directive.[122] From this interaction between the AG and the guidance in question we can see that this particular document seems to be rather vital in the framework of the Directive for the determination of concepts and key terms.

4. Soft Law as a Justification for a Decision or an Interpretation

The fourth theme we identified, relating to an even deeper engagement with soft law, is in cases where the Court uses soft law instruments not only to understand the problem but also as a means of substantiating its decision or interpretation. In contrast to the previous cases where the Court uses soft law as a scientific basis or as a tool to understand the problem, in the situations discussed in this section the Court instrumentalizes soft law in order to make a certain argument or to support a particular interpretation. This instrumentalization is of special interest here as it has a greater bearing—in comparison to the preceding two categories—on the legitimacy of the Court's decision-making and, ultimately, its decisions. We provide some examples below.

Going back to the *Waddenzee* ruling,[123] the Court used soft law for the purposes of determining the application of the notion of significant effects on the environment. It argued that the triggering of the environmental protection mechanism provided for in Article 6(3) of the Habitats Directive does not

[118] Ibid. para. 90.
[119] European Commission, 'Common Implementation Strategy for the Water Framework Directive Guidance Document No. 13 Overall Approach to the Classification of Ecological Status and Ecological Potential' (2005), https://circabc.europa.eu/sd/a/06480e87-27a6-41e6-b165-0581c2b046ad/Guidance%20No%2013%20-%20Classification%20of%20Ecological%20Status%20(WG%20A).pdf (last visited 12 February 2024).
[120] Ibid. para. 106.
[121] Ibid. para. 107.
[122] Ibid. para. 107.
[123] Case C-127/02, *Waddenvereniging and Vogelsbeschermingvereniging* (EU:C:2004:482).

presume that the plan or project considered definitely has significant effects on the site concerned but follows from the mere *probability* that such an effect attaches to that plan or project. In this context, the Court brought up the guidance on Article 6 of the Habitats Directive[124] as an authoritative source which 'clearly' supported the Court's interpretation,[125] more or less like a stamp of approval. This pattern seems to appear quite frequently. For instance, in the case *Grand Hamster II*,[126] the Court referred to the Commission's guidance on the strict protection of animal species in issuing its preliminary ruling concerning the adoption of administrative decisions on building works that lead to the deterioration or destruction of resting places or breeding sites of the European hamster.[127] In doing so, the Court used this guidance to support its interpretation of the terms 'breeding site', 'deterioration', and 'destruction'. Similarly to *Waddenzee*, in *Grand Hamster II* the Court presented its interpretation of the respective term and then used the guidance as a means of supporting and substantiating its view.

This type of usage also extends to the Opinions of AGs. In the case *Stadt Frankfurt (Oder) and FWA*,[128] concerning the interpretation—for the first time—of Article 7(3) of the Water Framework Directive concerning the establishment of safeguard zones for bodies of drinking water, AG Medina relied on the Commission's guidance to interpret a phrase in Article 7(3) of the Directive as well as to reach a decision on the possibility for Member States to establish safeguard zones.[129] Specifically, the AG took issue with the meaning of 'avoiding deterioration in [water] quality in order to reduce the level of purification treatment' contained in Article 7(3). According to AG Medina, the above phrase demonstrated that the aim the Member States must fulfil is to reduce the level of purification treatment required in the production of drinking water and the means to achieve that aim is the obligation that Member States should, as a minimum, avoid deterioration in the quality of bodies of water.[130] In making this argument, the AG quoted the 'Guidance on Groundwater in Drinking

[124] European Commission, 'Managing Natura 2000 sites: The provisions of Article 6 of the 'Habitats' Directive 92/43/EEC' (2000), https://op.europa.eu/en/publication-detail/-/publication/2c9f4a14-8f97-43ac-a274-4946c142b541 (last visited June 2024).

[125] Case C-127/02, *Waddenvereniging and Vogelsbeschermingvereniging* (EU:C:2004:482), paras 40–41.

[126] Case C-357/20, *Magistrat der Stadt Wien (Grand hamster—II)* (EU:C:2021:881), paras 26, 40, and 48.

[127] That dispute had previously given rise to a request for a preliminary ruling, on which the Court ruled in the judgment of Case C-477/19, *Magistrat der Stadt Wien (Grand hamster)* (EU:C:2020:517).

[128] Case C-723/21, *Stadt Frankfurt (Oder) and FWA* (EU:C:2023:264).

[129] Opinion of AG Medina in Case C-723/21, *Stadt Frankfurt (Oder) and FWA* (EU:C:2023:152).

[130] Ibid. paras 51–52.

Water Protected Areas',[131] and pointed out that it supported her interpretation of Article 7(3) and, in fact, added that the guidance document enjoyed significant authority as it represented a consensus position on best practice agreed by the Commission, all Member States, and other stakeholders.[132] In the same ruling, concerning the obligations for Member States stemming from Articles 7(2) and 4 of the Water Framework Directive and the relationship between the two provisions, AG Medina referred to soft law to corroborate her conclusions that Article 7(2) established additional obligations vis-à-vis those contained in Article 4.[133] In particular, AG Medina substantiated her argument through a direct quote of the same guidance document which explains,[134] in relation to Article 7(2) of the WFD, that the objectives of Article 4 (i.e. status, prevent or limit, implementation of trend reversal and other protected area objectives) must be met independently of meeting those of Article 7, including a general requirement to ensure that water is free from contamination that could constitute a danger to human health.[135] This type of engagement with soft law comes up time and time again. It is, seemingly, the most common way the CJEU uses soft law in its environmental adjudication.

While the great majority of the cases we have reviewed in this category seem to make wide use of soft law to support their arguments, we identified one instance where soft law was used as a springboard instead of a baseline. In his Opinion in the case *Association France Nature Environnement*,[136] AG Rantos took a bold approach.[137] The case, stemming from the Water Framework Directive, concerned the question of whether the Directive permitted the competent national authorities, during the authorization procedure for an individual programme or project, not to take into account temporary, short-term impacts on the status of a body of surface water which were without lasting consequences and, if so, under what conditions the derogations from the prohibition of deterioration of a body of water may be applicable. On this matter, the AG noted that the referring court mentioned the Commission's guidance on

[131] European Commission, 'Guidance Document No. 16 Guidance on Groundwater in Drinking Water Protected Areas' (2007), https://circabc.europa.eu/sd/a/aef48d98-7715-4828-a7ee-df82a6df4afb/Guidance%20No%2016%20-%20Groundwater%20in%20DWPAs.pdf (last visited June 2024).

[132] Opinion of AG Medina in *Stadt Frankfurt (Oder) and FWA* (EU:C:2023:152), para. 52.

[133] Ibid. para. 146.

[134] European Commission, 'Guidance Document No. 16 Guidance on Groundwater in Drinking Water Protected Areas' (2007), https://circabc.europa.eu/sd/a/aef48d98-7715-4828-a7ee-df82a6df4afb/Guidance%20No%2016%20-%20Groundwater%20in%20DWPAs.pdf (last visited June 2024).

[135] Opinion of AG Medina in *Stadt Frankfurt (Oder) and FWA* (EU:C:2023:152), para. 146.

[136] Case C-525/20, *Association France Nature Environnement (Impacts temporaires sur les eaux de surface)* (EU:C:2022:350).

[137] Opinion of AG Rantos in Case C-525/20, *Association France Nature Environnement (Impacts temporaires sur les eaux de surface)* (EU:C:2022:16).

exemptions to the Directive's environmental objectives,[138] according to which if there were no long-term adverse consequences for the water status, such fluctuations did not constitute deterioration. The AG continued by reinstating the non-legally binding nature of the guidance and, by looking only at the wording of the Water Framework Directive, concluded that the only criterion to be taken into account in an authorization procedure was whether or not 'deterioration' within the meaning of that provision was liable to occur. He therefore took the view that 'that document does not reflect the content of the directive, as interpreted by the Court' and proceeded to depart from it.[139] We deem that this constitutes a particularly environmentally friendly argument as the AG concluded that Article 4 of the Directive required Member States to take into account temporary, short-term impacts on the status of a body of surface water which were without lasting consequences when assessing whether an individual programme or project was compatible with the objective of preventing deterioration of water quality. In his Opinion, AG Rantos did not use the guidance to 'corroborate' his interpretation but instead utilized it as a benchmark to push for a more environmentally conscious reading of the Directive.

5. Soft Law as a Tool to Make a Decision

The last type of engagement we identified, although rare, not only uses soft law as a tool but also relies on it to make a decision. In these instances, by relying on the Commission's soft law instruments to reach a decision, the Court assigns great authority to such instruments. Even though the Court does—rather consistently—recognize the non-binding nature of soft law, in these instances, the Court somewhat blurs that line. Let us explore this further.

In the *Sahlstedt* case,[140] which is also the only case concerning an action for annulment in our dataset, an action was brought against the Commission list foreseen in the Habitats Directive declaring an area of Community interest. In order for their claim to be admissible under Article 263(4) TFEU, the applicants needed to prove direct concern. To do so, under the established case law of the CJEU,[141] it was necessary to prove that the Member States had no

[138] European Commission, 'Guidance Document No. 36 Exemptions to the Environmental Objectives according to Article 4(7) New modifications to the physical characteristics of surface water bodies, alterations to the level of groundwater, or new sustainable human development activities' (2017), https://circabc.europa.eu/sd/a/e0352ec3-9f3b-4d91-bdbb-939185be3e89/CIS_Guidance_Article_4_7_FINAL.PDF (last visited June 2024).

[139] Opinion of AG Rantos in Case C-525/20, *Association France Nature Environnement (Impacts temporaires sur les eaux de surface)* (EU:C:2022:16), para. 76.

[140] Case C-362/06 P, *Sahlstedt and Others v. Commission* (EU:C:2009:243).

[141] Joined Cases 21 to 24-72, *International Fruit Company* (EU:C:1972:115); Case C-152/88, *Sofrimport v. Commission* (EU:C:1990:259).

discretion in the implementation of the contested decision. In this context, AG Bot delivered an Opinion positing that inter alia the EU legislation established narrow limits on the discretion enjoyed by the competent national authorities under the Directive.[142] In his argument, AG Bot showed that this discretion was, indeed, limited by relying on the Commission's guidance on Article 6 of the Habitats Directive.[143] The AG outlined the content of the guidance explaining that it defines the meaning of the concepts of 'disturbance' and 'deterioration' of conservation sites and sets out an approach to be taken by the Member States when assessing conservation risks. In addition, the AG held that on the basis of the case law and the guidance in question, the Commission laid down the conditions and time limits in accordance with which the Member States were then required to adopt conservation measures.[144] In his argumentation, AG Bot considered this guidance to be able to limit the discretion of the national authorities and in fact treated it almost as if it was binding on the Member States. This represents an interesting case which goes well beyond the bounds of 'support' or 'corroboration' and instead uses soft law as the reason *why* a decision should be made in a certain way.

On similar grounds, *Holohan and Others*[145] was concerned with whether the Habitats Directive required that the potential impact on all species (as opposed to only protected species) which contribute to and are part of a protected habitat must be identified and discussed in an assessment under Article 6(3) of the Habitats Directive. In her Opinion, AG Kokott stated that the Habitats Directive provides only a rudimentary definition of the species that are typical of certain habitat types.[146] The AG made the point that scientific research and discussion of the different habitat types should make it possible to identify further typical species and essentially fill the 'gap' in the Directive.[147] In this context, AG Kokott noted the Commission's 'Interpretation Manual of Habitats'[148] and asserted that it contained valuable guidance in that regard, while also recognizing its non-binding nature.[149] Still, regardless of this caveat

142 Opinion of AG Bot in Case C-362/06 P, *Sahlstedt and Others v. Commission* (EU:C:2008:587).
143 European Commission, 'Managing Natura 2000 sites: The provisions of Article 6 of the 'Habitats' Directive 92/43/EEC' (2000), https://op.europa.eu/en/publication-detail/-/publication/2c9f4a14-8f97-43ac-a274-4946c142b541 (last visited June 2024).
144 Opinion of AG Bot in C-362/06 P, *Sahlstedt and Others v. Commission* (EU:C:2008:587), para. 97.
145 Case C-461/17, *Holohan and Others* (EU:C:2018:883).
146 Opinion of AG Kokott in Case C-461/17, *Holohan and Others* (EU:C:2018:649).
147 Ibid. para. 37.
148 European Commission, 'Interpretation Manual of European Union Habitats' (2013), https://circabc.europa.eu/ui/group/3f466d71-92a7-49eb-9c63-6cb0fadf29dc/library/37d9e6d9-b7de-42ce-b789-622e9741b68f/details (last visited June 2024).
149 Opinion of AG Kokott in *Holohan and Others* (EU:C:2018:649), para. 37.

of non-bindingness, AG Kokott used the Manual to show that there were more species than immediately apparent from the habitat type designation and considered it almost on a par with the other arguments in the case.[150]

5. A Double-Edged Sword: The Tension between Capacity and Authority

What general conclusions can we draw about the engagement of the CJEU with environmental soft law? Having delved into the use of EU environmental soft law by the CJEU in its adjudication, we now turn our attention to the—more conceptual—focus of this chapter and this volume: legitimacy. Our analysis shows that the Court's engagement with soft law at various stages of its reasoning relates to the legitimacy of the EU environmental governance system in three key ways.

First, and very much as expected, soft law measures are used to increase the scientific, methodological, and administrative capacity of the Court. As we saw in several cases, the Court—both through its rulings and the opinions of the AGs—lacks specialist knowledge to understand the context, content, and relevance of terms and concepts contained in directives stemming from the areas of biodiversity, environmental assessment, and water management. In these instances, without recourse to soft law, the Court is deprived of the necessary know-how to fully understand and decide on matters of environmental concern. In turn, without soft law, the Court would find itself in a position where its lack of expertise would result in decisions which lack epistemic legitimacy. Soft law is key in this regard. The specialist knowledge contained in soft law instruments which are aimed at aiding the implementation, application, and interpretation of EU law provisions—either by providing scientific fact or context, or by providing methodological guidance on *how* a rule is to be operationalized effectively—is vital to the legitimacy of the decisions of the Court.

However, this does not come without some clear risks. By increasing the scientific and administrative capacity of the Court through soft law, and therefore by increasing the epistemic legitimacy of its decisions, the political legitimacy of the decision can be put into question. As several AGs have pointed out in their Opinions, no matter how helpful a soft law measure may be, it is of a non-binding nature and a product of executive rule-making which does

[150] Ibid. paras 33–44.

not, necessarily, live up to the standards of scientific inquiry. Therefore, while soft law may exhibit a façade of expertise and knowledge, this might not always be the case. Here we recall the critical stance of the Court in *Commission v. Finland*,[151] where the relevance of the Commission's guidance on sustainable hunting, containing a list of species and their corresponding conservation status, was brought into question since it had not been updated in over a decade.[152] What is important to note at this point is that there are few requirements imposed on soft law regarding its adoption and review and, by extension, on the appropriateness of the information contained therein.[153] This makes the relationship between soft law and epistemic legitimacy a difficult one on which to draw definitive conclusions, as one should not disregard the expertise of soft law, but should also be wary of its status against standards of scientific and administrative knowledge.

Second, we see that in the broad need for expertise in the Court's adjudication, we can identify different types of specialist knowledge required when adjudicating environmental matters. For example, in *Commission v. France*,[154] AG Kokott turned to soft law to seek an interpretation of unclear terms relating to the protection of the European hamster. In *Commission v. Malta*,[155] AG Sharpston resorted to soft law to identify methodological guidance on applying derogations under the Birds Directive. In other examples, we can see the Court reaching out to find support, corroboration, or scientific evidence. What this points to is that, in response to the particular challenges posed by issues of environmental concern, there have emerged some—more or less—specific gaps in the Court's expertise. Addressing these gaps subsequently requires different approaches to capacity-building. As argued in the introduction to this volume, the ability of the Court, or in fact any institution, to promote or undermine the legitimacy of governance processes is very much dependent upon its capacity to effectively discharge the function attributed to it.[156] Through this two-step relationship, we argue that addressing the Court's knowledge gaps, for example in terms of scientific, methodological, or administrative know-how, through soft law increases the capacity of the CJEU to successfully fulfil its role

[151] See n. 102.

[152] European Commission, 'Guide to Sustainable Hunting Under the Birds Directive Council Directive 79/409/EEC on the conservation of wild birds' (2008), https://circabc.europa.eu/ui/group/3f466d71-92a7-49eb-9c63-6cb0fadf29dc/library/4b5dffd4-369c-4c4b-a249-625adc2a7545 (last visited June 2024).

[153] Petropoulou Ionescu and Eliantonio (n. 42).

[154] Case C-383/09, *Commission v. France* (EU:C:2011:23).

[155] Case C-557/15, *Commission v. Malta* (EU:C:2018:477).

[156] See Chapter 1, Section 1.

in adjudicating environmental matters, which in turn increases the Court's contribution to the legitimacy of the Union's environmental governance system. Specifically, in terms of the different types of reasons why the Court uses soft law, it may increase different types of legitimacy. For instance, when engaging with soft law as a means of understanding a problem or as scientific reference, the Court increases the epistemic legitimacy of its decisions. When engaging with soft law for matters of methodological guidance, it increases the legitimacy of its contribution to administrative practices.

The third issue that emerges from our analysis concerns the normative choices of the Court to engage with soft law. We recall once more the Commission's guidance document on sustainable hunting,[157] which was deemed useful by AG Sharpston in *Commission v. Malta* but rejected as outdated by the Court in *Commission v. Finland*.[158] Though this is the most obvious example of the normative tension that rules the relationship between soft law and the courts—which we addressed in depth in Section 3—there are many more normative choices that are made before a guidance makes it to the text of an opinion or a ruling. Courts must decide whether or not to use soft law, how to use it, in what way, whether or not they meaningfully engage with its content, whether they accept or reject its knowledge, and whether soft law can act as a reliable source. In short, the waters are rather muddied and, as the title of our chapter suggests, from the perspective of an external observer, the CJEU can be 'damned' if it does engage with soft law by endowing it with an 'epistemic force' which it was arguably not supposed to have and equally 'damned' if it disregards relevant scientific knowledge and only relies on its non-specialist background.

Regardless of the potential drawbacks relating to political legitimacy in using soft law as an authoritative source of specialist knowledge—either at the level of a footnote, a scientific reference, or as the basis for a decision—what we can say with certainty is that the Court makes wide use of it to serve a series of different purposes. By and large, and with *very* few exceptions, soft law instruments seem to be a useful addition to the Court's toolbox as they are used to better inform the CJEU in understanding, interpreting, and deciding on environmental matters. In this sense, its purpose in acting as a complementary aid for the CJEU and the Member States is well fulfilled. This purpose

157 European Commission, 'Guide to Sustainable Hunting Under the Birds Directive. Council Directive 79/409/EEC on the conservation of wild birds' (2008), https://circabc.europa.eu/ui/group/3f466d71-92a7-49eb-9c63-6cb0fadf29dc/library/4b5dffd4-369c-4c4b-a249-625adc2a7545 (last visited 1 June 2024).

158 See n. 102.

is particularly relevant in the environmental field, as we have seen again and again, where specialist knowledge is lacking, while, at the same time, the amount of vague terms and unsettled information is immense. In this way, an argument can be made that the Court does attempt to increase its capacity—and, by extension, the legitimacy of its decisions and ultimately of EU environmental governance—by meaningfully engaging with the Commission's soft law instruments.

6. Conclusions

This chapter set out to explore the intricate relationship between the EU Courts, soft law, and environmental matters—one that we have described as being akin to walking a tightrope. Through an analysis of the guidance documents adopted by the European Commission in the fields of biodiversity, environmental assessment, and water management, we have found that the CJEU in its adjudication, either through rulings or AG Opinions, makes broad use of soft law as a means to address some of the challenges posed by the presence of environmental matters in generalist courts such as the CJEU. As we have argued throughout this chapter, issues of environmental concern come with specific and complex 'baggage' and require generalist courts to go above and beyond their capacity. Soft law fills the knowledge gap which inevitably presents itself in environmental litigation.

Of course, this does not occur across the board, neither in terms of what soft law is used nor who uses it. As revealed by our quantitative analysis, some soft law instruments seem to enjoy a higher status than others, with a number of them being quoted time and time again. The same applies to the 'users' of soft law. As was shown in our qualitative analysis, there are certain 'usual suspects' who seem to quote soft law more than others—most notably, AG Kokott. These types of inconsistencies are bound to emerge given the context in which soft law can emerge. It is, ultimately, up to the discretion of the Court and the AGs to use or not use it, to agree or disagree with it, to accept or reject it. All in all, however, and within the remit of this necessarily incomplete analysis of environmental litigation, we can conclude that the way in which soft law has been used contributes to the capacity-building process of the CJEU, which in turn increases the legitimacy of the environmental rules on which the Court is called to adjudicate. Of course, the increase of this type of legitimacy also comes with certain drawbacks relating to political legitimacy. Thus, in any discussion regarding the interplay between courts and soft law—within the realm of environmental matters, and far beyond—we must take a bi-directional approach and consider how these instruments might increase the legitimacy of the CJEU's adjudication and of the governance framework on which it adjudicates, but also how their consideration by the Court in that process might endow them with more authority.

While our analysis here reveals some interesting patterns in the use of soft law by the CJEU in its environmental adjudication, we must also acknowledge certain limitations and avenues for further research. As we argued in the introduction to our chapter, the process of engaging with soft law is considerably dynamic, bottom-up, and—to a degree—rests on the discretion and goodwill of the Court. Due to this, one can only deduce a certain amount of information from the Court's output (the AG Opinions and the Court's rulings which explicitly refer to soft law instruments) without examining the interactional process closely or researching situations in which soft law might have made a meaningful contribution to the adjudicatory process but was not considered (at least explicitly) by the Court. A look into this would also address the normative choices now made by the Court only when engaging with soft law and identifying the appropriate measures to do so, but also when deciding not to engage. This is a side of soft law, and to an extent also of courts, that remains somewhat under-researched. Further research into this, including interviews with AGs and CJEU judges, could help us further understand the relationship between courts and soft law, and how their curious link might impact the CJEU's work in the field of environmental adjudication.

3

Environmental Principles and Legitimacy

Power-Allocation, Knowledge Gaps, and Coherence

Emma Lees

1. Introduction

The role of the environmental principles, both within and without the EU, has been extensively discussed in the literature.[1] The aim of this chapter is to examine whether, and how, their operation enhances the legitimacy of EU environmental governance, especially in the situations where the principles are invoked by the CJEU. In so doing, it is necessary to develop an understanding of how such principles work and their functions within the corpus of environmental jurisprudence before considering those functions in light of the legitimacy framework developed in the first chapter of this volume.

Section 2 explores the roles of the environmental principles. It draws upon Scotford's work, considering her three categories of 'policy cases', 'interpretive cases', and 'informing legal tests cases',[2] before exploring the additional categories of 'evaluating evidence' and 'power- and responsibility-allocation'. Section 3 will consider how these functions enhance the legitimacy of the operation of environmental law by examining whether the principles tend to obfuscate or resolve inconsistencies, to fill gaps or to render the legal landscape more obscure, or to enhance the role of justice and environmental protection. This section considers three recent cases in detail to show these functions in practice. I consider *Bayer v. Commission*,[3] *Austria v.*

[1] Most prominently: E. Scotford, *Environmental Principles and the Evolution of Environmental Law* (2017); Fisher, 'Precaution, Precaution Everywhere: Developing a "Common Understanding" of the Precautionary Principles in the European Community', 9 *Maastricht Journal of European and Comparative Law* (2002) 7; and N. de Sadeleer, *Environmental Principles: From Political Slogans to Legal Rules* (2nd edn, 2020). Scotford's work, in particular, examines in detail the contributions that principles can make to legitimacy.

[2] Scotford (n. 1) ch 4.

[3] Case C-499/18, *Bayer CropScience v. Commission* (EU:C:2021:367).

Emma Lees, *Environmental Principles and Legitimacy* In: *The Legitimacy of EU Environmental Governance and the Role of the European Courts*. Edited by: Mariolina Eliantonio and Emma Lees, Oxford University Press.
 DOI: 10.1093/oso/9780198972808.003.0003

Commission,[4] and *JP v. Ministre de la Transition*.[5] Section 4 concludes, emphasizing the entanglement between the principles and the rules of judicial review and administrative discretion and the methodological challenges faced by courts when resolving environmental problems. The principles, it will be shown, contribute to legitimacy by bypassing limited judicial capacity and by embedding expertise into a system which otherwise might lack direct scientific input. However, in making these two contributions, the use of the principles also generates risks in legitimacy terms.

Where the principles are used to allow action notwithstanding gaps in knowledge[6]—be that evidential as to the impact of any particular proposal, or doctrinal in terms of knowledge of the intended meaning or 'correct' meaning of a particular term used in legislation—the principles enhance the coherence of the legal system and, as such, enhance legitimacy. However, where the principles become a means to *avoid acknowledging* the existence of such uncertainties, facilitating a bypassing of questions mandated by legislation, or reassigning decision-making power, then the use of the principles not only undermines the coherence and clarity of the law but can also frustrate some of the goals of the environmental law rules. When, similarly, the environmental principles operate so as to dislodge state responsibility and capacity to strengthen the connection between decision-making and the democratic state, a turn to technocratic decision-making generates its own challenges in a field where there are, unfortunately, no clear answers.

2. Multiple and Contingent Roles

The question of the nature of the environmental principles can be asked both descriptively and theoretically. The descriptive question is relatively easy: what are the accepted principles of EU environmental law? The answer to this question determines the scope of the object under our gaze. The second—the theoretical question—is more complex. What *are* the principles of environmental governance? This is not easy to answer, for we must ask not only what legal principles are in general[7] but also whether the objects we are discussing in this chapter are *appropriately* referred to as principles. However, the answers

[4] Case C-594/18 P, *Austria v. Commission* (EU:C:2020:742).

[5] Case C-61/21, *JP v. Ministre de la Transition Écologique* (EU:C:2022:1015).

[6] See Lees, 'R (Wyatt) v. Fareham Borough Council: Worst Case Scenario and Habitats Protection', 24 Environmental Law Review (2022) 314.

[7] There is an extensive discussion of the nature of principles in Scotford (n. 1) 108–113.

to these questions are relatively settled even if, as we might expect, there are some questionable cases 'at the edges'. If we seek central case definitions both descriptively and normatively, then the starting point of our task is relatively straightforward.

In this chapter, I consider the environmental principles as contained in the EU Treaties: the precautionary principle, the polluter pays principle, the prevention principle, the principle of rectification at source (Art. 191(2) TFEU[8]), the principle of integration, and the principle of sustainable development (Art. 11 TFEU). These principles are notable not only for what was included but also for what was not included. There is no set of substantive principles covering, for example, intergenerational equity, ecological integrity, or environmental justice.[9]

To define 'principles' in this context, I defer to Dworkin.[10] By his account, legal principles are consolidation points between a range of values, more or less concrete and defined, and precise and predictable rules. I have utilized this definition of principles precisely because this 'version' of what principles might be well describes that which occurs in the use of the principles in the EU context. Such principles act as a shorthand for the expression of certain values and explain how the legal system balances those values. As such, the principles act as a reason for a decision to be made in a particular direction but do not demand that it be made in such a way.[11] They are a particularly heavy weight in the scales of justice but not a knockout blow. In the context of specific applications of the principles, however, it often becomes necessary to return to the underpinning values in order to interpret the meaning of the principle in its context. This creates the forms of contingency which Scotford discusses[12] and thus emerges the potential for incoherence in practice. The 'mediation' role (between values and rules) that the principles play is therefore both the source of their potential legitimizing power and the reason why they are not 'self-legitimizing'.[13]

[8] The Treaty on the Functioning of the European Union, OJ 2012 C 246/47.

[9] Contrast this with the ways in which the principles have been considered by e.g. the New South Wales Land and Environment Court (NSWLEC). See Scotford (n. 1) ch 5 and E. Fisher and B. Preston (eds), *An Environmental Court in Action: Function, Doctrine and Process* (2022).

[10] R. Dworkin, *Taking Rights Seriously* (1978) ch 2.

[11] Ibid. 24.

[12] E.g. Scotford (n. 1) 461.

[13] Scotford, 'Environmental Principles across Jurisdictions: Legal Connectors and Catalysts', in E. Lees and J. E. Viñuales (eds), *The Oxford Handbook of Comparative Environmental Law* (2019) 677.

A. The Roles Principles Play

With these points in mind, it is important to consider the multitude of roles that the principles can play. Before exploring these specific principles in detail, it is useful to start with a zoomed-out view.[14] Very often, environmental scholarship maps the principles and their effects, to chart the ways in which they operate within any particular legal system.[15] Indeed, both Scotford's and de Sadeleer's work achieve this goal within a range of jurisdictions. However, the best cartographers, as both Scotford and de Sadeleer are, see the landscape not as a fixed or static entity to be precisely described but as constantly in flux. As such, in describing the landscape as it *is*, we must also understand how it has come to be, and, as a result, how it is likely to change over time. Just as the forces of earth systems must be understood to accurately describe a landscape, so too it is recognized that this landscape generates forces of its own. A river is both a *consequence of* the landscape and a *reason why* the landscape is as it is. The environmental principles are a consequence of the shape of the law and of forces which shape that law in turn.[16] When understanding the role that the principles play in judicial decision-making in EU environmental law, therefore, we commence from the starting point that these roles are both determined by the prevailing legal culture and are themselves a determining feature of that culture.[17]

From this flows a second conclusion: that the role of the principles is contingent on the context within which they operate. They are 'nebulous, protean, and flexible'.[18] Scotford again has emphasized this contingency but, as Pedersen has argued, becoming too overwhelmed by contingency can blind us to the identifiable roles and meanings that the principles play and embody.[19] What this contingency means for this chapter, however, is that the roles that

[14] As discussed in Chapter 1, when viewed from a zoomed-out perspective, the relationship between decision-making and legitimacy in the modern administrative state is not susceptible to a precise articulation. However, it is important to establish the nature of the landscape being considered, locating particular instances or roles emerging within that landscape against which legitimacy can then be benchmarked. See Chapter 1, Section 2. See also Lees, 'Value in Comparative Law—3D Cartography and Analytical Description' in E. Lees and J. E. Viñuales (eds), *The Oxford Handbook of Comparative Environmental Law* (2019) 35.

[15] Fisher (n. 1) 7.

[16] De Sadeleer explores the relationship between the zoomed-out landscape of the law and the characteristics of the environmental principles in considering the transition from modern to post-modern law. See de Sadeleer (n. 1). Scotford (n. 1) 261.

[17] E. Lees and O. W. Pedersen, *Environmental Adjudication* (2020) 197. See also Nelken, 'Using the Concept of Legal Culture', 29 *Australian Journal of Legal Philosophy* (2004) 26.

[18] de Sadeleer (n. 1) 363.

[19] Pedersen, 'The Contingent Foundations of Environmental Law', 30 *Journal of Environmental Law* (2018) 359, at 364.

the principles play in the context of the jurisprudence of the CJEU will not be mirrored precisely in the courts of the Member States.[20] Rather, idiosyncratic approaches in terms of procedure, evidential rules, and approach to judicial review in the Member States will exert a subtle pressure onto even the interpretation of the principles in each context.[21] How the principles contribute to the legitimacy of EU environmental governance cannot, therefore, be judged in the abstract.

With these messages—the circular development of the principles in being shaped by, and shaping, legal culture and the fact that 'the ubiquitous environmental principles, despite their abundance, have very little content in the abstract'[22]—we can now consider the roles that the principles play in the reasoning of the CJEU. Scotford has identified three categories of role. These are policy cases, interpretive cases, and informing legal test cases. These categories, explained later, are convincing but not, I think, complete. Instead, there are additional roles that the principles play concerned with the allocation of decision-making power and responsibility[23] and with the interpretation and conclusions to be drawn from evidence.[24] Furthermore, as de Sadeleer explains, 'every principle represents a first step in ordering ideas'.[25] Scotford has convincingly shown that the principles do not perform this role systematically, or even very effectively, and do not indeed provide a stable foundation for the coherence of environmental law.[26] However, that does not mean that they do not provide this organizing or 'shortcut' role in expressing the more fundamental values of the system in a more haphazard way.

1. Policy Cases

In policy cases, 'environmental principles are raised in argument or mentioned or discussed by the EU courts but are legally irrelevant'.[27] In such cases as these, the principles are, in effect, devoid of normative power and are instead a shorthand expression of the goals or intention of a particular piece of legislation. This matches closely the definition of environmental principles outlined earlier but does not fully embrace the mediation role which principles

[20] See M. Eliantonio, E. Lees, and T. Paloniitty (eds), *EU Environmental Principles and Scientific Uncertainty Before National Courts* (2022) at Conclusions.
[21] Ibid. 354 ff.
[22] Pedersen (n. 19) 359.
[23] See Lees, 'Allocation of Decision-Making Power under the Habitats Directive', 28 *Journal of Environmental Law* (2016) 191.
[24] Lees (n. 6) 314.
[25] de Sadeleer (n. 18) 23.
[26] Scotford (n. 1) ch 6.
[27] Ibid. 255.

can (or should) play. Indeed, there is a powerful argument that when the 'principles' perform this role, they no longer have the required characteristics of principles at all. Rather, they become merely 'slogans'[28] explaining the goal of a particular regulatory instrument. It is crucial to note at this point, however, that the expression which is given to each principle in these policy cases is not homogenous. The fact that the principle is being referred to as a background justification for a particular approach does not render it more likely that the principles will be given a static meaning. Rather, they will still be expressed in line with the facts of the case. The principles may not have normative force but their justificatory or policy role remains a contingent and context-specific one.

This is important because while there is a legal irrelevance generated by principles in this 'mode', this irrelevance in terms of 'what the law is' does not equate to irrelevance in terms of the legitimacy of the law. This is clear with a thought example: a law based on a 'principle of inequality between genders' would be of highly questionable legitimacy even if a case concerning that regulation did not require reliance on the principle to assist in interpretation. In other words, the legitimacy of the content of the principles upon which law is based in *policy terms* still has an important role in determining the legitimacy or otherwise of a judicial decision based on that law. However, that role fades, to some extent, into the background given that there is a 'legislative intervention' which supersedes the principles. The principles play a supporting role and, as such, only play a supporting role in terms of legitimacy too.

The logic of principles being used only in this informational way lies in the separation of powers and the relationship between courts and democratic processes. Invocation of principles not present in the rules themselves is seen, in some cases, to inappropriately overstep proper boundaries. However, as Warnock has forcefully argued, the frame of the separation of powers is not an entirely convincing lens through which to assess the legitimacy of environmental law, for this way of looking at legitimate political action fails to take account of the kinds of rules that are needed to address complex, uncertain, and ever-changing legal problems.[29]

2. Interpretation Cases

More crucial, however, is the role the principles play in relation to interpretation. This is for two reasons. First, the multi-language reality of the EU means

[28] As the title of de Sadeleer, *Environmental Principles: From Political Slogans to Legal Rules* (n. 1) suggests.

[29] C. Warnock, *Environmental Courts and Tribunals: Powers, Integrity and the Search for Legitimacy* (2020).

that a purely linguistic approach to interpretation is certainly not possible.[30] The CJEU has always been faced with a different interpretive problem than that encountered by many of the Member State courts. The solution has been a teleological approach which is particularly apparent in the environmental context. What is important here is that the telos of environmental rules tends to be narrowly construed[31] to being about effective environmental problem-solving, and in a number of important cases this telos is explicitly stated to be represented by one or another of the environmental principles. This, in legitimacy terms, is both a positive and a negative attribute. On the one hand, as de Sadeleer argues, '[t]he existence of general principles thus authorizes interpretations of a teleological nature; that is, solutions are sought in the values that inspired the law-maker rather than solely on the basis of a legal formula'.[32] On the other, the failure to articulate the wider range of possible purposes of environmental legislation undermines the holistic operation of these rules, rendering them uncertain and disconnected from the other legal contexts within which they operate.[33]

3. Informing Legal Tests

Finally, there are cases in which the 'environmental principles have doctrinal roles in informing tests of legal review'.[34] They act as conferrers of legal power or duties in such cases. In the case of the CJEU, the principles can militate for more intensive standards of review, for more judicial control of the discretionary actions of administrative authorities, or for the reading of liability into ambiguous standards. This, as seen for example in relation to the Waste Directive,[35] has created regulatory approaches which are comprehensive and broad but not as precise and clear as compliance with the rule of law might warrant.[36]

[30] See Derlén, 'Multilingual Interpretation of CJEU Case Law: Rule and Reality', 39 *European Law Review* (2014) 295; Fennelly, 'Legal Interpretation at the European Court of Justice', 20 *Fordham International Law Journal* (1997) 656; and E. Paunio, *Legal Certainty in Multilingual EU Law—Language, Discourse and Reasoning* (2013).

[31] E. Lees, *Interpreting Environmental Offences: The Need for Certainty* (2015) 185ff.

[32] de Sadeleer (n. 1) 376.

[33] Lees (n. 31) 185ff.

[34] Scotford (n. 1) 289.

[35] Directive 2008/98/EC, OJ 2008 L 312/3.

[36] E.g. Joined Cases C-418/97 and C-419/97, *ARCO Chemie Nederland Ltd v. Minister van Volkshuisvesting, Ruimtelijke Ordening en Milieubeheer and Vereniging Dorpsbelang Hees, Stichting Werkgroep Weurt and Vereniging Stedelijk Leefmilieu Nijmegen v. Directeur van de dienst Milieu en Water van de provincie Gelderland* (EU:C:2000:318), paras 51 and 64; Joined Cases C-206/88 and C-207/88, *Criminal proceedings against G. Vessoso and G. Zanetti* (EU:C:1990:145), paras 12 and 13. For critique of this position, see e.g. Samuels, 'The Legal Concept of Waste', *Journal of Planning and Environmental Law* (2010) 1391; Ogley, 'A Wasted Opportunity?', *Journal of Planning and Environmental Law* (2011) 10; D. N. Pocklington, *The Law of Waste Management* (2nd edn, 2011); Cheyne and Purdue, 'Fitting

Scotford has examined in detail the legitimacy challenges created by this sort of use of the principles. She argues that these uses of the principles have not neatly met 'the high scholarly hopes of resolving legal and environmental problems'[37] and, given their rather nebulous nature, are perhaps not entirely suited to any such stabilizing roles.

4. Additional Roles

There are, however, further possibilities. What else could they be doing? This list of roles explained by Scotford is, in one sense, incomplete. On Scotford's account, the principles can operate (only) in three ways: they do not change the law; they help understand existing law; or they make new law. However, when we see them performing these roles, they may play two particular functions which have a different emphasis to Scotford's categories. These roles are both ones of weighing: the weighing of the evidence and the weighing of relative power and influence in reasoning.

First, the principles operate as modes through which evidence is read. The principles act as part of the judicial fact-finding role as well as the legal interpretation role. Second, the principles allocate the weight of decision-making power and responsibility in a particular case.[38] This does not change the legal rule in play but it changes where the benefit of the doubt is placed and how reasonableness is assessed. In these functions, principles may operate so as to hide conflict, to resolve inconsistencies in evidence, or to fill gaps in that evidence. They may also make sense of and structure the role of different actors within environmental decision-making. Finally, they may also operate so as to underpin these balancings of evidence and power with some sense of justice that has been explicitly integrated into the EU law system by the Treaty provisions themselves (one thinks here especially of the polluter pays principle). The use of the environmental principles encourages the reaction that it is *fair* that a particular individual be asked to bear the cost of some environmental harm, given the relationship between the Treaties and democratic processes.

The evidential role played by the principles is indeed critical to their success. Scotford, in explaining the roles the principles play in linking and connecting scholarship in relation to environmental law, argues that they may present

Definition to Purpose: the Search for a Satisfactory Definition of Waste', 7 *Journal of Environmental Law* (1995) 149; and Cheyne 'The Definition of Waste in EC Law', 14 *Journal of Environmental Law* (2002) 62.

[37] Scotford (n. 1) 192.
[38] Lees (n. 23) 191.

'legal solutions to the considerable methodological challenges faced by environmental law'.[39] This is true too in the practice of the law itself. The existence of evidence in court which is both uncertain and complex, and beyond the range of expertise of the majority of judges, creates a methodological challenge for that court.[40] The principles provide a means by which this challenge can be sidestepped, for the court is encouraged through the precautionary principle to read uncertainty as evidence of potential harm[41] or to read evidence relating to causation and connection generously to ensure that the polluter pays.[42] The principles, in so doing, build capacity.

Many of the clearest examples of this role in play come from the jurisprudence relating to biodiversity conservation. Here, courts are regularly required to assess evidence to demonstrate the likelihood or significance of a particular outcome.[43] As is seen from *Waddenzee*,[44] the terms of the Habitats Directive[45] as read 'through' the precautionary principle generate an approach to evidence which is to accept the presence of any risk as being significant[46] and any level of possibility as likelihood.[47] The legal test remains the same: on the balance of probabilities, is it likely that a harm will occur? But the way in which the evidence is read encourages a finding of such likelihood. This can indeed result in what is referred to here as a 'precaution-cubed' outcome. By this is meant that three levels of precaution operate in the same decision. First, an administrative authority reaches its expressed conclusions by reading the evidence it encounters through a precautionary lens. The court then reads the evidence relied on by that administrative authority through an additional layer of precaution. Finally, the decision made is then a precautionary one based on what, on the balance of precautionary possibilities, that evidence shows.

[39] Scotford (n. 13) 667.

[40] Warnock (n. 29) ch 1. See also Paloniitty, 'Scientific and Legal Mechanisms for Addressing Model Uncertainties: Negotiating the Right Balance in Finnish Judicial Review?', 33 *Journal of Environmental Law* (2021) 283.

[41] Case C-127/02, *Landelijke Vereniging tot Behoud van de Waddenzee v. Staatssecretaris van Landbouw, Natuurbeheer en Visserij* (EU:C:2004:482); Stokes, 'Liberalising the Threshold of Precaution—Cockle Fishing, the Habitats Directive, and Evidence of a New Understanding of "Scientific Uncertainty"', 7 *Environmental Law Review* (2005) 206; and Verschuuren, 'Shellfish for Fishermen or for Birds? Article 6 Habitats Directive and the Precautionary Principle', 17 *Journal of Environmental Law* (2005) 265.

[42] Case C-378/08 *Raffinerie Mediterranee (ERG) SpA, Polimeri Europa SpA and Syndial SpA v. Ministero dello Sviluppo economico* (EU:C:2010:126).

[43] Council Directive 92/43/EEC, OJ 1992 L 206/7, Art. 6.

[44] Case C-127/02 *Landelijke Vereniging tot Behoud van de Waddenzee v. Staatssecretaris van Landbouw, Natuurbeheer en Visserij* (EU:C:2004:48).

[45] Council Directive 92/43/EEC, OJ 1992 L 206/7.

[46] Verschuuren (n. 41) 265.

[47] Stokes (n. 41) 206.

The other role performed by the environmental principles which is focused on in this chapter is the power- (and responsibility-)allocation function. As with the discussion earlier, this role is one concerned with weight in decision-making processes. Because environmental law is polycentric, negotiated, and often operates via soft law provisions, the weight to be given to the views of any particular actor plays an important role in shaping the power flows relevant to environmental decision-making. The principles operate so as to include or exclude actors within such processes as well as changing their 'formal identity' within that process. For example, the interpretation given to the polluter pays principle may transform the role of an administrative agency from regulator to co-polluter. Similarly, the principle of rectification at source changes the lens through which local waste authorities are viewed and therefore how their respective responsibilities in relation to the Waste Directive[48] might be constructed. Finally, the precautionary principle may operate so as to render the weight of a scientific advisor's opinion more critical to a lawful decision than the views of a local community expressed through participative processes. The consequence of this role, and that of the evidential role, are discussion in Section 3.

B. Defining the Principles and the Roles They Play

So far, this section has outlined some of the roles the environmental principles can play. The existing literature explains some of these and the ways the principles therefore contribute to legitimacy, in relation to policy, interpretation, and legal test cases. This chapter contributes to that discussion by focusing instead on their role in the judicial fact-finding and weighing power and responsibility roles. Before moving on to make this examination, however, two important points remain to be made.

First, the relationship between the principles in these roles and wider concerns relating to environmental justice or intergenerational equity is important. The instrumental goal of environmental protection is usually adequately represented within a legislative scheme. So too, such schemes would tend to limit, for example, liability, to cases where such was warranted. What tends to be less present are the substantive levels of protection actually achieved in cases in the NSWLEC, for example.[49]

[48] Directive 2008/98/EC, OJ 2008 L 312/3.
[49] Fisher and Preston (n. 9).

Furthermore, the principles listed in the Treaties sit somewhere between substantive protection and procedural control. This ambiguity is important. It is important because when we look at how the principles operate in practice, whether their prevailing quality is perceived to be substantive protection, or whether it is perceived to be about following particular processes, their influence within the law will shift. Furthermore, because these are explicitly principles, the inclusion of them as principles infuses the law with standards which are deliberately malleable. The consequence of this is that any legitimizing force generated through the principles tends to be rather shallow. Protection of the environment can be perceived in rather simplistic terms but a true understanding of protection of the environment also engages with justice between groups of persons and wider issues related to the construction of space in the modern administrative state. These issues are rarely raised by the principles present in the TFEU. Any legitimacy generated through the principles, therefore, takes on this rather shallow form.

Second, despite their substantive potential, because of the judicial reluctance to allow the principles to generate an overstepping of the proper judicial role, there is a tendency to give them a procedural centre of gravity. That is not to say that the principles do not contribute to substantive environmental protection but rather the judicial interpretation of the principles is to encourage administrative authorities to generate processes which will likely produce such an outcome. The expectation is not that the judiciary will engage with the substance of the principles themselves, precisely because this is seen to be a role best left to administrative bodies. However, because the interpretation of the principles is driven by the judicial approach to defining their content and role, the procedural viewpoint which the judiciary bring to bear on what the principles can achieve will, to some extent, be internalized by those better placed to give them substantive weight.

These two points allow us to draw conclusions from Section 2. The environmental principles contained within the EU Treaties take on a rather shallow, procedural overtone when defined in the courts. With these characteristics at their foundations, the principles then perform different roles in shaping decision-making in relation to environmental protection: they act as summaries of wider policy; they assist in interpretation; they generate new or modified legal tests; they act as guides to courts when engaging in fact-finding; and they allocate power and responsibility between different actors in administrative processes. These latter two roles are not extensively discussed in the literature but in these two roles we can see the tensions that exist in the operation of the principles and legitimacy. As Section 4 will explain, ultimately, it is challenging to pursue all aspects of legitimacy at once: the internal and external dimensions will pull in different directions. The very nature of environmental problems creates an inherent tension between certainty and predictability, and effectiveness. However, by operating as they do—to weigh in favour of a particular outcome rather than demanding it—principles may be the best tools we have to cope with this inherent tension.

3. Principles and Legitimacy

This section considers how the sources of legitimacy, internal and external, are enhanced by the principles operating in this way. As explained in Section 2, the environmental principles perform a range of roles and are never precisely defined but rather defined only by reference to their particular context and by example. The consequence of this is that any assessment of the way in which they contribute to legitimacy will be done on a case-by-case basis: a global assessment is not possible. The only comprehensive conclusion that can be reached is indeed that of Scotford: that the principles do not contribute in a homogenous way and therefore do not provide the stable foundation for the development of environmental law that they may, on their face, promise.[50] The internal standard of legitimacy which is comprised of certainty, clarity, and coherence is not achieved through the use of the environmental principles in any global sense.[51] However, that does not mean that they do not make a valuable contribution to the overall legitimacy of EU environmental governance.

The second important general point is that because the principles do play such a range of roles, in writing about them each author may emphasize one role over others or use examples of that role in practice. This chapter also operates in this way since I am highlighting those cases where the principles contribute to the two additional roles I have identified. This does not mean that another perspective on the principles, which focuses instead on their undeniable contribution to the enhancement of environmental protection, is wrong, far from it. No one answer is 'right'.

As explained in Chapter 1, in this chapter the legitimacy assessment will be made according to a threefold division: institutional capacity; contribution to achieving 'the right' process; and tendency to lead to the correct outcome. In outline terms, for the environmental principles this means asking

[50] Scotford (n. 1) ch 6.
[51] For the 'upside' of this, see Pedersen (n. 19) 359.

three questions. First, does the way in which the environmental principles have developed facilitate or improve the capacity of the CJEU to understand and handle the complexity of the problem before it? Second, does the use of the principles render the decision more likely to comply with the rule-of-law principles of certainty, clarity, and coherence in a procedural sense? And, third, does the use of the principles make it more likely that a 'good' outcome will be reached, in particular one which enhances the protection of the environment in the EU? The section which follows answers these three questions briefly in general terms, and then in more detail in relation to the two additional functions (fact-finding and power- and responsibility-allocation) identified in Section 2.

A. Contributions to Legitimacy: General Considerations

Three points can be made in general about the principles and their contributions to legitimacy. First, the principles are asked, in effect, to help resolve problems which emerge not only from the nature of environmental problems themselves (unpredictability, complexity[52]) but also from the nature of the law that has developed to tackle these problems (malleable, responsive, uncertain). As de Sadeleer notes, 'because environmental law mirrors features of post-modern law where the clarity, rigidity, rationality, and certainty is giving way to fragmentation, flexibility, and dispersion, the principles of this legal branch provide a degree of underlying coherence and stability'.[53] However, these principles are themselves products of this form of lawmaking as well as being an attempt to resolve it. They are therefore asked to bound and restrain uses of discretion, whilst at the same time being blessed (or cursed) with malleable content themselves. In many ways, this is necessary both in capacity terms (too rigid rules would be almost impossible to work with in this context) and in outcome terms. As a result, de Sadeleer praises this feature of the principles:

> In this context, directing principles are preferable to rigid rules, since their flexibility makes it possible for divergent values and interests or contradictory policies to co-exist. Couched in extremely vague terms, directing principles are able to make an important contribution to the development of positive

[52] Warnock (n. 29).
[53] de Sadeleer (n. 32) 13.

law by providing conceptual flexibility for legislators, administrators, and courts in their practical work.[54]

The second general point is that the legitimacy of this constraining function is enhanced by the fact that the constraints on discretion come from within the law itself. The source of these constraints lies in primary legislation in the form of the Treaties and cannot thereby be criticized for not being the proper domain of the courts. Furthermore, it is important to recognize that the environmental principles are not deduced from individual regulatory instruments. They have not emerged *from* the stew of directives and regulations as summaries of the overarching structures within that mess of positive law. Rather, they are a justification *for* those individual regulatory structures, a means of understanding those regulations, and a point of criticism if the regulations do not in fact embody the principles. MacCormick's perspective on the value of principles in the law, therefore, does not apply here. He argues that 'working out the principles of a legal system to which one is committed involves an attempt to give it coherence in terms of a set of general norms'.[55] In EU environmental law, we do not work out the principles from the law: it is the other way around. This means that any tensions which might arise in relation to the judiciary generating their own 'coping mechanisms' for the exigencies of environmental adjudication do not apply if they use the environmental principles to help them solve environmental problems. As tools to enhance capacity, ensure coherence, and protect the environment, they are therefore *more legitimate* because the democratic processes have authorized the courts to use the principles in this way.

Finally, and conversely, as is perhaps shown by consideration of the debate around the legitimacy of EU environmental governance around which this book is structured, '[t]he legitimacy of the State is no longer acquired as of right but is rather a function of the relevance of State-generated programmes'.[56] In as much as the principles are themselves justified in their use by the fact that they have emerged from the legitimate processes of the democratic state, so too does their use in turn contribute to the legitimacy of that state. They do so because they represent more or less generalizable statements of values which underpin that state which can then be used to make the operation of the mechanisms of the state more coherent and more successful. We return to the circularity in the

[54] Ibid. 368.
[55] N. MacCormick, *Legal Reasoning and Legal Theory* (1978) 177.
[56] de Sadeleer (n. 1) 384.

role the principles play: they are a product of legal culture and contributors to it and they are a product of the legitimate use of power of the state and contributors to the legitimacy of that power.

These three points—that the principles allow for a more legitimate constraint of administrative discretion in relation to environmental problems, that they emerge from the law itself, and that they contribute to the wider legitimacy of state actions—set the tone for discussion of the two specific rules in the following sections.

B. Legitimacy and Evidential Lens: Sources of Knowledge Facing Up to Uncertainty

The first role examined here is the principles as tools to assist in the reading and interpretation of evidence. As de Sadeleer explains, the nature of the environmental principles is determined, in part, by their role in a post-industrial society where the nature of risks is characterized by high levels of uncertainty, and by cumulative and accumulated outcomes, generating across jurisdictions: 'characterised by on the one hand the general inability of scientists to make reliable predictions about hazards due to uncertainties (identifiable, but not quantifiable) or insufficient knowledge (ignorance) and, on the other hand, by the impossibility of assessing the character of damage that might occur'.[57] This means that the principles (especially the precautionary principle) take on a role which relates to these uncertainties.

The section which follows uses the decision in *Bayer v. Commission*[58] to demonstrate the ways in which the environmental principles—in this case, the precautionary principle—operate on how evidence is read and appropriately included in decision-making. Specifically, I examine three aspects of the case: the relationship between administrative guidance and other sources of scientific information; the relevance of the quality of such information to the weight it is given in administrative processes; and the role of administrative 'common sense'. These issues appear in many cases from the CJEU but *Bayer* provides a clear example of how the precautionary principle layers upon itself to shape judicial and administrative reasoning.

This case concerned the approval of pesticide use. In fact, between the initial challenge of the Commission and the appeal before the CJEU, all outdoor

[57] Ibid. 12.
[58] Case C-499/18, *Bayer CropScience v. Commission* (EU:C:2021:367).

use of the substances in question was prohibited in any case. Bayer's interest in continuing the process was twofold: first, it might have been entitled to compensation for the lack of authorization earlier in the process and, second, it wanted to challenge the Commission's decision-making *processes* when the precautionary principles and scientific information were in issue. It is this aspect of the Court's reasoning that is especially important here.

The Pesticide Regulation[59] in question was itself explicitly based on the precautionary principle. This was a case where the principle had been integrated into the 'hard rules' and as such takes on a legal force because of its presence within the Regulation. The normative status of the principle was not in question. What mattered was how its presence within the structure of the rules impacted upon the approach to be taken to decision-making under the Regulation. The challenge was to probe and analyse how the Commission should go about using scientific data in the approval process under Article 21(1) and Article 21(3) of the Regulation. Bayer alleged that the information which had been relied on by the Commission was inadequate.[60] It was seeking clarity on the types and extent of evidence needed within the review process. If the Court were to impose a very prescriptive approach, this would limit the Commission's discretion and would also provide manufacturers with a clearer sense of what data would be consulted during a review, giving them a greater ability to predict the outcome of the review.[61] This would have the potential for environmental benefits but also carried risks as seen, for example, in relation to the car industry and emissions data.

The first point of note relates to the relevance of the EU institutions' own guidelines relating to pesticide approval. AG Kokott had criticized the General Court for its approach to the guidelines.[62] However, the Court itself took the focus away from reliance on the guidelines—that is to say, a rather hands-off approach to judicial review which considered whether a decision-maker had complied with its own previously published policy statements—and instead placed the focus on the state of scientific and technical knowledge as a whole—and particularly new knowledge.[63] In other words, the source of that knowledge, whether in promulgated guidelines or otherwise, was less important than the content, certainty, and quality of that knowledge.[64] Risk assessment

[59] Regulation (EC) No. 1107/2009, OJ 2009 L 309/1.

[60] Case C-499/18, *Bayer CropScience v. Commission* (EU:C:2021:367), para. 45.

[61] Jennings, 'Probing the Scientific Evidence Base of the Plant Protection Regulation', 24 *Environmental Law Review* (2022) 191, at 193.

[62] Opinion of AG Kokott in Case C-499/18, *Bayer CropScience v. Commission* (EU:C:2020:735), para. 96.

[63] Case C-499/18, *Bayer CropScience v. Commission* (EU:C:2021:367), paras 66–71.

[64] Jennings (n. 61) 194.

was decoupled from guidelines allowing scientific knowledge to evolve. This impetus came directly from the precautionary principle as modulated into its formulations of 'best scientific information', 'most reliable', 'most rigorous', etc.

The consequences of this use of the precautionary principle are significant. First, the use of the principle shifts the burden of decision-making responsibility from the Commission as an administrative authority into the hands of scientific advisors and experts. In the context of the EU itself, where the Commission is rather disconnected in democratic terms from the constituencies it serves, this can be seen as a shift from a bureaucratic to a technocratic decision-making approach. In the context of a Member State, however, this may represent a different recalibration of power.

Second, the principle acts to shine a light on the quality of the scientific information being used. The Court, when asked whether new information ought to trigger a review of an authorization, reasoned that, 'in the context of the review of the approval of an active substance, the conclusion that the approval criteria laid down in Article 4 of Regulation No 1107/2009 are no longer satisfied may be based on any new knowledge, in so far as it is scientific or technical, regardless of the source or document from which it comes'.[65] The decision-maker is asked, actively, to interrogate the information at their disposal. This opening up of the scientific box[66] (rather than the hiding of scientific disagreement) is a positive contribution to the legitimacy of the law. This is potentially enriching, as Jennings notes:

> Minority science, dissenting science and studies on emerging risks are not readily accepted in mainstream scientific publications, therefore they would not readily fall within the categories of the 'best scientific information available' or 'most recent results'. Such studies, however, would be captured by a phrase such as 'new scientific and technical knowledge'. Minority and dissenting science act as an early warning system for human and environmental risks.[67]

Finally, Bayer had alleged that the Commission had not looked at all the relevant data—ignoring that relating to non-professional use.[68] The issue at hand

[65] Case C-499/18, *Bayer CropScience v. Commission* (EU:C:2021:367), para. 69.

[66] Fisher, 'Sciences, Environmental Laws, and Legal Cultures: Fostering Collective Epistemic Responsibility', in E. Lees and J. E. Viñuales (eds), *The Oxford Handbook of Comparative Environmental Law* (2019) 755.

[67] Jennings (n. 61) 196.

[68] Case C-499/18, *Bayer CropScience v. Commission* (EU:C:2021:367), para. 154.

was whether non-professional users would follow the instructions relating to the amount and mode of use. The CJEU said that in effect Bayer could not guarantee the safety of non-professional users taking account of the high degree of toxicity of the substance.[69] The reality here—as the AG also noted[70]—was that the Commission did not base this on data but rather on conjecture. There was no evidence that non-professional users would not follow the instructions on the packaging. However, per the Court, Bayer did not show that members of the public would use the product appropriately.[71] Neither position was justified in terms of scientific information—but the Court accepted that the Commission was entitled *in the face of a lack of evidence* to reach the decision that it did because of precaution. In other words, the precautionary principle here was used not as a lens through which to read the evidence but rather as an answer to a problem generated by a lack of evidence. The subtlety and multiplicity of roles that the principle can play in relation to reviews of evidence is clear here. The principle rendered justified the Commission's approach to evidence in risk management. Per the Court:

> Where it proves to be impossible to determine with certainty the existence or extent of the alleged risk, because the results of studies conducted are inconclusive, but the likelihood of real harm to the environment persists should the risk materialise, the precautionary principle justifies the adoption of restrictive measures.
>
> Thus, contrary to what Bayer Crop Science claims, an exhaustive risk assessment cannot be required in a situation where the precautionary principle is applied, which equates to a situation in which there is scientific uncertainty.[72]

In short, the principle overcomes the absence of evidence.

However, the case also serves to shine a light on the relationship between the environmental principles and other principles of EU law, particularly the principle of legal certainty. The principle of legal certainty is a well-established principle of EU law.[73] However, in the context of environmental law, the principle

[69] Ibid. para. 157.

[70] Opinion of AG Kokott in Case C-499/18, *Bayer CropScience v. Commission* (EU:C:2020:735), para. 167.

[71] Case C-499/18, *Bayer CropScience v. Commission* (EU:C:2021:367), para. 158.

[72] Ibid. paras 80–81.

[73] The principle of legal certainty appears very early in the jurisprudence of the CJEU: Case 13/61, *Kledingverkoopbedrijf de Geus en Uitdenbogerd v. Robert Bosch GmbH and Maatschappij tot voortzetting van de zaken der Firma Willem van Rijn* (EU:C:1962:11), para. 52; Case C-143/93, *Gebroeders van Es Douane Agenten BV v. Inspecteur der Invoerrechten en Accijnzen* (EU:C:1996:45), para. 27; Case C-248/04, *Koninklijke Coöperatie Cosun UA v. Minister van Landbouw, Natuur en*

tends to fade into the background in the face of the more obviously applicable environmental principles. Bayer had argued in this case that the breadth of the information that could be taken into account by the Commission severely limited the operation of legal certainty.[74] In particular, it argued that in cases of decisions to withdraw or amend an existing approval, legal certainty was especially important. In such cases, it argued, there needed to be a clear change in the factual situation.[75] Otherwise manufacturers would be constantly on the lookout for new reviews coming against then. But here again precaution 'won out'.

As explained earlier, the principles, in 'reading' evidence before decision-makers, can contribute both to the internal sources of legitimacy in the form of capacity, clarity, coherence, and legal certainty, and to the external source of achieving environmental protection. In what way do the four techniques discussed here enhance or threaten the legitimacy of the CJEU's decision from this perspective? It is argued here that there are two primary contributions. The first is that the principles represent a means to overcome a lack of judicial capacity to engage with scientifically complex arguments. The second is in relation to substantive environmental protection. By contrast, these approaches have the potential to diminish the clarity, certainty, and coherence of the law.

For the courts themselves, the ability to read evidence through the environmental principles has a clear impact on their fact-finding role. The task of the courts to resolve uncertainties in a set of facts before them is one of the core judicial functions. Its essence is to provide a forum within which contestation about what is true or otherwise can be resolved for the purposes of the state and its operations. That the courts are able to achieve this function is one of the key markers of their usefulness to a governance system as a whole. In an environmental context, the courts do not have a straightforward role in discovering what the facts are and their normal techniques to overcome complex or uncertain factual scenarios are not easily employed here. In 'traditional' cases, a court may be asked to hear witness testimony, to review written evidence, or through advocates to make use of cross-examination and the like. These techniques, relying as they do on the ability of the judge to identify convincing or

Voedselkwaliteit (EU:C:2006:666), para. 79; Case C-161/06, *Skoma-Lux sro v. Celní ředitelství Olomouc* (EU:C:2007:773), paras 38 and 67; Case C-205/82, *Deutsche Milchkontor GmbH and others v. Federal Republic of Germany* (EU:C:1983:233), para. 30; Case C-169/80, *Administration des douanes v. Société anonyme Gondrand Frères and Société anonyme Garancini* (EU:C:1981:171), para. 17; Case C-92/87, *Commission of the European Communities v. French Republic* (EU:C:1989:77).

[74] Case C-499/18, *Bayer CropScience v. Commission* (EU:C:2021:367), para. 73.
[75] Ibid.

unconvincing statements, are not useful in an environmental context since these are not situations where there are even necessarily diverging opinions so that a judge has to pick one; rather, all may agree *and still* uncertainty can remain. For this reason, in their fact-finding role, the courts can enhance their capacity by relying on the principles as a means to decide what evidence means.

Their second legitimizing potentiality in this context lies in their contribution to environmental protection. The way in which judicial fact-finding power is increased in a context of high uncertainty is not neutral in terms of the kind of outcome it is likely to produce. For example, it would be entirely possible to rely on a high burden of proof in relation to environmental protection, demanding a high level of knowledge that a particular action *will* cause harm to the environment in order to refuse to authorize it. This would also solve the difficulty of uncertainty here. By pushing the courts towards environmental protection, therefore, with all that entails for the resilience of food systems, of biodiversity and water networks, and of the climate, the chances of the right outcome being reached are also improved when the courts use the principles as a solution to their lack of scientific capacity, or the lack of certainty in the scientific position.

C. Sources of Legitimacy: The Allocation of Power

Just as the previous section used the decision in *Bayer* to provide insight into the range of roles the environmental principles can play in relation to the judicial fact-finding task, this section looks closely at *Austria v. Commission*[76] and *JP v. Ministre de la Transition Écologique*[77] to examine how the principles weigh relative power and responsibility. First, I consider how the principles may influence the division of labour between court and legislature. Second, I explore how the principles affect limits on Member State sovereignty in light of the Treaties. Finally, I examine what the principles have to say about the allocation of environmental responsibility. Elsewhere, I have used examples from biodiversity protection to demonstrate how the principles perform this role in relation to individual administrative decisions.[78] The discussion here, by contrast, considers the rather more systemic allocations of power and responsibility that the principles achieve.

[76] Case C-594/18 P, *Austria v. Commission* (EU:C:2020:742).
[77] Case C-61/21, *JP v. Ministre de la Transition Écologique* (EU:C:2022:1015).
[78] Lees (n. 23) 191.

The first case is *Austria v. Commission*.[79] In this case, the Commission had held that certain forms of financial support given to facilitate the construction of Hinkley Point C nuclear power station in the UK were indeed state aid. It decided, however, that the aid was accepted under Article 107(3)(c) TFEU because the UK was (a) pursuing the public interest objective of the promotion of nuclear energy and (b) because the measures were proportionate and necessary.[80] Austria challenged this decision. In particular, it shone a light on part (a) of the Commission's approach. On appeal to the CJEU, AG Hogan concluded that the appeal should be rejected on the grounds that the level of political debate over nuclear power was not for the CJEU to resolve as it had neither the competence nor would it be legitimate if it did so, not least because Article 194 TFEU explicitly preserves energy sovereignty.[81] Furthermore, the AG reasoned that all Member States were bound by the Euratom Treaty, a core objective of which was to develop nuclear power.[82] Finally, and importantly for this chapter, the AG stated that the Commission's job here was to assess aid in light of the single market and that environmental protection was not per se a component of the single market.[83] In doing so, the integration principle and its limits were examined. The CJEU reached the same conclusion, but by a different route.

First, the CJEU held that the Euratom Treaty did not preclude the application of EU environmental law to the nuclear sector.[84] It relied here on the integration principle and the sustainable development principle. These principles, in effect, shaped the operation of the TFEU and the Euratom Treaty but the CJEU did not explain what the principles meant in the context.

The CJEU also went further in stating: 'it [the Commission] must ... check that the activity does not infringe rules of EU law on the environment. If it finds an infringement of those rules, it is obliged to declare the aid incompatible with the internal market without any other form of examination.'[85] When the Commission checks whether state aid is intended to facilitate development and economic activity, it then needs to check whether that economic activity breaches EU environmental law. If this finding is made, then there is no scope for any further analysis—no proportionality test or assessment of the positive and negative aspects of trade. This case therefore represents a very big step

[79] Case C-594/18 P, *Austria v. Commission* (EU:C:2020:742).
[80] Ibid. para. 79.
[81] Opinion of AG Hogan in Case C-594/18 P, *Austria v. Commission* (EU:C:2020:352), para. 42.
[82] Ibid. paras 33–43.
[83] Ibid. para. 66.
[84] Case C-594/18 P, *Austria v. Commission* (EU:C:2020:742), para. 45.
[85] Ibid. para. 100.

forward in the integration of the single market rules and environmental law. Taken together, the principles here affect the balance of power between the Member States and the EU itself by bounding energy sovereignty in environmental rules.

However, what is also significant here is that the presence of a known risk to the environment was not enough to give rise to the intervention of the precautionary principle in this case. The AG stated:

> It is true, of course, that at a political level the merits (or, as the case may be, the demerits) of nuclear power are hotly debated in many Member States and it is an issue in respect of which there is presently no real consensus. Some may think that the shadow of Three Mile Island, Fukushima and, above all, Chernobyl, looms over the construction and development of every nuclear power plant and that that experience is sufficient to point to the existence of a grave environmental risk, the elimination of which is simply impossible. Others may think that as nuclear energy provides a sustainable, low-carbon source of energy it must accordingly be part of a mix of energy supplies if reliance on fossil fuels is to be ended and climate change targets are to be met.
>
> This Court has quite obviously neither the competence nor, just as importantly, the democratic legitimacy to rule on such issues.[86]

The Court agreed with this assessment, albeit in brief terms, stating that the environmental principles did not in all circumstances preclude the grant of state aid to nuclear power operators.[87] What is particularly notable here is that the 'non-intervention' of the precautionary principle, on the sparse wording of the Court's judgment, appears to be related to the Member State sovereignty relating to nuclear power. In other words, the fact that such sovereignty was maintained by the Treaty framework meant that although the risk and seriousness of environmental damage through nuclear operations are clear, this was taken 'outside' the scope of the precautionary principle because it was a matter for Member State judgement. This demonstrates clearly how the principle interacts with, and is itself shaped by, considerations about the allocation of decision-making control.

Furthermore, in the context of nuclear power in particular, the environmental arguments are complex. The potential of nuclear power to assist in the achievement of climate change goals is clear and so the pursuance of nuclear

[86] Ibid. paras. 41–42.
[87] Ibid. para. 49.

power, to some extent, can be seen as both beneficial to, and risky for, the environment. This makes the fourth criteria of the legitimacy framework highly elusive here: the 'correct' outcome from an environmental perspective is far from clear.

Whatever one thinks of this argument in either direction, it is clear that there is, in relation to nuclear power, not an uncertainty but rather a known risk. The consequences of failures in nuclear power plants are, certainly, catastrophic. Although the relevance of the precautionary principle was raised by Austria in its arguments, it is notable that it was not discussed in any detail by the AG. The CJEU was clear that the principle did not prevent investment in nuclear power. However, this is perhaps somewhat surprising. The basis, apparently, is that the TFEU explicitly reserves for the Member States their sovereignty in relation to energy sources but the Court apparently shows willingness to limit that sovereignty, giving rise to some ambiguity. This is also true of planning matters and the provision of housing, for example, which are also not under the purview of the EU. Nevertheless, the application of the precautionary principle through the Habitats Directive directly impacts upon such sovereignty precisely because the EU does have competence in relation to the environment. Indeed, an environmental impact assessment would be required to proceed with any development, including a nuclear power plant, meaning that EU law does indeed have the capacity to prevent the construction of such a plant on precautionary grounds. The rather more hands-off approach in relation to the *theoretical possibility* of state investment in nuclear power is, therefore, perhaps a little surprising. It also tells us something about the interaction between the precautionary principle and known risk, and the balance of democratic values, in contrast to the role this principle plays in handling unknowns and uncertainty, where it weighs in to read the evidence in such a way as to transform doubt into proof of risk.

The second relevant case considered here is *JP v. Ministre de la Transition Écologique*.[88] In this case, the CJEU's decision is not of great relevance in terms of the environmental principles and indeed the decision was greeted with a great deal of disappointment[89] given the promising nature of the AG's Opinion in the case.[90] However, the approach of AG Kokott in this case is useful in

[88] Case C-61/21, *JP v. Ministre de la Transition Écologique* (EU:C:2022:1015).

[89] See van Calster, '*JP v. Ministre de la Transition écologique.* The CJEU unlike its AG, rules out Frankovich liability for the EU air quality Directives' (12 January 2023), https://gavclaw.com/2023/01/12/jp-v-ministre-de-la-transition-ecologique-the-cjeu-unlike-its-ag-rules-out-frankovich-liability-for-the-eu-air-quality-directives/ (last visited 26 September 2024).

[90] Opinion of AG Kokott in Case C-61/21, *JP v. Ministre de la Transition Écologique* (EU:C:2022:359).

giving some insight into the polluter pays principle, a principle whose meaning is often assumed but rarely expounded by the courts. Even though the CJEU did not reach the same conclusions, it is a useful case for our discussion because it shows how it is not only the precautionary principle that has the power to shift the burden of responsibility in relation to environmental protection.

The case concerned the operation of the Ambient Air Quality Directive[91] for which compliance has, notoriously, been something of a problem.[92] This particular case involved assessing whether individual rights emerge through the Directive so that liability for harm arises in cases where there is a failure to comply with its provisions. In this case, the claim related to breaches of air quality limits in Paris. The claimants were seeking very substantial damages for health problems which started in 2003. The Versailles Administrative Court of Appeal had made a preliminary reference to ask whether there was a right to compensation in this case.

The answer turned on the *Francovich*[93] principles (and in the end the CJEU decided that the Directive was not intended to confer individual rights).[94] However, the Advocate General discussed the tension between polluter liability and state liability and how that tension was mediated through the polluter pays principle. She reasoned:

> It is true that the polluter-pays principle is a principle of Union policy on the environment referred to in Article 191(2) TFEU and must therefore also be observed when interpreting rules on ambient air quality. It is also true that, according to that principle, it is the air polluters who should primarily bear the costs, which is expressed even more clearly in other language versions than in the German 'Verursacherprinzip', with for example the English version using the wording 'that the polluter should pay' or the French version the wording 'principe du pollueur-payeur'.
>
> However, that principle cannot release Member States from their own responsibility if they allow, or fail to prevent, air pollution in breach of EU law. Moreover, the fact that the rules on ambient air quality impose that responsibility on Member States is justified because ambient air pollution generally results from various sources, with the result that the Member States must decide the extent to which certain polluters must reduce their emissions.[95]

[91] Directive 2008/50/EC, OJ 2008 L 152/1.
[92] See Case C-664/18, *Commission v. UK* (EU:C:2021:171).
[93] Joined Cases C-6/90 and C-9/90, *Francovich v. Italy* (EU:C:1991:428).
[94] Case C-61/21, *JP v. Ministre de la Transition Écologique* (EU:C:2022:1015), para. 65.
[95] Opinion of AG Kokott in Case C-61/21, *JP v. Ministre de la Transition Écologique* (EU:C:2022:359), paras 80–81.

To put this another way, the polluter pays principle and its mode of operation requires Member States and the EU institutions to ensure *not only* that any identified polluters do remediate any damage caused but also to engage in a reflective, and self-reflective, assessment as to who a polluter actually is in any particular case. The meaning of 'polluter' is not self-evident and the courts of the Union are therefore required to interpret this term and in doing so they, in effect, label certain actors as 'responsible for' environmental outcomes where there are often complex chains of action and reaction which contribute to the outcome in question. The principle opens up this avenue of discussion and requires courts to resolve it. In doing so, they can enhance their own legitimacy by utilizing this as a vehicle to ensure they are pursuing their core function (legitimacy criteria number one) by ensuring that actors are held to account but it also impacts upon the relationships between actors within the system and may therefore either enhance or limit the levels of environmental protection achieved.

Overall, this assessment of three specific instances of the roles the principles play as mediators of evidence and power shows the complex effects that the environmental principles have on the operation of the system as a whole and, thereby, of its legitimacy.

4. The Tensions in Legitimacy

This chapter has shown how the environmental principles operate to affect and enhance the capacity of the courts and help to contribute to good outcomes but that in doing so they may, on the other hand, compromise the legitimacy of the courts' contribution to the EU governance system as a whole by undermining the process values represented by certainty, coherence, and clarity. This section concludes the chapter by bringing together the threads of what has been said so far, to highlight two parts: the relationship between evidence and openness to ranges of views; and the tension that exists when environmental principles become entangled with rules which allocate decision-making responsibility and power.

A. Evidence and Openness

One feature of environmental cases, as noted earlier, is that they demand an engagement with uncertainty. The uncertainty in question here can be of many forms. It may be uncertainty in the underlying factual position or uncertainties around the shape of the law. Brian Preston's taxonomy of such uncertainties is useful here.[96] First, he refers to epistemic uncertainty. This, in the words of Regan *et al.*, is uncertainty which emerges from 'limitations of measurement devices, insufficient data, extrapolations and interpolations, and variability over time and space'.[97] This uncertainty is ever-present because the environment is 'a dynamic and not a static entity'.[98] Second, there are methodological uncertainties. These may arise due to 'excessive influence from lay audiences or non-scientific interest groups'[99] or, conversely, by an over-reliance on models which are a simplification of reality. Third, there are sociological uncertainties: 'environmental risks are not drawn from nature alone, but are socially constructed'.[100] Fourth, there is linguistic uncertainty which, clearly, is significant to the law.

The environmental principles operate, in part, to overcome some of these uncertainties. That they do so is a necessary function of rules which are supposed to operate in the face of evidential uncertainties. When a court is charged with the task of assessing on the balance of probabilities whether outcome x or y is likely to occur, in cases where there is simply a total absence of evidence as to the likely outcome, it is much better that the court resort to reliance on, for example, the environmental principles than, by contrast, simply guessing. The lack of judicial expertise in such areas is therefore remedied in part by the environmental principles. However, where the situation becomes more problematic is when the court uses the principles to obscure the presence of uncertainty: to render that which is uncertain into that which is certain and then to make a decision based on a position of certainty. This can occur when the court 'reads' the evidence using the principles. Evidence which is mixed, or open to a range of views, becomes evidence which *demonstrates the existence of a risk*. The existence of a risk then becomes the reason to make a precaution-based decision. The outcome may be the same in terms of result but the reasoning shifts. As discussed in *Bayer*, this becomes particularly important in cases if minority or emerging scientific information challenges the consensus. By papering over the uncertainty, the court fails

[96] Preston, 'Biodiversity in the Court: The Certainty of Contests about Uncertainty' in M. Eliantonio *et al.* (eds), *EU Environmental Principles and Scientific Uncertainty Before National Courts* (2022) 301 ff.

[97] Regan *et al.*, 'A Taxonomy and Treatment of Uncertainty for Ecology and Conservation Biology', 12 *Ecological Applications* (2002) 618, at 618.

[98] Preston (n. 96) 301.

[99] Ibid. 303.

[100] Ibid. 305.

to acknowledge tension in the scientific position, giving credence to scientific approaches which indeed may not be sufficiently robust. They are only treated as robust because they operate so as to favour environmental protection. Of course, in environmental terms such an outcome may be desirable but in the broader perspective of evidence-based decision-making, this approach of 'precaution cubed' risks the underlying soundness of the evidence relied upon. This conclusion becomes apparent when we consider the relationship between the courts' fact-finding roles and the way in which the principles operate.

B. Entanglement and Power Allocation

The second main conclusion emerging from the discussion here is that the entanglement of the use of the principles to achieve environmental protection, and their role in allocating decision-making power between different parts of the modern state, is telling. In de Sadeleer's work, his primary argument is that the environmental principles represent an indication that environmental law has shifted from the precise and clear rules of modern law into the more vague, negotiated, and value-centric rules of post-modern law. But this is developed on the premise that the state itself has become post-modern, eschewing expertise in favour of participation and negotiation; and moving from command and control to market forces. The use by the courts of the environmental principles, however, shows that the principles themselves, for all their post-modern flavour, have the tendency to integrate expertise above democratic preferences into decision-making relating to the environment. In particular, the CJEU's approach to the precautionary principle and its refusal to prioritize administration-sanctioned information and knowledge over other forms of knowledge in the public domain shows that the relationship between experts and legal decision-making is shaped by the approach of the Court, bringing scientific experts to the fore (see also Chapter 6 in this volume). As Corkin explains, this shows the ways in which:

> Science and democracy are latter-day totems that embody our will to master on the one hand the natural world and on the other hand ourselves. Usually complimentary, strains arise when, in mastering ourselves, we look to regulate risks (especially those resulting from our efforts to master the natural world)

> in ways that appear irrational to science. On such occasions, should we yield to a scientific 'rationality' that is increasingly complex, compartmentalised and difficult for the layman to grasp, or assign priority to lay 'irrationality'?[101]

On the other hand, the decisions in *JP* and *Commission v. Austria* are evidence of a willingness on the part of the CJEU to ensure that whilst the power to make decisions about the environment are science-led, the prioritization and therefore the responsibility for that priority, in terms of which kinds of environmental media are to receive the strongest protection, rests on the shoulders of the administrative state. Here too, therefore, we see how the environmental principles—the polluter pays and the integration principle—are used to ensure that the nation state retains its primary responsibility for remedying and avoiding environmental harms, even if it does not retain responsibility for the evidence and knowledge upon which those decisions are eventually based. This entanglement between experts and administrative agencies creates a complex power-allocation which is generated, in part, through the ways in which the environmental principles are given substance in a particular case.

5. Conclusions

Taken together, we can draw only contingent conclusions about how the environmental principles contribute to the legitimacy of the courts and thus to the courts' function in holding the modern administrative state to account. The conclusions are limited because the role of the principles is not homogenous and, as such, cannot be said to apply in all contexts. Furthermore, because the criteria for legitimacy will not always themselves pull in the same direction, when a principle has a tendency to, for example, increase judicial capacity but also fails to protect the environment, then it both enhances and detracts from the legitimacy of the system as a whole. However, even though the conclusions we can reach are only partial, that does not make them less useful in giving an insight into the principles, the role of the courts, or the legitimacy of the system as a whole. Both the fact-finding role of the courts

[101] Corkin, 'Science, Legitimacy and the Law: Regulating Risk Regulation Judiciously in the European Community', 33 *European Law Review* (2008) 359, at 359.

and their ability to interpret the allocation of decision-making responsibility and power embedded within environmental law rules are profoundly shaped by the operation of the environmental principles in ways which are often hidden by stark references to the principles without deep engagement with what the principles mean in the particular context at hand.

4

Environmental Protection in a Free Market

Member States' Room for Manoeuvre

Nicolas de Sadeleer

1. Introduction

In spite of the fact that industrial and energy production remains an important source of pollution emissions, the growth in pollutants and greenhouse gas emissions has been consumption-related. Indeed, there is a correlation between the rise in consumption of products and environmental impairment. Through their life cycle, all products cause environmental degradation in some way. Depending on their production method, their composition, and how they are transported, used, consumed, reused, recycled, or discarded, products can become a source of pollution. Focusing since the early 1970s on the regulation of 'point sources' of pollution, environmental policy gradually shifted through the 1990s towards the control of diffuse pollution thanks to environment-related product measures.

Furthermore, the rise of EU environmental policy was undeniably born out of the concern to avoid distortions of competition between undertakings. To give national authorities free rein to enact unilateral product and operating standards would entail the risk of a race to the bottom between states keen to attract polluting installations to the place where the cost of pollution is lowest. This would result in a generalized reduction of protection levels. In the absence of EU harmonization measures, several Western Member States have since the 1980s adopted a flurry of environment-related product measures. However, protecting the environment through national measures limiting the placing on the market or the use of hazardous products and substances might constitute a plausible alibi for reinforcing the competitiveness of national undertakings. What is more, such a strategy can be made all the more insidious by the use of measures that apply without distinction to both domestic and imported goods. If secondary law is not necessary for the implementation of the free movement

Nicolas de Sadeleer, *Environmental Protection in a Free Market* In: *The Legitimacy of EU Environmental Governance and the Role of the European Courts*. Edited by: Mariolina Eliantonio and Emma Lees, Oxford University Press. © Nicolas de Sadeleer 2025. DOI: 10.1093/oso/9780198972808.003.0004

of goods within the internal market, it remains complementary to it. Given that positive harmonization determines more precisely the room for manoeuvre left to the Member States than a changeable adjudicatory approach, it has been preferred by the EU institutions in environment-related matters, as well as in consumer safety, to negative harmonization. For this reason, over the last 30 years or so, numerous legal acts have been adopted by the lawmakers of the European Union with a view to harmonizing the conditions under which products posing a risk to the environment or to human health can be placed on the market.

The purpose of this chapter is not to revisit the controversies arising from the interpretation of the different TFEU provisions on the free movement of goods[1] but to explore, in light of recent Court of Justice of the European Union (CJEU) cases, the widely varying room for manoeuvre left by primary and secondary law to Member States. This discussion is crucial to the legitimacy and operation of EU law as a whole in relation to the environment, precisely because, as explained in Chapter 1, environmental protection is not the only aim underpinning EU governance. Environmental policy constantly competes with other public policies. To fully understand how the EU Courts contribute to the legitimacy of this governance system, therefore, it is crucial to examine how they attempt to balance environmental protection with other goals of the Union legal order.[2] This chapter sheds light on this by examining the reasoning which the CJEU endorses when balancing environmental protection and the free market.

Sections 2 and 3 analyse cases recently adjudicated by the CJEU concerning harmonization measures related to the marketing of biocidal and plant protection products. These acts—the Biocides Regulation[3] and the Plant Protection Products Regulation[4]—have been adopted on the basis of Article 114 of the Treaty on the Functioning of the EU (TFEU) and are based on similar administrative and scientific principles. Whenever these regulations expressly enshrine the precautionary principle, the Court makes use of it. In Section 4, we will look at the ways in which genetically modified organisms (GMOs) law restricts Member States' room for manoeuvre. In view of the limited space

[1] de Sadeleer, 'Environmental Measures as an Obstacle to Free Movement of Goods in the Internal Market', in E. Maître, C. Dalhammar, and H. C. Bugge (eds), *Preventing Environmental Damage from Products. An Analysis of the Policy and Regulatory Framework in Europe* (2018) 125–149.

[2] See Art. 3 of the Treaty on the European Union.

[3] Regulation (EU) No. 528/2012, OJ 2012 L 167/1.

[4] Regulation (EC) No. 1107/2009, OJ 2009 L 309/1.

available for our contribution, we have confined our analysis to a few recent CJEU judgments that have barely been commented on in law journals.

Our analysis will highlight that when the EU legislature harmonizes the placing on the market of a hazardous product, it does not regulate all aspects of that marketing. The Member States are thus endowed with some room for manoeuvre, subject to compliance with the internal market's fundamental freedoms that are strictly interpreted by the CJEU. Regarding the restrictions placed on the marketing or the use of hazardous products, the latitude left to the Member States is contained within limits, which are not always very clear. In this case, the fact that the domestic measures hindering the free movement of goods are underpinned by the principles of prevention and precaution may make some of these conditions more flexible.

Finally, in Section 5 we address the way in which the polluter pays principle is applied to energy products in the aftermath of the Green Deal. This once again raises the question of the extent of harmonization and the room for manoeuvre that remains for the Member States.

Taken together, the question of the 'room for manoeuvre' which Member States have with respect to environment-related measures puts into sharp relief the tensions in legitimacy that are explored in Chapter 1. On the one hand, the Court of Justice here is policing *not only* the balance between the environment and trade but also the relationship between the Union itself and the Member States. In the reasoning of the Court in these cases, there are therefore two pressures at play. On the other hand, the outcomes of these cases also have significant consequences for how far environmental protection measures can be pursued above and beyond what the EU itself has directed. Therefore, the Court's role in allocating power between the Member States and the Union has important consequences in that it allows or precludes a higher level of environmental protection than the harmonized EU standards.

2. Positive and Negative Harmonization

In order to explore the relationship between environment protection rules instigated by Member States and the Union's own legal measures, it is necessary to set the ground for how harmonization of product standards is achieved through the Union legal order. There are two ways to ascertain the compatibility of national environment-related product measures with the free movement of goods—from the perspective of positive harmonization or from that of negative harmonization. Either the domestic measure will be assessed only in the light of secondary legislation—as in the case of exhaustive harmonization—or it will be observed that the measure goes beyond the scope of existing directives and regulations, and its lawfulness will be assessed in the light of Treaty law. In this connection, Articles 28, 30, 34, 35, and 110 TFEU prohibit Member States from restricting free movement of goods (*negative harmonization*).

Against this background, a significant number of measures which have a direct impact on the internal market, and in particular those that lay down product standards, have been adopted on the basis of the former Article 100a EC Treaty and Article 95 EC Treaty (replaced by Art. 114 TFEU) within the perspective of the completion of the internal market. Accordingly, the EU measures addressing the environmental risks of chemical substances,[5] GMOs,[6] biocides,[7] objects or substances likely to become waste,[8] as well as acts encouraging the eco-design of products[9] have been founded exclusively on Article 114 TFEU.[10] Thus, the regulation of a flurry of hazardous products, ranging from GMOs[11] to motor vehicles,[12] is governed by directives and regulations adopted by the EU institutions (*positive harmonization*) in the framework provided for in the TFEU.

On the other hand, a residual category embraces all regulatory measures for which an analysis of their aim and their content shows that they seek to achieve a high level of environmental protection and that they, at most, affect the establishment of the internal market in a peripheral manner. Despite their direct or potential impact on the functioning of the internal market, these acts should be adopted on the basis of Article 192 TFEU.[13] This is the case of the directives aiming at protecting wildlife, different ecosystems, soils, marine, underground as well as surface water, air, and climate.[14] In addition, the acts regulating the

[5] See among others, Regulation (EC) No. 1907/2006, OJ 2006 L 396–851.

[6] With respect to GMOs, see Directive 2001/18/EC, OJ 2001 L 106/1 and Regulation (EC) No. 1830/2003, OJ L 2003 268/24.

[7] Regulation (EU) No. 528/2012 (n. 3).

[8] Proposal for a regulation of the European Parliament and of the Council on packaging and packaging waste, COM/2022/677 final.

[9] Directive 2009/125/EC, OJ 2009 L 285/10.

[10] The recourse to Art. 114 TFEU does not preclude the possibility to adopt an act on other legal bases such as Arts 43 and 168(4) TFEU. See Regulation (EC) No. 1107/2009, OJ 2009 L 309/1.

[11] Regulation (EC) No. 1829/2003, OJ 2003 L 268/1.

[12] Regulation (EU) 2019/2144, OJ 2019 L 325/1.

[13] Case C-155/91, *Commission v. Council* (EU:C:1993:98) and Case C-187/93, *European Parliament v. Council* (EU:C:1994:265), paras 24–26.

[14] For an overview of the different acts founded on Art. 192 TFEU, see N. de Sadeleer, *Commentaire Mégret. Environnement et Marché Intérieur* (2010) 247–329; L. Krämer, *EU Environmental Law* (8th edn, 2016) 223–267; P. Thieffry, *Traité de Droit de l'Environnement et Du Climat* (4th edn, 2020) 627–785.

pollution emitted by listed installations and waste management[15] have also been adopted on the basis of this provision.

Given that the EU lawmakers have adopted a vast body of legislation harmonizing the conditions under which goods are entitled to be placed on the market and to circulate within the EU, Member States' room for manoeuvre appears to be rather limited as regards the adoption of product standards. What room for manoeuvre is left to them? Can they adopt stricter standards than those provided for in EU secondary law? A priori, when directives and regulations have been adopted on the basis of Article 192 TFEU, they are empowered to adopt stricter standards by virtue of Article 193 TFEU. Therefore, the choice between Article 114 and Article 192 TFEU is of crucial importance given that internal market harmonization precludes Member State regulatory autonomy[16] whereas Article 193 allows Member States to adopt more stringent measures,[17] although they may be reluctant to exert their powers.

However, the possibility of adopting stricter standards is far more complex, as shown by the cases we will analyse later. As a matter of law, the free discretion of national authorities will be limited as harmonization deepens. 'Exhaustive' or 'full' harmonization[18] precludes the ability of the Member State to enact more stringent measures. It is settled case law that, where a matter has been the subject of exhaustive harmonization at the EU level, any national measure relating thereto must be assessed in the light of the provisions of that harmonizing measure and not in the light of primary law.[19]

Thus, in order to know whether the national measure falls within the scope of EU secondary law or Treaty law, it is necessary to assess the extent to which the regulation or the directive at issue gives rise to exhaustive or incomplete harmonization. It follows that the assessment of the consistency of national environmental measures with regard to the TFEU provisions requires a constant classification of the measures at stake, which may lead to difficulties regarding hybrid national measures, such as measures combining taxation and technical aspects. This is not an easy task. For instance, it is possible that an EU directive or regulation governs only some aspects of an issue, or only certain products, or only some stages in the life cycle of those products. Furthermore, the unilateral adoption of technical standards is also subject to a specific procedural

[15] N. de Sadeleer, *Droit des Déchets de l'UE. De l'Élimination à l'Économie Circulaire* (2016) 39–56.

[16] Art. 114(4) to (10) TFEU allows Member States to provide for reinforced protection under specific conditions. See N. de Sadeleer, *EU Environmental Law and the Internal Market* (2014) 359–380.

[17] de Sadeleer (n. 16) 350–358.

[18] The CJEU uses the two terms.

[19] Case C-573/12, *Ålands Vindkraft* (EU:C:2014:2037), para. 57 and the case law cited.

regime. In order to allow preventive control under the provisions on the free movement of goods and, in particular, in relation to the justification of the obstacles that could be created in that regard, Member States must communicate to the European Commission the draft provisions by which technical specifications are given binding effect before their entry into force.[20]

3. Free Movement of Biocidal Products and Possibility for Member States to Adopt Restrictive Measures Relating to Commercial and Advertising Practices

This section considers the rules relating to limitations on how, when, and through what means of advertising biocidal products can be sold within the Union. These rules define the ways in which Member State freedoms to restrict modes of selling are set against the goal of establishing the internal market, even in respect of products for which general Union-wide controls are in place.

Keck and subsequent case law narrowed down the scope of Article 34 TFEU in removing 'certain selling arrangements'—sales at a loss, rules on advertising, opening of stores on Sundays, etc.—from the scope of that provision as long as those arrangements were equal in impact on both domestic and foreign traders (1st condition) and on domestic and imported goods (2nd condition).[21] In so doing, the Court drew a distinction between selling arrangements and product requirements. On the one hand, the selling arrangements fulfilling the *Keck* conditions do not fall within the scope of Article 34 and, as a result, are not subject to any sort of justification. On the other, measures concerning the dimensions, weight, form, size, composition, designation, labelling, information about health effects and hazardousness, and presentation of goods do fall within the scope of Article 34. Table 4.1 distinguishes between the two sets of case law.

The rationale for this distinction is that these two categories have a different impact on intra-Union trade. The functioning of the internal market would be hindered if goods that comply with the legislation of the Member State of origin also need to comply with product requirements elsewhere in the Union. The impact of selling arrangements, on the contrary, is much more limited.

[20] Case C-433/05, *Sandström* (EU:C:2010:184), para. 42 and Case C-26/11, *Belgische Petroleum Unie and Others* (EU:C:2013:44), paras 49 and 50.

[21] Joined Cases C-267 and C-268/91, *Keck* (EU:C:1993:905).

Table 4.1 Case law for selling arrangements and the principle of mutual recognition

	Selling arrangements (*Keck and Mithouard* case law)	Principle of mutual recognition (*Dassonville* case law)
Scope	*De jure* or *de facto* restrictions on where, when, where, and by whom hazardous substances may be sold	Product requirements to be met by goods that have been 'lawfully manufactured and marketed' in other Member States, even if those rules are indistinctly applicable
Compatibility with Art. 34 TFEU	Presumption of legality provided that the arrangements apply to all traders operating within the national territory and affect in the same manner in law and in fact the selling of domestic products and those from other Member States	Given that these indistinctly applicable standards bar access to the domestic market to foreign goods, they breach Art. 34 TFEU, so long as they are not justified by an overriding general interest (Art. 36 TFEU)
Illustrations	E.g. restrictions on selling hazardous goods to qualified undertakings, advertising restrictions	E.g. product standards related to form, size, dimension, weight, trade description, composition, packaging, labelling and presentation of goods, safety requirements, thresholds of hazardous substances, dangerous properties

Arguably, given that the purpose of the latter measures is not to regulate trade, they are less likely to impose extra costs on the importers.

Insofar as EU environment-related product regulations primarily concern the characteristics of a good such as the toxicity of a chemical product, the origin or rarity of a plant or animal species,[22] the hazardousness of waste,[23] the labelling, the concentration of hazardous substances, specifications on health and environmental grounds concerning the flash point of diesel fuel,[24] rather than selling arrangements, the CJEU has seldom been faced with the case of a national measure on the selling arrangements for hazardous goods. For instance, the Court found that legislation requiring the marking of heavy metal concentration in batteries and accumulators before their sale in the Member State of origin, and thus before their marketing in the Member State of said

[22] Case C-510/99, *Tridon* (EU:C:2001:77) and Case C-659/20, *Ministerstvo životního prostředí* (EU:C:2022:642).

[23] Joined Cases C-241/12 and C-242/12, *Shell Nederland Verkoopmaatschappij BV and Belgian Shell NV* (EU:C:2013:821).

[24] Case C-251/14, *György Balázs* (EU:C:2015:687).

legislation, did not concern selling arrangements.[25] Indeed, such legislation entails an adaptation and new wrapping of the goods.

On 19 January 2023, the CJEU applied, for the first time, its 'selling arrangements' doctrine with respect to measures prohibiting commercial practices and commercial advertising for hazardous substances. With a view to enhancing public health and environmental protection, the French lawmaker decided that rodenticides and insecticides, two categories of biocidal products, could not be the object of certain commercial practices and restricted their advertisement. French trade committees operating in the essential oils sector and biocides manufacturers initiated an action for annulment against the measures at hand before the Council of State. The Council of State harboured doubts about whether the Biocides Regulation achieved exhaustive harmonization precluding the national rules at issue and considered, if such exhaustive harmonization had not been achieved, under what conditions those rules may be adopted. Of particular relevance was Article 1(1) of the Biocides Regulation, which states that the Regulation aims at improving 'the functioning of the internal market through the harmonisation of the rules on the making available on the market and the use of biocidal products, whilst ensuring a high level of protection of both human and animal health and the environment'. The Council of State referred the matter to the CJEU.

In addressing this case, the CJEU reasoned, first, that the French law prohibited certain commercial practices for biocides: discounts, price reductions, rebates, gifts of free units, etc.[26] The CJEU found that the Biocides Regulation was sufficiently broad to cover commercial practices 'linked to the sale of those products'.[27] However, the regulation, which provides for a system of prior authorization allowing biocides to be placed on the market and for uniform risk assessment principles, does not harmonize all aspects of the marketing of the products concerned.[28] The Biocides Regulation therefore did not preclude the French prohibition at issue.[29] In other words, exhaustive harmonization was not achieved in this case.

Given that harmonization was incomplete, the CJEU therefore had to assess the compatibility of the French measures in the light of Article 34 TFEU. It first had to determine whether the measures at issue fell within the scope of the *Keck and Mithouard* case law that precludes Article 34 TFEU. After recalling

[25] Case C-143/03, *Commission v. Italy* (ECLI:EU:C:2004:629), para. 29.
[26] Art. L522-18 of the Environmental Code.
[27] Case C-147/21, *CIHEF* (EU:C:2023:31), para. 33.
[28] Ibid. para. 33.
[29] Ibid. paras 31–35.

the conditions for implementing this case law,[30] the CJEU referred back to the national court the task of assessing whether the ban on commercial practices had a greater effect on access to the French market for biocidal products originating from other Member States.[31] To carry out such an assessment, the referring court was required to assess whether the ban covered a narrow range of marketing methods for the biocidal products concerned and whether, consequently, marketing methods which were not prohibited by those provisions ensured that products from other Member States were able to gain access to the domestic market.[32] If the answer was that such products would not be able to gain access to the domestic market, the French ban was liable to constitute a measure having equivalent effect within the meaning of Article 34 TFEU. Accordingly, the referring court would then have to determine whether the contested measures could be justified either on the basis of Article 36 or on the basis of the rule of reason.[33] Article 36 TFEU refers to the protection of human life and health that must be taken into account,[34] whereas the rule of reason encompasses the protection of the environment, which constitutes an overriding reason in the public interest capable of justifying a measure having an effect equivalent to a quantitative restriction.[35]

Thereafter, the CJEU set out the classic conditions—necessity and proportionality—for examining exceptions to the general prohibition of measures having equivalent effect.[36] Although it was for the referring court to verify the fulfilment of these various conditions,[37] the CJEU itself carried out this analysis, referring to the arguments put forward by the French government, the Opinion of Advocate General Emiliou and the indications of the referring court.[38] The CJEU stressed that the measure at hand was appropriate to achieve its health and environmental objectives. Indeed, in reducing the exposure of the public, animals, and the environment to the biocidal products concerned, the French ban aimed to prevent the accumulation of those products in the environment and the water pollution which may have resulted.[39]

On the basis of these various considerations, the CJEU concluded that Articles 34 and 36 TFEU did not preclude French legislation which prohibits

30 Ibid. paras 40–46.
31 Ibid. paras 42–45.
32 Ibid. para. 47.
33 Ibid. paras 49–58.
34 Ibid. para. 50.
35 Ibid. paras 51–52.
36 Ibid. para. 53.
37 Ibid. para. 54.
38 Ibid. paras 55–58.
39 Ibid. paras 55 and 56.

certain commercial practices. Thus, the application of the principle of prevention through restrictions placed on certain commercial practices corroborated the proportionality of the measure at hand.

On 21 April 2023, France's Conseil d'Etat ruled that while the French arrangements may restrict the total volume of sales of biocidal products, or even limit the market entry of new products, there was no evidence to consider these national measures to be such as to restrict access to the market of the biocidal products concerned originating in other Member States to a greater extent than that of such products originating in France.[40] Given that these arrangements fell under the *Keck* case law, there was no need to verify whether they violated Article 34 TFEU.

As regards the ban on all advertising to the general public for certain categories of biocides,[41] the CJEU reasoned in a similar way. The Court stressed that the EU lawmaker did not intend to regulate all aspects relating to the advertising of such products.[42] In particular, the legislature did not expressly exclude the possibility for Member States to prohibit advertising to the general public.[43] In the absence of exhaustive harmonization, the French measures had to be examined in light of Articles 34 and 36 TFEU.[44] Once again, the *Keck and Mithouard* case law on selling conditions applied.[45] As regards the de facto effect of the French ban on advertisement of imported products, the CJEU held that it had already decided that national legislation which restricts or prohibits certain forms of advertising for certain products may be liable to restrict their sales volume and, consequently, may have a greater impact on products from other Member States.[46] However, that finding is conditional on identification of a 'specific difficulty characterising a given product market with which an operator is confronted in order to enter the national market'.[47] France's Conseil d'Etat ruled also that these arrangements could not be regarded as being such as to restrict access to the French market of the biocidal products concerned originating in other Member States to a greater extent than that of such

[40] Conseil d'État, 5th and 6th Chambers [2023] no. 433889.
[41] Art. L522-5-3 of the Environmental Code provides that 'All commercial advertising shall be prohibited for certain categories of biocidal products defined by [Regulation No 528/2012].
[42] Case C-147/21, *CIHEF* (EU:C:2023:31), para. 69.
[43] Ibid. paras 68–70.
[44] Ibid. paras 71–83.
[45] Ibid. paras 72–75.
[46] Ibid. para. 78.
[47] Ibid. para. 78. See Case C-405/98, *Gourmet International Products* (EU:C:2001:135), paras 19 and 21; Case C-148/15, *Deutsche Parkinson Vereinigung* (EU:C:2016:776), para. 25; and Case C-190/20, *DocMorri* (EU:C:2021:609), para. 41.

products produced in France and that, consequently, they were not contrary to Articles 34 to 36 TFEU.[48]

Lastly, in sharp contrast to the previous measures, the CJEU held that a specific measure requiring the inclusion of a statement to professionals in addition to that provided for in Article 72 of the Biocide Regulation was precluded. Article 72 is intended to regulate, in a detailed and comprehensive manner, the wording of statements on the risks of using biocidal products which may appear in advertisements for those products.[49] Following the CJEU judgment in *CHIEF*, the French Conseil d'Etat annulled the French label on the grounds that it required additional information to that provided for in Article 72 of Regulation (EU) No. 528/2012 for advertising aimed at professionals.

From this case law, it is clear that the Court has utilized the environmental principles to shape the ways in which environmental risks are handled in the harmonization process. By emphasizing environmental protection within the proportionality test, the Court sees the Member States and the EU as working in tandem in that respect. Where the protective measure has already been decided in EU secondary law in an unambiguous way, as in the case of risk warnings, there is no need for the Member States to provide their own additional warnings.

4. Possibility for a Member State to Derogate from the Ban on Active Substances Posing High Risks to Bees

A similar 'environment first' approach is in evidence in relation to attempts by Member States not to impose more protective measures but rather to balance that environmental protection against other relevant concerns, such as agricultural competitiveness and food production. Furthermore, in considering the ban on neonicotinoids, the fact that most products have an impact on the environment, meaning that environmental measures seek to regulate their environmental risks rather than eliminate them completely, comes to the fore. As a result, product standards only rarely contain absolute prohibitions on harming the environment. Where regulations do enact a regime of prohibitions, it is generally subject to a flurry of derogations.[50] Environmental law is thus made of unresolved compromises. As a result, courts are constantly called

[48] Conseil d'État, 5th and 6th Chambers [2023] no. 433889, [5].
[49] Case C-147/21, *CIHEF* (EU:C:2023:31), para. 69.
[50] See e.g. Art. 60(4) REACH Regulation.

upon to weigh up the interests in play, particularly in considering and relying upon the principle of proportionality. However, in this case, the Court perhaps shifts its interpretive stance somewhat to see the environment less as a factor to be balanced and more as a goal to be reached which is not on an equal footing with other concerns in play. The proportionality assessment is thereby shifted to increase the weight of the environmental interest in the overall weighing of interests, at least where the prioritization of such protection emerges from a Union-wide measure.

Neonicotinoids are active substances used as insecticides in agriculture for the purpose of seed coating. After authorizing undertakings to place these active substances on the market, the European Commission first issued restrictions in 2013[51] and then prohibited the marketing and use of seeds treated with these active substances in 2018.[52] The CJEU dismissed actions for annulment brought by industry federations and companies against national bans on the marketing of neonicotinoids[53] as well as against the restrictions imposed by the European Commission.[54] Given that the EU ban on the marketing and use of neonicotinoids was not absolute, the CJEU had to rule on the possibility for a Member State to derogate from that ban.

In 2020–2021, the invasion of aphid colonies in sugar beet plantations had had major economic consequences for the sugar beet industry. Around ten Member States applied to activate the derogation provided for in Article 53(1) of the Plant Protection Products Regulation. In 2018, the Belgian authorities, relying on the temporary derogation regime provided for in Article 53(1), temporarily authorized the placing on the market of plant protection products containing two neonicotinoids—clothianidin and thiamethoxam—for the treatment of sugar beet seeds. In an annulment case based upon Article 53(1), considering such national measures, the Belgian Council of State referred questions to the CJEU for a preliminary ruling on the conformity of such a derogation. The referring court expressed doubts as to the scope of Article 53 and the scope of the derogation for which it provides. Article 53 of the Plant Protection Products Regulation allows Member States to authorize 'in special circumstances' the placing on the market, 'for a period not exceeding 120 days', of plant protection products that are in principle banned, 'for limited and

[51] Commission Implementing Regulation (EU) No. 485/2013, OJ 2013 L 139/12.

[52] Commission Implementing Regulation (EU) 2018/784, OJ 2018 L 132/35; Commission Implementing Regulation (EU) 2018/785, OJ 2018 L 132/40.

[53] Case C-514/19, *Union des industries de la protection des plantes* (EU:C:2020:803).

[54] Case C-449/18 P, *Bayer CropScience and Bayer v. Commission* (EU:C:2021:36).

controlled use, where such a measure appears necessary because of a danger which cannot be contained by any other reasonable means'.

In her opinion, Advocate General Kokott proposed that a balance be struck between protecting animal health and the environment on the one hand and pest control and agricultural competitiveness on the other. This led the AG to accept the possibility of derogating from the Commission's ban on the use of these products, provided that the benefits and risks of the products in question were weighed against each other. She concluded that Member States were authorized, in principle, to allow the use not only of active substances that had not yet been approved by the Commission but also the use of approved active substances that the Commission had expressly excluded by way of a restriction.[55]

However, the CJEU did not follow her opinion.[56] As it was firmly committed to defending the values associated with environmental protection, the Court endorsed a rigorous interpretation of the rules of secondary law founded on the principle of strict interpretation of derogations.

First, on the basis of the wording of the Regulation, the Court rightly concluded that the Member States could not derogate from provisions expressly prohibiting the placing on the market and the use of these plant protection products.[57]

In addition, a contextual analysis led the Court to rule that the EU lawmaker had in no way intended, through the possibility of derogation, to authorize the Member States to call into question an explicit ban on seeds treated with neonicotinoids.[58] The prohibitory measures laid down in the Commission's implementing decision were adopted 'bearing in mind the need to ensure a level of safety and protection consistent with the high level of protection of animal health that is sought within the EU'.[59] Such prohibitions were thus consistent with the objective of the Pesticides Regulation,[60] which is to ensure a high level of protection of human and animal health and the environment.[61] The opposite reasoning would render the European Commission ban nugatory.

Furthermore, the CJEU's reasoning was underpinned by the precautionary principle, which is one of the bases of the policy of a high level of protection pursued by the European Union in the field of the environment.[62]

[55] Ibid. para. 59.
[56] Case C-162/21, *Pesticide Action Network Europe* (EU:C:2023:30).
[57] Case C-449/18 P, *Bayer CropScience and Bayer v. Commission* (EU:C:2021:36), para. 36.
[58] Ibid. para. 42.
[59] Ibid. para. 45.
[60] Art. 1(3) and (4) and recital 8.
[61] Case C-162/21, *Pesticide Action Network Europe* (EU:C:2023:30), para. 46.
[62] Ibid. para. 47. See Case C-616/17, *Blaise and Others* (EU:C:2019:800).

Accordingly, as is clear from the explanatory memorandum to the Pesticides Regulation, the objectives of protecting human and animal health and the environment must take precedence over the aim of improving plant production. As a result, the traditional weighing of competing interests, which a proportionality test would provoke,[63] should be discarded in such cases. It follows that the national authorities must have demonstrated, before the plant protection products were placed on the market, not only that they presented a clear benefit for plant production[64] but also that they did not have any harmful effect on human or animal health.[65] This conclusion was all the more justified given that the marketing and use of the products concerned had been the subject of very clear prohibition measures following the scientific assessment of the European Food Safety Authority.[66]

The Court's conclusion is, therefore, crystal clear: Member States cannot authorize the placing on the market of plant protection products for seed treatment containing approved active substances which the Commission has excluded by way of a restriction or condition of approval. In this sense, the Courts have shown a clear willingness to police the relationship between the Member States' 'priorities' (in this case, protection of their farming industry) and those of the Union (in this case, the environment) by utilizing the environmental principles to support a restrictive field of autonomy for the Member States.

5. Free Movement of GMOs and National Coexistence Measures

This restricted field can also be seen when we consider not only the object of any particular national measure but also the logic underpinning it: the intention of the measure is relevant to the Member States' freedom. This can be seen in relation to local restrictions on GMOs. GMOs have repeatedly been a matter of much controversy, especially in Europe. The scepticism of many NGOs and several regulatory agencies has focused both on their impact on human health (allergenicity, genes expressing resistance to antibiotics in use for medical or veterinary treatment) as well as the impoverishment of biodiversity which

[63] de Sadeleer (n. 16) 308–318.
[64] Recital 24.
[65] Case C-162/21, *Pesticide Action Network Europe* (EU:C:2023:30), paras 48 and 49.
[66] Ibid. para. 52.

their cultivation could cause (wild species resisting GM plants, resistance to herbicides, hybrid plants, gene flow through pollen transfer, impacts upon soils, etc.).

Directive 2001/18 on the deliberate release into the environment of GMOs and Regulation No. 1829/2003 have been adopted on the basis of Article 114 TFEU. Directive 2001/18 makes the placing on the market of GMOs in a product, food, or feed subject to a system of prior authorization established at the EU level.[67] The objective of Directive 2001/18, as is clear from Article 1 thereof, is to approximate the laws, regulations, and administrative provisions of the Member States and to protect human health and the environment when carrying out the deliberate release of GMOs into the environment, whether by placing GMOs on the market within the European Union as products or for any purposes other than such placing on the market.[68] In accordance with Regulation No. 1829/2003, GMOs for feed use or feed containing or consisting of GMOs, or feeds produced from GMOs, on the other hand, may not be placed on the market where no authorization has been granted.[69]

Although MON 810 maize may be freely marketed within the European Union, its cultivation may be restricted in accordance with different safeguard clauses.[70] In particular, Article 26a of Directive 2001/18 empowers Member States to take appropriate measures to avoid the unintended presence of GMOs in other products.

In accordance with this provision, the Friuli region in Italy prohibited the cultivation of genetically modified maize on its territory in order to avoid the unintended presence of GMOs in conventional and organic maize crops. This regional ban was justified by the regional production models and farm structures that influence the degree of admixture between transgenic and non-transgenic crops.

The question arose as to whether this regional ban was consistent with Directive 2001/18, read in the light of Regulation No. 1829/2003 and the European Commission guidelines for the development of national coexistence measures to avoid the unintended presence of GMOs in conventional and organic crops.[71] In *Pioneer Hi Bred Italia*, the Court held that the cultivation of

[67] de Sadeleer, 'Centrifugal and Centripetal Forces in the Marketing and Cultivation of GMOs in the EU', 1 *European Journal of Consumer Law* (2016) 48.

[68] Case C-24/21, *Regione Autonoma Friuli Venezia Giulia* (EU:C:2022:526), para. 40.

[69] de Sadeleer, 'National Control of GMO Cultivation in the EU. The Path to Reconciliation of Opposed Interests', 1 *Nordic Journal of Environmental Law* (2018) 27–54.

[70] de Sadeleer, 'Marketing and Cultivation of GMOs in the EU. An Uncertain Balance between Centrifugal and Centripetal Forces', 4 *European Journal of Risk Regulation* (2015) 532–558.

[71] EC Recommendation of 13 July 2010.

GMOs, such as varieties of MON 810 maize, cannot be made subject to a national authorization procedure where the use and marketing of those varieties are authorized under Article 20 of Regulation No. 1829/2003. Article 26a of Directive 2001/18 may give rise to restrictions, or even geographically delimited bans, only as a result of coexistence measures actually adopted in compliance with the purpose of such measures.[72] In *Fidenato*,[73] an Italian court asked the CJEU whether the national authorization procedure applicable to the cultivation of varieties of MON 810 maize, authorized under EU secondary law, could itself constitute a coexistence measure for the purposes of Article 26a of Directive 2001/18 provided it was specifically intended to ensure compliance with the principle of coexistence. Along the same lines as in *Pioneer*, the CJEU interpreted Article 26a of Directive 2001/18/EC as not allowing a Member State to oppose the cultivation on its territory of GMOs that have already been authorized. Such a national authorization procedure cannot amount to a restriction, or even a geographically delimited ban, aimed at avoiding the accidental presence of GMOs in other crops.

If secondary law did not apply, the question arose as to whether that regional ban might constitute a measure having equivalent effect which is contrary to Articles 34 to 36 TFEU.

In *Regione Autonoma Friuli Venezia Giulia*, the CJEU stressed that the measures taken by the Member States, in accordance with Article 26a(1) of Directive 2001/18, must aim at avoiding the unintended presence of GMOs in other products, 'in order to enable producers and consumers to have the choice between organic production, conventional production and production using GMOs'.[74] Accordingly, in enacting these regional preventive measures, the authorities cannot have human health or the environment as their aim since these objectives are already ensured by the harmonized authorization procedures for the deliberate release of GMOs.[75]

In so doing, the CJEU drew a line between, on the one hand, the harmonization licensing process established by Directive 2001/18 and Regulation No. 1829/2003, which makes the grant of such authorizations subject to an environment and health risk assessment, and, on the other hand, the avoidance of the unintended presence of GMOs in other products, that is subject to an incomplete harmonization. The Court stressed that the measures aiming

[72] Case C-36/11, *Pioneer Hi Bred Italia* (EU:C:2012:534), para. 75.
[73] Case C-542/12, *Fidenato* (EU:C:2013:298).
[74] Ibid. para. 47.
[75] Case C-24/21, *Regione Autonoma Friuli Venezia Giulia* (EU:C:2022:526), para. 47.

Table 4.2 Differences between licensing of GMOs and measures relating to avoidance of the unintended presence of GMOs in other products

Approaches to ward off GMOs risks	Licensing process of GMOs	Avoidance of the unintended presence of GMOs in other products
Legal acts	Directive 2001/18 (Art. 4) and Regulation No 1829/2003 (Arts 3 to 7)	Directive 2001/18 (Art. 26a)
Goals	Protecting the environment and health	Enabling producers and consumers to have the choice between organic production, conventional production, and production using GMOs
Measures	Authorizations subject to an environment and health risk assessment	Coexistence measure designed to avoid the unintended presence of GMOs in other crops (Art. 26a of Directive 2001/18)
Harmonization	Exhaustive: impossibility for the Member State to rely upon Arts 34 to 36 TFEU to enact more stringent measures under Art. 193 TFEU	Incomplete: judicial review of the necessity of the regional measure prohibiting cultivation of GMOs

at the avoidance of the unintended presence of GMOs in other products 'are intended to preserve the plurality of crops and, in particular, in so far as possible, the coexistence between GMOs, on the one hand, and organic and conventional crops, on the other. Therefore, they involve taking account of the economic challenges for organic and conventional producers of the admixture of GMOs in their crops.'[76] Table 4.2 distinguishes the key differences between the two regimes.

In brief, the regional measure at hand must pursue the objective of guaranteeing consumers and producers the choice between the production of genetically modified maize and the production of organic or conventional maize. In other words, Article 26a(1) is about consumer protection rather than environmental protection.

Given that the measures of the Friuli region intended to preserve the plurality of crops were likely to hamper the authorization that had been granted

[76] Ibid.

by the European Commission to MON 810 maize, they were required to be reviewed by the Italian courts in light of the criteria determined by the CJEU:

- they cannot be based on considerations of protection of health or the environment;[77]
- they must be necessary, a requirement that obliges Member States not go beyond what is necessary and is the least detrimental to the objectives and principles laid down by that Directive;[78] and
- they must satisfy the conditions attached to the guidelines annexed to the recommendation of 13 July 2010, which were adopted by the Commission on the basis of Article 26a(2) of that Directive.[79]

The CJEU seemed to be aware of the technical difficulties in implementing such a ban with a view to enhancing consumer protection. Indeed, according to point 2.4 of the Commission guidelines, the degree of admixture is likely to vary according to various factors such as climatic conditions, topography, cropping patterns and crop rotation systems, or farm structures, including the surrounding structures.[80]

Against this background, the Court required the referring court to 'take into account the degree of admixture of genetically modified maize and the probability of admixture between that genetically modified maize and organically or conventionally grown maize'.[81] In particular, the referring court was also required to pay heed to the sources of the risk of mixing and the effectiveness of the methods of crop separation, which must be assessed in the light of, inter alia, the geographical and climatic constraints and characteristics of the region and the methods of cultivation used there.[82] That being said, the determination of zones of exclusion from GMO cultivation, the separation of organic fields from those that do not contain GMOs, and the effectiveness of the prohibition of the cultivation of all GMOs are embedded in uncertainty. Unlike the previous judgments on active substances, the Court of Justice did not make use of the precautionary principle, which is enshrined in the Directive.[83]

In this case, therefore, we can see that the context of the particular decision at hand changes the mixture of reasons upon which the Court will rely. Whilst

77 Ibid. para. 46.
78 Ibid. para. 49.
79 Ibid. para. 50.
80 Ibid. para. 55.
81 Ibid. para. 56.
82 Ibid. para. 57.
83 Arts 1 and 4, Annex IIB. As regards the application of the precautionary principle to this field, see N. de Sadeleer, *Environmental Principles* (2nd edn, 2022) 232–247.

the precautionary principle was arguably very relevant here, the Court's primary concern was to delineate which areas of concern were appropriately within the 'realm' of the Member States and which had already been accounted for by the Union. The precautionary principle was, in this sense, part of the Union calculation that did not need to be called upon again in relation to the Member States' own freedoms.

6. Higher Excise Duties Rates under the Energy Taxation Directive and the Prohibition of Tax Discrimination

Finally, carbon taxes warrant special attention. There is no carbon tax in force today at the EU level. The Emissions Trading Scheme (ETS)[84] is the only scheme where greenhouse gas (GHG) emissions are subject to a price for the polluter, regardless of the origin, the activity, or the fuel. Currently, the ETS covers only around 45 per cent of emissions from industrial activities. It does not encompass the emissions from other economic sectors such as small and medium-sized enterprises (SMEs), transport, or agriculture that fall within the scope of the Effort Sharing Regulation.[85]

In 2011, the European Commission attempted to revise the Energy Taxation Directive (ETD)[86] with a view to reinforcing its environmental character. The taxation of energy products would have had two different bases; a large share of the taxation being based on the product quantity and the other on the carbon content. However, seven years later, the Commission withdrew its proposal due to the absence of political consensus.

The European Green Deal and the subsequent Fit-for-55 package target all sectors where energy consumption is high. Against this background, in 2021 the European Commission considered revising the ETD, which in itself is neither a carbon tax nor an environmental tax.[87] A new proposal was submitted by the European Commission to the European Parliament and the Council, with a strong focus on achieving substantive change in consumption patterns, implementing the polluter pays principle, and increasing the price of some untaxed or less-taxed energy consumption. The proposal aimed, among others, at removing outdated exemptions and incentives for the use of fossil fuels while promoting clean technologies. The proposal also aimed at fostering

[84] Directive 2003/87/EC, OJ 2003 L 275/32.
[85] Regulation (EU) 2018/842, OJ 2018 L 156/26.
[86] Council Directive 2003/96/EC, OJ 2003 L 283/1.
[87] S. Wolff, *Should EU Energy Taxation Contribute More to Sustainability?* (2024) 551.

investment in new and innovative green industries. Moreover, the proposal aimed at facilitating the transition away from fossil fuels towards clean fuels and supporting the EU's delivery of its ambitious targets on the reduction of GHG emissions and energy savings.

Since the ETD was adopted on the basis of Article 113 TFEU, any modification is subject to a special legislative procedure, which requires unanimity within the Council of the European Union. It soon became apparent that the Member States disagreed with the European Commission's proposal.

Faced with the impossibility of increasing energy excise duty rates by amending the ETD, the European lawmaker implemented the polluter pays principle in certain energy-intensive economic sectors by amending the ETS. Given that Directive 2003/87/EC establishing a scheme for GHG emission allowance trading within the EU ETS was adopted on the basis of Article 192(1) TFEU, which provides for the ordinary legislative procedure, a limited number of Member States could not impeach a qualified majority of Member States within the Council to apply the polluter pays principle. As a result, a new emissions trading system (ETS2) was created, separate from the existing EU ETS.[88] This new carbon market, which will become operational in 2027, will oblige fuel distributors to hold allowances for all fuels released for consumption, independent of their final use (for heating or for propelling a vehicle).[89] Given the impossibility of increasing excise duties by modifying the ETD, the polluter pays principle will be applied to the economic sectors that have not achieved their emission reduction targets due to environmental harmonization.

The mandatory surrendering of emissions allowances by operators for those activities is rather similar to the obligation to pay duties under the excise legal framework.[90] The similarity between the two regulatory schemes is mainly related to the absence of connection and time correspondence between the holding of the allowance and the release of the emissions into the environment.[91]

While the obligation to submit the building and road transport sectors to a new carbon market restricts the Member States' room for manoeuvre, Member States still retain a large portion of their sovereignty in the field of taxation. Indeed, Article 110 TFEU does not prohibit them from adopting differentiated taxation regarding similar products, insofar as they aim to achieve legitimate

[88] Directive (EU) 2023/959, OJ 2023 L 130/134, Arts 3g–a.
[89] Ibid.
[90] Wolff (n. 87) 491.
[91] Ibid. 492.

economic and social objectives. EU law does not restrict the freedom of each Member State to establish a tax system which differentiates between certain products 'on the basis of objective criteria, such as the nature of the raw materials used or the production processes employed'.[92]

Nevertheless, the 2003 ETD allows Member States to increase excise duties rates for energy. Consequently, tax harmonization is not exhaustive. This raises the question of the compatibility of higher tax rates with the functioning of the internal market.

In this connection, *Outokumpu Oy* is a case in point. Finnish law provided for a differentiated taxation scheme for electricity depending on the nature of the energy used for its generation. A favourable tax treatment was granted for renewables but only for electricity produced nationally. The CJEU condemned this system of differentiated taxation on the grounds that it taxed imported electricity at a flat rate. Though this flat rate was lower than the highest rate applicable to electricity of domestic origin, it could lead, 'if only in certain cases, to higher taxation being imposed on imported electricity'.[93] The technical difficulty of applying differentiated rates to imported electricity was not taken into account.[94]

Given that tax harmonization in relation to excise duties is not exhaustive, Member States must ensure that they do not breach Article 110 when increasing their excise duties to implement the polluter pays principle.

Insofar as the Member States must implement several legal instruments, such as bans, excise duties, eco-taxes, and carbon markets (ETS1 and 2), in order to achieve climate neutrality by 2050, it is important to identify the room for manoeuvre they have for each of these instruments. Table 4.3 compares the room for manoeuvre that EU harmonized product standards, excise duties, and the ETS leaves to Member States in relation to their climate change policies.

7. Conclusions

Thanks to the Green Deal for Europe, the European Union is currently developing a new generation of legal instruments that will enable it to achieve climate neutrality by 2050. The implementation of these numerous regulations

[92] Case C-213/96, *Outokumpu Oy* (EU:C:1998:155), para. 30.
[93] Ibid. para. 41.
[94] Ibid. para. 39.

Table 4.3 Room for manoeuvre for bans, taxation, and cap-and-trade measures

	Ban	Taxation	Cap-and-trade
Legal acts	Fluorinate GHG Regulation 517/2014	Excise Duties Directive 2003/96	ETS Directive 2003/87
Legal basis and procedure	Art. 192(1) TFEU; ordinary legislative procedure	Art. 113 TFEU; special legislative procedure	Art. 192(1) TFEU; ordinary legislative procedure
Legal effects	Transposition	Directly applicable	Transposition
Harmonization	Maximal *de jure*	Minimal rates	Maximal de facto
Personal scope	Economic operators placing on the market CFC	Consumers	Economic operators (listed installations, aviation, maritime transport, fuel)
Enforcement (control, criminal penalties)	Member States	Member States	Member States

and directives will oblige Member States to do more to restore biodiversity, to mitigate the impacts of the climate crisis, and to develop a low-carbon and circular economy. The question will soon arise as to whether the Member States will be able to adopt measures that are stricter than the new EU standards in order to achieve climate neutrality by 2050.

The various judgments analysed in this chapter show just how complicated this exercise can be. The choice of legal basis can certainly have a significant influence on the possibility of adopting stricter domestic standards. However, as we have seen earlier, even in the context of the functioning of the internal market, several key EU rules only partially harmonize the matter. If the matter is not exhaustively harmonized, the question arises as to whether the national measure can be qualified as a selling arrangement and fall outside the scope of Article 34 TFUE. Whenever the conditions of the *Keck* case law are not fulfilled, the national measure likely to restrict the free movement of goods is to be regarded as a measure having equivalent effect within the meaning of Article 34 TFUE. Such a measure can only be justified if it is consistent with the objective of protecting human or animal health (Art. 36 TFEU) or the environment (rule of reason). Furthermore, in contrast to the uniform authorization procedures stemming from the acts regulating the authorization of GMOs, regional bans on GMOs cultivation escape total harmonization. Accordingly, compatibility with EU law must be assessed in the light of Articles 34 to 36 TFEU.[95]

A priori, it is not easy to meet the conditions required to demonstrate that the restrictive national measures are necessary and proportionate to achieve the preventive objectives. However, the judgments commented on in this chapter show that the Court of Justice is sensitive to the preventive nature of these measures, which are often called upon to counter an uncertain risk. In addition, the Court restrictively interprets the derogations allowing Member States to allow the use of substances that have been banned by the European Commission. Finally, as it is impossible for the Council to amend a tax directive adopted on the basis of Article 113 TFEU, due to the absence of unanimity, it is now an economic instrument—ETS2—that makes it possible to implement the polluter pays principle in relation to two energy-intensive sectors: buildings and land transport. The Member States' room for manoeuvre in this environmental area is severely limited.

Crucially, this demonstrates that the relationship between the free market and environmental protection is not always resolved either with the same balance struck or by reference to the same legal techniques. In some cases, the environmental principles come to the fore, resulting in an interpretation which finds an explicit Treaty basis for the prioritization of the environment in this balance. In others, the task of the Court appears to be less about the relationship between trade and the environment than it is about the relative allocation of power between the Union and the Member States. From the perspective of legitimacy, therefore, this means that the courts are resolving a complex web of interconnected questions for which, as noted in Chapter 1, a simple 'legitimate' or 'illegitimate' conclusion is inadequate to address the ways in which legitimacy is enhanced or otherwise by the actions of the courts.

95 Case C-24/21, *Regione Autonoma Friuli Venezia Giulia* (EU:C:2022:526), para. 66.

5

Fundamental Rights to Climate Protection in Europe

Can the Judiciary Leverage the Legitimacy of Environmental Governance?

Gerd Winter

1. Introduction

Do courts that test climate protection legislation against fundamental rights encroach on the political sphere or do they have a genuine role to play?[1] The question of the relationship between political and judicial powers has incited discussion among academics and courts for many years and across jurisdictions. In doctrinal terms, a general consensus seems to have emerged in democratic states that broad discretion rests with the legislator, whilst the courts ought to practice self-restraint. Nevertheless, that consensus operates very differently depending on legal cultures and the personal attitudes of judges and scholars. My opinion is that courts contribute to the legitimacy of the system, bringing an additional dimension to an election-based democratic legislator. They act as a forum for independent evidential inquiry and reasoned argumentation that differs from the struggles about interests and ideas in the political arena.[2] The US Supreme Court has defined this proper realm of the

[1] The author was counsel for the applicants in *Carvalho* (n. 10) and for intervenors in *KlimaSeniorinnen* and *Duarte Agostinho* (n. 8). Parts of this chapter were previously published in Winter, 'Climate Protection before the European Court of Human Rights: The Cases *KlimaSeniorinnen* and *Duarte Agostinho* in Perspective', 84(3) *Zeitschrift für ausländisches öffentliches Recht und Völkerrecht (ZaöRV)* (2024) 457.

[2] See on legitimation through principled reasoning, R. Dworkin, *Taking Rights Seriously* (1978) 22–31, 184–205; on legitimation through deliberative proceedings, see J. Habermas, *Faktizität und Geltung* (1992) 272–291; and on autonomous historical roots of courts, parliaments, and governments, see Smend, 'Das Bundesverfassungsgericht', in R. Smend (ed.), *Staatsrechtliche Abhandlungen* (1955, 3rd edn, 1994) 582–583. On the broader debate on the legitimation of courts see further Chapter 1 in this volume. For my own views see Winter, ‚*Armando Carvalho et alii versus Europäische Union*: Rechtdogmatische und staatstheoretische Probleme einer Klimaklage vor dem Europäischen Gericht', 5 *Zeitschrift für Europäisches Umweltrecht* (2019) 259.

Gerd Winter, *Fundamental Rights to Climate Protection in Europe* In: *The Legitimacy of EU Environmental Governance and the Role of the European Courts*. Edited by: Mariolina Eliantonio and Emma Lees, Oxford University Press. © Gerd Winter 2025. DOI: 10.1093/oso/9780198972808.003.0005

judiciary as any question for which 'judicially discoverable and manageable standards for resolving it' exist.[3] This comes down to the simple observation that the courts have a role to play as long as their standpoint can reasonably be related to existing rules and presented in doctrinal terms rather than political language. Of course, this does not exclude that courts may be more or less inclined to tread new paths.

In order to explore the contribution of the judiciary to the legitimacy of the governance system, it is important to appreciate the details of that role. It is only by examining the precise fault lines of the courts' reasoning that the balance drawn in the relationship between legislator and judiciary can be identified and analysed. This chapter, therefore, approaches the theme of legitimacy from the point of view that the detail of the law is critical.

From this starting point, the chapter will not aim at enhancing the theoretical debate but rather steps down to the level of doctrinal constructions. I shall examine the content and interpretation of pertinent fundamental rights and examine how they direct climate governance. Analysing exemplary court cases, it will be shown that in Europe the fundamental rights doctrine has developed productively, albeit with a different innovative readiness of different courts. With those observations in mind, I will explore how the fundamental rights doctrine can be developed further to better cope with the particular characteristics of climate change and its effects.

My focus will be fundamental rights as standards for the testing of climate protection legislation. This means I will not address proceedings about sub-legal norms, programmes, and administrative acts (or omissions of the same) and their compatibility with ordinary climate legislation.[4] Moreover, I will concentrate on legislation that fixes overall emissions reduction targets for greenhouse gas emissions. Such targets assemble the individual reduction amounts to be achieved by various sectoral or cross-sectoral instruments. Addressing such summary targets facilitates litigation because, when actions are brought to contest individual climate protection measures, courts will be

[3] This criterion is one of a set of five indicators the court established in *Baker*, 369 US 217 (1962). The entire set that has since been coined as the Baker criteria reads as follows: 'Prominent on the surface of any case held to involve a political question is found a textually demonstrable constitutional commitment of the issue to a coordinate political department; or a lack of judicially discoverable and manageable standards for resolving it; or the impossibility of deciding without an initial policy determination of a kind clearly for non-judicial discretion; or the impossibility of a court's undertaking independent resolution without expressing lack of the respect due coordinate branches of government; or an unusual need for unquestioning adherence to a political decision already made; or the potentiality of embarrassment from multifarious pronouncements by various departments on one question.'

[4] The clarification of the content of fundamental rights can nevertheless be useful for this kind of litigation because fundamental rights are often invoked as guidance for the interpretation of indeterminate ordinary laws or for an incidental constitutionality test of the same.

confronted with a great number of alternative options, among which they will be reluctant to decide. In comparison, the summary character of overall targets is more convenient to be tested against fundamental rights.

2. The Court Cases Discussed and Overview of Analysed Issues

The cases I will discuss are exemplary for an analysis centred around fundamental rights in climate litigation on three constitutional levels: the German Basic Law (Grundgesetz, GG) as an example of a national constitution; the European Convention on Human Rights (ECHR); and the EU Charter of Fundamental Rights (ChFR). The German case illustrates a system that has a tradition of genuine and active development of fundamental rights by the Constitutional Court. The case of the ECHR is exemplary of mutual cooperation in the development of rights by the European Court of Human Rights (ECtHR) and national courts, especially when the state (such as in the Belgian case) has not adopted a fundamental rights code of its own. Finally, the case of the ChFR shows how, in a unique system of semi-federalism, the Court of Justice of the European Union (CJEU) has cautiously developed a body of fundamental rights for its own state-like law in combination with national law that implements EU law. All of these different systems are confronted with a sweeping problem—climate change. This challenges them to adjust their bodies of fundamental rights. As will be shown, the response can be moderately innovative—the cases of the German Federal Constitutional Court (Bundesverfassungsgericht, BVerfG) and ECtHR being exemplary in that regard. In the CJEU case the response has so far been evasive, but, as will be shown, there is potential to catch up.

First, concerning the German GG, in *Neubauer* individual persons living both in Germany and abroad, and an NGO, asked the BVerfG to annul parts of the Climate Protection Act (Klimaschutzgesetz, KSG).[5] The KSG had set a target for the reduction of yearly greenhouse gas (GHG) emissions by 55 per cent to be reached by 2030, referenced to 1990. In addition, the KSG laid out a table that listed the maximum allowable yearly GHG emissions from 2020 until 2030 for each of the six emission source sectors. The applicants alleged

[5] BVerfG order of 24 March 2021, 1 BvR 2656/18, 78, 96, 288/20 (*Neubauer et al.*), BVerfGE 157, 30. English translation at www.bundesverfassungsgericht.de/SharedDocs/Entscheidungen/EN/2021/03/rs20210324_1bvr265618en.html (last visited 27 September 2024).

that the permitted emissions were too high if measured against their fundamental rights to health, occupation, and property. Relying on a new concept of 'advance effect of future encroachment of freedom rights', the Court found a violation of such rights insofar as it only regulated emissions until 2030 without taking into account emission needs post-2030. The decision is also noteworthy for examining the transnational reach of fundamental rights to the two applicant families living abroad in Bangladesh and Nepal.

Second, concerning the ECHR, the *Klimaatzaak* case concerned an action filed by an association—Klimaatzaak—and thousands of named individuals against the Kingdom of Belgium and its regions of Brussels Capital, Wallonia, and Flanders. The action alleged that the climate protection measures taken or omitted by the respondents violated their human rights. The Brussels Appellate Court, largely upholding the decision of the court of first instance, interpreted the rights to life (Art. 2 ECHR) and to a private life (Art. 8 ECHR) as positively obliging the state to reduce GHG emissions.[6] It drew a distinction between measures taken between 2013 and the present day and measures planned until 2030, holding that there was violation in the past period, except for the Walloon Region, while the planned measures did not undershoot the state's margin of appreciation.[7]

Again with regard to the ECHR, the *KlimaSeniorinnen* and *Duarte Agostinho* cases involved an action filed by five elderly ladies and their association against Switzerland and an action filed by six young persons against Portugal and 32 other European states claiming that the respondent states had taken insufficient climate protection measures thereby violating their rights to life and to a private life (Arts 2 and 8 ECHR).[8] The core question was whether the Court would further develop its doctrinal construction of Articles 2 and 8 ECHR, possibly relying on its evolutive approach.[9] The ECtHR joined the cases and rendered its judgments in April 2024. It dismissed the application in

[6] Court of Appeal of Brussels, arrêt de 30 November 2023, Case 2021/AR/1589, 2022/AR/737, 2022/AR/891 *(Klimaatzaak et al. v. Belgium et al.)*, https://climatecasechart.com/wp-content/uploads/non-us-case-documents/2023/20231130_2660_judgment-1.pdf (last visited 27 September 2024). Unauthorized English translation at https://climatecasechart.com/wp-content/uploads/non-us-case-documents/2023/20231130_2660_judgment-2.pdf (last visited 27 September 2024).

[7] *Klimaatzaak et al. v. Belgium et al.* (n. 6) paras 214–216.

[8] ECtHR, *Verein KlimaSeniorinnen et al. v. Switzerland*, Appl. no. 53600/20, Judgment of 9 April 2024; ECtHR, *Duarte Agostinho et al. v. Portugal et al.*, Appl. no. 39371/20, Decision of 9 April 2024, available at https://climatecasechart.com/wp-content/uploads/non-us-case-documents/2020/20201126_Application-no.-5360020_application-1.pdf (last visited 16 October 2024). All ECtHR decisions are available at http://hudoc.echr.coe.int/.

[9] Kobylarz, 'The European Court of Human Rights: An Underrated Forum for Environmental Litigation', in H. T. Anker and B. E. Olsen (eds), *Sustainable Management of Natural Resources. Legal Instruments and Approaches* (2018) 99, 112.

Duarte Agostinho as inadmissible. In relation to the non-Portuguese respondents, it denied the reach of their human rights for causing extraterritorial effects of their emissions while, in relation to Portugal, it found that the national remedies were not exhausted. Concerning *KlimaSeniorinnen*, the Court denied standing for the individual applicants but granted standing to their association, the Verein KlimaSeniorinnen, as representing the collective interests of those affected. In substance, the Court developed an ambitious set of state obligations which Switzerland was found not to have fulfilled.

Third, concerning the EU ChFR, the case *Carvalho and Others v. EP and Council*[10] dealt with an action brought to the EU Courts by ten families living in different regions of the EU and some in Kenya and Fiji and an association, all engaged in peasant agriculture and/or adapted tourism. They claimed that they, both in the present and certainly in the future, would suffer serious health and economic damage as a result of climate change and that this was partly due to the greenhouse gas emissions allowed by certain EU legal acts.[11] Alleging that these acts violated their fundamental rights in the ChFR, including rights to health, occupation, property, and equal treatment, they applied for annulment of the relevant provisions.[12] The EU General Court (GC) and, on appeal, the European Court of Justice (ECJ) rejected the action as inadmissible, holding that the plaintiff families were not individually concerned by the challenged legal acts. As the defendant institutions contented themselves with only addressing admissibility questions, leaving open the merits of the case, I will need to discuss the substance on the basis of the allegations the plaintiffs and intervenors actually submitted and my own assessment of how EU fundamental rights might be interpreted to cope with climate change.

While this analysis concentrates on the merits of climate litigation, Section 3 briefly discusses admissibility issues. With regard to the substance, I shall concentrate on the general construction of rights as negative and positive obligations of the state, the scope of rights, the notion of interference with them, and the possibilities of justification of interference in Section 4.

[10] Case T-330/18, *Carvalho et al. v. EP and Council* (EU:T:2019:324), paras 33 et seq; upheld on appeal by Case C-565/19, *Carvalho v. EP and Council* (EU:C:2021:252), para. 77.

[11] Directive (EU) 2018/410, OJ 2018 L 76/3; Regulation (EU) 2018/842, OJ 2018 L 156/26; and Regulation (EU) 2018/841, OJ 2018 L 156/1 (LULUCF).

[12] See in more detail, Winter, '*Armando Carvalho and Others v. EU*: Invoking Human Rights and the Paris Agreement for Better Climate Protection Legislation', 9 *Transnational Environmental Law* (2020) 137; the application and appeal are accessible at https://climatecasechart.com/wp-content/uploads/non-us-case-documents/2018/20180524_Case-no.-T-33018_application.pdf and https://climatecasechart.com/wp-content/uploads/non-us-case-documents/2019/20190711_Case-no.-T-33018_appeal-1.pdf (last visited 16 October 2024).

3. Admissibility

This section will focus on whether there is a remedy for challenging climate legislation in terms of fundamental rights, the conditions of standing, and whether other remedies must have been exhausted.

A. Availability of a Remedy

With regard to remedies, the first question is whether the court is competent to assess a legislative act against fundamental rights and, in the case of incompatibility, declare it void. An answer in the affirmative is now a general standard in European countries, with variations concerning whether all courts or only a constitutional court have competence. Judicial review of legislative acts has even been introduced in those countries with a tradition of parliamentary supremacy. Notably, in France (ex post) review by the Conseil Constitutionnel of legislative acts was introduced in 2008.[13] In the UK, review by the courts was established in 1998, although with limits since a court cannot annul a legislative act but only declare it to be incompatible with human rights.[14] With regard to the ECHR system, the ECtHR has routinely tested the legislative acts of the contracting states, although it cannot annul them but only declare them to be incompatible with a human right.[15] Likewise, the CJEU is competent to check EU legislative acts since the term act in Article 263(4) TFEU embraces all legal acts, including legislation. It has also not hesitated to test the compatibility of Member State legislation with applicable EU primary law.

Provided that an annulment or a declaration of incompatibility is possible in principle, there can be different routes to obtaining such a decision. The most straightforward for individuals is a direct action brought by a person before a constitutional court, also called a

[13] Art. 61-1 of the Constitution; see Jouanjan, 'Constitutional Justice in France', in A. von Bogdandy, P. M. Huber, and C. Grabenwarter (eds), *The Max Planck Handbooks in European Public Law Volume III: Constitutional Adjudication: Institutions* (2020) 223, 259–263.

[14] Human Rights Act 1998, s. 4(1), (2), (5), and (6).

[15] P. Leach, *Taking a Case to the European Court of Human Rights* (4th edn, 2017) para. 3.22. In cases of 'systemic Convention violations', the Court may, however, give more general guidance applying what is called the 'pilot judgment procedure'. See ibid. paras 3.23–3.39. It could be questioned whether the court could qualify the general lack of climate protection of the respondent states as a systemic violation and formulate principles that go beyond the mere declaration of incompatibility of specific measures.

constitutional complaint. Such action is, for example, available in Austria,[16] Belgium,[17] Germany,[18] Poland,[19] and Spain[20] but not in France or the UK.[21]

B. Legal Standing

As a preliminary observation, there is no perfectly clear line between the standing of individuals as an *admissibility* question and the individual character of fundamental rights as a question of *substance*. Commonly, it is sufficient for legal standing to claim and substantiate to some degree an individual concern. Whether the right is actually violated is then a matter of the merit of the claim. Such a neat distinction is difficult, however, in cases where not the facts but the content of the right itself is unclear and needs to be construed in more detail. In such cases, courts sometimes leave the question of standing open and interpret the right at the merits stage.[22] When they find a rights violation, this implicitly affirms that the complainants have standing. In contrast, if the courts plan to reject the application, they sometimes examine the scope and content of the right in depth at the admissibility stage, which implies that they ask for more than just the substantiated claim of concern at that stage.

Even if the substantiated claim of concern is sufficient to confer standing, there are differences among legal systems as to the 'level' of individual concern required to allow the claim to be brought and the intensity with which courts review that question, as can be seen from the cases discussed in this chapter.

The BVerfG in *Neubauer* conferred standing on all the individual applicants. It required personal, present, and direct concern but found that the nature of climate change required a broad understanding of the criteria so that 'personal concern' included the concerns of many people, that future damage can be regarded as present if irreversibly caused at present, and that the allowance of emission quantities causes a kind of direct concern. However, the

[16] Art. 140(1) no. 1c Bundesverfassung; see Grabenwarter, 'The Austrian Constitutional Court', in von Bogdandy, Huber, and Grabenwarter (n. 13) 19, 48.

[17] Art. 142 Constitution Belge; see Behrendt, 'The Belgian Constitutional Court', in von Bogdandy, Huber, and Grabenwarter (n. 13) 71, 97–99.

[18] Art. 93(1) no. 4a Grundgesetz.

[19] Art. 79(1) Constitution. See Tuleja, 'The Polish Constitutional Tribunal', in von Bogdandy, Huber, and Grabenwarter (n. 13) 619, 636–638.

[20] Art. 24 Constitucion, Art. 41 (2) Ley Orgánica del Tribunal de Garantías Constitucionales.

[21] Art. 61-1 Constitution; see Jouanjan (n. 13) 263–267. It is noteworthy that the annulment has effect only *ex nunc*, as opposed to other systems like the German one which, in principle, provides for annulment *ex tunc*.

[22] For an example, see ECtHR, *Kurt v. Austria*, Appl. no 62903/15, Judgment of 15 June 2021, para. 160.

association's action was found inadmissible on the ground that the personal character of fundamental rights excludes an action of a legal person representing a collective interest.[23]

The Brussels Appeal Court in *Klimaatzaak* ruled equally liberally for individuals and even more so for the applicant association. The relevant provisions, Articles 17 and 18 Code judiciaire, require that the applicant must show an 'existing and actual interest' ('*intérêt né et actuel*') in the action. In the court's interpretation, the plaintiff must 'demonstrate, on the one hand, the existence of a serious and grave threat likely to create, from the outset of the action, a specific disturbance and, on the other hand, that the requested decision presents a concrete utility for him'.[24] Referring to Article 17(2) Code judiciaire and also citing Article 9(3) of the Aarhus Convention, the court found that Klimaatzaak, as an environmental organization, had a sufficient moral interest in climate protection. Concerning the individual applicants, the court applied a generalized test accepting that 'the extent of the consequences of global warming and the scale of the risks it entails mean that it can be considered, with sufficient judicial certainty, that each of the natural persons who are validly involved in the case has an interest of their own in obtaining the convictions that are sought against the public authorities'.[25]

The ECtHR has traditionally applied a narrower test of standing. According to Articles 13 and 34 ECHR, an individual applicant must be a victim of a violation of a Convention right which is interpreted as requiring that an applicant must be personally and seriously concerned.[26] The Court retained this line in *KlimaSeniorinnen*, finding that the individual applicants had not proved that they met this standard. An action by an association had previously been admitted when the association represented persons with individual victim status.[27] In *KlimaSeniorinnen*, the Court extended the realm of representation to collective interests without requiring that all individual members must be victims. It is unclear whether non-members may be represented.[28]

An extremely narrow concept of standing is applied by the CJEU. The requirement under Article 263(4) TFEU that the applicant must be individually

[23] *Neubauer et al.* (n. 5) para. 136.
[24] *Klimaatzaak v. Belgium et al.* (n. 6) para 119.
[25] Ibid. paras 127 and 133.
[26] See e.g. ECtHR, *Cordella v. Italie*, Appl. nos 54414/13 and 54264/15, *Définitif* of 24 June 2019, paras 100–109.
[27] ECtHR, *Gorraiz Lizarraga and others v. Spain*, Appl. no. 62543/00, Judgment of 10 November 2004, para. 38; ECtHR, *Asselbourg et autres v. Luxembourg*, Appl. no. 29121/95, Decision of 29 June 1999.
[28] ECtHR, *KlimaSeniorinnen v. Switzerland*, Appl. no. 53600/20, Judgment of 9 April 2024, para. 489

concerned is interpreted formally as distinctive and unique, not materially, and as a personal and severe concern.[29] This has the paradoxical consequence that the impact of climate change, which will be and already is catastrophic for many people, cannot be brought by anyone because of the generality of damage.[30] Concerning actions brought by an association, the Court has denied standing referring to its ruling that such action is only admissible if all members are individually affected or the association has by law been granted a special procedural position or was itself materially affected.[31]

As climate change affects a multitude of persons, the question arises with particular emphasis of whether a class action is admissible. As noted, the ECtHR has accepted this, as has the Belgian Appellate Court, but not the CJEU or the BVerfG. However, when applying human rights, national courts will have to reconsider their practice in view of Article 6(1) ECHR. This Article guarantees access to judicial review, which, in principle, the ECtHR interprets to include an action by an association, although a state may weigh up the admissibility of a collective action against other concerns such as the separation of powers.[32]

C. Exhaustion of Other Remedies

Exhaustion of other remedies is a precondition for a German constitutional complaint.[33] In its climate judgment, the BVerfG understood this leniently, accepting that contesting the targets set and emission amounts allocated by the KSG was not possible through actions before administrative or civil courts.[34]

Exhaustion of other remedies is also required by Article 35 ECHR. The applicants in *Duarte Agostinho* argued that in many of the respondent states no appropriate action was available, that it was a disproportionate burden to follow the process through 32 jurisdictions, and that climate protection was too urgent to wait for such time-consuming testing through national proceedings. The ECtHR did not respond to this argument because the case was dismissed on another ground, namely, as said, the lack of extraterritorial jurisdiction.

[29] See in more detail, Chapter 7 in this volume.

[30] Winter, 'Plaumann Withering: Standing before the EU General Court underway from Distinctive to Substantial Concern', 15 *European Journal of Legal Studies* (2023) 85–123.

[31] Case C-565/19, *Carvalho v. EP and Council* (EU:C:2021:252), para. 85.

[32] *KlimaSeniorinnen v. Switzerland* (n. 28) para. 631.

[33] § 90(2) Act on the Federal Constitutional Court—BVerfGG.

[34] *Neubauer et al.* (n. 5) para. 138.

The direct action before the EU General Court does not presuppose exhaustion of other remedies. The narrow concept of standing can, however, be interpreted to refer plaintiffs to legal protection in the national courts and invite them to try the preliminary reference procedure under Article 267 TFEU if they do aim at the annulment of EU legal acts.[35]

4. General Construction of Fundamental Rights

Turning now to questions of merits, I shall first, in Section A, discuss the general construction of fundamental rights as negative and positive obligations, also including any consequences for the intensity of court review. In Section B, I discuss the methodology of rights application.

A. Rights as Negative and Positive Obligations

Human rights were originally conceived of as generating negative obligations for states. Citizens were enabled to defend themselves against encroachments on their freedoms by the state. Such rights have been termed *status negativus* or negative obligations. With the development of the interventionist welfare state, rights were established—or rather interpreted as contained in *status negativus*—which entailed positive obligations to protect resting on the state and the right to seek legal protection in case of inaction. Such rights have been called *status positivus*.[36] With the rise of democracy, procedural rights were introduced—or interpreted as being contained in *status negativus*—that provide rights of participation in political and administrative proceedings. They could be named *status activus*.

Applying the difference of status *negativus* and *positivus* to our case of greenhouse gas emissions, four different constructions of fundamental rights can be imagined: negative obligations concerning state-based emissions, positive obligations to protect, negative obligations concerning future interferences, and negative obligations concerning the allocation of emission rights.

[35] Winter (n. 30).

[36] The distinction between *status negativus* and *positivus* goes back to the German constitutional lawyer Georg Jellinek, *Das System der öffentlichen Rechte* (1892). While Jellinek applied the *status positivus* only to rights to the observance of ordinary laws (109–129), the BVerfG upgraded it to the level of fundamental rights that may trigger better legislation. See (for environmental cases), BVerfG 8 August 1978, 2 BvL 8/77, BVerfGE 49, 89, 141–142.

1. Negative Obligations Concerning State-Based Emissions

This notion covers emissions from public services, such as an airport or power-generation installation run by the state.[37] State-based emissions make up only a small share of the overall emissions in market-based societies. They are, of course, much higher in states with large state property in industry, services, and buildings.

2. Positive Obligations to Protect

This concept builds on the fact that most greenhouse gases are emitted from private sources. While fundamental rights are not applicable to such 'horizontal' interferences in most legal systems, they have been interpreted as containing principles of protection that the state must implement, both as an objective obligation and as a subjective right of the persons concerned.

The ECtHR has often relied on positive obligations derived from Articles 2 and 8 ECHR in various policy areas, including general environmental law.[38] In *KlimaSeniorinnen*, it also applied the concept to climate law.[39] In *Klimaatzaak*, the Brussels Appeal Court likewise took this step.[40]

In *Neubauer*, the BVerfG also tested positive obligations with regard to climate legislation, deriving them from the fundamental rights to health and property (Arts 2(2) and 14 GG). However, it concluded that considering the measures the German legislator had already taken, the margin of political discretion was not over- (or under-)stepped. The positive obligation was additionally examined in relation to two complainant families domiciled in Bangladesh and Nepal. Whilst denying a breach of obligations, the Court could leave open to what extent it was willing to recognize the transboundary reach of positive obligations.

The CJEU has not been active in transforming negative into positive obligations, however some steps can nevertheless be observed. First, the Court did establish positive obligations as a dimension of the basic freedoms. In particular, it has ruled that Member States must ensure the free movement of goods, including their transportation on transit highways.[41] Regarding

[37] See for a state-owned airport, ECtHR, *Flamenbaum et autres v. France*, Appl. nos 3675/04 and 23264/04, Judgment of 13 December 2012, para. 141.

[38] See Council of Europe, *Manual on Human Rights and the Environment* (3rd edn, 2022).

[39] *KlimaSeniorinnen v. Switzerland* (n. 28) para. 519.

[40] *Klimaatzaak et al. v. Belgium et al.* (n. 6) paras 139–143.

[41] Case C-112/00, *Schmidberger* (EU:EC:C:2003:333), para. 57: 'In this way the Court held in particular that, as an indispensable instrument for the realisation of a market without internal frontiers, Article 30 does not prohibit only measures emanating from the State which, in themselves, create restrictions on trade between Member States. It also applies where a Member State abstains from adopting the measures required in order to deal with obstacles to the free movement of goods which are not caused by the State.'

fundamental rights, the Court has held that the fundamental right to human dignity and integrity must be observed in relation to bio-patents concerning human embryos, which can be taken as a statement regarding such positive obligations.[42] Likewise, in a case concerning restrictions of copyright, the Court demanded that a balance be struck 'between (i) copyrights and related rights, which are intellectual property and are therefore protected under Article 17(2) of the Charter, (ii) the freedom to conduct a business, which economic agents such as internet service providers enjoy under Article 16 of the Charter, and (iii) the freedom of information of internet users, whose protection is ensured by Article 11 of the Charter'.[43]

Remarkably, the CJEU, more so than the ECtHR and BVerfG, is inclined to accept the horizontal effect of fundamental rights. Victims of climate change might then be able to claim a violation of their right to health in an action directly against an emitter. However, the CJEU has acknowledged horizontal effect only insofar as the relevant Charter provision addresses relationships between two private persons, such as safe working conditions according to Article 31 ChFR which can only be viewed as concerning relationships between employees and employers.[44] Although the rights to climate protection discussed here also address relationships between private parties, namely between emitters and victims, this is not explicitly assumed or stated in the text of the relevant rights, such as the rights to health and to property.

3. Negative Obligations Related to Future Interferences

This construction is an unfamiliar concept that was invented by the BVerfG in *Neubauer*. It relies on fundamental rights as negative obligations, holding that if emissions are not reduced sufficiently at present, life conditions will emerge in the future which will force the state to drastically restrict energy use and thus encroach on fundamental rights. These expected future restrictions have an 'advance effect' (Vorwirkung) obliging the state not to allocate emission amounts that will predetermine the future.[45]

The BVerfG construct has consequences for the transboundary scope of fundamental rights. According to the BVerfG, the fact that future restrictions by a state must be prevented implies that only the inhabitants of that state can

[42] Case C-377/98, *Netherlands v. European Parliament and Council* (EU:C:2001:253), para. 70.

[43] Case C-314/12, *UPC Telekabel Wien* (EU:C:2014:192), para. 47.

[44] Joined Cases 569/16 and C-570/16, *Bauer* (EU:C:2018:871), paras 88–92. Lenaerts and Guterriérrez-Fons, 'The Place of the Charter in the European Legal Space', in S. Peers *et al.* (eds), *The EU Charter of Fundamental Rights. A Commentary* (2nd edn, 2021) at 17.11, para. 55.31.

[45] *Neubauer et al.* (n. 5) para. 183.

apply for prevention because those living outside Germany are not subject to the jurisdiction of that state.[46]

4. Negative Obligations Related to the Allocation of Emission Rights

This concept draws on the fact that the climate legislation of many states, including the EU, has moved from protecting victims against 'horizontal' emissions to actively managing emissions, most visibly if emission rights are allocated to emitters. This new role of states and the EU suggests that they take responsibility for the emissions. For example, in the EU Emissions Trading System (ETS), emission allowances are allocated by the EU Commission to the Member States and by the Member States to private actors on the basis of a sharing scheme, by auction, for free, or other means.[47] Likewise, the climate protection laws or sub-legal regulations of several states lay out permissible emissions for the main emitting sectors.[48] Moreover, the issuance by states of authorizations for emitting sources, such as fossil fuel exploitation and energy-intensive industries, can be interpreted as enabling emissions.[49] Although the emissions and their effects are ultimately 'horizontal', the state actively enables them and can therefore be regarded as indirectly causing the interference.

5. Combined Negative Obligations

The two versions of negative obligations could be combined into one. The negative character of the right, in other words, the obligation of the state to stay away from an action, is characteristic of both versions. Both require that the allocation of emission allowances is avoided or reduced. They also overlap in looking to the future and recognizing the increasing intensity of harmful effects. The difference is only related to the kinds of harm caused and the corresponding protective content of the rights. In the BVerfG's construct, this is the availability of energy as a component of almost all freedoms, considering that a broad range of activities from production to consumption of goods and

[46] Ibid. para.132.

[47] E. Woerdman, M. Roggenkamp, and M. Holwerda, *Essential EU Climate Law* (2nd edn, 2021) 44–73.

[48] See e.g. § 4 with Annex II of the German Climate Protection Act; Arts 3 and 6A of the Irish Climate Action and Low Carbon Development Act.

[49] On a similar line, see the decision of the Montana First Judicial District Court, Lews and Clark County in *Rikki Held et al. v. State of Montana et al.* of 14 August 2023, Case No. CDV-2020-307, https://climatecasechart.com/case/11091/,(last accessed 27 September 2024) where the court states: 'The State issues permits, licenses, and leases that result in GHG emissions without considering how the additional GHG emissions will contribute to climate change or be consistent with the standards the Montana Constitution imposes on the State to protect people's rights' (para. 261); 'The State's actions exacerbate anthropogenic climate change and cause further harms to Montana's environment and its citizens, especially its youth' (para. 268).

services depend on energy use.[50] Enjoyment of the related rights is endangered if, in future, energy use must be drastically curbed. In contrast, in the other construct, the endangered interests are material goods such as human health, occupation, property, children's welfare, etc. These are increasingly being harmed because the allowed emissions cause droughts, flooding, violent storms, heatwaves, etc.

There is no reason to draw a systematic difference between the two approaches. Both can be combined in order to facilitate the full protective scope of rights. I believe that the material interest approach is preponderant, however. The relevant trajectory ranges from emissions and changes in weather patterns to human diseases, parched or flooded land, dying forests, and damaged houses, installations, and infrastructure, etc. In addition, the relevant rights depend on energy availability. For example, farmers who seek to water their dried-out soil will need energy to pump groundwater. Healthcare will need energy to run hospitals. Occupational activities need energy to be performed. Crucially, the concern for life conditions in the future could also be integrated into this unitary concept. With continued GHG emissions, human welfare deteriorates both with regard to the material and the energy aspects, and future regulatory restrictions are to be expected concerning the satisfaction of both. Restrictions are imaginable, for example, concerning the production and consumption of energy-intensive products, transportation for leisure purposes, services for non-essential healthcare, land use for meat production, etc.

In conclusion, both kinds of negative rights can be integrated into one if the protected interests are conceived of as including both material and energy components.

B. Consequences of the Choice of Concept

1. Intensity of Court Review

In the jurisprudence of the BVerfG, fundamental rights as negative obligations invite a rather intensive review of state conduct, while fundamental rights as positive obligations imply a broader margin of discretion for the state. According to the BVerfG, this is because, in the first case, a specific and already implemented measure is under scrutiny thus allowing the judge to clearly approve or quash it while, in the second case, a variety of options are possible, among which the judge should not make a choice owing to the principle of

[50] *Neubauer et al.* (n. 5) para. 37.

separation of powers. By contrast, the ECtHR does not see much difference in review when applying negative or positive obligations.[51] The CJEU has a practice of conceding a broad margin of appreciation to the EU institutions, even concerning constellations of negative obligations.[52] Overall, as will be explained later,[53] I suggest that the structural difference between negative and positive obligations does have a certain effect on the weighing up of the interests of right holders and public interests. Anyway, whether self-restraint is practised with more or less zeal is also a question of the characteristics of the individual case, as well as the legal cultures and attitudes of judges.

2. Methodology of Rights Application

Rights as negative obligations typically have a two-step structure. They are breached if (1) there is an interference with a right and (2) there are no reasons to justify the interference.[54]

Step (1) is sometimes split into two, asking whether (1a) the case falls within the scope of protection of a right and, if so, (1b) whether the act concerned constitutes an interference. Step (2) can also be divided into two, namely examining (2a) the existence of a legitimate objective and (2b) the necessity of pursuing the same.[55] Furthermore, the legitimate objectives of interference can be divided into public interests and the conflicting fundamental rights of third parties.[56] In a simplified version, the methodology would comprise three steps: examining scope, interference, and possible justification. Nevertheless, overlaps are unavoidable, in particular between scope and interference. In particular, the substantive and procedural content of rights can be categorized as issues of scope or interference, while the extraterritorial reach of human rights is rather a question of scope.

With regard to positive obligations, the methodology of application is less firmly settled. Courts rather tend to merge the steps into a single one that

51 ECtHR, *Hatton v. UK*, Appl. no. 36022/97, Chamber Judgment of 2 October 2001, para. 96. See further Krieger in O. Dörr, R. Grote, and T. Marauhn, *EMRK/GG Konkordanzkommentar* (3rd edn, 2022) Part I, ch. 6, paras 25–79.

52 Wollenschläger, 'Article 17(1)', in Peers *et al.* (n. 44) 489, at 17.1, paras 54–56 (concerning the right to property).

53 See Section 5.C.

54 For an example of ECtHR practices, see ECtHR, *Flamenbaum et autres v. France*, Appl. nos 3675/04 and 23264/04, Judgment of 13 December 2012, paras 142–154. Rights of fundamental importance (e.g. Art. 2 ECHR) are sometimes guaranteed without the possibility of justification. But, even then, some weighing of competing interests is acknowledged, in particular if the protective scope is broadened to include more remote causes of danger to life such as in the climate realm. See *Klimaatzaak et al. v. Belgium et al.* (n. 6) para. 139.

55 ECtHR, *Flamenbaum et autres v. France*, Appl. nos 3675/04 and 23264/04, Judgment of 13 December 2012, paras 146–154.

56 See for an example, Case C-275/06, *Promusicae v. Telefónica* (EU:C:2008:54), paras 62–66.

balances various concerns. In the words of the ECtHR, a 'fair balance has to be struck between the competing interests of the individual and of the community as a whole' and 'in striking the required balance States must have regard to the whole range of material considerations'.[57] Nevertheless, a certain structuring can be noticed.

Upon closer scrutiny, courts often first determine the scope of protection of a fundamental right. For example, in *Hatton*, the ECtHR implicitly accepted that the right to health protects against disturbances caused by airport noise.[58] In a similar case about airport noise from Düsseldorf airport, the BVerfG discussed whether the right to health only covers physical suffering or embraces psychological well-being in a broader sense.[59] In *Neubauer*, the BVerfG argued that the protective scope of the right to health extends to the harmful effects of climate change, including those occurring in the future.[60]

As a second consideration, courts frame and examine the individuality and seriousness of harm when looking at one side of the balance to be struck. For example, in *KlimaSeniorinnen*, the ECtHR established a high standard requiring 'a particular level and severity of the adverse consequences affecting the applicant concerned'.[61]

As a third consideration, the harm caused to right holders is weighed with other public interests, including the ways and means of minimizing the harm. For example, in *Hatton*, the ECtHR balanced the health interests of residents with the general economic interest in air transportation.[62] Such weighing up normally raises the question of the interrelation between the political and judicial branches, requiring courts to determine when the discretionary margin of appreciation is over- (or under-)stepped. One limit to such discretion is the standard of the necessity of interference. In *KlimaSeniorinnen*, the ECtHR concretized this, formulating an ambitious range of measures a state must take before an interference can be accepted.[63]

In conclusion, a certain structure is also possible and, in fact, is partly practised with regard to positive obligations. It appears that the three steps known from negative obligations can be relied on with certain specific aspects coming to the fore. First, there is nothing different in requiring that the scope of the

[57] ECtHR, *Hatton v. UK*, Appl. no. 36022/97, Chamber Judgment of 2 October 2001, para. 96; ECtHR, 'Guide on Article 8 of the ECHR' (2024), para. 5

[58] ECtHR, *Hatton v. UK*, Appl. no. 36022/97, Chamber Judgment of 2 October 2001, para. 103.

[59] BVerfG order of 14 January 1981, 1 BvR 612/72 (*Flughafen Düsseldorf*), BVerfGE 56, 54, 73–78.

[60] *Neubauer et al.* (n. 5) para. 146.

[61] *KlimaSeniorinnen v. Switzerland* (n. 28) para. 531.

[62] ECtHR, *Hatton v. UK*, Appl. no. 36022/97, Chamber Judgment of 2 October 2001, paras 96 and 97.

[63] *KlimaSeniorinnen v. Switzerland* (n. 28) para. 550.

right must be determined. Second, interference is to be tested but is, in such cases, subdivided into testing the intensity of interference and the grounds of responsibility of the respondent authority. Third, as an operation to work out the duties of the state to protect, the interference is weighed against other concerns, including public interests and the rights of third parties. Ways and means of minimizing interferences are to be examined, leaving a broad margin of appreciation for the political branches of government. This structure would, I believe, increase the clarity of argumentation and emphasize that the right is the principle and any justification of interference the exception.[64]

5. Scope of Protection

There are four questions of interest here: what fundamental rights are pertinent in climate cases; what state action or omission is covered by their protective sphere; whether, considering the transboundary effect of domestic GHG emissions, fundamental rights have an external reach; and, if such external reach can be affirmed, whether a state is also responsible for emissions that originate abroad but are in some ways controlled by it.

A. Relevant Fundamental Rights

Several fundamental rights are relevant in climate cases, but not all of them are granted by all of the three human rights bodies discussed here. Human health is protected by all of them, including Article 2 (2) GG, Article 2 ECHR, and Articles 2 and 3 ChFR. The right to occupation is protected by Article 12 GG and Articles 15 and 16 ChFR. It is not granted by the ECHR, although to some extent such activities are nevertheless included in the right to property insofar as there is an 'underlying business' which the Court is prepared to call a 'possession' in the sense of Article 2 1st Protocol ECHR.[65]

The right to property is protected by Article 14 GG, Article 17 ChFR, and Article 1 1st Protocol ECHR. It was invoked by the applicants in *Neubauer* and

[64] This was also suggested by Judge Wildhaber in ECtHR, *Stjerna v. Finland*, Appl. no. 18131/91, Judgment of 24 October 1994, Concurring Opinion of Judge Wildhaber. The BVerfG largely follows this line.

[65] See e.g. ECtHR, *O'Sullivan McCarty Mussel Development Ltd v. Ireland*, Appl. no. 44460/16, Judgment of 7 May 2018, para. 88.

Carvalho but not in *Klimaatzaak* or *Duarte Agostinho*.[66] It is noteworthy that farmers whose land is suffering from drought or flooding have not yet brought any cases, although they could claim an interference with their property rights. The ECtHR has only cursorily been confronted with similar claims. For example, in *Budayeva et al. v. Russia*, the risk of mudslides was considered under both Article 2 and Article 1 1st Protocol to the Convention.

Equal treatment may also be invoked considering the inequality of the life chances of younger generations compared to the present adult generations. Special rights of children can be found in Article 24 ChFR, while they are not expressly mentioned in the GG and ECHR but do figure as part of other rights such as to health, equal treatment, choice of education and occupation, and property. In general, the ECHR is concerned with human rights in the sense of protecting persons and small businesses, while large economic players have rarely brought cases. In contrast, fundamental rights at the EU level have been applied to big business without much reluctance. A similar practice can be noted in the German Constitution.[67] However, some secondary differentiation of the levels of protection may be found.[68] The inclusion of industry in the scope of protection may be a reason why, in climate matters, the CJEU and the BVerfG, but not the ECtHR, have been approached by actors who allege that climate protection measures are *too strict*. It is only with the 'rights turn' (since about 2010) that actors seeking *stricter* measures have gained ground.

B. Substantive and Procedural Dimensions

The fundamental rights to human health and property are, first of all, substantive rights in the sense that health and property are protected at a certain level, for instance against diseases or loss of property. In addition, however, the courts have developed a procedural component. The ECtHR has repeatedly held that 'appropriate investigations and studies' must be made[69] based on 'detailed and

[66] It was invoked in ECtHR, *The Norwegian Grandparents' Climate Campaign and others v. Norway*, Appl. no. 19026/21, Case adjourned. See http://climatecasechart.com/non-us-case/the-norwegian-grandparents-climate-campaign-and-others-v-norway/ (last visited 27 September 2024).

[67] On this uneven buttressing of economic interests with constitutional protection, see (exemplified with biotechnology regulation) Winter, 'Cultivation Restrictions for Genetically Modified Plants. On Variety of Risk Governance in European and International Trade Law', 7 *European Journal of Risk Regulation* (2016) 120, at 122–123.

[68] See e.g. BVerfG judgment of 1 March 1979, 1 BvR 532, 533/77, 419/78, 1 BvL 21/78 (*Mitbestimmung*), BVerfGE 50, 290, 340–347.

[69] ECtHR, *Tătar v. Romania*, Appl. no. 67021/01, Decision of 5 July 2007; ECtHR, *Budayeva v. Russia*, Appl. no. 11673/02, Judgment of 28 February 2008, para. 136.

rigorous data'[70] and that the public must be given opportunities to comment.[71] For instance, in its first decision on *Hatton*, the Court's observation was that the authorities did not sufficiently examine, on the one hand, the noise effects on the sleeping conditions of residents and, on the other hand, the economic importance of an additional runway.[72] But there are, of course, also cases that have been decided on material grounds. For example, in *Cordella*, the court based its decision on the finding that the protective measures taken by the respondent state were materially insufficient.[73] Also, in *KlimaSeniorinnen*, the Court focused on the substantive standards requiring a state to adopt effective emission reduction targets and measures.[74]

Insofar as procedures are emphasized, the reason may be that the related rules are normally relatively precise while substantive criteria are often more generally framed, especially if opening up possibilities of weighing up conflicting interests. Courts can then avoid replacing political judgement with their own. A constitutional reason has been added by the BVerfG. Observing that judicial review of a governmental decision that has already been taken may come too late, it has held that the protection of rights is better ensured if those potentially affected by a decision have a right to comment early on in the decision-making procedure.[75] Such advanced legal protection (vorgezogener Rechtsschutz) means, for example, that the right to health not only protects against falling ill but also entitles participation in prior risk assessment procedures.

C. Transnational Reach of Fundamental Rights

An increasingly important aspect of the scope of protection is whether fundamental rights have a transnational reach. This question is a general one, environmental cases being only a subcategory of many other fields of application.

A traditional argument against transnational reach is the international customary principle of territoriality of jurisdiction. A state shall not be allowed to regulate matters situated in another state. However, this strict interpretation

[70] ECtHR, *Fadeyeva v. Russia*, Appl. no. 55723/00, Judgment of 19 May 2005, para. 128.

[71] ECtHR, *Taşkın et autres v. Turquie*, Appl. no. 46117/99, Judgment of 21 October 2004, paras 118–119.

[72] ECtHR, *Hatton v. UK*, Appl. no. 36022/97, Chamber Judgment of 2 October 2001, paras 100 and 103.

[73] ECtHR, *Cordella v. Italie*, Appl. nos 54414/13 and 54264/15, *Arrêt Définitif* of 24 June 2019, para. 172.

[74] *KlimaSeniorinnen v. Switzerland* (n. 28) para. 550.

[75] BVerfG judgment of 20 December 1979, 1 BvR 385/77 (*Mülheim Kärlich*), BVerfGE 53, 30, 59–61.

has become more and more flexible. For instance, in one case, the marriage between a formerly divorced German woman and a Spanish man was disallowed by the competent German authority because, at the time, Spanish law disallowed marriage with a divorced partner. The couple challenged that decision, arguing that their right to protection of marriage and family (Art. 6 GG) included marriage between divorced partners and was also applicable to transboundary marriages. The Hamm Appellate Court (Oberlandesgericht (OLG) Hamm), relying on a previous judgment of the Federal Court of Justice (Bundesgerichtshof, BGH), upheld the decision on the ground that the German human right of freedom to marry did not extend beyond the German borders.[76] However, the BVerfG quashed the BGH decision, establishing that transborder marriage and the weight of the right to free marriage were a sufficient link to allow the German fundamental right to extend to the Spanish restriction, thus entitling both the German woman and her Spanish partner to rely on that right.[77] This means that the German fundamental right is permitted to encroach on the sovereign realm of a foreign state, albeit, as the BVerfG pointed out, this should be done with respect and caution.

The territoriality principle is interfered with even less consequentially if the foreign fundamental right provides a citizen with an advantage. This is the normal case in environmental contexts where fundamental rights protect against possibly harmful encroachments. For example, the BVerfG acknowledges such an external reach by arguing that the text of fundamental rights does not set territorial limits. For instance, the rights to health and property protection are not formulated to end at the German border. The court nevertheless lowers the level of protection in comparison with inhabitants within the German territory, reasoning that—with regard to its advance effect doctrine—persons living abroad will not be subject to future German restrictions of energy use and—with regard to the positive obligation doctrine—German mitigation and adaptation measures will not be valid abroad.[78] Such reasoning—which appears to be an excuse for inaction anyway—would not apply in the construct of the negative obligation suggested here, that is, the obligation to reduce the allocation of emission allowances. That obligation would equally benefit residents and those living abroad.

A different concept applies to the external reach of ECHR rights. The basis is Article 1, which reads: 'The High Contracting Parties shall secure to everyone

[76] OLG Hamm Judgment of 3 September 1968—IV VA 4/67.
[77] BVerfG order of 4 May 1971, 1 BvR 636/68, BVerfGE 31, 58, 72–77.
[78] *Neubauer et al.* (n. 5) paras 173–181.

within their jurisdiction the rights and freedoms defined in Section I of [the] Convention.' In *Banković*, the ECtHR decided that jurisdiction can also mean the jurisdiction of a state in another state, but that such a situation is exceptional. The Court has accepted such a situation when the respondent state exercises public powers normally belonging to the foreign government, for instance as a consequence of military occupation or through the consent, invitation, or acquiescence of the government of that territory. In the case cited—families suffered from the bombing of Belgrade by NATO forces—the Court decided that the bombing itself did not constitute effective control of the relevant territory and therefore dismissed the action.[79]

After *Banković*, a second exception was accepted, that is, control through state agents, such as in *Öcalan*, where Turkish officials had detained a person in Kenya and the Court found Turkish human rights to be applicable.[80]

The ECtHR summarized the two exceptions as constituting spatial or personal control, holding that 'The two main criteria established by the Court in this regard are that of "effective control" by the State over an area (spatial concept of jurisdiction) and that of "State agent authority and control" over individuals (personal concept of jurisdiction).'[81]

A third exception has emerged under the notion of 'special features'. These are not defined *in abstracto* but case by case. One such case was *Hanan v. Germany* where the parents of two sons killed by armed forces in Afghanistan alleged that Germany had, in violation of Article 2, not effectively prosecuted the soldiers who were responsible. The Court saw three grounds for a special jurisdictional link: the obligation of Germany relating to criminal prosecution under humanitarian international customary law, the impossibility for the Afghan authorities to institute criminal investigations, and the obligation under German law to do so.[82]

In *Duarte Agostinho*, the ECtHR was asked to apply its doctrinal concept of 'jurisdiction' to transboundary environmental impacts.[83] The applicants claimed that transnational control exists if any activities originate in, and can be controlled by, the responsible state, have serious, lasting, and foreseeable transboundary effects, and cannot be repelled by the affected state. Such

[79] ECtHR, *Banković et al. v. Belgium et al.*, Appl. no. 52207/99, Grand Chamber Decision of 12 December 2001, para. 71.

[80] ECtHR, *Öcalan v. Turkey*, Appl. no. 46221/99, Grand Chamber Judgment of 12 May 2005, para. 91.

[81] ECtHR, *Duarte Agostinho et al. v. Portugal et al.*, Appl. no. 39371/20, Decision of 9 April 2024, para. 170.

[82] ECtHR, *Hanan v. Germany*, Appl. no. 4871/16, Grand Chamber Judgment of 16 February 2021, paras 136–139.

[83] Annex to the Application, paras 18–25, https://climatecasechart.com/wp-content/uploads/non-us-case-documents/2020/20200902_3937120_complaint-1.pdf (last visited 16 October 2024).

responsibility could also be built on the three circumstances of special features the Court acknowledged in *Hanan*: the respondent states are all under the obligation of the customary harm rule to prevent transnational damage; the affected state is unable to suppress such effects; and the national law of the acting state has specific regulations to reduce emissions.

This approach could be supported by considerations of a 'European legal space' for the Convention states and by 'European public order'. The 'legal space' would bind the Convention states to more stringent obligations to each other than to non-Convention states.[84] On the other side, this would discriminate against non-European citizens. A more basic argument in favour of extending extraterritorial reach would be that it would reflect a general movement in international law that establishes a more principled correlation between the external exertion of power and its legal framing, including through the guarantee of human rights.[85] Such correlation has been acknowledged in fora other than the ECtHR[86] and, in particular, the Inter-American Court of Human Rights (IACtHR) with its *Opinion on the Environment and Human Rights*,[87] as well as the Committee on the Rights of the Child (CRC) with its decision in the case of *Chiara Sacchi et al.*[88] Both bodies draw a distinction between the territoriality and jurisdiction of a state, defining jurisdiction as the control of a state over causal processes that originate in that state and cause extraterritorial harm.[89]

One further doctrinal concept relies on an observation former ECtHR Judge Serghides proposed in his partly concurring opinion in *Georgia v. Russia*.[90] He suggested that Article 1 ECHR should be understood only to rule on positive obligations of states to protect and not on negative obligations to desist from an activity. This implies that the external reach of negative obligations must be

[84] ECtHR, *Cyprus v. Turkey*, Appl. no. 25781/94, Grand Chamber Judgment of 21 March 2001, para. 78; ECtHR, *Banković et al. v. Belgium et al.*, Appl. no. 52207/99, Grand Chamber Decision of 12 December 2001, para. 42. One element of 'European public order' has been suggested to be peaceful living conditions; see Dissenting Opinion of Judge Chanturia in ECtHR, *Georgia v. Russia*, Appl. no. 38263/08, Grand Chamber Judgment (Merits) of 21 January 2021, Partly Dissenting Opinion of Judge Chanturia, paras 53–54.

[85] Giegerich, 'Extraterritoriale Wirkung von Grund- und Menschenrechten', 50 *Europäische Grundrechtezeitschrift (EuGRZ)* (2023) 17–39, at 31.

[86] Ibid.

[87] Inter-American Court of Human Rights (IACtHR), Advisory Opinion OC-23/17 of 15 November 2017, requested by Colombia, entitled 'The Environment and Human Rights'.

[88] Committee on the Rights of the Child (CRC), Decision adopted by the Committee under the Optional Protocol to the Convention on the Rights of the Child on a communications procedure, concerning communication No. 104/2019, Communication submitted by Chiara Sacchi *et al.* (CRC/C/88/D/104/2019).

[89] IACtHR (n. 87) chs VI and VII; CRC (n. 88) paras 10.1–10.14.

[90] ECtHR, *Georgia v. Russia*, Appl. no. 38263/08, Grand Chamber Judgment (Merits) of 21 January 2021, Partly Concurring Opinion of Judge Serghides.

derived from the interpretation of the various basic rights themselves rather than from Article 1. As a consequence, Article 1 would lose part of its filtering function. This concept would also challenge the ECtHR's standing opinion that negative and positive obligations are largely equivalent in terms of their level of protection. Negative obligations would gain new ground. Any state-based activity that intervenes with a right would be covered, whether the victims live within or outside the jurisdiction of the responsible state. This would also apply to victims of climate change from greenhouse gas emissions.

However, all of these reasons were rejected by the ECtHR, with its major concern being opening the floodgates for actions. Indeed, numerous persons would be brought into the protective realm of fundamental rights. Nevertheless, an *actio popularis* could be prevented by various means that could be developed by case law, including that control by a state of emissions must meet certain preconditions, victim status is restricted, collective action is accepted, and procedural safeguards are established such as terms for application, joining of actions, selection of test cases, *res iudicata* effect, etc.

D. Transnational Reach Concerning Causation of Emissions Abroad

In both *KlimaSeniorinnen* and *Duarte Agostinho*, the applicants alleged that the defendant states had extraterritorial jurisdiction not only for the external effects of domestic emissions but also for the external emissions caused by the defendant states through the importation of products produced abroad with GHG emissions and the exportation of products or services that cause emissions abroad. These external emissions are called scope 3 emissions.[91] The ECtHR denied the claim for the same reasons as stated previously but, distinguishing between responsibility and jurisdiction, acknowledged that a state is responsible for its transborder impacts. It is, however, not clear how this materializes. It may be interpreted as a non-subjectivized objective obligation, such as if an environmental impact assessment is extended to the climate effects of a project.

A cautious step in this direction was taken by the Norwegian Supreme Court in a case concerning the exploitation of mineral oil in the Barents Sea.[92] The

[91] Scope 1 means domestic and external effects of domestic emissions, scope 2 means external emissions caused by imported energy, and scope 3 means external emissions caused by exported products.

[92] Supreme Court Judgment of 22 December 2020, HR-2020-2472-P, unofficial English translation, para. 149. Contrastingly, the Appeal Court while also accepting responsibility for external emissions extended this to external effects. Cf. ibid. para 13, https://climatecasechart.com/wp-content/

court held that the right to a healthy environment established by Article 112 of the Norwegian Constitution extended to activities abroad that the Norwegian authorities directly influenced or could control, such as emissions from the combustion of exported fuel. However, the court was only prepared to accept responsibility for the reverse effects on the domestic territory. This nevertheless implies that the court accepted responsibility for emissions caused abroad if the state in some way controlled the activity.[93]

More indirectly, and without much reference to transnational jurisdiction, the Dutch Rechtsbank interpreted the duty of care of Royal Dutch Shell for emissions from gasoline combustion abroad to be, among other bases, also framed by the fundamental rights to human life and health (Arts 2 and 8 ECHR).[94] The German District Court (Landgericht) Stuttgart was, in a similar way, approached to rule that the car manufacturer Mercedes was responsible for emissions, including from Mercedes cars exported to other countries. The court rejected the action, arguing that the climate effects of emissions are uncertain and that, in any case, the legislator, and not the courts, was competent to decide the issue. It thus avoided addressing the question of the transborder reach of fundamental rights.[95]

An even more extensive transnational responsibility of states could have been invoked in the *KlimaSeniorinnen* case. The direction and financing of emission-intensive activities abroad by Swiss concerns and banks is a core business model that permeates and supports the Swiss economy. Extraterritorial emissions caused by projects financed by those enterprises are enabled by pertinent authorizations and oversight of the state. By doing this, the state can be regarded as taking responsibility for emissions from activities abroad. This responsibility can be integrated into the concept of positive obligations of the state. Alternatively, in terms of the concept of negative obligations, one could construe that by authorizing the related activities, the state enables emissions abroad and, through these, interferes with the rights of those affected.

The ECtHR denied such responsibility in a case concerning the participation of German and Austrian companies in a consortium implementing a

uploads/non-us-case-documents/2020/20201222_HR-2020-846-J_judgment.pdf (last visited 14 February 2025).

[93] The Oslo District Court relied on this concept in a follow-up case on exploration and exploitation of petroleum fields when requiring that the environmental impact assessment has to include emissions from the combustion of exported oil. Oslo District Court, judgment of 18 January 2024, Case no. 23-099330TVI-TOSL/05 (*Greenpeace and Natur of Ungdom v. Government*), ch. 3.5.3.

[94] Rechtbank Den Haag, Judgment of 22 May 2021 (*Milieudefensie et al. v. The Netherlands*), ECLI:NL:RBDHA:2021:5339 (English version).

[95] Landgericht Stuttgart, 13 September 2022, 17 O 789/21 (*Mercedes*).

Turkish hydroelectric project affecting the archaeological site of Hasankeyf. According to the Court, the German and Austrian governments could not be held responsible because the Turkish authorities had exclusive jurisdiction over the project.[96] One might think this position to be somewhat formalistic because foreign companies often have a decisive influence on a project. When such companies are authorized and supervised by their state of origin, that state may therefore be held responsible for their activities.[97]

Transboundary responsibility may also be supported by the customary no-harm rule. The rule has been accepted as establishing responsibility for the transnational effects of national emissions. The extension of this responsibility to scope 3 emissions has not yet been much discussed. However, it could be defended, arguing that the rule addresses any causation of harm, not only pollution from domestic sources. Looking further into Treaty law, Article 3 (1) of the UN Framework Convention on Climate Change (FCCC) could be interpreted to cover all climate-relevant activities of states when very comprehensively stipulating that the Parties 'should protect the climate system for the benefit of present and future generations of humankind'.

6. Interference

Once it has been determined that the contested climate legislation falls within the scope of fundamental rights, interference with the relevant rights must be examined. In constellations of *status negativus*, it has become common opinion that the notion of interference covers both legal acts imposing an obligation and burdensome factual conduct (such as noise caused by a government-owned airport). However, if the burdening activity is 'horizontally' caused by private actors, such as GHG emissions, interference must address two issues and establish pertinent criteria, namely criteria concerning (A) the physical causation of the harm and (B) the responsibility of the state.

[96] ECtHR, *Zeynep Ahunbay et al. v. la Turquie, l'Autriche et Allemagne*, Appl. no. 6080/08, Decision of 21 June 2016, para. 94.

[97] See further Kobylarz, 'Anchoring the Right to a Healthy Environment in the European Convention on Human Rights: What Concretized Normative Consequences Can Be Anticipated for the Strasbourg Court?', in G. Antonelly *et al.* (eds), *Environmental Law Before the Courts: A US–EU Narrative* (2023) 153.

A. Physical Causation

Environmental cases brought to courts have largely been concerned with linear or 'but for' causality of interference with fundamental rights. Criteria of interference, such as personal concern, serious harm, direct causation, imminent threat, lasting effect, etc., have been developed to delimit the relevant causation. In contrast, the causal chain of climate change is much more complex, including the following stages: GHG emissions by actors; an increase of concentrations in the atmosphere; (global and local) temperature increase; changes in the thermohaline earth system; changes in weather patterns; changes in natural life conditions; damage to the health, occupation, property, etc. of citizens. This poses the question of whether the established criteria of relevant causation shall be applied or need to be further developed.

I will examine five dimensions: certainty, intensity, individualization, time, and directness of causation. The criteria are discussed here as issues of the merits of a case but it should be remembered that they are already important at the admissibility stage, although in principle as a matter of a substantiated claim rather than a final determination.[98]

1. Certainty

In principle, the causal nexus must be 'proven' in factual terms, ruling out abstract statements or hypotheses.[99] Yet, probabilistic research results, such as those concerning risks of accidents of dangerous installations or dose-response relations of dangerous substances, are common ground for national courts,[100] but less so for the ECtHR,[101] though in *Tatar* they were accepted concerning the occurrence of asthma by sodium cyanide[102] and in *Budayeva* concerning the occurrence of devastation through an insufficiently dammed mudslide.[103] The reports of the Intergovernmental Panel on Climate Change (IPCC) certainly meet this standard concerning the relationship between human GHG emissions and a broad range of detrimental effects. However, when it comes to precise quantification of correlations, the law is required to determine the level of certainty required. For example, the global emissions allowed before the

[98] See Section 3.B.

[99] ECtHR, *Asselbourg et al. v. Luxembourg*, Appl. no. 29121/95, Decision of 29 June 1999.

[100] See Chapter 6 in this volume. For an example of the standard of review concerning the risk assessment of nuclear power facilities, see BVerfG 2 BvL 8/77, BVerfGE 49, 89.

[101] See as an instance, ECtHR, *Tatar v. Romania*, Appl. no. 67021/01, *Arrêt* of 27 January 2009, para. 102 on causation of asthma by sodium cyanide.

[102] Ibid.

[103] ECtHR, *Budayeva et al. v. Russia*, Appl. nos 15339/02 etc., Judgment of 28 February 2008, paras 147–160.

warming ceiling of 2°C is reached have been calculated to be, from 2020, 1,150 gigatonnes (Gt) with a probability of 66 per cent.[104] This means that the calculated amount is too high (or too low) with a probability of 34 per cent. The legal question is whether such a large margin of error is agreeable or whether precaution demands a margin of error of only 5 or 10 per cent, which would lead to a significant reduction of the available budget.[105]

2. Individualization

The ECtHR and most national jurisdictions construe fundamental rights as protecting individual persons. At the merits stage, this individual dimension is commonly more broadly conceived of than where it is narrowly defined at the admissibility stage. For example, when examining the compatibility of the Climate Protection Act with fundamental rights, the BVerfG has in mind the fate of the younger generations at large rather than the individual circumstances of the applicants, which act as a precondition for standing.[106] Even the CJEU, with its narrow definition of standing, treats the right holders as representing a type rather than as uniquely affected persons.[107] The practice of the ECtHR appears to have been similar in environmental cases.[108]

It is nevertheless doubtful whether the individual character of fundamental rights fits well with situations like climate change where the risk is of a collective nature, meaning that the causation of damage is certain but the individuals who will be hit are difficult to predict. For example, in *KlimaSeniorinnen*, the applicants argued they, as elderly persons, were exposed to an increased probability of suffering from heatwaves. They claimed that this was already an interference with their rights.[109] However, as noted, the ECtHR insisted on a narrow conception of standing thereby denying admissibility and thus desisting from opening up individual rights on the merits.

It appears that in cases where the harm caused is of a collective nature, the representation of the interest by an association is better suited than if an

[104] IPCC, '2021: Sixth Assessment Report, Working Group I, Summary for Policymakers' (cited as IPCC AR6 WGI SPM), p. 29, Table SPM.2.

[105] According to ibid., the 2°C budget would shrink from 1150 Gt to 900 Gt if an 83 per cent likelihood was required.

[106] *Neubauer et al.* (n. 5) passim.

[107] See e.g. Joined Cases C-402/05 P and C-415/05 P, *Yannin Abdullah Kadi and Al Barakaat International Foundation* (EU:C:2008:461), paras 331–367, where the Court develops the right to judicial review and the right to property having in mind the interests of all right holders who may find themselves in similar situations as the applicants in the case.

[108] ECtHR, *Cordella v. Italie*, Appl. nos 54414/13 and 54264/15.

[109] Similar ibid. para. 160 where the Court accepted individual concern without insisting that the effects of pollution were to be quantified and distinguished from other factors for each individual situation of the applicants. Similar *Klimaatzaak et al. v. Belgium et al.* (n. 6) para. 133.

individual acts on behalf of many others. As already mentioned, neither the BVerfG nor the CJEU have held a collective action representing a collective interest as admissible, thus avoiding a discussion of rights as collective rights at the merits stage. However, as also already mentioned, the ECtHR did accept an action by an association precisely in order to cope with the collective nature of the interference.

3. Intensity

The interference with a right must be severe, excluding merely superficial harm. The ECtHR has required this with regard to Article 8 ECHR.[110] In *Klimaatzaak*, the Brussels Appeal Court, reiterating ECtHR jurisprudence, demanded that a 'minimum level of seriousness' must be reached but found that the interference did not need to be locality-specific.[111] Applying the standard, the ECtHR found the threshold not to be crossed in *KlimaSeniorinnen*.[112]

In *Carvalho*, some of the applicant farmers proved that they were indeed severely harmed because of continuing drought, while others claimed that their land was overflooded and salinized by seawater. It is imaginable that had the CJEU accepted standing, it might, at the merits stage, have affirmed that the right to property was interfered with.

4. Time

The interference with a right has been required to be 'present', 'imminent', or 'immediate'. These criteria are challenged by situations of causes that will have their effect in the future. The ECtHR has already implicitly accepted the relevance of such future effects by holding that, in relation to future harm, it is not enough to claim an increased risk in the abstract. Instead, some degree of probability must be proven.[113] The Court has held such situations to exist in the climate realm because of the longevity of CO_2 in the atmosphere and the associated irreversible warming effect.[114] It has also extended the protective scope of Article 8 ECHR to the future of present generations.[115]

[110] See ECtHR, *López Ostra v. Spain*, Appl. no. 16798/90, Judgment of 23 November 1994, para. 51; ECtHR, *Hatton v. UK*, Appl. no. 36022/97, Chamber Judgment of 2 October 2001, para. 118; ECtHR, *Marchis and Others v. Romania*, Appl. no. 38197/03, Decision of 28 June 2011, para. 33; *KlimaSeniorinnen v. Switzerland* (n. 28) para. 531.

[111] *Klimaatzaak et al. v. Belgium et al.* (n. 6) para. 141.

[112] *KlimaSeniorinnen v. Switzerland* (n. 28) para. 533.

[113] ECtHR, *Aly Bernard et al. v. Luxembourg*, Appl. no. 29197/95, Décision of 29 June 1999, En Droit para 1.

[114] *KlimaSeniorinnen v. Switzerland* (n. 28) para. 533.

[115] Ibid. para. 420.

The construct of a 'negative obligation in respect of future interference' is particularly suited to capturing such future effects. However, it is not impossible to incorporate the idea in a positive obligation setting. The notion of advance effect could be used to conceive present-day positive obligations as being particularly stringent in view of future restrictions on livelihoods.

If the future is incorporated in the notion of interference, it remains to be decided to what extent future generations will be the beneficiaries of such rights. According to the BVerfG, human rights protection is granted only to the present generations (including existing embryos) because only they can be holders of human rights. National constitutions may nevertheless go further, such as Article 20a of the German Basic Law, which establishes a non-subjectivized obligation of the state to protect the natural conditions of human life, including for-not-yet-existing future generations.[116] The CJEU has not so far addressed this issue. However, the ECtHR has extended the protective scope of Article 8 ECHR to the future of the present generations but not to those who are not yet born.[117]

5. Directness

Directness as related to physical causation[118] can be understood as requiring a close connection between the holder of a right and the environment, the protection of which is at stake. Such a connection can be rather loose in legal systems that provide a general right to a healthy environment. For example, as already mentioned,[119] such a right is guaranteed in Norway by Article 112 of the Constitution.

Even without such a general right, environmental conditions are relevant with regard to fundamental rights that protect more concrete legal interests such as human health, children's welfare, occupation, and property. This means that the environment enters into the protective scope of rights because air pollution, droughts, flooding, etc., cause damage to human life, the cultivation of land, or the energy supply of industry. This has been recognized by the ECtHR in cases of air pollution, for example by recognizing air quality as a condition for good health.[120] Both the ECtHR and the BVerfG have acknowledged that

[116] *Neubauer et al.* (n. 5) paras 108–109.

[117] *KlimaSeniorinnen v. Switzerland* (n. 28) para. 420.

[118] Directness is also applied to causation by law requiring that the effect of a legal act must be caused without the intervention of a second legal act implementing the first. See in this sense, *Neubauer et al.* (n. 5) para. 108. Directness in this sense to some extent coincides with exhaustion of other remedies because it serves to direct legal action to contesting the intervening acts. See for a related case, BVerfG order of 15 July 2015, 2 BvR 2292/13, BVerfGE 140, 42, paras 60–64.

[119] See Section 3.D.

[120] ECtHR, *Cordella v. Italie*, Appl. nos 54414/13 and 54264/15, *Arrêt* of 18 December 2018, paras 157–160.

the same should apply to climate change effects, which are included in the protective reach of fundamental rights insofar as they affect human health and other rights.[121] The CJEU has not been seized of an opportunity to form an opinion on the issue.

B. Responsibility: Concretizing a State's Share

So far, causality has been treated as an issue of linking harm to emissions. In addition, and further upstream in the causation chain, it must be determined whether the emissions can be attributed to a state (or the EU). The answer is somewhat different depending on the chosen doctrinal structure of rights. In the setting of positive obligations, the state is obliged to reduce emissions because, as already explained, the human rights concerned contain underlying commitments for values such as human health, property, etc. Insofar as these values protect individuals and not just the public interest at large, they provide individuals with subjective rights to demand protection by the state. By contrast, in a setting of a negative obligation, the state is obliged to desist from an interference with freedoms, which in the climate context is to refrain from authorizing emissions.

The obligation, be it positive or negative, may need to be qualified as to the time when it starts to run. One could refer, objectively, to the date when the harmful causation started. This could go back as far as the beginning of industrialization, considering its reliance on fossil energy. However, the ECtHR jurisprudence, followed by the Brussels Appeal Court in *Klimaatzaak*, introduced a subjective component presupposing that the state must have had the relevant knowledge in order for duties to emerge. The Brussels Appeal Court suggested that Belgium knew or should have known in about the first decade of the new millennium that it had to take effective mitigation measures.[122] One could also argue that with the conclusion of the FCCC in 1992, climate change and its anthropogenic causes had become evident to anyone.[123]

However, an individual state cannot be made responsible for all the harm caused by all states. Three questions arise here: whether the state can invoke the *de minimis* argument, whether it is only responsible for the proportion of its contribution, and how the amount of that contribution can be determined.

[121] *KlimaSeniorinnen v. Switzerland* (n. 28) paras 425 and 465; BVerfGE 157, 30 para. 148.
[122] *Klimaatzaak et al. v. Belgium et al.* (n. 6) paras 165–169.
[123] See for the relevance of dating back responsibility, Section 6.B.3.

1. The *de minimis* Argument

In the climate cases before the ECtHR, many respondent states have argued that their share of global emissions is small and, therefore, their responsibility is negligible. Many national courts, including the Dutch Hoge Raad, the Brussels Court of Appeal, and the German BVerfG, have also been confronted with similar arguments. They have rejected them.[124] This can be understood to mean that causality is not simply a question of fact but a normative concept that can determine that any contribution is relevant because other small emitters could claim an equal privilege so that the sum of many small emissions would be significant. In addition, the BVerfG has construed a procedural obligation of the state to engage in international climate protection negotiations.[125] In terms of fundamental rights, this can be understood as introducing an element of global responsibility into the bilateral relationship between the affected individual and the state.

Another doctrinal construct may be derived from environmental law in general. For instance, in a case decided by the German Federal Administrative Court (BVerwG), the operator of a coal power plant emitting sulphur dioxide argued that its individual contribution to air pollution was small and therefore legally negligible. Rejecting this plea, the court held that if there is an overall 'concept' of reducing emissions, any contribution covered by it is of relevance.[126] This so-called 'concept requirement' (*Konzeptgebot*) is, I suggest, also applicable in climate law. International law requires all states to jointly reduce emissions. This 'concept' renders emission reductions of all states a relevant component, including states with relatively small overall shares. Even these small emitters are, therefore, obliged to reduce emissions. This obligation then shapes the content of the fundamental rights of the state's citizens. They can stipulate that their state fulfils its obligation even if this is only a small contribution to the necessary global effort.

2. Pro Rata Responsibility

Concerning the second issue of the share of responsibility, it appears that responsibility pro rata is preferable as a criterion. The alternative, that a state is jointly and severally liable for the entire contributions of all states, would lay an excessive burden on the liable state, even if it is given the right to have recourse against other states. Along that line, the Dutch Hoge Raad was of the opinion

[124] *KlimaSeniorinnen v. Switzerland* (n. 28) para. 439; *Neubauer et al.* (n. 5) para. 199; Hoge Raad, decision of 20 December 2019, case 19/00135 (ECLI:NL:HR:2019:2007), para. 5.7.1.

[125] *Neubauer et al.* (n. 5) paras 200–201.

[126] BVerwG judgment of 17 February 1984, 7 C 8.82, BVerwGE 69, 37, 45.

'that, under Articles 2 and 8 ECHR, the Netherlands is obliged to do "its part" in order to prevent dangerous climate change, even if it is a global problem'.[127]

Pro rata responsibility can even be regarded as a rule of international customary law. Article 47(1) of the Draft Articles on Responsibility of States for Internationally Wrongful Acts, as proposed by the UN International Law Commission (ILC) and adopted by the UN General Assembly, reads: 'Where several States are responsible for the same internationally wrongful act, the responsibility of each State may be invoked in relation to that act, ...' The ILC adds an explanatory note that 'The general rule in international law is that of separate responsibility of a State for its own wrongful acts.'[128]

3. Determination of the (Pro Rata) Contribution

When determining the precise share in the interference with fundamental rights for which a state (or the EU) is responsible, it must first be clarified whether that interference consists of harm caused in a real sense or if it is defined as exceedance of an abstractly defined fair share of the global emissions. I shall discuss the second variant first and then return to the real harm approach.

The fair share approach proceeds in two steps: the calculation of the global budget and the allocation of shares to states.

The global budget is calculated on the basis of specific upper limits for temperature increases. It is based on the well-proven fact that GHG emissions remain in the atmosphere for a long time, building increasing concentrations and causing the atmosphere to warm. From this combination of factors, the emission quantities—the global 'budgets', that are still possible up to certain temperature limits—can be derived. The IPCC Working Group I estimated that the global CO_2 budget remaining from the beginning of 2020 amounted to 500 Gt with a 50 per cent likelihood and 300 Gt with an 83 per cent likelihood for up to 1.5°C warming, while for up to 2°C warming 1350 Gt with a 50 per cent likelihood and 900 Gt with an 83 per cent likelihood remained.

While these estimations take the temperature limits as scientific assumptions, the legal question is whether the limits are legally binding. Such limits have been set by the Paris Agreement (PA), which, according to Article 2, calls for 'efforts' to stay below 1.5°C and definitely to stay 'well below' 2°C. The BVerfG reads 'well below 2°C' as aiming at 1.75°C, referring to a proposal by

[127] Hoge Raad, decision of 20 December 2019, case 19/00135 (ECLI:NL:HR:2019:2007), para. 5.7.1.

[128] International Law Commission (ILC), 'Responsibility of States for Internationally Wrongful Acts, with commentaries' (2001) Art. 47(6).

the German Environmental Scientific Advisory Board (SRU). The SRU explains this choice of temperature limit by the fact that, during the Paris negotiations, 2°C was chosen on the basis of 66 per cent confidence of no intolerable harm and 'well below' was added to indicate that a higher confidence level should be required in order to protect against harm occurring before 2°C has been reached. Obviously, such higher confidence would be achieved by reducing 2° to a lower degree, such as to 1.75°C.

With regard to the 1.5°C limit, it has often been argued that making 'efforts' implies that states enjoy a broad margin of discretion. The applicants in both *KlimaSeniorinnen* and *Duarte Agostinho* insisted that 1.5°C should be seen as binding, while the Court, although sympathizing with this understanding, did not regard it as a strict obligation.[129] Indeed, the closer the world gets to this limit, the more urgent it becomes to reflect on the reasons why the limit may be construed as being binding. The margin of appreciation must be regarded as having shrunk to zero, given the heavy damage that will already be caused if a rise of 1.5°C is reached. This has been abundantly proven by the IPCC report SR1.5°C.[130] It should also be noted that the 'Glasgow Climate Pact' which was concluded at COP 26, '*resolves* to pursue efforts to limit the temperature increase to 1.5 °C' and '*recognizes* that limiting global warming to 1.5 °C requires rapid, deep and sustained reductions in global greenhouse gas emissions . . . .'[131] This can be regarded as a 'subsequent agreement' within the meaning of Article 31 (3) (a) of the Vienna Convention.

In addition, it should be noted that the PA has not overruled the customary no-harm rule. This rule prevails at least insofar as the Treaty leaves room to be filled in, as is the case, for instance, concerning the interpretation of the 1.5°C limit.[132] Considering that damage will already be caused if the 1.5°C limit is transgressed, this supports the interpretation of the limit as binding.

In a second step, the global budget must be distributed among states. Many criteria have been discussed for how this should be done. Some are proposed but not made binding by the Paris Agreement, including equity, common but differentiated responsibility, and respective capabilities.[133] When applied, these criteria result in very different amounts of permitted emissions. A developed country receives a modest budget if 'respective capabilities' is chosen in

[129] *KlimaSeniorinnen v. Switzerland* (n. 28) para. 436.
[130] IPCC 2018, 'Global warming of 1.5°C' (2019).
[131] 'Decision-/CP.26 Global Climate Pact', para. 16, https://unfccc.int/sites/default/files/resource/cop26_auv_2f_cover_decision.pdf?download (last visited 16 October 2024).
[132] N. L. Dobson, *Extraterritoriality and Climate Change Jurisdiction* (2021) 26 and 153.
[133] Arts 2(2) and 4(4) Paris Agreement.

relation to GDP, but almost nothing is left if equity is understood to mean that past emissions are deducted from that budget on a per capita basis. At least, there is a broad consensus that grandfathering must be excluded.[134] This criterion would allow a state's share of the remaining global budget to be the same as its share in the past.[135] For instance, with its estimated 18 per cent of overall historical emissions, the EU could claim the same percentage of the remaining budget, even though its population share is only about 9.8 per cent. This would clearly violate the principle of equal treatment.

In addressing this issue, the BVerfG relied on an equal per capita basis as related to the budget remaining in 2020. This led to an amount of 6.7 Gt for Germany, which would be used up by about 2030 if normal yearly emissions were to continue.

By contrast, the applicants in *KlimaSeniorinnen* and *Duarte Agostinho* submitted that a combination of criteria should be applied. They relied on the methodology of the Climate Action Tracker (CAT), which is a widely used tool for assessing the climate protection performance of states. The criteria proposed are responsibility for past emissions, capability in terms of GDP, need for development, and a present equal per capita basis.[136] The ECtHR did not discuss this approach, adhering to an equal per capita approach as a principle it found to be legitimate.

I will nevertheless describe the CAT methodology because it may be taken up by other courts and also because it has influenced public discourse. If the mentioned set of criteria is applied to an individual country, this results in a range of different emission amounts for that country because (in the example of an industrialized, highly populated state) past responsibility may result in a very small or negative budget while present equal per capita may result in a larger budget. Likewise, a developing country that has a high potential for renewable energy will receive a large amount on the basis of the 'right to development' but a smaller one based on capability. The spread of budgets resulting from different criteria is referred to a state's 'fair share range'.

Each country's fair share range is determined based on available empirical studies about the country's socio-economic conditions. Once this range is identified, the lowest and highest emissions within a state's fair share range

[134] Rajamani, 'National "Fair Shares" in Reducing Greenhouse Gas Emissions Within the Principled Framework of International Environmental Law', 16 *Climate Policy* (2021) 1.

[135] Buser, 'Of Carbon Budgets, Factual Uncertainties, and Intergenerational Equity—The German Constitutional Court's Climate Decision', 22 *German Law Journal* (2021) 1409, at 1421.

[136] Climate Action Tracker, 'CAT rating methodology', https://climateactiontracker.org/methodology/cat-rating-methodology/ (last visited 27 September 2024).

are added together with the lowest and highest emissions within all other states' fair share ranges, respectively. As a result, a global range is represented by a worldwide equity best case scenario and a global equity worst case scenario.[137] The impacts of the lowest and highest emission aggregates on global warming are then evaluated. Applying the 1.5°C and 2°C limitations yields three categories: below 1.5°C, 1.5°C to 2°C, and above 2°C.

As the highest aggregate (or the least effort of all states combined) will reach well above 2°C, and the lowest aggregate may not even fall below 1.5°C, the entire package then needs to be compressed in order to be compliant with the 2°C and possibly 1.5°C restrictions. The reduction percentage necessary to reduce the package is equally applied to each state without further differentiation, considering that equity criteria have already determined the fair share range of the individual states. By starting at the top end of each state's fair share range and descending to each state's fair share range by the same percentage until the aggregate over all states reaches the emission level that is consistent with a temperature level, the global range of fair shares is mathematically reduced in line with the required temperature level.[138]

As a result of this process, fair share ranges for each country's three temperature categories—<1.5°C, 1.5°–2°C, and >2°C—are established, with the >2°C category further subdivided into <3°C, < 4°C, and >4°C. Each of these six categories corresponds to the temperature outcomes that would result if all other governments were to put forward emissions reduction commitments with the same relative position on their respective fair share range or the same ambition level.

This normative profile makes it possible to calculate the emissions quantities or budgets available for a state if it wants the world to keep global temperatures below certain temperature limits.

In summary, states have different amounts of allowable emissions at their disposal depending on how the global budget is calculated and allocated. In any case, under any single criterion or combined set of criteria, developed states will be left with very small residual amounts, with the effect that they can easily be found to exceed them and thus interfere with the fundamental rights of affected persons.

The fair share approach is difficult for non-scientists to understand. The factual basis is also subject to uncertainty at various points, particularly in relation

[137] Wachsmuth *et al.*, 'Fairness- and Cost-Effectiveness-Based Approaches to Effort-Sharing under the Paris Agreement', 39 *Climate Change* series (2019), available at https://www.umweltbundesamt.de/en/publikationen/fairness-cost-effectiveness-based-approaches-to (last visited 27 September 2024).

[138] Rajamani (n. 134).

to the probability of available budgets in relation to different temperature limits. The normative assumptions, particularly the temperature limits and allocation criteria, can be and have long been debated. Courts may, therefore, perceive this to be a political question and stay away from taking a position.[139] As mentioned, neither the ECtHR nor the BVerfG have discussed the approach in its complexity. They have nevertheless accepted the equal per capita principle as a legitimate (though not binding) option. Both of them found the remaining budget to be small and the respondent states not to have taken sufficiently effective abatement measures.

Alternatively, a simpler and more easily understandable approach can be taken. The threshold of interference is then determined not by reference to abstractly defined parameters (such as temperature limits, methods of budget calculation, and allocation principles) but in a concrete sense of harm to human health, occupation, and property, respectively. If the protection of these goods is interpreted as the prevention of serious harm and GHG emissions are found to cause such harm, this then per se constitutes an infringement of the right.

As the harm has not been caused entirely by an individual state but by a large number of states, the respondent state's share must be identified. This share corresponds to its part in actual global emissions, not to its fair share in the abstractly defined sense. This means that a state's share of emissions over a given period of time must be calculated. That period should be determined by reference to the time since a state became aware—or negligently ignored—that its conduct had to be brought in line with international law.[140] One possibility is to refer to the period since 1992 when the FCCC was concluded. By 1992, at the latest, the need to curb emissions had become common knowledge to virtually all states.

This reference to actual harm, as defined by the wording of the relevant human rights, appears to be more practicable than the highly sophisticated fair share approach. It does not relax the level of protection. On the contrary, it is even stricter. It also allows the scientific and political community to avoid

[139] See e.g. Ontario Superior Court of Justice, Case No. CV-19-00631627-0000, judgment of 14 April 2023 (*Sophia Mathur et al. v. Ontario*), para 109: 'The factors that have been identified by Dr. Matthews as relevant to the determination of a country's or province's fair share—population, historical responsibility, wealth, access to inexpensive low carbon energy sources, economic and energy generation choices—as well as the factors referred to in Article 2(2) of the Paris Agreement—equity, common but differentiated responsibilities, respective capabilities and different national circumstances—do not have a sufficient legal component to warrant the judicial intervention of an Ontario court. The selection of the appropriate allocation approach to determine a jurisdiction's fair share is an issue that should be determined in another forum, not in a domestic court in Ontario.'

[140] For an elaboration of the criterion in relation to climate protection, see *Klimaatzaak et al. v. Belgium et al.* (n. 6) para. 139.

endless and time-consuming transnational debates about temperature thresholds, budgets, and allocation criteria.

In conclusion, it must unequivocally be stated that the climate crisis is a fact that is already interfering with human rights. Any individual state has contributed to the interference either because its available budget, if any, was overspent or because it has contributed to already existing concrete damage. The simple consequence is that all further emissions, including small ones, must be stopped immediately. Nevertheless, a second step is available—the possible justification of interference—which can be used to place emissions reductions in a gradual structure.

7. Justification of Interference in the Public or Third Parties' Interest

A. General Considerations

The constitutional texts analysed here formulate the possible justification of interference as follows.

Article 8 (2) ECHR reads, concerning the right to a private sphere, that:

> There shall be no interference by a public authority with the exercise of this right except such as is in accordance with the law and is necessary in a democratic society in the interests of national security, public safety or the economic well-being of the country, for the prevention of disorder or crime, for the protection of health or morals, or for the protection of the rights and freedoms of others.

Article 51(1) CFR states, in relation to all fundamental rights, that:

> Subject to the principle of proportionality, limitations may be made only if they are necessary and genuinely meet objectives of general interest recognised by the Union or the need to protect the rights and freedoms of others.

The GG provides in Article 2(2) that '[E]very person shall have the right to life and physical integrity. Freedom of the person shall be inviolable. These rights may be interfered with only pursuant to a law.' Article 12(1) GG further states that '[A]ll Germans shall have the right freely to choose their occupation or profession, their place of work and their place of training. The practice of an occupation or profession may be regulated by or pursuant to a law.' Finally, Article 14(1) GG provides that '[P]roperty and the right of inheritance shall be guaranteed. Their content and limits shall be defined by the laws.'

The essence of these formulations and their interpretation by courts is that interference with a right is justifiable when there is a legitimate public interest or where the interest of holders of competing fundamental rights comes into conflict with the right under consideration. Further, if such legitimate interest exists, an interference with the right must be proportionate in relation to it, which means that the interference must be effective and necessary to serve the relevant interest, and the interest must be predominant when balanced against the interference.

As this possibility of justification is an exemption to the protection of fundamental rights, general methodological principles would require that it is interpreted narrowly.

In any case, the weighing up of the interest of affected right holders with public and third-party interests primarily belongs to the political sphere. The judiciary must therefore practice self-restraint. The relevant reasons can be found in different theoretical bases elaborated on at some length by the Brussels Appeal Court in *Klimaatzaak*.[141] One is, of course, the separation of powers between democratically elected bodies and the judiciary when generally formulated legal provisions will be applied. Another is scientific expertise, which is located primarily within the executive branch rather than within the courts. A third is concerned with subsidiarity of jurisdictional levels: the ECtHR acknowledges the plurality of national solutions, both political and judicial, rather than imposing its own appreciation.[142] Finally, as already demonstrated, whether positive obligations open up a broader margin of appreciation than negative ones is under dispute.

Whatever doctrinal basis is chosen, all approaches will end up with some middle-range criteria that will delineate the realm of the judiciary. The BVerfG makes use of three of them, that is, whether measures are completely missing, unsuitable, or insufficient to achieve the protective goal, concluding that the margin of appreciation was not overstepped.[143] The ECtHR increases its intensity of review the more the Contracting States have already found converging solutions, a criterion that was of importance when the Court assessed the climate legislation of the respondent states in *Duarte Agostinho*.[144] The Brussels

[141] *Klimaatzaak et al. v. Belgium et al.* (n. 6).

[142] See, in more detail on the subsidiarity aspect, Marauhn and Mengeler in O. Dörr, R. Grote, and T. Marauhn (eds), EMRK/GG Konkordanzkommentar (2022) Part I, ch. 7, paras 58, 59.

[143] *Neubauer et al.* (n. 5) paras 152–170.

[144] ECtHR, *Goodwin v. UK*, Appl. no. 28957/98, Judgment of 11 July 2022, para. 74.

Appeal Court in *Klimaatzaak* developed a kind of threshold approach according to which a '*minimum minimorum*' degree of protection may not be undershot, a criterion that led the court to require a 55 per cent reduction of GHG emissions by 2030 instead of the 80 per cent or more requested by the applicants and suggested by scientific reports.[145] The Norwegian Supreme Court spoke of a 'safety valve' that the judiciary should operate. English courts apply the so-called *Wednesbury* test, the core of which is the notion of unreasonableness.[146] In sum, it appears that none of these formulae give precise direction. The deciding court will, rather, look at the circumstances on a case-by-case basis and will be heavily influenced by the legal culture in which it is based, and also by the personal attitudes and political affiliations of the judges.

B. Prevailing Interests

A major public interest is, among others, the supply of fossil energy as long as it has not yet been replaced by renewables. This can also be regarded as an element of the fundamental rights of third persons since the availability of energy is a prerequisite for almost all freedoms. An example of an illegitimate interest would be purchasing and operating an oversized energy-intensive car. This is neither a public interest nor protected by a fundamental right.[147]

The BVerfG proposed a formula that gives climate protection not an absolute but a step-by-step preponderance. The court stated:[148]

> Once the constitutionally relevant limits of global warming have been reached, the constitutional obligation to take climate action will make it mandatory to restrict greenhouse gas emissions to levels that have a net zero impact on greenhouse gas concentrations in the Earth's atmosphere (cf. § 1 third sentence and § 2 no. 9 KSG). Art. 20a GG does not however take absolute precedence over other interests. In cases of conflict, it must be balanced against

[145] *Klimaatzaak et al. v. Belgium et al.* (n. 6) para. 202.

[146] *Associated Provincial Picture Houses Ltd v. Wednesbury Corporation* [1948] 1 KB 223, 229. See further W. Wade, C. Forsyth, and J. Gosh, *Wade & Forsyth's Administrative Law* (12th edn, 2014) 310–313.

[147] This may be seen differently in the German basic rights doctrine. The BVerfG has interpreted Art. 2(1) Grundgesetz which guarantees everyone the '*freie Entfaltung seiner Persönlichkeit*' (free unfolding of their personality) as providing '*allgemeine Handlungsfreiheit*' (general freedom of conduct) which implies that an extremely broad array of activities comes under the umbrella of basic rights, ranging from the consumption of any desired product to the business activities of a multinational corporation. The step was taken as early as 1957 by the BVerfG in judgment of 16 January 1957, 1 BvR 253/56 (*Elfes*), BVerfGE 6, 32, 36–42.

[148] *Neubauer et al.* (n. 5) para. 198.

> other constitutional interests and principles. ... However, given that climate change is almost entirely irreversible as things currently stand, any overshoot of the critical temperature for preventing climate change would only be justifiable under strict conditions—such as for the purpose of protecting fundamental rights. Within the balancing process, the obligation to take climate action is accorded increasing weight as climate change intensifies.

In short, according to the Court, climate protection does not take absolute precedence over other interests but must be balanced against them, although climate protection is accorded increasing weight as climate change intensifies.[149]

Biodiversity is a competing public interest that becomes more important as more land is occupied by measures mitigating climate change, such as wind parks, biomass production, and solar farms.

C. Necessity

If the supply of fossil energy (as long as it has not been replaced) is regarded as a legitimate interest, the necessity test requires that the use of fossil energy must be reduced to a minimum. The key question is how to determine this minimum. One way is to use the IPCC and CAT methodology to calculate modelled pathways of emissions reduction, which I will now examine in Subsection 1. An alternative approach, called 'best possible means', will be described in Subsection 2.

1. Modelled Mitigation Pathways

Modelled pathways, as proposed by the IPCC and CAT, were submitted by the applicants in both *KlimaSeniorinnen* and *Duarte Agostinho*. They result from a two-step approach.

First, at a global level, scenarios are compiled for five different world regions that combine different cost-effective sectoral and cross-sectoral emission reduction measures, all of which comply with certain upper temperature limits.[150] The benchmark is the pathway that ensures compliance with the

[149] In its subsequent practice, the German Federal Administrative Court has tended to level this differentiated concept down to a simple weighing up on an equal footing of climate protection with any other public interest. E.g. the court approved the construction of a new highway, giving the generation of additional emissions less weight than the benefit of accelerated individual transportation. I suggest this disregards the dynamic element in the BVerfG formula.

[150] IPCC, AR 6 WG III, 'Climate Change 2022. Mitigation of Climate Change' (2022). For a recent compilation of scenarios, see: J. Jaeger *et al.*, 'Methodology Underpinning the State of Climate Action

1.5°C limit with no or limited overshoot above 1.5°C and minimized carbon dioxide removal (CDR).

Second, these effective regional pathways are downscaled to national pathways, taking into account the conditions of the individual states, such as population size and GDP. The pathway of a state corresponding to the 1.5°C limit can then be plotted as a curve that shows the decrease of emissions from a base year to a year by which a level of net zero emissions must be achieved. The curve corresponds to the median of the entire set of the state's pathways. The actual performance of a country can be measured against this curve. If a state's actual measures describe a national curve exceeding the modelled curve, the state is deemed not to have taken the necessary measures to avoid an interference with the fundamental right.

The reduction commitments resulting from fair shares and modelled emission pathways may differ. In industrialized countries, fair shares will usually impose stronger reduction burdens than modelled pathways. This is because fair shares strictly require that reduction measures up to certain warming limits must be implemented, while modelled emission pathways allow for substituting financial transfers for reduction measures that are considered to be achievable at lower cost in another state.

The question then arises of which budget should be used. Economic modelling suggests going by modelled pathways plus financial transfers. By contrast, legal reasoning instead speaks in favour of fair shares. First, cost-effectiveness with its shift of obligations from industrialized to developing states is incompatible with equity principles. Second, fundamental rights provide protection in kind, not in cash. This means that the emissions causing interference with rights must be reduced physically rather than having to be suffered and compensated. Third, modelled pathways may prove to be unsuitable because monetary offsets do not guarantee that the forgone reduction will actually be realized elsewhere. It is true that an appropriate legal framework could require strict and monitored conditions such as additionality[151] and permanence of the supported project. But its implementation is questionable given the negative experience with the clean development mechanism (CDM) in the Kyoto Protocol system. The CDM mainly supported projects in emerging economies

Series' (2023 update), https://doi.org/10.46830/writn.23.00043; the Climate Action Tracker (CAT), see https://climateactiontracker.org/methodology/ (last visited 16 October 2024).

[151] Additionality was required by the Kyoto Protocol, Art. 12 (5) (c) for projects within the Clean Development Mechanism (CDM). This means that a supported project must be in addition to projects that a country would undertake in any event.

that were not in addition to what the country could and should have afforded anyway.[152] As a matter of course, financial support by developed countries for developing countries remains crucial but should not be based on offset grounds.[153]

2. Best Possible Means

As with fair shares, modelled pathways are difficult for non-scientists to understand. They, too, involve uncertainties and evaluations. As an alternative or complement, applicants in *Carvalho*[154] and interveners in *KlimaSeniorinnen*[155] and *Duarte Agostinho*[156] proposed a more practical approach called the 'best possible means' standard. It is divorced from specific limits relating to temperature rise and thus freed from the endless and fruitless debates, evasions, and delays of unwilling states. It is based on the observation that damage has already been caused even below 1.5°C warming. This implies that a legitimate budget is no longer available. Any budget calculation can only determine which emissions are unavoidable. An amount identified in this way can therefore only constitute an emergency, not a merited, budget.

The 'best possible means' standard, as suggested here, would require each individual state to reduce GHG emissions: from all source sectors; to the greatest extent that is technically, economically, socially, geographically, and institutionally feasible; and using the most effective instruments.

Most importantly, the approach would be in line with the current practice of the ECtHR in environmental law cases. As explained earlier, the ECtHR looks at whether the respondent state has carried out appropriate investigations and taken legislative and administrative measures designed to provide effective prevention of threats to human rights, with the public given opportunities to comment. An instructive example of how the ECtHR applies this test is *Cordella v. Italy* where the Court carefully scrutinized the research and measures undertaken by the respondent government, concluding that they

[152] For an assessment of CDM practices, cf. IPCC AR6 WG III (n. 150) ch. 16.5.3.

[153] See for such grounds, Winter, 'Indicators for the Implementation of International Climate Protection Law', in J. Fromageaux *et al.* (eds), *Measuring the Effectiveness of Environmental Law Through Legal Indicators and Quality Analyses*, IUCN Environmental Policy and Law Paper No. 91 (2023) 57, 71–72.

[154] Application of 13 May 2018, T-330/18, ch. J4, available at https://climatecasechart.com/wp-content/uploads/non-us-case-documents/2018/20180524_Case-no.-T-33018_application.pdf (last visited 27 September 2024).

[155] Third party intervention of CAN-E, ch. E (2) (d), https://climatecasechart.com/wp-content/uploads/non-us-case-documents/2022/20221205_Application-no.-5360020_na.pdf (last visited 27 September 2024).

[156] Third party intervention of CAN-E, ch. II 3. b), https://climatecasechart.com/wp-content/uploads/non-us-case-documents/2021/20210506_3937120_na-3.pdf (last visited 27 September 2024).

were insufficient.[157] In *KlimaSeniorinnen*, the Court followed the same line and even went further by compiling a list of requirements such as the setting and monitoring of emission reduction targets as well as the adoption and implementation of effective abatement and adaptation measures.[158]

In numerous reports, the IPCC has applied a similar approach in putting together studies about sectoral emission reduction potentialities and appropriate instruments.[159] However, a difference in methodology should be noted. The IPCC has developed mitigation options in a top-down manner, from the global and regional to the national level.[160] In contrast, the 'best possible means' approach looks at each country individually without immediately calculating the overall impact on warming limits. It also does not apply criteria of comparative transnational cost-effectiveness. It is a last resort and an urgent appeal to states to at least do what they can. As a second step, though, accompanying studies can add up all bottom-up efforts and compare the total remaining emissions with assumed temperature limits. Any exceedance could then be used as a further warning sign.

In more detail, the sectors to look at include energy, industry, transport, buildings, agriculture, waste, and consumers. Land use, land-use change, and forestry (LULUCF) would also be included as a bottom-up perspective does not require a transnationally agreed count; it is sufficient for a state to understand that LULUCF should reduce emissions and enhance GHG removal as far as possible.

The evaluation criteria would have to include more dimensions than the technical and economic components. They would embrace socio-cultural feasibility in order to address acceptability to citizens, especially where sufficiency measures are concerned. In addition, geophysical feasibility suggests taking into account the natural conditions of a state (e.g. in terms of sun, soil, and water availability). Institutional feasibility must be respected in terms of powers of government vis-à-vis vested interests. Finally, economic feasibility

157 ECtHR, *Cordella v. Italie*, Appl. nos 54414/13 and 54264/15, *Définitif* of 24 June 2019.

158 ECtHR, *Verein KlimaSeniorinnen et al. v. Switzerland*, Appl. no. 53600/20, Judgment of 9 April 2024, para. 550.

159 IPCC AR4 WGIII, 'Climate Change 2007. Mitigation of Climate Change' (2007) chs 4–13; IPCC, AR 1.5°C, 'Cross Chapter Box', 3; IPPC AR6 WGIII, 'Technical Summary', chs TS.4 and TS.5.

160 To be accurate, the modelled pathways approach uses both global and domestic scenarios. According to the IPCC, this double strategy combines top-down and bottom-up possibilities. However, before being scaled down, the national scenarios are incorporated into global pathways (IPCC, 'Climate Change 2007. Synthesis Report' (2007) 58, fn. 21). Alternatively, 'best possible means' would see national studies as such, i.e. as evidence of whether a state's potential was utilized to its fullest extent or more could be done.

would have to consider a country's transnational competitiveness in order to avoid carbon leakage.

In terms of instruments, the usual types need to be examined, including capping emissions, regulation, emissions pricing, emissions trading, financial incentives, voluntary agreements, and information.

Interestingly, the EU's Scientific Advisory Board on Climate Change (ESABCC) recently used a sort of 'best possible means' approach that focused on bottom-up feasibility as a complement to fair share reasoning.[161] A difference nevertheless remains because the ESABCC's primary aim is to feed a number of emissions reduction scenarios into three core pathways and derive from them EU-wide overall reduction targets for 2040, 2050, and so on. The best possible means, as suggested here, would instead focus on the reduction capacity of any individual state. However, when related analyses are undertaken, the dimensions and parameters the ESABCC has used could be employed as heuristic tools. Of course, the focus on individual states can be stimulated by transnational comparisons of measures taken and emissions reduced by different states.

8. Summary and Conclusions

This chapter has discussed how climate legislation is tested against fundamental rights, taking the perspective of persons suffering from the effects of climate change. The doctrinal issues that are in its focus at the same time raise the question of the role of the judiciary within the system of separation of powers. The chapter has discussed exemplary court cases that apply fundamental rights to health, occupation, property, and equal treatment on three constitutional levels: the German *Grundgesetz* (GG) as an example of a national constitution, the European Convention on Human Rights (ECHR), and the EU Charter of Fundamental Rights (ChFR).

Issues of procedure and substance of actions arise in this analysis. While the chapter concentrates on the substance of rights, it nevertheless offers a few findings about procedural issues.

[161] European Scientific Advisory Board on Climate Change (ESABCC), 'Scientific advice for the determination of an EU wide 2040 climate target and a greenhouse gas budget for 2030–2050' (2023), https://climate-advisory-board.europa.eu/reports-and-publications/scientific-advice-for-the-determination-of-an-eu-wide-2040/scientific-advice-for-the-determination-of-an-eu-wide-2040-climate-target-and-a-greenhouse-gas-budget-for-2030-2050.pdf/@@display-file/file (last visited 16 October 2024).

On procedure, it is shown that the competence of courts to assess a legislative act against fundamental rights and, in the case of incompatibility, declare it void, is now a general standard in European countries, with variations concerning whether all courts or only a constitutional court have such powers. However, there can be different routes to obtaining such a decision, ranging from implicit powers of the ordinary courts to referral to a constitutional court and further to a direct constitutional complaint which usually presupposes the exhaustion of other remedies. Second, concerning the *locus standi* of applicants, individual concern is required in most systems, though *actio popularis* is available in some. Individual concern is interpreted very differently, ranging from severe harm, as required by the ECtHR and BVerfG, to unique harm, as required by the CJEU. As climate change affects many persons, the question arises with particular emphasis when asking whether a class action is admissible. The ECtHR has accepted this, but neither the CJEU nor the BVerfG has done so. However, when applying human rights provisions, national courts will have to reconsider their practice in view of Article 6(1) ECHR. This Article guarantees access to judicial review, which the ECtHR interprets to, in principle, include collective actions representing victims of rights violation, although a state may weigh up their admissibility against other concerns such as the separation of powers.

As to the substance of fundamental rights, in looking at the *basic construction* of rights as the negative and positive obligations of a state, this chapter has suggested a novel approach. When states allocate emission allowances to GHG-emitters that cause harm to 'third' persons this can be construed as an interference of the state with the fundamental rights of those persons. Such framing as a negative obligation of the state legitimizes a more intense court review than in the case of positive obligations.

Considering the transnational effects of GHG emissions the *transnational application* of fundamental rights is obviously significant in determining whether individuals can make claims in relation to harms they have suffered through emissions. While on a national and an EU level, this is answered by the text of the individual rights themselves, which usually does not limit rights to national territories, the applicability of ECHR rights according to Article 1 ECHR presupposes the external jurisdiction of a state. The ECtHR refused to conceive of extraterritorial jurisdiction as control of a state over emissions having external effects for fear of opening the floodgates for actions. Arguably, however, an overload of legal actions could be avoided by procedural means.

Furthermore, doctrinal innovation is needed in relation to the *notion of interference* with rights. It is submitted that the physical causation of harm should be distinguished from construing responsibility of states for the same.

Concerning *physical causation*, fundamental rights have commonly been developed for linear neighbourhood constellations, while climate change effects result from remote sources and more complex chains of causality. Such innovation has largely been developed by the ECtHR and BVerfG but not (yet) by the CJEU. It is done through reinterpretation of several criteria, which can be categorized by the dimensions of certainty, individualization, severity, presence, and directness of harm.

In relation to *certainty*, the ECtHR and BVerfG, relying on IPCC information, found the relationship between human GHG emissions and a broad range of detrimental effects to meet this standard. Other propositions are less certain, such as the emission budget available until certain warming limits are reached. However, the enhanced legitimacy in outcome that is achieved by 'certainty' in legal rules and their application is not an end in itself. Instead, some reassessment of what kinds and levels of certainty can be achieved in the context of climate change is required. Neither the ECtHR nor the BVerfG have ruled on the degree of likelihood required in legal terms. Precaution would require an error probability of less than 10 per cent. The 50 per cent likelihood commonly accepted for the 1.5°C limit and the 33 per cent accepted for the 2°C limit would far exceed that level. If reduced to 10 per cent, the related budgets would be much smaller or even negative.

Regarding *individualization*, litigation of an individual person for another person or a collective of potentially affected persons, or *actio popularis*, is not accepted by the courts considered in this chapter. Applicants must show that they are personally affected. However, as the impact of climate change, while being certain collectively, is difficult to predict individually, an action by an association representing such collective risk gives more appropriate access to justice. This has been recognized by the ECtHR. The CJEU and BVerfG will need to consider whether to follow suit, based on the ECtHR's interpretation of Article 6(1) ECHR.

The *severity of harm* will also come under the microscope as the differentiated impacts of climate change are felt over time. For now, a certain severity is required for an activity or omission to be classified as interference. Such severity undoubtedly does exist for many people whose health, occupation, or property is damaged by heatwaves, droughts, flooding, and other extreme events.

Concerning the *temporal dimension*, while fundamental rights are commonly considered to be interfered with only if the harmful effects are present or imminent, the ECtHR and BVerfG take future harm to the present generations into account, considering that causation currently enacted will irreversibly result in damage in the foreseeable future.

Finally, concerning the requirement of *directness*, a general right to a healthy environment is not acknowledged in the jurisdictions considered in this chapter. Nevertheless, general court practice acknowledges that the environment, including the climate, enters into the scope of rights insofar as it impacts the goods protected by the right, such as human health, occupation, and property.

Physical causation by emissions of adverse effects does not by itself establish the responsibility of a state. Rather, *responsibility for causation paths* depends on how the fundamental rights are construed. If construed as positive obligations to protect, the state is obliged to reduce emissions because the relevant right contains underlying commitments for values such as human health, property, etc. If construed as negative obligations, the state itself is the causer and as such is obliged to refrain from authorizing emissions in order to avoid active, though indirect, interference with freedoms. In any case, an individual state cannot be made responsible for the entirety of states contributing to climate change. Rather, a state should be made responsible *pro rata*. Its share can be determined as its relative contribution to the damage caused in a concrete sense. Alternatively, the contribution can be determined by defining damage abstractly as an excess of a state's 'fair share'. 'Fair share' means that, taking two steps, the global budget of emissions is derived from certain temperature limits and allocated to states according to a choice of equity criteria including a present or past equal per capita basis, common but differentiated responsibility, respective capabilities, etc. As the remaining budget is tiny by any calculation, industrialized states presently exceed their budget, or they will in the near future, thereby interfering with rights. Likewise, and with even more evidence, interference is a given if defined as concrete damage to goods protected by rights, such as human health, occupation, and property. Such damage has already been caused in multiple ways.

In principle, a given interference has the consequence that any further emissions must immediately be stopped. However, a certain continuance of interference may be justifiable. Such *justification of interference* depends on whether the interference is necessary in the public interest or in the rights-based interest of third parties. The weighing up of an interference with the *public interest* or interests of other right holders is primarily a competence of the political institutions. Nevertheless, the courts are obliged to check whether the margin of appreciation has been overstepped. Various criteria have been suggested to mark such limits but decisions will be made on a case-by-case basis and depend on the legal culture of jurisdictions and the personal attitudes of judges.

If considerable public interest in the continued utilization of fossil fuels is assumed, the *necessity test* requires that such utilization and related emissions must be reduced to a minimum. The minimum can be identified by either of two methods: emission reduction pathways modelled on the basis of the comparative cost-effectiveness of measures and reduction pathways based on an in-depth inquiry into what is technically, economically, and socially possible for an individual state. The former method follows economic modelling but raises equity and effectivity concerns. The latter method is easier to understand and better corresponds to current court practices, including that of the ECtHR in *KlimaSeniorinnen*.

Returning, then, to the general question of *legitimacy*, I submit that the climate protection demanded by victims of climate change is not only a question of politics. Relevant fundamental rights are simply in existence and binding on all political institutions. They are framed in general language but can and must be concretized through professional legal reasoning; in other words, by reconstructing the facts in view of the law, interpreting the law in view of the facts, and resolving whether the law has been observed or breached. As shown, such legal reasoning has shaped and will further develop the criteria of the admissibility of actions, the concept of rights as negative and positive obligations, the scope of rights, interference with them, and the possible justification of interference. Professional legal reasoning in a setting of judicial independence carries its own source of legitimacy. Nevertheless, it needs to respect the margin of appreciation of political institutions that is based on the judiciary's democratic deficit, limited scientific expertise, and subsidiary role in quasi-federal structures. The related judicial self-restraint has its place in the weighing up of the interference with preponderant public interests and in the choosing of mitigation measures. However, this should not amount to fundamentally denying the judiciary from assuming its proper role as the guardian of fundamental rights.

6

Scientific Uncertainty before the EU Courts, Boards of Appeal, and National Courts in Environmental Matters

George Iordachescu and Michał Krajewski[*]

1. Introduction

Do science and law still serve as sanctuaries of 'certainty'? Science used to be conceived of as providing infallible, empirically verified truths. Law, unfolding in adjudication, made a strong claim to rationality. Nowadays, we realize that science, especially when harnessed for regulatory purposes, rarely provides unequivocal or perfectly certain propositions, which would allow decision-makers to dissociate themselves from any value judgements.[1] At the same time, legal frameworks employ indeterminate notions to address various risks, the knowledge of which rapidly evolves.[2] Scientific uncertainty exacerbates legal uncertainty when uncertain science reaches judicial fora, as in environmental cases.

EU legal studies, traditionally court-centric, perceive courts and adjudication as default and optimal mechanisms for solving disputes between public authorities and private entities in view of ensuring the legal accountability of the former,[3] as well as between EU and national

[*] This chapter expresses the personal views of the author and cannot be attributed to the European Ombudsman.

[1] See S. Jasanoff, *The Fifth Branch: Science Advisers as Policymakers* (1992); S. Jasanoff, *Science at the Bar: Law, Science, and Technology in America* (1995). For a critical and common-sense view of science, see S. Haack, *Defending Science—Within Reason: Between Scientism and Cynicism* (2007). See for instance of an analysis of how values permeate expert assessments, Millstone and Clausing, 'Reasons for Reinforcing the Regulation of Chemicals in Europe', 14 *European Journal of Risk Regulation* (2023) 78.

[2] See G. C. Leonelli, *Transnational Narratives and Regulation of GMO Risks* (2021).

[3] Judicial review is usually considered the necessary condition for the rule of law and the driving force behind the development of EU law. See F. Jacobs, *The Sovereignty of Law: the European Way* (2007) 43–50. This is why EU legal scholars are often concerned with whether the EU Courts and judicial review keep pace with evolving forms of exercising public authority in view of ensuring 'checks and balances', legal accountability, the rule of law, effective judicial protection, or similar goals. See, among many, Gentile, 'Ensuring Effective Judicial Review of EU Soft Law via the Action for Annulment before

George Iordachescu and Michał Krajewski, *Scientific Uncertainty before the EU Courts, Boards of Appeal, and National Courts in Environmental Matters* In: *The Legitimacy of EU Environmental Governance and the Role of the European Courts*. Edited by: Mariolina Eliantonio and Emma Lees, Oxford University Press.
 DOI: 10.1093/oso/9780198972808.003.0006

authorities.[4] When courts shy away from delving into complex and uncertain empirical assessments linked to legal issues,[5] despite such assessments appearing significant for the outcome of the disputes, the goals of judicial proceedings, such as upholding the rule of law or effective judicial protection, seem to be at risk.[6] In such cases, a natural juristic reflex may be to plead for more 'intense' judicial review[7] and look for ways to enhance the epistemic ability of judges[8] or other adjudicators to rule on such assessments.

Hence, scholars explore how judges engage with science and how they can moderate this engagement. For instance, there have been examinations of how international judges 'frame' the disputes before them, deciding to what extent

the EU Courts: a Plea for a Liberal-Constitutional Approach', 16 *European Constitutional Law Review* (2020) 466 (arguing that EU judicial review should encompass proliferating EU soft law); Xanthoulis, 'Administrative Factual Conduct: Legal Effects and Judicial Control in EU Law', 12 *Review of European Administrative Law* (2019) 39 (arguing that EU judicial review should also encompass 'factual acts', and not only formal legal acts, as public authority subjected to EU law is also exercised through the former); De Bellis, 'Multi-Level Administration, Inspections and Fundamental Rights: Is Judicial Protection Full and Effective?', 22 *German Law Journal* (2021) 416 (concerning the judicial review of 'inspection powers' of EU authorities); Eckes and Mendes, 'The Right to Be Heard in Composite Administrative Procedures: Lost in between Protection?', 36 *European Law Review* (2011) 651; Brito Bastos, 'An Administrative Crack in the EU's Rule of Law: Composite Decision-Making and Nonjusticiable National Law', 16 *European Constitutional Law Review* (2020) 63; Röttger-Wirtz, 'From Integration to Exclusion: EU Composite Administration and Gaps in Judicial Accountability in the Authorisation of Pharmaceuticals', 10 *European Journal of Risk Regulation* (2019) 393 (the latter three articles analysing how the strict division of jurisdiction between the EU and national judicature, despite the increasingly prevalent practice of composite decision-making, may result in gaps in judicial review). See also on the EU requirements of effective judicial protection in matters covered by EU law at the national level and the myriad of functions that this principle plays, Safjan and Düsterhaus, 'A Union of Effective Judicial Protection: Addressing a Multi-Level Challenge through the Lens of Art 47 CFREU', 33 *Yearbook of European Law* (2014) 3; Gentile, 'Effective Judicial Protection: Enforcement, Judicial Federalism and the Politics of EU Law', 2 *European Law Open* (2023) 128.

[4] L. Prete, *Infringement Proceedings in EU Law* (2017).

[5] 'Complexity' implies a resource- and effort-intensive process of analysis due to a variety of relevant factors, whereas 'uncertainty' implies the absence of a single, objectively 'correct' answer. Opinion of AG Emiliou in Case C-389/21 P, *ECB v. Crédit lyonnais* (EU:C:2022:844), paras 49–50.

[6] In particular, a serious concern in EU competition law has been a 'marginal review' of complex economic evidence and assessment by the EU Courts, despite the fact that such evidence and assessments have decisive influence on the rights, duties, and even sanctions imposed on private undertakings. See Jaeger, 'The Standard of Review in Competition Cases Involving Complex Economic Assessments: Towards the Marginalisation of the Marginal Review', 2 *Journal of European Competition Law & Practice* (2011) 295. As regards the need for thorough judicial review of scientific assessments in EU risk regulation to ensure 'rational' and 'evidence-based' decision-making, see Alemanno, 'Case C-79/09, Gowan Comércio International e Serviços Lda v. Ministero della Salute, Judgment of the Court of Justice (Second Chamber) of 22 December 2010, nyr', 48 Common Market Law Review (2011) 1329.

[7] See analyses of why and how the EU Courts intensified judicial review in areas involving complex and uncertain empirical assessments in Mendes, 'Discretion, Care and Public Interest in the EU Administration: Probing the Limits of Law', 53 *Common Market Law Review* (2016) 419; Dąbrowska-Kłosińska, 'Risk, Precaution and Scientific Complexity before the Court of Justice of the European Union', in Ł. Gruszczyński and W. Werner (eds), *Deference in International Courts and Tribunals* (2014) 192; Ioannidis, 'The Judicial Review of Discretion in the Banking Union: From "Soft" to "Hard(Er)" Look?', in C. Zilioli and K.-P. Wojcik (eds), *Judicial Review in the European Banking Union* (2021) 130.

[8] See Chapter 3 in this volume.

they focus on legal or empirical issues and, consequently, how much science enters the judicial forum.[9] Judges can also solve science-intense disputes by interpreting the rules regarding the burden of proof, thereby deciding who should bear the consequences of the uncertainty of empirical assessments and to what extent the precautionary principle can justify regulatory action despite uncertainty.[10] Moreover, judges dealing with the judicial review of legal acts adopted by public authorities can decide on the applicable standard of review. Complex and uncertain scientific assessments can be subject to limited review only.

However, 'process-oriented' strategies have been proposed, especially with regard to EU judicial review, allowing judges to dissect the successive elements of the decision-making process and assess its rationality, logic, intelligibility, or consistency.[11] Some argue that EU judicial review should moreover ensure that decision-making involving uncertain science be more inclusive and deliberative,[12] considering that the evidence informing EU decision-making often comes from the regulated industries.[13] When it comes to national models of judicial review and their engagement with science, they seem to vary across the EU. Even in those systems in which judges face few legal obstacles to delve into empirical issues, including in environmental cases, judicial practice depends on the specific type of cases and accessibility to the necessary expertise.[14] Overall, the complexity and uncertainty of specialist knowledge remain an epistemic challenge to judicial legitimacy. This is why EU Boards of Appeal (BoAs) have recently attracted scholarly attention. These are partly specialized

[9] K. Sulyok, *Science and Judicial Reasoning: The Legitimacy of International Environmental Adjudication* (2021) 45.

[10] Eliantonio and Krajewski, 'Scientific Uncertainty before the Court of Justice and the General Court: Is the Judicial Toolbox Sufficient?', in M. Eliantonio, E. Lees, and T. Paloniitty (eds), *EU Environmental Principles and Scientific Uncertainty Before National Courts: The Case of the Habitats Directive* (2023) 327.

[11] Scott and Sturm, 'Courts as Catalysts. Re-Thinking the Judicial Role in New Governance', 13 *Columbia Journal of European Law* (2006) 565; Vos, 'The European Court of Justice in the Face of Scientific Uncertainty and Complexity', in M. Dawson, B. de Witte, and E. Muir (eds), *Judicial Activism at the European Court of Justice* (2013) 142; Sulyok, 'Science, Legitimacy and the Judicial Function—A Need for More Intrusive Standards of Review', in G. Kajtár, B. Çali, and M. Milanovic (eds), *Secondary Rules of Primary Importance in International Law—Attribution, Causality, Evidence, and Standard of Review in the Practice of International Courts and Tribunals* (2022) 83.

[12] Morvillo and Weimer, 'Who Shapes the CJEU Regulatory Jurisprudence? On the Epistemic Power of Economic Actors and Ways to Counter It', 1 *European Law Open* (2022) 510.

[13] In Case C-616/17, *Blaise* (EU:C:2019:800), the referring court had doubts whether it was compatible with the precautionary principle that the tests, studies, and analyses required in the procedures for the EU approval of pesticides were submitted by the applicants with no independent counter-analysis. In response, the Court held that the competent authorities are nonetheless required to 'take account of the most reliable scientific data available and the most recent results of international research' rather than 'giving in all cases preponderant weight to the studies provided by the applicant'. Ibid. 94.

[14] See an overview of such models in Eliantonio, Lees, and Paloniitty (n. 10).

and functionally independent adjudicatory bodies, set up in certain EU agencies vested with direct decision-making powers. Their goal is to keep the bulk of cases requiring specialist assessments outside the EU Courts, offering tailor-made and quicker administrative review.[15]

This chapter examines the boundaries of the contributions of courts and similar adjudicatory bodies to the legitimacy of EU environmental governance when faced with scientific uncertainty, which especially underlies legal disputes about the natural environment. It understands 'legitimacy' as relative to whether adjudicatory bodies can rationally inspire a justifiable belief in the 'certainty' of propositions relating to empirics that are contained in their rulings. As will be shown, courts cannot always offer such certainty about all such propositions relevant to the solution of legal disputes brought before them. However, this does not mean that their rulings contribute to rendering the system 'illegitimate'. Rather, the conclusion offered in this chapter is that we should be aware of the boundaries of the judicial contribution to legitimacy and realistic in expectations that we entertain towards courts, given their non-specialist composition, limited time, and resources—all of which limit the extent to which courts can engage—as well as the extent of politically-laden scientific disputes brought to adjudication.

The chapter begins by conceptualizing the main types of 'certainty' expected of adjudication and how scientific uncertainty challenges its primary goals (Section 2). Subsequently, it examines the case law of the EU Courts, including the requirements expressed by the Court of Justice towards national courts, and discusses the decision-making practice of the Board of Appeal of the European Chemicals Agency. It analyses whether and on what grounds a reader can rationally form a justifiable belief in the certainty of propositions linked to complex and uncertain scientific assessments presented in the rulings. Thus, it reveals the boundaries of certainty offered therein. The specific sections of this chapter follow the types of 'certainty' expected of adjudication: the 'stability' of legal propositions (Section 3), the 'truth' of empirical propositions (Section 4), and the 'acceptability' of both (Section 5). The final section wraps the different lines of the argument together and reinstates the merits of paying attention to the socio-political entanglements of various

[15] M. Chamon, A. Volpato, and M. Eliantonio (eds), *Boards of Appeal of EU Agencies: Towards Judicialization of Administrative Review?* (2022). See the recent cases in which the EU Courts analysed the legal nature of BoAs and the scope of their tasks: Case T-125/17, *BASF v. ECHA* (EU:T:2019:638); Case T-735/18, *Aquind v. ACER* (EU:T:2020:542); Case C-46/21 P, *ACER v. Aquind* (EU:C:2023:182); Case T-133/08, *Schräder v. CPVO* (EU:T:2012:430); Case C-546/12 P, *Schräder v. CPVO* (EU:C:2015:332).

environmental issues to contextualize the boundaries of certainty offered by adjudication (Section 6).

The chapter discusses in detail politically-laden scientific controversies underlying several illustrative cases. It incorporates perspectives from political ecology, an interdisciplinary field that questions power dynamics and the ways in which policies can enact environmental injustices. Bringing a political ecology approach to court proceedings can illuminate the contention around scientific uncertainty in two complementary ways. First, political ecologists show the complex ways in which diverse and sometimes marginal actors are affected by public policies or decisions that courts also deal with. Second, political ecology scholarship can help understand how scientific controversies over environmental governance are enmeshed with power struggles involving decision-makers at various levels. In particular, scientific uncertainty in environmental matters and the difficulty of assessing legality or illegality stem from the ways humans attach different values to nature.[16]

Political ecologists can bring these complex values into legal disputes by showing the impact of various pieces of legislation on local livelihoods and on species conservation or by illuminating how uncertainty prevents effective collaboration between stakeholders (including between adjudicators and experts).[17] Nonetheless, political ecologists see courts as instrumental in remedying environmental injustices.[18] Lawyers might benefit from engaging with political ecology to better understand the entanglement of the political and scientific stakes of the disputes that they engage with, as well as the reasons for suboptimal law enforcement. For instance, research on wildlife trafficking and environmental crime showed that uncertain scientific knowledge both obscures and facilitates the production of environmental harms,[19] hinders international synergies between enforcement and control authorities,[20] and impacts public trust[21] by creating and maintaining a crisis of scientific authority.[22]

[16] See Intergovernmental Science-Policy Platform on Biodiversity and Ecosystem Services, 'The Assessment Report on Diverse Values and Valuation of Nature' (2022), https://www.ipbes.net/the-values-assessment (last visited 20 December 2023).

[17] P. Robbins, *Political Ecology: A Critical Introduction* (2012), at 20.

[18] Phelps *et al.*, 'Environmental Liability Litigation Could Remedy Biodiversity Loss', 14 *Conservation Letters* (2021) e12821.

[19] Iordachescu *et al.*, 'Political Ecologies of Green-Collar Crime: Understanding Illegal Trades in European Wildlife', 32 *Environmental Politics* (2023) 923.

[20] G. Iordachescu, 'Uncertain Scientific Knowledge and European Illegal Wildlife Trade' (2023), https://beastlybusiness.org/wp-content/uploads/2023/02/Uncertain.pdf (last visited 20 December 2023).

[21] Popescu, Pop, and Rozylowicz, 'Trophy Hunting Undermines Public Trust', 372 *Science* (2021) 1049.

[22] See on the appropriate level at which to establish the conservation status, and how to establish if it is 'favourable', etc., Trouwborst and Fleurke, 'Killing Wolves Legally: Exploring the Scope for Lethal

Therefore, the chapter will bring to the fore a range of political ecology studies to show how scientific uncertainty affects the goals of adjudication and, as a result, how it affects the legitimacy of EU environmental governance.[23]

2. Certainty and Uncertainty in Adjudication

Adjudication has traditionally been seen as providing certainty regarding the meaning of applicable laws and determining and assessing relevant facts. Fuller argued that adversarial adjudication, in which two opposing parties confront each other before a neutral arbiter, maximizes the chances of obtaining accurate propositions about law and facts thanks to the separation of tasks. The task of the parties is to advance the best arguments and adduce pertinent evidence, whereas that of the arbiter is to choose the more convincing account. Unlike in inquisitorial settings, the judges are not distracted by the additional task of investigating the case *for* the parties.[24]

This goal of adversarial adjudication seems hindered by indeterminate legal notions referring to science and the elusiveness of empirical truth. Science can no longer be persuasively conceived of as a set of absolute truths. It is, rather, a social practice concerned with an inquiry to corroborate or disqualify propositions about some external reality, as well as a betterment of methods of such an inquiry.[25] Scientists usually generate propositions that are not perfectly certain and it is often the case that scientific knowledge is closely enmeshed with value judgements when harnessed for regulatory purposes.[26] Epistemic communities of experts advising regulators share both knowledge and value-laden beliefs about appropriate regulatory action, which influences the 'objectivity' of their reasoning or regulatory advice.[27] Uncertainty of scientific propositions is relative to simplifications inherent in theoretical frameworks, imperfections of measurement, the non-representativeness of samples, controversial

Wolf Management under European Nature Conservation Law', 22 *Journal for International Wildlife Law and Policy* (2019) 231.

[23] Green *et al.*, 'Barriers and Bridges to the Integration of Social-Ecological Resilience and Law', 13 *Frontiers in Ecology and the Environment* (2015) 332.

[24] Fuller, 'The Forms and Limits of Adjudication', 92 *Harvard Law Review* (1978) 353.

[25] See Haack (n. 1).

[26] See Ashford, 'Science and Values in the Regulatory Process', 3 *Statistical Science* (1988) 377; Jasanoff, 'The Practices of Objectivity in Regulatory Science', in C. Camic *et al.* (eds), *Social Knowledge in the Making* (2011) 307.

[27] Haas, 'Ideas, Experts and Governance', in M. Ambrus *et al.* (eds), *The Role of Experts in International and European Decision-Making Processes* (2014) 19, 29–32.

extrapolations, inferences based on fallible models simplifying reality, and the complexity of causality.[28]

Adversarial adjudication is not the optimal setting for settling scientific controversies. Judges, unlike scientists, are constrained to search for workable solutions within a limited time frame. The parties advocate for their case rather than engaging in the pursuit of scientific truth. Some parties are more powerful in socio-economic terms than others, so they may be able to produce and present more persuasive, even though not perfectly objective, evidence.[29] Admittedly, law deals with uncertainty by, among other things, allocating the burden of proof and establishing the required threshold of proof. In particular, it may accept the facts to be established according to the 'balance of probabilities' rather than 'beyond reasonable doubt'.[30] However, an autonomous and persuasive assessment of the balance of probabilistic scientific statements and counterstatements usually requires access to specialized knowledge, so it nonetheless constitutes a challenge to the legitimacy of judicial decision-making. At the same time, adjudicators cannot leave complex and uncertain empirical assertions and legal issues requiring specialist knowledge unaddressed. Otherwise, they may undermine the persuasiveness of their rulings.[31]

Some could argue that the response is that 'legal truth', with which adjudication is concerned, does not have to perfectly correspond to 'empirical truth'. However, this view seems to alienate law from our lives. In the specific context of environmental litigation in the EU, court rulings may affect not only the parties represented before the court but all the present and future generations.[32] Therefore, social expectations that adjudication will prompt public authorities to more radically address environmental challenges in the 'objectively' right way and based on 'empirical truth' seem to be mounting. This is evidenced by the phenomenon of climate litigation, which expresses an expectation towards courts that they will address the insufficiency of reactions by political institutions to the climate crisis.[33]

[28] Walker, 'The Myth of Science as a "Neutral Arbiter" for Triggering Precautions', 26 *Boston College International and Comparative Law Review* (2003) 197, at 205–211.

[29] S. Haack, *Evidence Matters: Science, Proof, and Truth in Law* (2013) 35–36.

[30] See A. Kalintiri, *Evidence Standards in EU Competition Enforcement: The EU Approach* (2020) 72 ff, regarding the concept of the standard of proof and its significance.

[31] Sulyok (n. 9) 15.

[32] See e.g. litigation launched by an individual manufacturer against the European Chemical Agency concerning the classification of a so-called 'forever chemical', in which a Member State and civil society organizations acted as interveners on the side of the Agency, Case C-293/22 P, *Chemours Netherlands v. ECHA* (EU:C:2023:847).

[33] For an overview of such litigation, how it reflects dissatisfaction with actions by democratically elected institutions, but also how it constitutes a challenge to judicial legitimacy also due to possible scientific uncertainty, see Besselink, 'The National and EU Targets for Reduction of Greenhouse

Inquisitorial court procedures are not easy solutions to the problems mentioned here. Such procedures are intended to provide certainty primarily thanks to the independence of judges, tasked with investigating the 'truth', and the multi-instance procedure, in which the courts of higher instance, composed of more experienced judges, meticulously verify decisions of lower-instance courts.[34] However, complex and uncertain empirical assessments are usually left to the 'lowest instances', as being supposedly best equipped to assess the facts 'on the ground'. Higher-instance judges are usually tasked with solving more general questions of law. Nonetheless, specialized courts are sometimes set up,[35] including environmental courts,[36] or legal systems come up with other ways of equipping judges with access to neutral scientific expertise.[37]

This chapter views the contribution to legitimacy made by courts and quasi-judicial bodies in the context of EU environmental law cases as relative to whether they can, despite scientific complexity and uncertainty, provide some degree of certainty regarding legal and empirical propositions linked to science. Certainty, thus understood, has at least a few interrelated dimensions.

First, the 'certainty' that courts are expected to offer implies the 'stability' of their legal propositions. We should be able to safely assume that public authorities will respect legal propositions offered by courts so that we can find these propositions reliable and plan our conduct accordingly.[38] Article 19(1) TEU stipulates that the EU Courts ensure the observance of law in the interpretation and application of the EU Treaties. Therefore, the EU institutions and Member States should observe their rulings. The BoAs do not have such strong legal mandates. Nonetheless, they are vested with an appellate jurisdiction over their agencies. They are deemed to express the final position of their

Gas Emissions Infringe the ECHR: The Judicial Review of General Policy Objectives', 18 *European Constitutional Law Review* (2022) 155.

[34] M. Damaška, *The Faces of Justice and State Authority: A Comparative Approach to the Legal Process* (1986), at 47-56.

[35] See e.g. Paloniitty and Nieminen-Finne, 'The EU Nature Conservation Law in Finnish Judicial Review: Various Avenues, Coalescing Case Law?', in Eliantonio, Lees, and Paloniitty (n. 10) 213.

[36] See C. Warnock, *Environmental Courts and Tribunals: Powers, Integrity and the Search for Legitimacy* (2020).

[37] See e.g. Fleurke, 'Judicial Review of the Application of Art. 6(3) Habitats Directive: How the Dutch Council of State Integrates Science, Expertise and Scientific Uncertainty', in Eliantonio, Lees, and Paloniitty (n. 10).

[38] In case law and legal doctrine, this requirement is often expressed through the notion of legal certainty, which implies 'on the one hand, that rules of law must be clear and precise and, on the other, that their application must be foreseeable by those subject to them'. Case C-231/15, *Polkomtel* (EU:C:2016:769), para. 29 and the earlier case law cited. This dimension of certainty corresponds to the *internal* criterion of output-related legitimacy discussed in the introduction. According to this criterion, courts increase the overall legitimacy of the governance structure by ensuring the clarity and consistency of law, among other things.

agencies. Hence, we can reasonably assume that the relevant agencies should comply with the decisions of their BoAs unless these decisions are contested by the EU Courts.[39]

The long-term stability of courts' propositions about law may be somewhat affected if lawmakers decide to amend the relevant legal instruments in response to court rulings. Such 'overruling' is not a problem in and of itself. In a democracy, members of representative bodies can always change their minds about how the law should address specific issues, while analysing the evolution of case law. Nonetheless, if overly frequent or concerning major societal issues, 'overruling' might erode the rational belief in the stability of judicial pronouncements. The EU context seems to be somewhat special in this regard. Because of its unprecedented success in fostering European integration, the Court of Justice is usually expected to 'get things right' at least for a relatively long time, as it often relies on policy principles enshrined in the Treaties.[40] In addition, EU legislative instruments are difficult to change as the EU legislative process involves remarkable political hurdles, given its reliance on intergovernmental and inter-institutional negotiations.[41]

Moreover, the stability of the Court's legal propositions can also be affected by their incoherent implementation by national courts. The Court is supposed to ensure the uniformity of EU law across jurisdictions. If national courts implement the Court's preliminary rulings in a significantly divergent way, the rational perception of the stability of these rulings would be adversely affected. An additional layer of this problem may be present in legal areas heavily reliant on the appropriate determination and assessment of facts, as in environmental law, given sundry national models of how judges engage with complex and uncertain empirical claims.

Second, the 'certainty' that courts should offer implies the 'truth' of empirical propositions with which the courts are faced and which may constitute, in particular, the empirical basis for the contested regulatory or administrative action. Litigants often expect courts to indicate an accurate or possibly the most plausible account of empirical factors relevant to the case at hand.[42]

[39] Case T-735/18, *Aquind v. ACER* (EU:T:2020:542), paras 23–34.

[40] S. Schmidt, *The European Court of Justice and the Policy Process: The Shadow of Case Law* (2018); Davies, 'Legislative Control of the European Court of Justice', 51 *Common Market Law Review* (2014) 1579.

[41] Horeth, 'The Least Dangerous Branch of European Governance? The European Court of Justice under the Checks and Balances Doctrine', in B. de Witte, E. Muir, and M. Dawson (eds), *Judicial Activism at the European Court of Justice* (2013) 32.

[42] Krajewski, 'On Crosswords and Jigsaw Puzzles: The Epistemic Limits of the EU Courts and a Board of Appeal in Handling Empirical Uncertainty', 2 European Law Open (2023) 784. See also cases discussed by Morvillo and Weimer (n. 12).

However, courts or even partly specialized BoAs are not scientific institutions. It is not realistic to expect them to determine the 'truth' when even scientists disagree. Nonetheless, to maintain the epistemic legitimacy of their rulings, they are at least expected to verify the minimum consistency and plausibility of impugned scientific assessments relevant to the resolution of the case.[43]

Comparative literature reveals a variety of judicial strategies addressing complex and uncertain empirical propositions. As mentioned, courts may frame legal disputes in such a way as to eschew scientific questions. They may also moderate the required threshold of proof and the intensity of judicial review.[44] Courts that scrutinize scientific appraisals in more detail do not always assess their plausibility head-on. Instead, they sometimes verify the credentials of scientific experts involved in making the contested appraisals, whether the sources used in these appraisals have been subject to peer review or whether the accepted propositions correspond to the majority view in the relevant scientific community.[45]

Third, 'certainty' implies 'acceptability' by the affected parties. Courts must observe the principles of procedural fairness, which aim not only to maximize the accuracy of court rulings but also to reassure the affected parties that they can genuinely participate in decision-making and influence its outcome. Ideally, courts might also consider socio-economic inequalities between the parties that affect their ability to commission and present evidence, among other things. Legal procedures should lead at least to a 'rational acceptability' if not, ideally, to the 'actual acceptance' of rulings by all the parties. Through fair procedures, courts should ascertain that the parties, if they were able to look at their own case impartially and detach themselves from their own interests,

[43] This dimension of certainty corresponds to the *external* criterion of output-related legitimacy discussed in the introduction. According to this criterion, courts increase the overall legitimacy of the governance structure by ensuring that regulatory and administrative action is based on sufficiently plausible empirical accounts, which is a prerequisite for this action to advance the normative goals of the legal order.

[44] Sulyok (n. 9) 44 ff; Eliantonio and Krajewski (n. 10); Eliantonio, Lees, and Paloniitty, 'Conclusions', in Eliantonio, Lees, and Paloniitty (n. 10) 349.

[45] Ky, 'Qualifications, Weight of Opinion, Peer Review and Methodology: A Framework for Understanding the Evaluation of Science in Merits Review', 24 *Journal of Environmental Law* (2012) 207; Vinuales, 'Legal Techniques for Dealing with Scientific Uncertainty in Environmental Law', 43 *Vanderbilt Journal of Transnational Law* (2010) 437. The EU Courts also hear allegations concerning conflicts of interest of experts involved in EU decision-making. See e.g. Case T-594/18, *Pharma Mar v. Commission* (EU:T:2020:512).

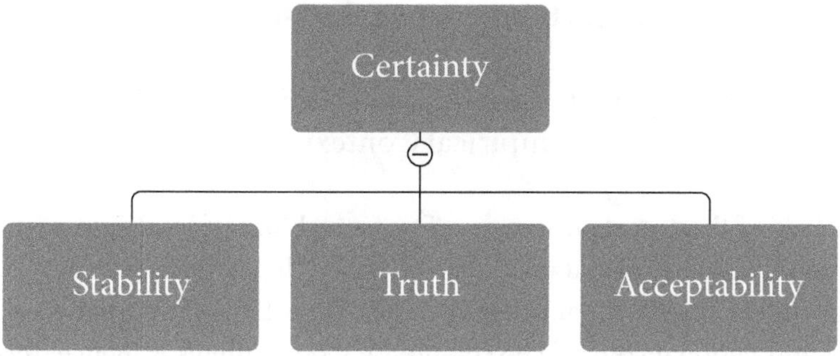

Figure 6.1 Dimensions of certainty of adjudication

would have good reasons to accept the ruling, given how the judicial procedure has been conducted.[46]

As courts decide on cases affecting a wide range of parties, as well as the general public, such as in environmental law, expectations of the openness and inclusivity of their proceedings grow significantly.[47] On the one hand, by opening their proceedings, courts can agglomerate specialist knowledge. By engaging in supplementary fact-finding, such as commissioning additional expert evidence, they can assuage socio-economic inequalities between the parties, including industry, public administration, and civil society. On the other hand, by doing so, they may increase the time and cost of proceedings.[48] Therefore, they must strike a delicate balance in how they conduct their proceedings. Otherwise, they might undermine the certainty and rational acceptability of the judicial process itself by excessive time and cost.

Figure 6.1 shows the three dimensions of certainty that adjudication is expected to offer: the stability of legal notions, the truth of empirical propositions, and the acceptability of judicial process and its outcomes.

[46] See generally on the theory of procedural justice, Solum, 'Procedural Justice', 78 *South California Law Review* (2004) 181; see also on different schools of thought about procedural justice ('due process'), D. Hovell, *The Power of Process: The Value of Due Process in Security Council Sanctions Decision-Making* (2016) ch. 4, 'A "Value-Based" Approach: Three Models of Due Process'.

[47] With regard to expectations towards the increased transparency and procedure of the Court of Justice, see C. Krenn, The Procedural and Organisational Law of the Court of Justice: An Incomplete Transformation (2022) ch. 5, 'Completing the Transformation: Proposals for Democratising the ECJ'.

[48] See with regard to fact-finding by the EU Courts and the standard of judicial review, Barbier de la Serre and Sibony, 'Expert Evidence Before the EC Courts', 45 *Common Market Law Review* (2008) 941; F. Castillo de la Torre and E. Gippini Fournier, *Evidence, Proof and Judicial Review in EU Competition Law* (2017) ch. 5, 'Procedure and Evidence in Court'.

3. Certainty as Legal Stability

A. Interpreting Indeterminate Legal Notions in an Uncertain Empirical Context

The rulings of the Court of Justice offer the stability of legal interpretation thanks to the Court's formal mandate. However, this stability in practice also depends on the responses of other actors, such as the EU and national lawmakers, and national courts. The stability of Court rulings is, hence, relative to both the Court's formal authority and the substantive persuasiveness of its reasoning. In particular, the Court interprets some legal notions in the context of the evolving state of scientific knowledge, so legal interpretation may also require an engagement with science. EU lawmakers frequently use indeterminate legal notions referring to specialist knowledge explicitly or implicitly.[49] For instance, while interpreting the EU Habitats Directive,[50] the Court of Justice is faced with such uncertain notions as 'favourable conservation status', 'natural range', or 'a habitat of a species'. As García-Ureta notes, legal interpretation must incorporate scientific findings.[51]

A compelling example is *Confédération paysanne*.[52] This case shows that, faced with profound politically-laden scientific disputes, courts may be able to offer only relative stability of legal notions, framing their reasoning in such a way as to keep a distance from the merits of the scientific dispute itself. This case has been an important element in the multi-layered debate about the status of genetically modified organisms (GMOs) in the EU.[53] The release of such organisms into the environment and their use in food and feed is subject to EU rules requiring prior authorization. However, the conclusion of the EU authorization procedure frequently encounters significant obstacles due to politico-scientific controversies between the Member States, some of which remain sceptical about introducing genetically modified plants.[54]

[49] Such as the notion of 'mutagenesis'. See Case C-528/16, *Conféderation paysanne (I)* (EU:C:2018:583) and Case C-688/21, *Conféderation paysanne (II)* (EU:C:2023:75), and the controversies regarding the Court's interpretation, such as Garnett, 'Hold your Pipettes: The European Court of Justice's Findings in *Confédération Paysanne & Others* stirs GMOtions', 28 *Review of European, Comparative, International & Environmental Law* (2019) 349.

[50] Council Directive 92/43/EEC, OJ 1992 L 206/7.

[51] García-Ureta, 'The European Court of Justice's Approach to Scientific and Factual Matters in the Habitats Directive—Between Uncertainty and Precaution', in Eliantonio, Lees, and Paloniitty (n. 10) 31, 33; Preston talks in this regard about linguistic uncertainty. Preston, 'Biodiversity in the Court: The Certainty of Contests about Uncertainty', in Eliantonio, Lees, and Paloniitty (n. 10) 297.

[52] Case C-528/16, *Confédération paysanne* (EU:C:2018:583).

[53] See Chapter 4 in this volume.

[54] See in more detail, M. Weimer, Risk Regulation in the Internal Market: Lessons from Agricultural Biotechnology (2019) 115, ch. 4, 'EU Authorisation of GMOs—The Failure of Deliberation'.

Controversies concern the very basic question of whether GMOs involve risks to the natural environment. Some see this technology as a chance to create more sustainable food systems, whereas others are concerned about the increased use of pesticides on new pesticide-resistant crops, the possibility of crop-to-crop gene flow, and the broader adverse effects of genetic modification on biodiversity. The scientific questions in this debate are closely linked to socio-economic ones concerning, for instance, the effects of genetic modification on organic farming by small and medium-sized farms in Europe or fostering the economic power of big industry actors.[55] Research informed by political ecology approaches has addressed GMOs as a serious environmental and political issue,[56] acknowledging that this debate is often intimately tied with moral and speculative judgements about technology's role in today's society.[57] For instance, there have been debates over transgenic maize in Mexico, where robust scientific knowledge informed the political contention, but the ensuing political discussions could not be resolved by science alone.[58]

This specific case concerned the meaning of 'mutagenesis', a technique used to obtain GMOs. Organisms obtained through mutagenesis were exempted from regulatory duties under the Directive on the deliberate release of GMOs into the environment[59] because this technique had a history of safe use when the Directive was adopted. However, new mutagenesis techniques had since appeared. They allowed for much more precise and significant modifications of the genome. Nonetheless, they lacked a history of safe use. Hence, the national court asked, among other things, whether the notion of 'mutagenesis', as employed in the Directive, should be understood as covering these new techniques, exempting them from the regulatory framework in question.

The Advocate General focused on the legislative intention and considered that the EU lawmakers, when adopting the Directive, must have anticipated that the techniques of mutagenesis would quickly evolve. As a result, that notion should be interpreted broadly, thereby exempting organisms obtained through novel techniques from regulatory duties. At the same time, according to this

[55] Leonelli (n. 2) 2–7; Wainwright and Mercer, 'The Dilemma of Decontamination: A Gramscian Analysis of the Mexican Transgenic Maize Dispute', 40 *Geoforum* (2009) 345; Velicu and Ogrezeanu, 'Quiet No More: The Emergence of Food Justice and Sovereignty in Romania', 89 *Journal of Rural Studies* (2022) 122.

[56] Wainwright and Mercer, 'Transnational Transgenes: The Political Ecology of Maize in Mexico', in R. Peet, P. Robbins, and M. Watts (eds), *Global Political Ecology* (2011) 412.

[57] Flachs, 'Redefining Success: The Political Ecology of Genetically Modified and Organic Cotton as Solutions to Agrarian Crisis', 23 *Journal of Political Ecology* (2016) 49, at 50.

[58] Wainwright and Mercer (n. 56).

[59] Art. 3 of Directive 2001/18/EC, OJ 2001 L 106/1.

view, national lawmakers could cover the exempted organisms by stricter rules on their territories subject to the general free movement principles.[60]

However, the Court of Justice emphasized that the case concerned an exception from the GMO regulatory framework, so the scope of the exception must be interpreted restrictively and in line with the precautionary principle. Crucially, the key interpretive argument for the Court was of an 'empirical' rather than a purely 'legal' nature. The Court openly deferred to the empirical assessment of the referring court, according to which, first, the risks linked to the use of the new mutagenesis techniques might prove to be similar to those which result from techniques in which foreign genes are introduced into an organism (known as 'transgenesis') and, second, thanks to the new techniques it is possible to produce genetically modified organisms at an unprecedented rate and in much larger quantities.[61] Based on this empirical assessment, subsequently contested,[62] the Court decided that the regulatory exemption for mutagenesis did not cover the novel techniques.

The Member States participating in these proceedings had highly divergent views on the empirical question of risk.[63] Moreover, the judgment stirred up a heated debate, which was not surprising given the existing politico-scientific controversies regarding how genetically modified organisms could affect the natural environment. While the judgment of the Court seemed to strictly follow the precautionary principle, some criticized the Court for ignoring science and hindering scientific progress.[64]

Crucially, given the heated controversy, the Court deferred to the empirical assessment of the national court, invoking the formal division of jurisdiction within the preliminary reference procedure.[65] This formal argument offered the Court a strategy to fulfil its legal mandate while eschewing the need to authoritatively solve the underlying politico-scientific dispute. A degree of legal

[60] Opinion of AG Bobek in Case C-528/16, *Confédération paysanne* (EU:C:2018:20).

[61] Case C-528/16, *Confédération paysanne* (EU:C:2018:583), para. 48.

[62] Commission, 'Statement by the Group of Chief Scientific Advisors: A Scientific Perspective on the Regulatory Status of Products Derived from Gene Editing and the Implications for the GMO Directive' (2018), https://op.europa.eu/en/publication-detail/-/publication/a9100d3c-4930-11e9-a8ed-01aa75ed71a1/language-en (last visited 22 December 2023).

[63] Opinion of AG Bobek in Case C-528/16, *Confédération paysanne* (EU:C:2018:20), paras 69–78.

[64] E.g. Purnhagen was concerned that if novel genomic techniques 'were subject to the scrutiny of GMO legislation, the high approval costs carry the danger that business and research in NPBTs will forego the EU market, with the result that this very promising technology is developed and applied elsewhere'. Purnhagen, 'How to Manage the Union's Diversity: The Regulation of New Plant Breeding Technologies in *Confédération paysanne and Others*', 56 *Common Market Law Review* (2019) 1379, at 1380; Urnov, Ronald, and Carroll, 'A Call for Science-Based Review of the European Court's Decision on Gene-Edited Crops', 26 *Nature* (2018) 800; Callaway, 'EU Law Deals Blow to CRISPR Crops', 560 *Nature* (2018) 16.

[65] Case C-528/16, *Confédération paysanne* (EU:C:2018:583), para. 48.

stability was achieved without necessarily increasing certainty regarding the controversial empirical assessment of risks entailed by genetic modification.

However, the question is how stable a legal interpretation dissociated from the underlying scientific contention may turn out to be. The Commission has recently proposed to somewhat liberalize the regulatory framework for targeted mutagenesis and other novel techniques, considering that the existing scientific evidence demonstrates their safety.[66] In this context, one could argue that the Court's attempt to engage with the underlying scientific issue to a limited extent only allowed it to achieve relative legal stability. However, had it engaged further and autonomously performed its own 'risk assessment' of the novel techniques, it might have restricted the freedom of EU lawmakers to perform their assessment. Others might argue that endorsing the Advocate General's strategy to focus on the legislative intent and the internal logic of legislation[67] while considering empirical developments only marginally[68] would leave even more freedom to the EU and national lawmakers. However, the Court might have been concerned that this approach would have undermined the precautionary principle by exempting too many types of genetically modified plants from regulatory duties, with possible reactions by national lawmakers being too uncertain.

Be that as it may, from the Court's internal perspective on the matter, the middle-ground solution of engaging with the scientific question, albeit only indirectly through a reference to the national court's empirical assessment, might have seemed cautious and workable. One could arguably defend that solution as providing as much certainty as possible in these circumstances, given the Court's limited epistemic capacity to engage with politically-laden scientific controversies, even though that solution might have produced relative legal stability only.[69]

The Court may also be called on to enhance legal stability despite an almost complete absence of empirical data that would allow it to anticipate

[66] Proposal for a Regulation of the European Parliament and of the Council on plants obtained by certain new genomic techniques and their food and feed, 2023/0226 (COD). The Commission justified its proposal by saying, among other things, that 'the European Food Safety Authority … concluded that, as regards risks for human and animal health and the environment, there are no specific hazards linked to targeted mutagenesis or cisgenesis'. A different scientific opinion was published by the German Federal Agency for Nature Conservation, 'New developments and regulatory issues in plant genetic engineering' (2021), https://www.bfn.de/sites/default/files/2021-10/Viewpoint-plant-genetic-engeneering_1.pdf (last visited 20 December 2023).

[67] Opinion of AG Bobek in Case C-528/16, *Confédération paysanne* (EU:C:2018:20), paras 90–107.

[68] Ibid. para. 149.

[69] For a different assessment, see Somsen, 'Scientists Edit Genes, Courts Edit Directives. Is the Court of Justice Fighting Uncertain Scientific Risks with Certain Constitutional Risks?', 9 *European Journal of Risk Regulation* (2019) 701.

the long-term effects of different interpretive options. An example of such a case is *Alianța pentru combaterea abuzurilor*. It concerned a wolf captured in Romania in a village without prior authorization granted by the competent national authority under the Habitats Directive to relocate a protected species outside human settlement. Those who captured the wolf were criminally charged. The national criminal court asked the Court of Justice whether the Directive applied in this case as it protected the relevant species within their 'natural range' and 'in the wild',[70] also using the concept of 'habitats of a species'.[71] The Court applied a literal and systematic interpretation to find that the Directive does not condition the protection offered to the relevant species depending on the geographical area covered by the protected sites or natural habitats.[72] Considering the normative goals of improving biodiversity and favourable conservation status, the Court ruled that the concept of a 'habitat of a species' (the 'environment defined by specific abiotic and biotic factors, in which the species lives at any stage of its biological cycle') 'is not a territory with fixed and immutable boundaries', even though the Directive mentioned the protection of the species 'in the wild'.[73]

Also in this case, the Court considered the empirical context, albeit again to a limited extent only. It confined itself to note that in many EU regions, wolves are forced to live in the immediate vicinity of humans and that their territories shrink because of developing infrastructure, unlawful logging, farming, and industrial activities. Therefore, according to the Court, it would not serve the purpose of the Directive to limit the protection afforded to the relevant species because of the expansion of human settlements and other activities.[74]

It may come as no surprise that the Court did not delve more into the empirical context, given the great politico-scientific uncertainty surrounding the protection of wolves in Europe. Engaging more into this context would probably not be helpful, as it would only expose the great uncertainty of long-term consequences of choosing a narrower or broader interpretation of the environmental notions at issue. In this case, the interpretation of the legal notion of 'habitat' carried important consequences for managing this species in human-dominated landscapes and for the wider human–wolf coexistence, both themes central to political ecology research. Far from being a wilderness area, the Southern Carpathian Mountains, where the event underpinning this

[70] Case C-88/19, *Alianța pentru combaterea abuzurilor* (EU:C:2020:458), para. 28.
[71] Ibid. paras 35–36.
[72] Ibid. paras 33–34.
[73] Ibid. paras 36–49.
[74] Ibid. para. 50.

case occurred in 2016, have been modified for centuries by human uses such as logging, grazing and transhumance, hunting, and game management.[75] Large carnivores, including the wolf (*Canis lupus lupus*), have always been present in the area and have adapted to land changes and different regimes of managing the mountains.[76] Recent development of infrastructure and intense forest extraction, coupled with the intensification of tourism and ecotourism in the area, posed new pressures on the wolf population, including habitat fragmentation, which in turn might have made wolf incursions into human settlements more frequent.[77]

The dispute is further complicated by the uncertain scientific knowledge about the ecology and population of large carnivores like wolves and bears, a reality which is particularly relevant to the Romanian context.[78] In 2016, the country's technocratic government imposed a hunting ban, which put an end to active management of the species through culling. The ban, still in place today, was supposed to last until robust scientific knowledge could inform a sound management plan.[79] The ban created conflicts not only between hunters (for whom hunting was a source of income) and conservation practitioners (largely in favour of the ban) but also between farmers and local and national authorities. The Court's attempt to give a decision in favour of wolf conservation had to navigate these complex socio-ecological and political entanglements.

However, the Court's decision has more profound implications for wolf management and conservation in the wider European context. It has been widely argued that assessing 'natural range' and, implicitly, what 'habitat' means becomes more challenging in the context of large carnivores' dispersal and ongoing expansion in Europe.[80] Wolves, among other protected species, have been very successful at establishing permanent populations in countries

[75] J. Linnell *et al.*, 'Biodiversity Assessment of the Fagaras Mountains, Romania' (2016), Norwegian Institute for Nature Research, https://brage.nina.no/nina-xmlui/handle/11250/2394029 (last visited 20 December 2023), 21–23. See also on the production of the 'wilderness' narrative in these region, Iordachescu, 'The Shifting Geopolitical Ecologies of Wild Nature Conservation in Romania', in E. Krasznai Kovacs (ed.), *Politics and the Environment in Eastern Europe* (2021) 185.

[76] Linell *et al.* (n. 75) 17.

[77] For a recent assessment of wolf population dynamics in this area, see Dyck *et al.*, 'Dracula's Menagerie: A Multispecies Occupancy Analysis of Lynx, Wildcat and Wolf in the Romanian Carpathians', 12 *Ecology and Evolution* (2022) e8921.

[78] For an overview of the state of knowledge, see European Parliament, 'Large carnivore management plans for protection: best practices in EU Member States', Report commissioned by PETI Committee (2018), https://www.europarl.europa.eu/RegData/etudes/STUD/2018/596844/IPOL_STU(2018)596844_EN.pdf (last visited 20 December 2023).

[79] On the need for robust data, see Popescu *et al.*, 'Assessing Biological Realism of Wildlife Population Estimates in Data-Poor Systems', 53 *Journal of Applied Ecology* (2016) 1248.

[80] Popescu *et al.*, 'Romanian Carnivores at a Crossroads', 364 *Science* (2019) 1041.

such as Germany, the Netherlands, and even Belgium, where they have been absent for more than a century. As most farmers in these countries are late in implementing measures to prevent attacks on livestock, conflicts have increased and even triggered high-level discussions about lowering the protection status for wolves.[81] Understanding how the species occupies new habitats calls for a scientific reassessment of how their ecological dispersal takes advantage of complex socio-economic transformations such as the decline of traditional land uses, land abandonment,[82] increase in protective measures, and an upsurge in rewilding initiatives. Hence, after acknowledging the limitations of existing scientific knowledge, the European Commission has recently launched a wide consultation to address the challenge posed by the species' return, inviting local communities, scientists, and other stakeholders to contribute up-to-date data on wolf populations and their impacts with the aim of updating current legislation or introducing measures for more flexible management of the species.[83]

This context shows that, when it comes to the Court's case concerning the capturing of a wolf in Romania, although the Court somewhat increased the level of legal certainty by endorsing the strict protection of wolves and other species wherever they occur, its decision will surely have consequences for the wider discussion on human–carnivores coexistence and conflict. In the context of uncertain scientific knowledge about species ecology and population dynamics, effective management and collaboration of actors involved in their management remains only an aspiration.[84]

B. Uncertain Implementation by National Courts

The stability of legal interpretations provided by the Court depends also on their implementation by national courts. Advocate General Bobek recently argued that, in the preliminary reference procedure, the Court should concern itself only with uniform 'interpretation', in line with the wording of Article 267 TFEU, accepting that the 'application' of uniformly interpreted EU law

[81] Foote, 'EU parliament votes to blow big, bad wolves' protection down', *Euractiv*, 25 November 2022, https://www.euractiv.com/section/agriculture-food/news/eu-parliament-votes-to-decrease-big-bad-wolves-protection-status/ (last visited 20 December 2023).

[82] Pettersson *et al.*, 'Who Must Adapt to Whom? Contested Discourses on Human–Wolf Coexistence and their Impact on Policy in Spain', 5 *People and Nature* (2023) 1989, at 1993.

[83] European Commission, 'Wolves in Europe: Commission urges local authorities to make full use of existing derogations and collects data for conservation status review' (4 September 2023), https://ec.europa.eu/commission/presscorner/detail/en/ip_23_4330 (last visited 20 December 2023).

[84] Iordachescu (n. 20).

may differ somewhat between the Member States. Although the difference between abstract 'interpretation' and concrete 'application' often hinges upon the purely formal framing of the legal problem, it is arguable that the Court should be concerned with sufficiently generalizable legal problems rather than the minutiae of specific cases.[85]

However, different standards of judicial review by national courts may affect the perception of certainty of formally uniform EU legal notions, including those employed in EU environmental law. In particular, to attain the environmental goals, the Court requires national authorities to base their decisions concerning actions interfering with the environment on 'best science' or 'rigorous data' to achieve a high level of empirical certainty and leave 'no reasonable doubt' that envisaged actions could adversely affect the environment.[86] When verifying these conditions, national courts may need to scrutinize complex and uncertain scientific evidence and reasoning advanced by specialist administrations. However, different national traditions shape how national courts engage with such empirical issues. Also, notions such as 'best' or 'rigorous science' are fairly abstract. Due to these jurisdictional limits and diverse traditions, it would be challenging for the Court to offer more guidance on exactly how national courts should assess scientific evidence in specific cases.[87] As this layer of decision-making is not easily susceptible to harmonization led by the Court of Justice, it may result in a degree of 'legal instability' of formally uniform EU law among the Member States.

Although judicial review courts are usually tasked with reviewing the 'legality' of administrative acts, including those concerning the natural environment (and only some with reviewing their 'merits'), the specific understanding of what 'legality' implies differs across jurisdictions. Some courts will concern themselves only with entirely unreasonable conclusions drawn from the evidence and manifest errors or assessments. Other courts may be vested with a formally unlimited duty of thoroughly examining all relevant facts.[88]

The recent cases of wolves in Finland and European bison in Poland show how national courts may approach the scrutiny of uncertain scientific

[85] Opinion of AG Bobek in Case C-561/19, *Consorzio Italian Management* (EU:C:2021:291), paras 147–149.

[86] Case C-304/05, *Italy v. Commission* (EU:C:2007:532), para. 59; Case C-674/17, *Luonnonsuojeluyhdistys Tapiola Pohjois-Savo—Kainuu ry* (EU:C:2019:851), paras 45 and 71.

[87] The Court of Justice accepts limited judicial review. See Case C-71/14, *East Sussex County Council* (EU:C:2015:656), paras 53 and 58; Joined Cases C-211/03, C-299/03 and C-316/03 to C-318/03, *HLH Warenvertrieb and Orthica* (EU:C:2005:370), para. 79.

[88] M. Eliantonio, E. Lees, and T. Paloniitty, 'Conclusions', in Eliantonio, Lees, and Paloniitty (n. 10) 349, 355–357.

appraisals.[89] These two cases do not account for the great variety of ways national courts engage with science but aim to illustrate possible approaches. Notably, in analysing the intensity of judicial review in science-intense cases, it is important to keep in mind that judicial statements of reasons may not allow the readers to easily deduce to what extent the courts expressed their own independent view on the probative value of the evidence and the soundness of complex and uncertain scientific reasoning or, instead, to what extent they deferred to the assessments of the expert administration, repeating the main points of these assessments and merely upholding them as 'reasonable' or 'consistent'.[90]

In the case of wolves in Finland,[91] the Finnish Supreme Administrative Court asked the Court of Justice whether it was possible, under the Habitats Directive, to grant derogations from the prohibition on the culling of wolves in view of combatting illegal poaching. A Finnish authority granted such derogations to mitigate wolves' depredations on livestock and to prevent adverse reactions from the local population. According to the Habitats Directive, granting such derogations was possible if there was no satisfactory alternative (such as deterrence or relocation), the derogations would not be 'detrimental to the maintenance of the populations of the species concerned at a favourable conservation status in their natural range', as well as if the culling was carried out 'under strictly supervised conditions, on a selective basis and to a limited extent'.[92]

According to the referring court, poaching (i.e. illegal killing) was a significant threat to wolf conservation in Finland. Indeed, the Court of Justice found that combating poaching can be a legitimate aim for granting derogations under the Habitats Directive. However, the question of whether selective culling (legal hunting) can actually limit poaching was surrounded by uncertainty. Hence, the national authorities were required to provide 'rigorous scientific data ... on the effects of legal culling for population management purposes on the conservation status of wolves', showing that selective culling 'is actually capable of reducing illegal hunting to such an extent that it would have a net positive effect on the conservation status of the wolf population'.[93] The

[89] Finland seems to provide an example of the model of the judicial review of administrative acts characterized by 'intense' review (see ibid.), whereas the Polish model is characterized by a deferential review on factual matters. Bar, 'Scientific Knowledge in Environmental Litigation before Polish Administrative Courts: A Problem of Compliance with EU Law?', 27 *European Energy and Environmental Law Review* (2018) 169.

[90] On the notion of 'concealed' judicial deference, see Krajewski (n. 42).

[91] Case C-674/17, *Luonnonsuojeluyhdistys Tapiola Pohjois-Savo—Kainuu ry* (EU:C:2019:851).

[92] Ibid. paras 28 and 35.

[93] Ibid. para. 45.

Court of Justice left this empirical question about the effectiveness of the contested measure to be determined by the national court. However, it provided its 'preliminary view', according to which there was 'no scientific evidence that the legal hunting of a protected species reduces poaching to an extent that it would have an overall positive effect on the conservation status of wolves'.[94] Moreover, the Court clarified that national authorities must verify—'taking account ... of the best relevant scientific and technical evidence'—that there is no alternative solution, that the planned measure will not adversely affect the favourable conservation status of the species, and whether the selected specimen of the species will be eliminated under strictly monitored conditions. Crucially, the Court referred to a wealth of empirical information provided by the Commission and other parties to express its doubts as to whether these conditions had indeed been satisfied in this case. The referring court subsequently found that the conditions were not satisfied.[95]

By referring to notions such as 'the best relevant scientific and technical evidence', and even by providing its preliminary view on empirical issues, the Court of Justice seems to expect national courts, most often administrative courts, to form an independent view on the probative value of evidence presented by expert administration in such cases to justify derogations from the strict protection. Arguably, the national courts cannot simply defer to the administration, given the great complexity and uncertainty of the matter. This is a challenging task for judicial bodies because, among other things, scientific knowledge and evidence concerning the conservation and management of protected species is rarely certain.

For example, in a recent report on the prosecution of wildlife crime in Europe produced by civil society, the authors show how the poor monitoring of endangered species populations on the continent puts the conservation of these species at risk by preventing effective international collaboration between enforcement authorities and experts.[96] The uncertain scientific knowledge about the ecology and demography of certain species could also result in the adoption of inconsistent legislation across Member States and hinder the tasks of supervisory and enforcement authorities. Another academic report

[94] Ibid. para. 46.

[95] For an overview of the follow-up case, see Epstein and Kantinkoski, 'Non-Governmental Enforcement of EU Environmental Law: A Stakeholder Action for Wolf Protection in Finland', 8 Frontiers in Ecology and Evolution (2020), https://www.frontiersin.org/articles/10.3389/fevo.2020.00101/full (last visited 20 December 2023).

[96] Engel, 'Uncovering the Invisible: Successes and Challenges for Wildlife Crime Prosecution in Europe' (2023), at 45, https://wwfeu.awsassets.panda.org/downloads/swipe_european_summary_report_july_2023.pdf (last visited 20 December 2023).

shows how incomplete or inaccurate data creates criminogenic opportunities that green-collar crime offenders can exploit across diverse sectors such as hunting tourism, aquaculture, and ecotourism.[97] Taken together, these reports point to the lack of robust empirical assessment of the status of many species as a structural problem that affects the conservation and effective management of wildlife in Europe, including through derogations from important pieces of environmental legislation.

As in other cases detailed in this chapter, wolves are a symbol in Finland of conflicting ways of valuing wildlife. Current research on human–wolf conflict and coexistence in the country points towards wider socio-economic controversies that have a direct impact on people's tolerance towards large carnivores.[98] Wolves' territories in Finland have been changing rapidly over the last decades, partly due to an increase in the number of reindeer (their natural prey), changes in land use, and transboundary natural dispersal from Russia.[99] Because they cause significant damage to farmers' property and their predation challenges the socio-cultural sustainability of reindeer husbandry,[100] they have become political populations;[101] that is they are central elements of political discussions about nature management, conservation, and agricultural development within the country. As noted by political ecologists, agricultural production (including livestock production) is in crisis and exposed to ever-growing global challenges, including climate change and extreme weather events,[102] which makes the wolf population's rapid expansion into agricultural landscapes an easy target for populist discourses.[103] Therefore, tolerance towards wolves touches upon complex societal issues. In the context of such uncertainty, it is understandable that the Court, in the above case, did not focus on the broader empirical issue of whether and to what extent culling could help combat poaching but demanded specific evidence to support the adoption of such measures, putting the burden of proof fully on the shoulders of competent public authorities.

[97] Duffy *et al.*, 'Examining Illegal Wildlife Trade in Europe. Final Report' (2023), https://beastlybusiness.org/2023/09/06/beastly-business-final-report/ (last visited 20 December 2023).

[98] Komi and Nygren, 'Bad Wolves? Political Ecology of Responsibility and More-Than-Human Perspectives in Human–Wildlife Interactions', 36 *Society & Natural Resources* (2023) 1238.

[99] Komi and Kröger, 'Predators in the Web of Life: World-Ecology of Historical Human–Wolf Interactions in Finland', 23 *Journal of Agrarian Change* (2023) 500, at 510.

[100] Rasmus *et al.*, 'Mission Impossible? Pursuing the Coexistence of Viable Predator Populations and Sustainable Reindeer Husbandry in Finland', 80 *Journal of Rural Studies* (2020) 135.

[101] Darimont *et al.*, 'Political Populations of Large Carnivores', 32 *Conservation Biology* (2018) 747.

[102] Komi and Kröger (n. 99).

[103] Komi and Nygren, 'Bad Wolves? Political Ecology of Responsibility and More-Than-Human Perspectives in Human–Wildlife Interactions', 36 *Society & Natural Resources* (2023) 1238.

Administrative courts in some Member States are expected to thoroughly engage with 'facts', and not only with 'law', so they may face fewer obstacles in fulfilling the task of thorough engagement with complex and uncertain empirical evidence. However, in some jurisdictions, the judicial review of administrative action is traditionally deferential on empirical matters in view of safeguarding the constitutional separation of powers between the administration and administrative courts.[104] For instance, Polish administrative courts cannot, in principle, hear new evidence in the courtroom. They only verify the consistency of the account of facts and evidence provided in the administrative case file. Therefore, they do not independently establish facts but only verify whether the way in which the administration has established the facts complies with the law.[105] This way of engaging with the facts of the case corresponds to the remedy that Polish administrative courts can grant. In principle, they do not change the merits of faulty administrative decisions but can only annul them, referring the case back to the competent administrative authorities. Traditionally, Polish administrative courts are careful not to impinge upon the discretionary powers of administrative authorities, which they recognize whenever the applicable law states that an administrative authority 'may' (rather than 'must') issue a specific administrative act.[106] Nonetheless, even in such a legal context, courts have ample opportunities to verify whether the administrative authorities have diligently established and assessed all the relevant empirical factors, depending, of course, on the arguments raised by the applicants.

Polish administrative courts have recently dealt with cases concerning European bison (*Bison bonasus*). These cases did not involve preliminary references to the Court of Justice as the legal disputes primarily concerned the determination and assessment of facts. One of the cases was brought by environmental organizations against a decision of a Polish authority allowing the culling of some individuals due to the increasing population of the species in Poland, the harm they caused to human settlements, and diseases spreading in these populations. The administrative authority considered it necessary to cull sick, injured or aggressive individuals. The authority also argued that

[104] Bar (n. 89).

[105] The Supreme Administrative Court of Poland, Case II FSK 72/06, https://orzeczenia.nsa.gov.pl/doc/EB09234487 (last visited 20 December 2023).

[106] M. Wojtuń, *Sądowa Kontrola Uznania Administracyjnego z Perspektywy Komparatystyki Prawniczej* [The Judicial Review of Administrative Discretion from the Perspective of Comparative Law] (2020).

the density of the species in a specific forest was excessive in relation to the carrying capacity of that specific habitat.[107]

However, the environmental organizations argued that there was no evidence that individuals matching the indicated criteria of being sick, injured, or aggressive existed in the forest in question. Moreover, they argued that an alternative solution existed, such as resettlement. They also expressed a more general view that the growth of the species' population was due to the fact that the management authorities fed the bison during the winter and, subsequently, intended to cull some individuals for commercial purposes.[108]

The court found the justification provided by the authority as sufficient regarding the absence of alternative solutions. It opined that leaving the sick individuals would only prolong their suffering and would risk spreading the diseases, while relocating aggressive individuals was not a viable option as the animals might return to their previous habitat. Also, the decision concerned only a small percentage of the overall population of bison, which continued to grow, so in the court's view, there was no risk to the favourable conservation status of these animals. Moreover, the decision set only a maximum rather than a minimum number of animals to be taken down and introduced monitoring conditions to be fulfilled in individual cases.

Readers of this ruling might wonder to what extent a court that does not hear independent experts in the courtroom might have been able to assess in a reliable way whether the conditions for granting derogations from strict protection have been fulfilled, including whether there were genuinely no alternative options, such as systemic changes in the management's practice of feeding the animals during the winter. Moreover, the organizations argued that no sick animals had actually been properly identified. The court noted an expert opinion of a national advisory council for environmental protection but did not seem to have scrutinized its merits in light of the EU standard of 'best scientific evidence'.

Undoubtedly, this case raises very complex and politically-laden scientific issues. The recovery of the European bison is considered an uncontested story of conservation success. The species, strictly protected in the EU, experienced almost a century of intense human management and care, which included

[107] Regional Administrative Court in Warsaw, Case IV SA/Wa 1654/20, available at https://orzeczenia.nsa.gov.pl/doc/60D50BA5CB (last visited 20 December 2023). See also a parallel case, Supreme Administrative Court, Case III OSK 7731/21, available at https://orzeczenia.nsa.gov.pl/doc/1BE2FBF6E1 (last visited 14 March 2024).

[108] 'Prawnicy walczą o żubry. "Nie dla ochrony przez zabijanie"' ['Lawyers fight for bison: "No" to protection through killing'], *OKO Press*, 21 March 2019, https://oko.press/prawnicy-walcza-o-zubry-nie-dla-ochrony-przez-zabijanie (last visited 20 December 2023).

both intervention and non-intervention, in the attempt to save it from extinction. For decades, Poland has been at the centre of recovery efforts, which included captive and selective breeding, supplementary feeding over wintertime, predator control, and the development of veterinary knowledge to increase the bison's chances of survival.[109] Although, over recent years, efforts to conserve the species have moved away from a controlling towards a hands-off approach, conservation practitioners, including game managers, are maintaining a delicate balance between intervention and non-intervention. Once reintroduced in the wild, the bison are expected to behave in a certain way, use their natural instincts, and contribute to creating healthier and more diverse ecosystems, such as by opening closed canopies and influencing forest regeneration.

Research on the actual unfolding of reintroduction programmes paints a messier picture. Often, the assumptions of conservation practitioners are contradicted by the bison's behaviour.[110] Bison often come close to villages and farms seeking food, feed on the fodder reserved for domestic cattle, roam outside assigned forestlands into the open fields, and are extremely prone to a range of diseases.[111] Their poor health may be a result of genetic inbreeding over decades of experimentation in an attempt to save the species from extinction[112] or it may be dependent on uncertain causes. One particular disease, *posthitis*, which affects 6 per cent of bison males, is still puzzling the scientific community despite years of study.[113]

The environmental organizations argued that, as the species is strictly protected under the Habitats Directive, culling should only be permitted after resettling or other options have been ruled out.[114] But resettling bison, also known as translocation, is a complicated and costly affair which involves teams of scientists, geneticists, conservation practitioners, and game managers. The process cannot happen ad hoc, as mandated by the urgency of the cull derogation, but in accordance with strict protocols in order to satisfy genetic diversity criteria, dynamics within the newly formed groups, and fitness to survive in

[109] De Bont, 'Extinct in the Wild. Finding a Place for the European Bison, 1919–1952', in J. Lachmund and R. De Bont (eds), *Spatializing the History of Ecology: Sites, Journeys, Mappings* (2017) 165.

[110] Ibid. 172.

[111] Vasile, 'The Vulnerable Bison: Practices and Meanings of Rewilding in the Romanian Carpathians', 16 *Conservation and Society* (2018) 217.

[112] Larska and Krzysiak, 'Infectious Disease Monitoring of European bison (*Bison bonasus*)', in M. Feretti (ed.), *Wildlife Population Monitoring* (2019) 147.

[113] Olenski *et al.*, 'Genome-Wide Association Study for Posthitis in the Free-Living Population of European Bison (*Bison bonasus*)', 10 *Biology Direct* (2015).

[114] ClientEarth, 'We have joined the fight to stop Polish bison cull' (2019), https://www.clientearth.org/latest/latest-updates/news/we-have-joined-the-fight-to-stop-polish-bison-cull/ (last visited 20 December 2023).

the new habitat, which can sometimes be very different to the one from which the individuals were translocated.

Although the recovery of European bison throughout Europe is considered a successful conservation story for now, there are important uncertainties about the species' ecology and interactions within human-dominated landscapes. Most programmes that aim at reintroducing the species involve experimental phases,[115] including experiments with purifying their genetics, which makes the survival of the species as such marred by uncertainties. In such a context, adjudication did not seem capable of significantly improving certainty around these complex and uncertain empirical issues. Thus, the case has revealed a risk to the stability of EU legal notions such as 'rigorous science' and 'best scientific evidence' as instrumental to the fulfilment of EU environmental law objectives.[116]

4. Certainty as Truth and Objectivity

A. Navigating Around Uncertain Science

The EU Courts are frequently called on to independently assess whether legislative, regulatory, or administrative action by EU or national public authorities has been underpinned by accurate empirical assessments and whether that action has been objectively adequate to fulfil legitimate goals. Such issues may arise especially in infringement proceedings concerning EU environmental law or in annulment proceedings concerning EU legal acts addressing uncertain risks to the environment and public health.

The infringement proceedings are based on an adversarial legal framework, in which it is for the Commission to prove the existence of the alleged infringement, without relying on 'presumptions or schematic causalities',[117] and to provide the Court with the information necessary for it to determine whether the infringement has occurred.[118] Sometimes, the Court can rule in

[115] Tanasescu, 'Restorative Ecological Practice: The Case of the European Bison in the Southern Carpathian Mountains, Romania', 105 *Geoforum* (2019) 99.

[116] See also, however, a case concerning bison in which the Polish administrative courts seem to have engaged with the evidence and reasoning of the environmental authority more thoroughly. Judgment of the Supreme Administrative Court, Case III OSK 7041/21, available at https://orzeczenia.nsa.gov.pl/doc/5E622CCC6C (last visited 14 March 2024).

[117] Case C-443/18, *Commission v. Italy* (EU:C:2019:676), para. 80. See also Case C-153/16, *Commission v. Slovenia* (EU:C:2017:275), paras 50–55, where the Court made it clear that arguments 'based on mere probability' could not be accepted.

[118] Case C-504/14, *Commission v. Greece* (EU:C:2016:847), para. 111.

such cases by pointing out weaknesses in evidence provided by one of the parties.[119] The Court's task of solving scientific problems may be facilitated if the EU legislation provides indications as to the required evidence.[120] But, crucially, the Commission is relatively limited in its capacity to gather evidence of non-compliance with EU environmental law. The Commission does not conduct independent investigations and mostly relies on the data provided by the Member States themselves.[121] The Court of Justice is not oblivious to this institutional context. It considers this context while interpreting the required burden and threshold of proof.[122] For instance, where the Commission has adduced 'sufficient evidence to establish that the national provisions transposing a directive are not applied correctly in practice in the territory of the defendant Member State, it is for the latter to challenge in substance and in detail the information produced, and the inferences drawn'.[123]

Apart from moderating the burden and required threshold of proof, the EU Courts may also reframe the dispute in a way that would render uncertain scientific issues not central to its resolution.[124] For instance, in a case in 2019, the Court assessed Italy's alleged infringement of EU law through its failure to remove plants infected by *Xylella fastidiosa*, a harmful bacteria causing the death of a large number of plants, and to monitor and prevent it spreading. The Commission alleged, among other things, that relevant inspections of plants were carried out at inappropriate times of the year when the probability of detecting the bacterium was low. Italy relied on scientific information, counter-arguing that the chosen time was in fact still appropriate. The CJEU eschewed direct engagement with the scientific controversy by focusing on the legal duty of Italy to take effective measures to prevent the spread of the disease. Even if Italy had been right that the bacteria could be detected throughout the year, it would have been too late for the competent authorities to take any effective measures due to the late timing of the monitoring.[125]

Depending on the case, the strategy of avoiding purely scientific disagreements may be quite useful in helping the judges focus on issues with regard to which they can genuinely enhance the level of certainty, such as with regard to the legal duty to take effective action, as in the previous example. But it also

[119] Case C-142/16, *Commission v. Germany* (EU:C:2017:301), paras 29–45.

[120] Case C-636/18, *Commission v. France* (EU:C:2019:900), paras 44–45.

[121] Case 97/17, *Commission v. Bulgaria* (EU:C:2018:285), para. 70; Case C-668/19, *Commission v. Italy* (ECLI:EU:C:2021:815), para. 75.

[122] See Case C-559/19, *Commission v. Spain (Doñana II)* (EU:C:2021:512), paras 155 and 170–171.

[123] Case C-502/15, *Commission v. the United Kingdom* (EU:C:2017:334), para. 24.

[124] E.g. Case C-543/16, *Commission v. Germany* (EU:C:2018:481), paras 54–61.

[125] Case C-443/18, *Commission v. Italy* (EU:C:2019:676), paras 56–62.

risks leaving significant aspects of the disputes unaddressed, especially in cases in which the legality of the challenged activities of public authorities hinges upon an underlying empirical assessment.

The case of the Białowieża, a Polish primeval forest, provides an illustrative example. The forest was designated as a Site of Community Importance and a Special Area of Conservation under the Habitats Directive, and a special protection area under the Birds Directive[126] and, as such, part of the Natura 2000 network of protected areas. According to the Commission, the forest was 'one of the best-preserved natural forests in Europe, characterised by large quantities of dead wood and old trees, in particular trees a century old or more'.[127] In 2016, the Polish Minister for the Environment approved an appendix to the ten-year Forest Management Plan (2012–2021) increasing the harvesting volume of the main forest products, resulting from pruning prior to felling and felling and the envisaged area of afforestation and reforestation.[128] The Minister justified this decision with the need to mitigate serious damage caused by the spread of bark beetle (*Ips typographus*). The infestation called for an increase in salvage logging to remove colonized trees, ensuring the health and sustainability of ecosystems and natural habitats, as well as ensuring public safety since the accumulation of dying trees was interpreted as a public danger.[129] The accompanying environmental impact assessment stated that the measures proposed did not entail a significant negative impact for the environment and the integrity of the site.[130]

The legal issue concerned whether the 2016 appendix constituted a 'plan' or a 'project' not directly connected with or necessary to the management of the site but likely to have a significant adverse effect thereon, which the Polish authorities failed to ascertain prior to the adoption of the measure.[131] According to the Commission, the Polish authorities should have aimed at preserving the site's constitutive characteristics, such as the natural ecological processes, including bark beetle outbursts, the natural regeneration of trees, natural species selection uncontrolled by humans and natural ecological succession, the diversity of species and their age structure, the abundance of dead wood, etc.[132]

[126] Directive 2009/147/EC, OJ 2010 L 20/7.
[127] Case C-441/17, *Commission v. Poland (Białowieża Forest)* (EU:C:2018:255), para. 17.
[128] Ibid. para. 28.
[129] Ibid. paras 29–30.
[130] Ibid. para. 31.
[131] Art. 6(3) of the Habitats Directive required competent authorities to ensure that a plan or project not directly connected with or necessary to the management of the site concerned but likely to have a significant effect on it was authorized only to the extent that it would not adversely affect the integrity of that site.
[132] Case C-441/17, *Commission v. Poland (Białowieża Forest)* (EU:C:2018:255), para. 82.

In fact, removing dead and dying trees coincided with the potential threats listed in the management plan adopted in 2015, unlike the activity of the bark beetle.[133] The Commission argued that the 'outbreaks of the spruce bark beetle form part of the natural cycle of old forests that contain spruce trees' (*Picea abies*).[134]

The crux of scientific dispute lay in the assessment of active management practices sought by the Polish government. According to the government, 'the Commission failed to consider the fact that the integrity of that site has been shaped for centuries by human activities' (hunting, foraging, reforestation, industrial logging). In the government's view, it was the drastic reduction, under pressure from the Commission, conservationists, and UNESCO,[135] of logging in ageing forest stands that led to their die-back due to the resulting spread of the spruce bark beetle. Accordingly, it was 'the interruption of the conservation measures which [threatened] the integrity of that site and the continuity of the habitats found there'. Active forest management as a measure to mitigate the impacts of bark beetle outbreaks was also opted for in other Member States.[136] Overall, the government argued that it was rather 'the absence of a response to the spruce bark beetle' that posed a 'high probability of serious and irreparable harm' for Białowieża.[137]

The scientific dispute was not only between two opposing types of management, that is, salvage logging as active management to tackle the bark beetle outbreaks versus inaction and increased conservation as a way to let the natural processes unfold without foresters' intervention. It was also interpreted as a contention over who held the legitimate knowledge to decide the future of this complex ecosystem. As aptly remarked by political ecology researchers, environmental knowledge-making is intimately linked to decision-making,[138] and in the case of Białowieża, the National Council on Nature Protection, which was in favour of active management, was composed of newly-appointed forestry specialists after the Minister of Environment had dismantled the previous board, which had been more in favour of conservation and a reduction

[133] Ibid. paras 83–84.
[134] Ibid. para. 85.
[135] E. Blavascunas, *Foresters, Borders and Bark Beetles. The Future of Europe's Last Primeval Forest* (2020) 163.
[136] Case C-441/17, *Commission v. Poland (Białowieża Forest)* (EU:C:2018:255), paras 98–99. Thorn *et al.*, 'Impact on Salvage Logging on Biodiversity: A Meta-Analysis', 55 Journal of Applied Ecology (2018) 279.
[137] Case C-441/17, *Commission v. Poland (Białowieża Forest)* (EU:C:2018:255), paras 97–99, 105. For a general discussion about interventions to address bark beetle infestations, see Jonasova and Prach, 'The Influence of Bark Beetle Outbreak vs. Salvage Logging on Ground Layer Vegetation in Central European Mountain Spruce Forests', 141 Biological Conservation (2008) 1525.
[138] Turnhout, 'The Politics of Environmental Knowledge', 16 *Conservation and Society* (2018) 363.

in logging.[139] As demonstrated by Blavascunas, an anthropologist who has done over two decades of research in Białowieża, ecology and politics have become integral parts of the forest.[140] It was precisely the increase in the allowed logging quota in the old-growth forest stands that the Commission challenged. Supporting the Commission's actions, civil society rapidly mobilized against the government's plans through demonstrations across Europe, setting up camps in the forest and organizing blockades. Conservationists and forest scientists around the world sympathized with the social movement and took a stance by bringing their own scientific expertise into the debate, which doubled the efforts of citizen scientists collecting data on the ground.[141]

The spruce bark beetle is native to the Białowieża forest and has shaped the ecology of the site for millennia (like many other species), often by producing impressive amounts of dead spruce, such as during outbreaks in 1995, 2003, 2008, and 2012.[142] However, these outbreaks have recently become more violent and unpredictable, which deepens the uncertainty about appropriate management interventions. Ecologists and scholars across Europe have demonstrated that bark beetle outbreaks are getting more severe as the climate regimes spin out of control, which translates in the case of Poland to hotter and drier weather that weakens the natural defence of spruce stands.[143] Uncertainty related to managing these outbreaks is further complicated in the case of the Białowieża forest as significant areas under the administration of the State Forests (Lasy Państwowe) have been planted with spruce monocultures, a species that is highly productive from an economic point of view, but increasingly susceptible to climate-induced disturbances.[144] One of the natural predators of this insect is the three-toed woodpecker (*Picoides tridactylus*), an endangered species that needs old-growth forest as a nesting habitat, which excludes the type of active management such as the one adopted by the Polish government. In other regions of Europe, similar processes are decimating plantation forests. There is no scientific consensus about how the bark beetle outbreaks should be addressed, which in turn has complex political implications for the

[139] Blavascunas (n. 135) 174.

[140] Ibid. 162.

[141] Blavascunas and Konczal, 'Bark Beetles and Ultra-Right Nationalist Outbreaks: Białowieża, Poland', in S. Brian and V. Pál (eds), *Environmentalism under Authoritarian Regimes: Myth, Propaganda, Reality* (2018) 96.

[142] Blavascunas (n. 135) 161.

[143] Fahse and Heurich, 'Simulation and Analysis of Outbreaks of Bark Beetle Infestations and their Management at Stand Level', 222 *Ecology Modeling* (2011) 1833.

[144] See Grodzki, 'Mass Outbreak of Spruce Bark Beetle *Ips typographus* in the Context of Białowieża Forest', 77 *Forest Research Papers* (2016) 324.

development of the forestry economy and available scenarios for tourism and conservation.[145]

The Court of Justice was put at the centre of this heated politico-scientific controversy, the crux of which it eschewed in view of, arguably, delivering the kind of certainty that a court in such a situation can deliver. It seems to have focused primarily on the consistency of arguments and successive actions by the Polish authorities to assess compliance with the relevant decision-making procedure and rules regarding the burden and threshold of proof.

The Court classified the 2016 appendix increasing the volume of harvestable timber as not connected with conservation objectives as 'it does not lay down in the slightest the conservation objectives and measures relating to that site'. The competent Polish authority had set out the conservation objectives slightly earlier, in the 2015 management plan, which had stipulated 'that the removal of spruces colonized by the spruce bark beetle must be regarded as a potential threat' to habitats.[146] Moreover, the Court focused on the rules for plans or projects likely to have an impact on a site, but not necessarily connected to its management. It recalled its previous case law requiring a very high threshold of proof, removing 'all reasonable scientific doubt as to the effects of the proposed works on the protected site concerned'.[147] The Court held that, in fact, the Polish government did not dispute that it had been required to undertake an impact assessment of the envisaged active management forest operations. Instead, this government contended that it had complied with that duty by carrying out an impact assessment in 2015.[148] However, the Court pointed out several issues with that impact assessment, such as outdated information,[149] noticeable gaps or inconsistencies,[150] and actions by the Polish authorities following the adoption of the 2016 appendix, which suggested that the impact assessment process was continued and relevant data was still collected.[151] Moreover, the Court noted that the Commission was not obliged 'to prove a causal relationship between the active forest management operations at issue and the adverse effect on the integrity of those habitats and species', as establishing the probability or risk was enough in light of the precautionary principle.[152]

[145] S. Petrova, *Communities in Transition. Protected Nature and Local People in Eastern and Central Europe* (2013), at 128.
[146] Case C-441/17, *Commission v. Poland (Białowieża Forest)* (EU:C:2018:255), paras 123–126.
[147] Ibid. paras 113–114.
[148] Ibid. para. 131.
[149] Ibid. paras 136–138.
[150] Ibid. paras 140–144.
[151] Ibid. paras 145–150.
[152] Ibid. para. 158.

Importantly, the Court recognized that active management measures in view of stopping the spread of a 'harmful organism' within a Natura 2000 site can be legitimate.[153] It also acknowledged scientific uncertainty ('controversy') regarding the most appropriate methods to stop the spread of the spruce bark beetle, which related, in particular, to the 'very desirability of combating its spread'. However, it concluded that, because of the uncertainty, the Polish authorities could not adopt the 2016 appendix as reasonable doubts about the risks entailed by active management of the site at issue still remained. Moreover, the Court found that the measures undertaken by the Polish authorities were disproportionate as they were not targeted only at spruce colonized by the bark beetle.[154]

Overall, the Court solved this aspect of the case[155] based on procedural rules, those concerning the burden and threshold of proof, and an analysis of inconsistencies in the acts, actions, and arguments of the Polish government.[156] The politico-scientific controversies about the extent to which the Białowieża forest had or had not been shaped by humans for centuries and whether active management measures were justified in the fight against the bark beetle were somewhat put aside. On the one hand, it could be argued that avoiding a scientific controversy of such a degree safeguarded the Court's contribution to the legitimacy of the system. It allowed the Court to offer certainty regarding non-compliance with procedural and burden-of-proof rules rather than the substance of the underlying empirical assessment that was extremely contentious. On the other hand, one could be concerned about the future readiness of the Commission to bring similar actions for infringement of EU environmental law involving the need to assess highly uncertain and contentious empirical questions, where establishing non-compliance with clear formal rules may not be sufficient to win the case.

[153] Ibid. para. 171.

[154] Ibid. paras 160–192, in particular, paras 171 and 179. It should be added that despite the ongoing proceedings and the massive social mobilization against their plans, the foresters had logged the entire quota projected for 2021 by 2018, which meant over 140,000 trees of which about one-third were in the old-growth forest stands. Blavascunas (n. 135) 164.

[155] Moreover, the Court found that Poland had failed to comply with other provisions of the Habitats Directive and the Birds Directive. See Case C-441/17, *Commission v. Poland (Białowieża Forest)* (EU:C:2018:255), paras 194 ff.

[156] The apparent weaknesses of the parties' submissions may generally offer a way out of scientific conundrums. See e.g. Case C-526/16, *Commission v. Poland* (EU:C:2018:356), paras 69–71 (Poland made general statements about its geological structure while admitting that a case-by-case analysis was necessary); Case C-502/15, *Commission v. United Kingdom* (EU:C:2017:334), para. 44 (the UK claimed that its waste-water collecting systems already complied with the requirement of 'best technical knowledge' while, at the same time, embarking upon a large programme of works in that regard); Case C-336/16, *Commission v. Poland* (EU:C:2018:94), paras 93–104 (where the Court assessed the adequacy of air quality plans through the prism of the excessive time necessary to achieve the goals).

At the same time, some argue that when courts delve too much into the uncertain scientific assessments underpinning EU action, they may undermine the precautionary principle. For instance, in the *Doñana* case, the Court examined whether an upgrade of a country road through the Doñana National Park in Spain without taking appropriate protective measures had seriously altered the ecological characteristics of that protected site, essential for the Iberian lynx (*Lynx pardinus*). The Court meticulously verified somewhat conflicting empirical evidence concerning, for instance, the likelihood of animals being struck by vehicles travelling at high speed and the effectiveness of wildlife crossing the road, as measures intended to protect the Iberian lynx population from further habitat fragmentation. The Court noted that a few of these animals had recently been born in captivity, which 'represents a step forward in the preservation of current genetic variability'. The Court also pointed out that few killings of these animals by vehicles had, in fact, been reported. Ultimately, it found the Commission's evidence insufficient to prove that the implementation of the project for upgrading the country road placed the Iberian lynx in great danger.[157]

Some criticized this relatively thorough approach to the analysis of empirical evidence as insufficiently considering the precautionary principle faced with irreducible uncertainty.[158] Notably, the Court itself admitted that 'certain elements in the case file appear to indicate that the overall situation of the Doñana site might not be satisfactory in the light of the requirements relating to conservation of the Iberian lynx'.[159] But even if the road development alone did not seem to place the species in great danger, new changes in the land use associated with the development of infrastructure in the area could seal the fate of the species. Recent research has pointed to an even more grim picture for the Iberian lynx in Doñana—showing that the species' future indeed hangs by a thread. Increasing gas extraction and the expansion of illegal farms that have exhausted the freshwater reserves of the area represent serious threats to the survival of Europe's most endangered cat.[160]

[157] Case C-308/08, *Commission v. Spain* (EU:C:2010:281).
[158] García-Ureta (n. 51) 31, 41–42.
[159] Case C-308/08, *Commission v. Spain* (EU:C:2010:281), para. 52.
[160] Camacho *et al.*, 'Groundwater Extraction Poses Extreme Threat to Doñana World Heritage Site', 6 *Nature Ecology and Evolution* (2022) 654.

B. Between Procedural and Substantive Review

The Article 263(4) TFEU action for annulment is another procedure in which scientific evidence and specialist reasoning may be put directly before the EU Courts, in particular the General Court, which examines direct actions brought by private parties in the first instance. This legal avenue serves predominantly to review the 'legality' of administrative acts adopted by the EU institutions and bodies. However, the notion of EU 'legality' currently encompasses elaborate standards operating in the interstice between procedure and substance, the so-called 'duty of care'. This notion results from the pursuit of more 'intense' judicial review at the EU level in response to the expectations of litigants, scholars, and national courts.[161] As regards complex and uncertain empirical issues, according to the standard formula, the EU Courts cannot substitute their own assessment for that of the expert EU administration. However, EU judicial review can be concerned with whether all the relevant factors have been examined carefully and impartially, whether the evidence substantiates the conclusions drawn from it, whether there has been a manifest error of assessment, and whether the procedural rules have been complied with (process-oriented review).[162] Nonetheless, the procedure is predominantly adversarial so it is the applicant who should advance the relevant arguments and adduce evidence to enable judicial review.[163] Therefore, the intensity of judicial review is, in practice, relative to the comprehensiveness, clarity, and persuasiveness of the material provided by the applicant.[164]

Complex and uncertain assessments are relatively often put on the EU judges' docket. In practice, when it comes to the judicial review of the scientific reasoning of expert committees and bodies, the EU Courts often explicitly limit themselves to verifying the internal consistency of scientific reasoning.[165] They analyse whether the scientific committees' opinions are comprehensive,

[161] Mendes, 'Discretion, Care and Public Interest in the EU Administration: Probing the Limits of Law', 53 *Common Market Law Review* (2016) 419, 430. See also, Hofmann, 'Between Discretion and Proportionality: The Duty of Care in EU Judicial Review', *University of Luxembourg Law Working Paper* (2020) 9.

[162] Case 269/90, *Technische Universität München* (EU:C:1991:438); Case T-257/07, *France v. Commission* (EU:T:2011:444), paras 85–87; Case T-204/11, *Spain v. Commission* (EU:T:2015:91), paras 32–33 and the earlier case law cited.

[163] See in general, Case C-122/16 P, *British Airways v. Commission* (EU:C:2017:861), paras 86–90.

[164] The EU Courts may identify a manifest error of assessment if 'the evidence adduced by the applicant [is] sufficient to make the factual assessments used in that measure implausible'. See e.g. Case T-584/13, *BASF v. Commission* (EU:T:2018:279), para. 94. See also Joined Cases T-337/18 and T-347/18, *Laboratoire Pareva & Biotech 3D v. Commission* (EU:T:2021:594), paras 130–131.

[165] Case T-189/13, *PP Nature-Balance Lizenz v. Commission* (EU:T:2014:1056), para. 52; Case T-611/18, *Pharmaceutical Works Polpharma v. Commission* (EU:C:2021:241), para. 169.

consistent, and intelligible[166] and whether the background documentation contains a prima facie plausible response to the applicant's arguments.[167] They may rely upon the agency's general scientific guidance.[168] They often invoke the burden of proof and persuasion resting on the applicant to highlight that the applicant's arguments, or merely general assertions, have not managed to convince them of a substantive error.[169] In many cases, the judges invoke a great deal of information in the administrative case file, often uncontested by the applicant, to counter the applicant's allegations.[170] In recent cases in which environmental organizations contested the conclusions drawn by the Commission and the European Food Safety Authority regarding the safety of genetically modified plants, the EU Courts attributed a strong presumption of correctness of complex and uncertain assessments made by the EU expert administration. The organizations could rebut this presumption only by adducing evidence that this administration had omitted.[171]

Overall, it is uncertain to what extent the EU judges express their own opinion about the reliability and probative value of the evidence and the soundness of specialist reasoning, and to what extent, instead, they verify the logical consistency and intelligibility of complex and uncertain assessments, which may imply deference to the expert administration.[172] Some favour this limited judicial review of 'consistency' of scientific opinions as a 'hybrid' concept allowing the judges to meaningfully scrutinize the outer layers of complex and uncertain empirical assessments without second-guessing their deeper substance.[173] However, internal consistency and the prima facie plausibility of such opinions is not a warrant for their correctness. Generalist adjudicators

[166] Case T-115/15, *Deza v. Commission* (EU:T:2017:329), para. 161; Case T-189/13, *PP Nature-Balance Lizenz v. Commission* (EU:T:2014:1056), paras 52 ff; Case T-400/17, *Deza v. Commission* (EU:T:2018:712), paras 46–54 and 57; Case T-672/14, *Dr August Wolff v. Commission* (EU:T:2016:623), paras 143–163; Case T-556/20, *D&A Pharma v. Commission* (EU:T:2022:111), paras 188–236; Case T-303/16, *Mylan IRE Healthcare v. Commission* (EU:T:2022:25), paras 135–141.

[167] Case T-539/10, *Acino v. Commission* (EU:T:2013:110), paras 95–98 and 101–103.

[168] Case T-177/19, *Exxonmobil Petroleum & Chemical v. ECHA* (EU:T:2021:336), paras 127 ff.

[169] Case T-115/15, *Deza v. Commission* (EU:T:2017:329), paras 198–199; Case T-472/19, *BASF v. Commission* (EU:T:2020:432), paras 77–79; Case T-719/17, *FMC Corporation v. Commission* (EU:T:2021:143), paras 165–170; Case T-303/16, *Myre IRE Healthcare v. Commission* (EU:T:2022:25), paras 61–63.

[170] Case T-783/17, *GE Healthcare v. Commission* (EU:T:2019:624), paras 66 ff; Case T-115/15, *Deza v. Commission* (EU:T:2017:329), paras 193 ff; Case T-672/14, *Dr August Wolff v. Commission* (EU:T:2016:623), paras 143–163; Case T-629/20, *Delifruit v. Commission* (EU:T:2022:448), paras 45–48.

[171] Case T-177/13, *TestBioTech v. Commission* (EU:T:2016:736). See Leonelli, 'GMO authorisations and the Aarhus Regulation: Paving the Way for Precautionary GMO Governance', 26 *Maastricht Journal of Comparative and European Law* (2019) 505.

[172] Krajewski (n. 42).

[173] Sulyok (n. 9) 352–353.

may not be able to conceive of alternative methodologies and substantive counterarguments or they may not be aware of previous studies and critiques, to independently assess the degree of reliability of complex and uncertain scientific assessments. Overall, a scientific opinion appearing internally consistent and prima facie plausible to a non-specialist may ultimately turn out to be biased, incomplete, tendentious, or even outright incorrect to a specialist who possesses relevant background knowledge.[174] Notably, the appellants before the Court of Justice allege increasingly often that the standard of review by the General Court has been insufficient. They allege that the General Court has imposed on the applicants an impossible burden of proof in demonstrating 'manifest' errors in the EU administration's specialist reasoning rather than expressing its own view on the soundness of that reasoning.[175]

Nonetheless, there are cases in which the General Court seems to have been confident enough to express its own view on what counts as good or better evidence and correct reasoning, even if this reasoning involved a modicum of specialist knowledge. Perhaps, those issues were characterized by a somewhat lower level of complexity and uncertainty so they were epistemically 'easier'. For instance, the General Court seems to have expressed an independent view on the value of monitoring data regarding the effects of pesticides on bees, noting why this data did not indicate causality.[176] Also, the General Court seems to have considered the difference between the value of studies using randomized, placebo-controlled and double-blind pharmaceutical trials and those not complying with these standards.[177]

Moreover, there are cases in which the EU Courts venture to scrutinize, based on the arguments presented by the applicants, whether the EU administration has properly considered 'all relevant factors'. This review technique may seem 'procedural' in nature and, as such, not entailing the risk of the Court second-guessing substantive assessments of the administration. But it has been argued that the review of all relevant factors may bring the EU Courts quite close to expressing their own view on the contentious empirical issues.[178] After all, that a factor is 'relevant' in an assessment means that it can change its

[174] See Haack (n. 1) 236, on why exactly it is difficult for non-specialists to assess the evidence and reasoning of specialists. Haack uses an analogy of a crossword puzzle to explain how we form justified beliefs. To solve crossword puzzles, not only do we need clues (experience or information coming from the outside) but we also need to check how well new entries fit existing entries (propositions we already hold to be true or our background knowledge).

[175] E.g. Case C-82/17 P, *TestBioTech v. Commission* (EU:C:2019:719), para. 62.

[176] Case T-584/13, *BASF Agro v. Commission* (EU:T:2018:279), paras 130–136.

[177] Case T-472/19, *BASF v. Commission* (EU:T:2020:432), paras 66–70.

[178] Mendes, 'Law and Discretion in Monetary Policy and in the Banking Union: Complexity Between High Politics and Administration', 60 *Common Market Law Review* (2023) 1579.

conclusion.[179] Therefore, it does not seem possible to disassociate a verification of 'all relevant factors' from the assessment of the merits. In recent cases concerning potential risks posed by chemical substances to the environment and public health, the EU Courts found 'manifest errors', considering that the EU administration had disregarded relevant factors in the legal framework of the risk regulation of chemical substances. These factors were the low solubility of a potentially aqua-toxic substance[180] and the agglomeration of the particles of another substance influencing its density and impact on laboratory animals.[181] Taking these factors into account could have resulted in a lower assessment of the risk of the substances to the benefit of the chemical companies that had requested judicial review. Readers of these rulings could wonder whether the EU bodies had, indeed, completely 'overlooked' these factors or, rather, decided to consider them not decisive, thereby making some precautionary although uncertain assumptions without, perhaps, adequately justifying them. Importantly, the EU Courts examined these cases under the duty of care rather than only the duty to state reasons, which suggests that the EU administration was subsequently required to include these factors in its risk assessment, which might, however, affect the assessment's overall result.

On the one hand, a limited judicial review, focused only on the 'consistency' of scientific assessments, may result in tolerating the risk of insufficiently evidence-based measures, either overly or insufficiently restrictive. On the other hand, thorough judicial review—even if formally limited to the verification of 'all relevant factors'—may inadvertently restrict the legitimate technical discretion of expert administrators or even result in epistemic trespassing by courts. Therefore, in the reality of contemporary EU litigation, it is not easy for the EU Couts to navigate between procedural and substantive review to ensure an adequate empirical basis for EU regulatory action. In this context, judicial strategies aimed at avoiding direct engagement with science may be considered a measure to avoid overstepping the appropriate, and indeed possible, judicial role.

[179] S. Haack, *Evidence Matters: Science, Proof and Truth in the Law* (2013), 61: 'a piece of evidence is relevant to a conclusion if it affects the degree of supportiveness of the evidence overall; i.e. if adding it either contributes to or detracts from the explanatory integration of evidence-plus-conclusion . . .'.

[180] Case T-689/13, *Bilbaina v. Commission* (EU:T:2015:767) and Case C-691/15 P, *Bilbaina v. Commission* (EU:C:2017:882). See also Leonelli, 'The Fine Line Between Procedural and Substantive Review in Cases Involving Complex Technical-Scientific Evaluations: *Bilbaína*', 55 *Common Market Law Review* (2018) 1217.

[181] See Joined Cases T-279/20, T-288/20 and T-283/20, *CWS Powder Coatings v. Commission* (EU:T:2022:725).

C. The Added Value of Administrative Review

This is also why partly specialized adjudication has appeared at the EU level, as mentioned, to provide for more thorough administrative review of complex and uncertain assessments. BoAs are functionally independent adjudicatory units set up in certain EU agencies vested with direct decision-making powers vis-à-vis private parties. An appeal to the BoA is mandatory before bringing a case to the General Court, as the BoA formally expresses the final position of the agency. The legal and procedural frameworks of specific BoAs differ from each other to some extent. In particular, some boards are permanent structures, whereas others adjudicate on an ad hoc basis. Some boards can only annul an unlawful agency act, whereas others can also modify it.[182] The common features are the legally enshrined independence of its members from the rest of the agency, the duty of impartiality,[183] the accessibility of appellate proceedings to the addressees of contested decisions and third parties 'directly and individually concerned',[184] and the predominantly adversarial character of the appellate proceedings resembling the procedural rules of the General Court in the annulment avenue.[185]

At least two approaches could be adopted in analysing the BoAs. According to the top-down approach, the nature of the boards of appeal can be explained by means of concepts derived from national laws, such as 'judicial' and 'administrative review' or the review of 'legality' or 'merits' of the impugned acts. According to this approach, such concepts have a more or less established meaning and can be transplanted to the EU legal order.[186] In this view, the BoAs are clearly not 'judicial' bodies as they are not part of the EU judicature, so it may be inappropriate to include them in the analysis of a judicial engagement with science.

However, according to an alternative approach, the concepts of 'judicial' and 'administrative' are not necessarily 'stabilized' within the EU legal order. Suffice it to mention again the notion of 'legality', which has significantly evolved in

[182] P. Chirulli and L. de Lucia, *Non-Judicial Remedies and EU Administration Protection of Rights versus Preservation of Autonomy* (2021) ch. IV, 'Administrative Review before the EU Agencies' Boards of Appeal'.

[183] E.g. Art. 90 of Regulation 1907/2006, OJ 2006 L 396/1 (the REACH Regulation).

[184] E.g. Art. 92(1) REACH Regulation.

[185] M. Krajewski, *Relative Authority of Judicial and Extra-Judicial Review* (2021) 129–136.

[186] The traces of this approach can be seen in Ritleng, 'Boards of Appeal of EU Agencies and Article 47 of the Charter: Uneasy Bedfellows?', in M. Chamon, A. Volpato, and M. Eliantonio (eds), *Boards of Appeal of EU Agencies: Towards Judicialization of Administrative Review?* (2022). Nonetheless, P. Craig, *EU Administrative Law* (2018) 281, classifies BoAs as courts, considering their substantive characteristics rather than formal designation only.

recent decades for the purpose of intensifying EU judicial review.[187] At the same time, the models of judicial review of administrative action vary across Europe, making it very difficult to distinguish the features of 'judicial review' as opposed to 'administrative review'. According to this alternative approach, it is then crucial to consider what these formally non-judicial bodies offer in terms of the legal and administrative arrangements for their functional independence, their powers and techniques of review, their accessibility to the interested parties, and the conduct of proceedings. It turns out that BoAs may operate in a similar way to courts or even offer a 'fair trial' and an 'effective remedy'. In terms of their added value, it seems crucial that the BoAs can benefit from the proximity of the agency and its expert resources and that they may adopt a less formalist procedural practice, allowing for a more intense and direct scientific debate between the parties and the interveners.[188]

The BoA of the European Chemicals Agency (ECHA) deals particularly often with complex and uncertain assessments underpinning ECHA's decisions for further data or tests concerning chemical substances marketed in the EU but giving rise to concerns about their impact on the natural environment or public health.[189] Apart from verifying whether ECHA has correctly interpreted the relevant legislative framework[190] and complied with the procedural rules,[191] this BoA is often called on to scrutinize whether ECHA has complied with its duty of care and whether it has committed errors of substantive assessment. Thanks to its partial specialization, this BoA often seems to express its own independent view on the probative value of the scientific evidence adduced before it and the cogency of scientific reasoning presented in the impugned decisions. For instance, it may analyse the value of scientific studies adduced by the registrants of chemical substances, on the one hand, and ECHA, on the other hand, to decide which are more reliable in light of their shortcomings and deviations from methodological guidelines.[192] It may also assess the value of a predictive model concerning the metabolites of a

[187] Mendes (n. 7); Dąbrowska-Kłosińska (n. 7).

[188] Krajewski (n. 185).

[189] For a comprehensive restatement of the case law of ECHA BoA, see 'Digest of Decisions of the Board of Appeal of the European Chemicals Agency', https://echa.europa.eu/documents/10162/2314761/digest_of_decisions_of_boa_en.pdf/cad5c04e-1888-9ac3-5718-eb6f17a395a8?t=1694089430069 (last visited 20 December 2023).

[190] See e.g. a recent case in which the BoA interpreted the relationship between the REACH Regulation and Cosmetics Regulation, Case A-009-2018, *Symrise*, paras 116–117; Case A-010-2018, *Symrise*, paras 117–118. See also Case T-655/20, *Symrise v. ECHA* (EU:T:2023:736).

[191] See e.g. a case in which the BoA clarified how the right to be heard should be applied in ECHA proceedings, Case A-009-2014, *Albemarle Europe*, para. 225; Case A-004-2015, *Polynt*, para. 65; Case A-009-2016, *Symrise*, paras 53 and 112.

[192] Joined Cases A-003-2018 to A-005-2018, *BASF SE and Kemira Oyj v. ECHA*, paras 103–110.

substance, as proposed by the registrants in the absence of experimental data on the metabolites.[193] Moreover, it may assess the chances that a specific study required by ECHA will generate the necessary data considering the specific properties of the substance at issue.[194] Arguably, in performing such assessments, the ECHA BoA applies its own specialized knowledge, benefiting from thorough exchanges with the parties and their expert consultants.

Occasionally, this BoA also acts with deference when considering that a dispute between the appellant and ECHA amounts to a 'difference of scientific opinion' regarding the interpretation of the available data. In such situations, the appellants have not managed to convince the BoA of substantive errors of assessment on the side of ECHA, so the BoA recognizes ECHA's discretion and defers to the latter's scientific position.[195] The General Court has confirmed that the ECHA BoA does not have to perform a de novo review of all empirical issues under its consideration but only identify 'errors' (as opposed to 'manifest errors' with which the EU Courts are concerned).[196] As it turns out, an in-depth, partly specialized administrative review does not need to rule out deference to the expert administration. Arguably, if the disagreement between the parties in such cases is of a 'scientific' nature, the BoA implies that the level of certainty of ECHA's empirical assessment is sufficient for it to undertake administrative action.

Overall, the added value of a BoA may consist not only in its ability to provide a quicker and less formalistic means of review, while keeping the bulk of complex cases outside the docket of EU Courts, but also in its ability to assess, in an independent and reliable manner, the probative value of scientific evidence and the soundness of specialist reasoning underpinning EU regulatory or administrative action. The increasing position of BoAs in the EU system of remedies seems to be confirmed by their recognition as a form of legal redress in the Statute of the EU Courts, which justifies the lesser engagement of the Court of Justice as the apex appellate authority in cases that BoAs have already dealt with.[197]

[193] Case A-026-2015, *Envigo Consulting*, paras 52–60.

[194] Ibid. paras 118–125 and 133–142.

[195] E.g. Case A-018-2014, *BASF Grenzach*, para. 134; ECHA BoA, Case A-015-2015, *Evonik Degussa*, para. 174; ECHA BoA, Case A-007-2019, *Chemours v. ECHA*, paras 64 and 67.

[196] Case T-125/17, *BASF v. ECHA* (EU:T:2019:638).

[197] Art 58a of the Statute of the Court of Justice of the European Union. See also a proposal to amend the Statute made by the President of the Court on 30 November 2023 to extend the requirement for leave to appeal from the General Court to the Court of Justice regarding appeals against decisions of the General Court concerning the decisions of BoAs.

5. Certainty as Rational Acceptability

Last but not least, court rulings are expected to provide certainty, which is understood as their rational acceptability by the affected parties. Courts are subject to requirements of procedural fairness, including the duty to allow the affected parties to actively participate in the court proceedings by adducing and discussing relevant evidence and advancing reasoned arguments. This way, courts are supposed to examine the different points of view on the matter and ascertain how their ruling would affect the legally protected interests represented by the affected parties. These requirements of procedural fairness can be deemed particularly important in cases involving complex and uncertain evidence and assessments, in which non-specialist adjudicators can evidently greatly benefit from the specialist information provided by the parties, although it may be challenging for them to distinguish between plausible and implausible empirical accounts. In practice, the initiative and activity of the parties in proceedings before the EU Courts is crucial. In particular, infringement and annulment proceedings, in which the EU Courts are often called on to assess the empirical accounts and specialist assessments, are predominantly adversarial.

Evidently, the formally adversarial procedural framework does not make the parties before the court equal in their practical ability to obtain, produce, and present the relevant evidence and formulate relevant arguments based on it. As mentioned, sometimes the Commission may be rather constrained in its ability to gather the necessary evidence against the Member States, and sometimes the private applicants, especially civil society, appear much weaker vis-à-vis the resourceful EU administration supported by the specialist scientific committees or Member States' competent authorities.[198] The unequal ability of the parties to participate effectively in the judicial procedure may adversely affect procedural fairness and the rational conviction of the parties that they should consider the procedure's outcome as rationally acceptable.

Another challenge for certainty as a rational acceptability of court rulings may stem from the limited range of actors admitted to participate in the procedure. Annulment proceedings are usually open mainly to members of

[198] E.g. in Case C-82/17 P, *TestBioTech v. Commission* (EU:C:2019:719), para. 62, the civil society organizations lamented that the General Court imposed on them an impossible burden of proof. Similar allegations are sometimes raised by the industry. See e.g. Case C-119/21 P, *PlasticsEurope v. Commission* (ECLI:EU:C:2023:180), para. 41.

industries affected by the EU regulatory and administrative action.[199] As EU regulatory and administrative action is usually also underpinned by the assessment of studies provided by the regulated industries, the EU Courts are primarily confronted with this type of scientific evidence. The techniques of judicial review that they apply, as analysed earlier, foster bilateral exchanges between the EU administration and the industry rather than a broader opening of EU regulatory processes in view of making them more inclusive and deliberative.[200]

When it comes to infringement proceedings, private parties, including individuals and organizations—even those that have brought relevant complaints to the Commission against Member States—cannot join the subsequent infringement proceedings as interveners.[201] Preliminary reference proceedings are somewhat more open as the parties to the main proceedings, including interveners, may submit observations to the Court of Justice.[202] However, in practice, the possibility to intervene in these proceedings before the Court depends on national rules and, sometimes, the discretion of national judges. Nonetheless, intervention opportunities for environmental organizations have recently been broadened in annulment proceedings.[203] Broader opportunities for interventions also exist before the ECHA BoA.[204]

Could the EU Courts address the issues of the unequal status of certain parties and the limited openness of the proceedings to the affected parties with a view to improving the rational acceptability of their rulings? Theoretical solutions exist, but their effectiveness remains uncertain, and they may always provoke other negative effects. According to its rules of procedure, the General Court can commission independent expert reports.[205] Arguably, it could also directly question members of the EU scientific committees advising the EU administration.[206] However, employing such measures could prolong the length

[199] This finding also applies to the BoAs due to the criterion of 'individual and direct concern', which is replicated in the legal provisions governing the access to BoAs. See e.g. Art. 92(1) REACH Regulation. Krajewski (n. 185) 76–81.

[200] Morvillo and Weimer (n. 12).

[201] Art. 40, second para. of the Statute of the Court of Justice of the European Union. Case C-301/17, *Commission v. Romania* (Order of 10 April 2018, EU:C:2018:232), paras 4–5.

[202] Art. 96–97 of the Rules of Procedure of the Court of Justice of 25 September 2012, OJ 2012 L 173/65.

[203] Case C-499/18 P, *Bayer v. Commission* (Order of 7 February 2019, EU:C:2019:107); Case C-471/18 P, *Germany v. ESSO and ECHA* (Order of 12 March 2019, EU:C:2019:198); Case C-611/22 P, *Illumina v. Commission* (EU:C:2023:205).

[204] See an overview of criteria for animal welfare organizations, which frequently intervene before the ECHA BoA in Case A-013-2016, *BASF Personal Care and Nutrition GmbH* (decision on intervention of 3 May 2017).

[205] Art. 91(e) of the Rules of Procedure.

[206] Based on Art. 24 of the Statute, the Court can require the parties and other bodies of the EU not being parties to the case to supply all information which the Court considers necessary for the

of proceedings, replicating the earlier decision-making stages, without any guarantee of improving the substantive accuracy of the ruling. The length of proceedings is often crucial, especially in cases concerning responses to risks to the natural environment and public health.[207] Another challenge for the EU Courts arises when conflicting expert opinions are presented in the courtroom. At the same time, the experience of the ECHA BoA shows that a direct and less formalistic engagement with experts representing both parties (not necessarily lawyers) during oral hearings may be an effective way of clarifying contentious scientific issues.[208]

6. Conclusion

This chapter has explored the different ways in which scientific uncertainty poses a challenge to the contribution to the legitimacy of EU environmental governance from the judicial and quasi-judicial rulings applying EU environmental law. Legitimacy has been conceived of in terms of a rational belief in the certainty of propositions about law and empirics offered in the rulings: the stability of legal propositions, the truth of empirical propositions, and the rational acceptability of both in view of the conduct of the judicial process and participation opportunities for the parties concerned. The chapter has incorporated insights from political ecology scholarship to elucidate how scientific complexity and uncertainty can be closely enmeshed with political controversies, exacerbating the challenges that adjudication faces in environmental matters.

proceedings. According to Art. 91(a) of the Rules of Procedure, the General Court can also order the personal appearance of the parties and, according to Art. 91(d) of the Rules of Procedure, it can order oral testimony. The procedure for the examination of witnesses is described in Art. 94 and the examination of the expert's report in Art. 96 of the Rules of Procedure.

207 It important to note whether court actions or extra-judicial appeals have an automatic suspensive effect. If so, the time taken to decide on the court action or the appeal lodged by an industry member may exacerbate the risks to the natural environment and public health because, as in the case of the ECHA BoA, the examination of the appeal will delay the provision of additional scientific information and ensuing risk-management measures. The action for annulment does not produce an automatic suspensive effect but the appeal to the ECHA BoA does do so (Art. 91(2) REACH Regulation). This is why the ECHA BoA attaches great importance to the time taken to issue decisions. See 'Annual Report from the Chairman of the Board of Appeal' (2022), https://echa.europa.eu/documents/10162/17085/mb_26_2022_boa_chairman_annual_report_en.pdf/b34b9751-0d28-9bae-53aa-544c1af02e3b?t=1661152141395 (last visited 22 December 2023), 7 and 19. It could be argued that if the time of the appellate process were to be excessively long, it would adversely affect the legitimacy of BoA decisions because the potential benefit of empirical and legal certainty offered by BoA decisions would be outweighed by the risk to the public interest stemming from the length of the appellate procedure.

208 Krajewski (n. 185) 133–136.

It has shown that the EU Courts, national courts, and boards of appeal have some discretion to moderate the degree of complex and uncertain science entering the adjudicatory process, by deferring to empirical assessments of other bodies, invoking the precautionary principle, focusing on the rules regarding the burden of proof or the logical consistency of submissions made by the parties and the impugned empirical assessments by expert administration. Some cases, however, may require adjudicators to express an independent view on the probative value of the evidence and the soundness of expert reasoning. This is where more specialized adjudicatory bodies, such as boards of appeal, can bring added value.

While there is always a concern that courts decreasing their degree of engagement with uncertain science will undermine the persuasiveness of their rulings, by leaving certain issues unaddressed or not fully addressed, this strategy may also help to ensure that courts do not step beyond what they are able or well-suited to achieve, thereby enhancing the legitimacy of the system as a whole. Courts identify issues where they can offer a relatively high level of certainty, although they may be able to offer only relative certainty regarding issues linked to complex and uncertain science enmeshed with heated political controversies. This is why it is necessary to express realistic expectations of adjudication as the legitimacy with which it contributes to the broader governance structure is inherently limited by that which courts have the capacity to achieve.

7

EU Environmental Law

A Complete and Effective System of Remedies before the Courts of the European Union?

Luca Prete

1. Introduction

The topic of the present volume is the legitimacy of EU environmental governance, with a special focus on the *judicial* contribution to that governance.[1] In the introductory chapter of the volume, it is argued that the Courts of the European Union can positively contribute to environmental governance to the extent that they fulfil a number of criteria. The present chapter intends to provide some elements for reflection, particularly as regards the importance of the scrutiny provided by courts, their compliance with the values of legal process in so doing, and, crucially, the role that the remedial outcome of judicial decision-making has in the wider governance of environmental problems. Indeed, the objective of the chapter is to investigate whether, with regard to EU environmental law, the system of legal remedies set up in the EU Treaties is actually *complete* and generally *effective*.

By 'complete', I refer to the possibility to ensure, directly or indirectly, judicial review of the legality of EU acts producing legal effects and of national acts that apply EU law. By 'effective', I refer to the existence of *adequate* remedies[2] of a judicial nature against any decisions of the EU or national authorities that may breach the rights and freedoms that individuals derive from EU law. Both requirements can, in my view, be considered to follow from the principle of the effective judicial protection of individuals' rights under EU law, referred to in the second subparagraph of Article 19(1) of the Treaty on European Union (TEU), which is a general principle of EU law, stemming from the

[1] Views expressed are personal to the author.
[2] The term 'adequate' covers, in principle, all the relevant elements of the proceedings (existence, accessibility, foreseeability, interim protection, costs, etc.) which may render it impossible or excessively difficult for the individuals to obtain judicial protection of their rights.

Luca Prete, *EU Environmental Law* In: *The Legitimacy of EU Environmental Governance and the Role of the European Courts*. Edited by: Mariolina Eliantonio and Emma Lees, Oxford University Press.
 DOI: 10.1093/oso/9780198972808.003.0007

constitutional traditions common to the Member States, also enshrined in Articles 6 and 13 of the European Convention for the Protection of Human Rights and Fundamental Freedoms (ECHR), and now reaffirmed by Article 47 of the Charter of Fundamental Rights of the European Union (Charter).[3] In particular, the latter provision states inter alia that 'everyone whose rights and freedoms guaranteed by the law of the Union are violated has the right to an effective remedy before a tribunal'. Crucially, by defining the key terms by reference to the Treaty frameworks themselves, the contribution that the courts make in legitimacy terms already brings into play some of the wider themes of this volume: legal context, allocation of power between state actors, and the appropriate judicial role in the face of environmental degradation.

Having clarified the above, I wish to make clear that the present chapter, as with the other chapters in this volume, rather than attempting to suggest a straightforward and objective answer to the research question—assuming one were to be possible—begins from the premise that it is only in the detail of the cases themselves that the contribution which the courts bring to the legitimacy or otherwise of EU environmental governance can be properly assessed. That said, it cannot be overlooked that there has been an abundance of literature on this matter in the past years which brings to light the challenges that the EU legal order faces in respect of remedies.[4] The present chapter will thus focus on the most recent decisions of the Court of Justice of the European Union (CJEU). In that respect, it is, arguably, important to stress if those decisions are consistent with past case law or, conversely, appear to bring some innovative elements. Indeed, in the last 15 years, a number of significant changes to the EU constitutional and legislative framework saw the light of the day.[5] In addition, it

[3] See e.g. Case C-64/16, *Associação Sindical dos Juízes Portugueses* (EU:C:2018:117), para. 35.

[4] See, inter alia, Bogojevic, 'Judicial Protection of Individual Applicants Revisited: Access to Justice through the Prism of Judicial Subsidiarity', 34 *Yearbook of European Law* (2015) 5; Cheneviere-Mesdag, 'La Cour de Justice de l'Union Européenne, les Justiciables et la Justice Climatique', *Annales de droit de Louvain* (2022) 123; Hadjiyianni, 'Judicial Protection and the Environment in the EU Legal Order: Missing Pieces for a Complete Puzzle of Legal Remedies', 58 *Common Market Law Review* (2022) 777; Hartmann and Willers, 'Protecting Rights in Climate Change Litigation before European Courts', 13 *Journal of Human Rights and the Environment* (2022) 90; M. Hedemann-Robinson, *Enforcement of European Union Environmental Law: Legal Issues and Challenges* (2nd edn, 2015); Krämer, 'Climate Change, Human Rights and Access to Justice', 16 *Journal for European Environmental & Planning Law* (2019) 21; Krämer, 'The Environment before the European Court of Justice', in C. Voigt (ed.), *International Judicial Practice on the Environment—Questions of Legitimacy* (2019) 25; Schoukens, 'Access to Justice before EU Courts in Environmental Cases against the Backdrop of the Aarhus Convention: Balancing Pathological Stubbornness and Cognitive Dissonance?', in Voigt, ibid. 74; M. Peeters and M. Eliantonio (eds), *Research Handbook on EU Environmental Law* (2020); Winter, 'Not Fit for Purpose. Die Klagebefugnis vor dem Europäischen Gericht angesichts allgemeiner Gefahren', 3 *Europarecht* (2022) 367.

[5] To give but a few examples: the entry into force of the Treaty of Lisbon which, inter alia, amended Art. 263 TFEU and rendered the Charter legally binding (December 2009); the conclusion by the

is also interesting to note whether—within the CJEU—diverging points of view were expressed in those cases (e.g. General Court and/or Advocate General *vs* Court of Justice). That would signal that the legal issues at stake were controversial or, at the very least, not totally straightforward.

That detailed case-based analysis of the EU Courts' contribution to EU environmental governance will reveal, inter alia, that, when it comes to remedies, the case law is largely embedded within the wider context of remedies available within the EU legal order. Even with the addition of the Aarhus rules, the processes and standards prioritize, it seems, the process values of consistency and certainty, over the environmental outcomes. In this sense, close consideration of remedies shows how legitimate governance is often about striking a balance between competing values.

The present chapter is structured as follows. After a few preliminary remarks highlighting the specific features of the EU judicial system (Section 2), I will briefly explain the main forms of actions—before the CJEU and the national courts—which are available to persons whose rights have allegedly been breached and refer to the most important cases relating to environmental protection (environmental litigation) recently decided by the CJEU (Sections 3 and 4). Subsequently, a global evaluation of the EU system of remedies will be carried out (Section 5), before finally drawing conclusions (Section 6).

2. Preliminary Remarks: The Specific Features of the EU Judicial System

At the outset, it should be emphasized that, according to settled case law, the European Union is a Union based on the *rule of law* in which its institutions are subject to judicial review of the compatibility of their acts with, inter alia, the EU Treaties and the Charter. The EU Treaties have, to that end, established a *complete system* of legal remedies and procedures designed to permit the CJEU to review the legality of acts of the EU institutions. Individuals are therefore entitled to effective judicial protection of the rights they derive from the EU legal order.[6]

European Union of the Aarhus Convention (2005); and the adoption first (2006), and then amendment (2021), of the so-called Aarhus Regulation (Regulation (EC) No. 1367/2006, OJ 2006 L 264/13).

[6] See e.g. Joined Cases C-663/17 P, C-665/17 P and C-669/17 P, *ECB v. Trasta Komercbanka* (EU:C:2019:923), para. 54 and the case law cited.

In turn, pursuant to Article 17(1) TEU, the European Commission (Commission) is to promote the general interest of the Union and take appropriate initiatives to that end. Inter alia, the Commission is required to 'ensure the application of the Treaties, and of measures adopted by the institutions pursuant to them' and to 'oversee the application of Union law under the control of the [CJEU]'. In particular, pursuant to Articles 258 and 260 of the Treaty on the Functioning of the European Union (TFEU), the Commission may start 'infringement proceedings' against Member States that fail to comply with EU law and, in certain cases, ask the Court of Justice (Court) to impose financial penalties for the breaches. An adverse ruling is, vis-à-vis the Member State concerned, that of a prohibition having the full force of law on the competent national authorities against applying a national rule recognized as incompatible with the Treaties and, if the circumstances so require, an obligation on them to take all appropriate measures to enable EU law to be fully applied.[7] As the Court stated in one of the first cases brought before it under Article 258 TFEU, the infringement procedure 'is a procedure far exceeding the rules heretofore recognized in classical international law to ensure that obligations of States are fulfilled'.[8]

The EU Treaties thus provide for a number of specific legal remedies meant to ensure that EU institutions' and Member States' compliance with EU law may be subject to judicial review. However, the completeness and effectiveness of the EU judicial system cannot be assessed by focusing only on the proceedings taking place before the CJEU. Indeed, the EU judicial system has a peculiar structure which follows, primarily, from the (generally accepted) fact that the European Union is neither a typical international organization nor a nation state, but something in between.[9] As stated in Article 1 TEU, the Member States establish among themselves the European Union and, by dint of the Treaties, confer competences on it to attain objectives they have in common. The Court has consistently emphasized that 'the founding treaties of the EU, unlike ordinary international treaties, established a new legal order, possessing its own institutions, for the benefit of which the Member States thereof have limited their sovereign rights, in ever wider fields, and the subjects of which comprise not only those States but also their nationals'.[10] In Opinion 1/13, the

[7] Case 48/71, *Commission v. Italy* (EU:C:1972:65), para. 7.

[8] Case 20/59, *Italy v. High Authority* (EU:C:1960:33), p. 339.

[9] See e.g. von Bogdandy, 'Neither an International Organization Nor A Nation State: The EU as a Supranational Federation', in E. Jones *et al.* (eds), *The Oxford Handbook of the European Union* (2013) 761, ch. 53.

[10] See e.g. Opinion 2/13 *(Accession of the European Union to the ECHR)* (EU:C:2014:2454), para. 157.

Court has also stressed the fact that the EU gave rise to 'a new kind of legal order, the nature of which is peculiar to the EU, [and possesses] its own constitutional framework and founding principles, a particularly sophisticated institutional structure and a full set of legal rules to ensure its operation'.[11]

There is no need to delve further into this matter for the purposes of the present chapter. Suffice to recall two constitutional features of particular significance in this context: (i) according to the principle of conferral, the European Union can act only 'within the limits of the competences conferred upon it by the Member States in the Treaties to attain the objectives set out therein' and 'competences not conferred upon the Union in the Treaties remain with the Member States' (Arts 4(1) and 5(2) TEU); and (ii) each institution must 'act within the limits of the powers conferred on it in the Treaties, and in conformity with the procedures, conditions and objectives set out in them' (Art. 13(2) TEU).

The peculiarity of the EU judicial system is revealed, in particular, by Article 19(1) TEU, which—after laying down the CJEU's mission to 'ensure that in the interpretation and application of the Treaties the law is observed'—provides that 'Member States shall provide remedies sufficient to ensure effective legal protection in the fields covered by Union law'. In fact, the CJEU has a clearly defined jurisdiction: under Article 274 TFEU, 'save where jurisdiction is conferred on the [CJEU], disputes to which the Union is a party shall not on that ground be excluded from the jurisdiction of the courts or tribunals of the Member States'. Arguably, national courts have jurisdiction in all disputes which concern situations involving EU institutions, EU measures, or EU rules in respect of which the drafters of the EU Treaties did not grant any jurisdiction to the CJEU.[12] Those provisions clearly show the existence of an un-dissociable link and mutual interdependence between the EU judiciary and the Member States' judiciary. Indeed, in Opinion 1/09 the Court stated that, 'as is evident from Article 19(1) TEU, the *guardians* of [the EU] legal order and the judicial system of the European Union are the Court of Justice *and* the courts and tribunals of the Member States'; and that the national courts, in collaboration with the Court of Justice, fulfil 'a duty entrusted to *them both* of ensuring that in the interpretation and application of the Treaties the law is observed'.[13] In fact, according to settled case law, under the principle of sincere cooperation

[11] Ibid. para. 158.

[12] Cf. Opinion of AG Mengozzi in Case C-354/04 P, *Gestoras Pro Amnistía and Others v. Council* (EU:C:2006:667), para. 104; View of AG Kokott in Opinion procedure 2/13 (EU:C:2014:2475), para. 96; and Opinion of AG Wahl in Opinion procedure 2/15 (EU:C:2016:657), paras 41 to 43.

[13] Opinion 1/09 (EU:C:2011:123), paras 66 and 69 (emphasis added).

laid down in Article 4(3) TEU, it is generally for the Member States to ensure judicial protection of an individual's rights under EU law.[14]

Having emphasized those specific characteristics of the EU judicial system, I shall now turn to the main forms of actions—before the CJEU and the national courts—which are available to persons whose rights under EU law have allegedly been breached and refer, in that regard, to the most recent cases relating to environmental protection.

3. Judicial Review by the CJEU

The EU Treaties provide, in the first place, for various forms of proceedings intended to permit the CJEU to review, *ex ante* or *ex post*, the conduct—action or inaction—of the EU institutions. With regard to environmental litigation, the most relevant forms of proceedings are: (i) the action for annulment and (ii) the action for failure to act (Arts 263 and 265 TFEU, respectively) which allow direct review of the institutions' conduct; (iii) the preliminary ruling procedure (Art. 267 TFEU) which allows, inter alia, review of the validity of the relevant EU acts; (iv) the action for non-contractual liability (Arts 268 and 340 TFEU); and (v) the procedure for interim measures.[15] Those forms of proceedings are meant, in the view of the Court, to constitute a coherent whole; that is so especially in respect of the actions for annulment and the preliminary ruling procedure. As the Court has consistently held, in the complete system of legal remedies and procedures established by the EU Treaties—with a view to ensuring judicial review of the legality of acts of the institutions—where natural or legal persons cannot, by reason of the conditions for admissibility laid down in Article 263 TFEU, directly challenge acts of the European Union of general application, they are able, depending on the case, either indirectly to plead the invalidity of such acts before the EU judicature under Article 277

[14] See e.g. Case C-404/13, *ClientEarth* (EU:C:2014:2382), para. 52 and the case law cited.

[15] Other forms of proceedings which are not particularly relevant in the context of environmental litigation—such as the request for an Opinion on the compatibility of an international agreement (Art. 218(11) TFEU), which allows for an *ex ante* check of the compatibility with EU law of envisaged agreements, or the plea of illegality (Art. 277 TFEU), which allows for an *incidental* control of legality of EU acts—will not be discussed in this chapter. With respect of the plea of illegality, I would only add that, in legal scholarship, it was recently noted that such a mechanism has only rarely been used in challenges before the EU Courts and has almost invariably been used unsuccessfully. On that basis, it was argued that, insofar as 'the direct means to judicial review through Article 263 TFEU and indirect review through Article 267 TFEU are ... heavily criticised as not offering significant relief to natural and legal persons in addressing possible errors in EU law ..., the plea of illegality is the missing piece of the jigsaw that, in hindsight, does not fit' (Eliantonio, 'The plea of illegality in European Union law—The missing piece in the puzzle of a "complete system of remedies"?' REALaw.blog, 7 March 2023).

TFEU[16] or to do so before the national courts and ask them, since they have no jurisdiction themselves to declare those acts invalid, to make a reference to the Court of Justice for a preliminary ruling on validity. In the second place, the Treaties also provide for two procedures which permit the CJEU to rule on Member States' compliance with EU law: directly, by means of infringements proceedings (Arts 258 to 260 TFEU), and indirectly, via the preliminary ruling procedure on interpretation. These forms of proceedings will now be described in turn.

A. Actions for Annulment

An action for annulment based on Article 263 TFEU is available against all measures adopted by the EU institutions or bodies, whatever their nature or form, which are intended to have binding legal effects. Article 263 TFEU provides for four cumulative conditions for the admissibility of such an action: (i) the act is open to challenge; (ii) the party has standing; (iii) the grounds of illegality invoked are those mentioned therein; and (iv) the application is submitted within the time limit set by the Treaties. Pursuant to Articles 264 and 266 TFEU, if the action is well founded, the CJEU declares the act concerned to be void and the institution whose act has been declared void is required to take the necessary measures to comply with the judgment.[17] Jurisdiction for this action is shared between the General Court and the Court of Justice: whereas the latter hears most actions lodged by the Member States and EU institutions, actions commenced by physical and legal persons are always heard at first instance by the General Court.[18] The decisions given by the General Court can then be appealed on points of law before the Court, pursuant to Article 256 TFEU. If an appeal is successful, the Court can annul, partially or totally, the first instance decision and, if the case can be decided on the substance, will

[16] Art. 277 TFEU provides that 'notwithstanding the expiry of the period laid down in Article 263, sixth paragraph, any party may, in proceedings in which an act of general application adopted by an institution, body, office or agency of the Union is at issue, plead the grounds specified in Article 263, second paragraph, in order to invoke before the [CJEU] the inapplicability of that act'. As explained in the previous footnote, that provision will not be discussed in the present chapter.

[17] More generally, on this form of action, with references to case law, see R. Barents, *Remedies and Procedures Before the EU Courts* (2nd edn, 2020) chs 5 and 6.

[18] Actions lodged by Member States or EU institutions in this area are relatively rare. For one such case, see Case C-144/21, *Parliament v. Commission (Authorisation of a substance of very high concern)* (EU:C:2023:302).

rule on the parties' claims; otherwise, the Court will refer the case back to the General Court for a fresh assessment.[19]

Most conditions set out in Article 263 TFEU for an action to be admissible only rarely raise interpretative issues albeit that, as explained in Chapter 5 of this volume, the overall threshold for admissibility is nevertheless a high one. In particular, the concept of 'act open to challenge' is interpreted quite broadly as encompassing any act that may produce legal effects. An interesting issue which has arisen in a recent case in that regard is whether a letter in which the European Investment Bank (EIB) rejected as inadmissible a non-governmental organization's (NGO) request to review, pursuant to Article 10(1) of the Aarhus Regulation, the resolution of its Board of Directors (BoD) approving the financing of a biomass power-generation plant in Spain could be challenged before the EU Courts. The General Court considered that: (i) the letter was an 'act open to challenge' under Article 263 TFEU; (ii) the EIB acted as a public authority; (iii) the resolution in question was a measure under environmental law; and (iv) that resolution had legally binding and external effects. On that basis, the General Court annulled the contested letter.[20] On appeal, the Court, following the Opinion of AG Kokott, endorsed the approach retained by the General Court. In essence, the Court found that Article 271(c) TFEU—which sets out the limits to the CJEU's jurisdiction with regard to the measures adopted by EIB's BoD—did not preclude, as a matter of principle, an NGO from requesting, in accordance with Article 10(1) of the Aarhus Regulation, an internal review of a resolution of the BoD, or from bringing an action for annulment, on the basis of Article 12(1) of that Regulation, against a decision declaring inadmissible such a request.[21]

By contrast, a procedural aspect that has often been considered problematic in the context of environmental litigation is that of standing. The Treaties identify three different groups of subjects, which have to meet different standing requirements to be able to start proceedings: 'privileged' applicants (Commission, Council, European Parliament, and the Member States) that can challenge *any* act that is open to challenge; 'semi-privileged' applicants (European Central Bank, Court of Auditors, Committee of the Regions) that can challenge any act provided that the action aims at protecting their

[19] More generally, on the appeal procedure, with references to case law, see C. Naômé, *Appeals Before the Court of Justice of the European Union* (2018).

[20] Case T-9/19, *ClientEarth v. EIB* (EU:T:2021:42), paras 80 ff.

[21] Joined Cases C-212/21 P and C-223/21 P, *EIB and Commission v. ClientEarth* (EU:C:2023:546), paras 32 ff, and Opinion of AG Kokott in the same cases (Joined Cases C-212/21 P and C-223/21 P (EU:C:2022:1003), paras 41 ff).

prerogatives; and 'non-privileged' applicants, that is, any natural or legal person (individuals, companies, associations, organizations, public bodies, territorial communities, etc.), that can only challenge EU acts when the conditions provided for in the fourth paragraph of Article 263 TFEU are satisfied. That provision sets out three alternative situations in which non-privileged applicants are entitled to challenge the validity of an EU act directly before the CJEU: (1) the act is *addressed* to them; (2) the act is of *direct* and *individual concern* to them; and (3) the act is a *regulatory act* which is of direct concern to them and does not entail implementing measures. The nature and meaning of those conditions have been the object of a rich case law[22]—not to mention of an endless academic debate[23]—that dates back to the early years of the CJEU's activity and that was progressively refined over the following decades. The third situation set out in Article 263(4) TFEU was, however, added only with the Treaty of Lisbon, after an equivalent provision had been included in the draft treaty establishing a constitution for Europe, following the discussions held within the Convention on the Future of Europe, in turn inspired by the well-known *Jégo Quéré/UPA* judicial saga.[24]

In essence, the concept of 'individual concern' has been defined by the Court with reference to the so-called *Plaumann* test:[25] the measure must affect the applicants by reason of certain attributes which are peculiar to them or by reason of circumstances in which they are differentiated from all other persons, and by virtue of these factors distinguishes them individually just as in the case of the person addressed ('the distinctive test').[26] Next, 'direct concern' has been defined by the Court as the ability of the challenged measure to directly affect the legal position of the applicants, leaving no discretion to the addressees of the measure. In other words, direct concern exists if there is no need for intermediate (EU or domestic) rules for the measure in question to deploy its legal effects vis-à-vis the applicants.[27] Finally, the concept of

[22] See, at that time, Albors-Llorens, 'The Standing of Private Parties to Challenge Community Measures: Has the European Court Missed the Boat?', 62 *The Cambridge Law Journal* (2003) 72. More recently, see Arnull, 'Protecting the Rights of Individuals: Opinion of Advocate General Jacobs in UPA', in G. Butler and A. Łazowski (eds), *Shaping EU Law the British Way* (2002) ch. 33.

[23] See, among others, the cases mentioned later in nn. 26 to 29, 32, 47, and 50.

[24] Cf. Opinion of AG Jacobs in Case C-50/00 P, *Unión de Pequeños Agricultores v. Council* (*UPA*) (EU:C:2002:197), paras 31 ff, and judgment in Case T-177/01, *Jégo-Quéré v. Commission* (EU:T:2002:112), paras 22 ff, with judgments in Case C-50/00 P, *Unión de Pequeños Agricultores v. Council* (EU:C:2002:462), paras 32–47, and Case C-263/02 P, *Commission v. Jégo-Quéré* (EU:C:2004:210), paras 29 ff.

[25] Name deriving from Case 25/62, *Plaumann v. Commission* (EU:C:1963:17), p. 107.

[26] For a recent application: Case C-348/20 P, *Nord Stream 2 v. Parliament and Council* (EU:C:2022:548), para. 156.

[27] See e.g. Joined Cases C-622/16 P to C-624/16 P, *Scuola Elementare Maria Montessori v. Commission* (EU:C:2018:873), para. 42.

'regulatory act' encompasses, according to the Court, all non-legislative acts of general application (i.e. delegated acts, implementing acts, acts adopted following special procedures);[28] and the requirement that they do not 'entail implementing measures' means that the specific legal effects altering the position of the applicants materialize vis-à-vis that person as a result of the EU act challenged and not of any other act adopted by the EU or the Member State in question.[29]

In that respect, a number of recent decisions of the CJEU are particularly noteworthy. Those decisions can be grouped into two main strands of case law. The first one concerns the standing of private persons (individuals, companies, associations, etc.) and the second the standing of regional or local entities.

1. Standing: Private Applicants

As far as the first strand of case law are concerned, the *Carvalho* case is important. The applicants were several individuals and an association operating in the agricultural or tourism sectors from various EU Member States and the rest of the world. They sought (i) the annulment of several legislative acts governing greenhouse gas (GHG) emission reductions by Member States from 2021 to 2030 and (ii) compensation in the form of an injunction for the damage that they claimed to have suffered. In their view, the EU's target for GHG reduction was insufficient to combat climate change and thus threatened the applicants' fundamental rights of life, health, occupation, and property, as enshrined in a number of legal instruments (inter alia TFEU, Charter, United Nations Framework Convention on Climate Change, and the Paris Agreement). By its order, the General Court dismissed the actions as inadmissible for lack of individual concern.[30] On appeal—ruling without an Opinion of the Advocate General[31]—the Court confirmed the General Court's analysis. The General Court had emphasized that:

> [i]t is true that every individual is likely to be affected one way or another by climate change, that issue being recognised by the EU and the Member States who have, as a result, committed to reducing emissions. However, the fact that the effects of climate change may be different for one person than they

[28] See e.g. Case C-583/11 P, *Inuit Tapiriit Kanatami and Others v. Parliament and Council* (EU:C:2013:625), paras 58–61.

[29] See e.g. Case C-274/12 P, *Telefónica v. Commission* (EU:C:2013:852), paras 30 and 31.

[30] Case T-330/18, *Carvalho and Others v. Parliament and Council* (EU:T:2019:324), paras 33–55.

[31] Pursuant to the fifth paragraph of Art. 20 of the Statute of the Court, 'where it considers that the case raises no new point of law, the Court may decide, after hearing the Advocate General, that the case shall be determined without a submission from the Advocate General'.

are for another does not mean that, for that reason, there exists standing to bring an action against a measure of general application.

According to the General Court, a different approach would have the result of rendering the requirements of the fourth paragraph of Article 263 TFEU meaningless and of creating standing for all without the criterion of individual concern within the meaning of the *Plaumann* case law being fulfilled. In that regard, the Court added that the protection conferred by Article 47 of the Charter (effective remedy and fair trial) does not require that an individual should have an unconditional entitlement to bring an action for annulment of a legislative act of the EU directly before the EU Courts. Although the conditions of admissibility laid down in Article 263 TFEU must be interpreted in the light of Article 47 of the Charter, such an interpretation cannot—the Court stated—have the effect of setting aside the conditions expressly laid down in that Treaty.

As regards actions for annulment brought by associations, the Court recalled that such actions have been held admissible in three types of situation: (i) where a legal provision expressly grants a series of procedural powers to associations; (ii) where the association represents the interests of its members, who would themselves be entitled to bring proceedings; and (iii) where the association is distinguished individually because its own interests as an association are affected, in particular because its negotiating position has been affected by the act in respect of which annulment is sought. Yet, none of those situations was found applicable with regard to the association acting in the case. With respect to the argument that the General Court should have recognized the existence of another situation in which associations would be entitled to bring proceedings, namely 'the action of a collective defending a collective good', the Court found that that argument was not put forward at first instance and should therefore be rejected as inadmissible in the context of the appeal.[32]

In *Sabo*, certain individuals and associations sought the partial annulment of the 2018 Directive on the promotion of the use of energy from renewable sources, insofar as it included forest biomass among the sources of renewable energy. The General Court, confirmed by the Court of Justice on appeal, rejected the action as inadmissible for lack of individual concern. Those courts found that, contrary to the applicants' submissions, it was not possible to identify a limited category of persons concerned by the provisions of the contested directive that were at issue. As an act of general application, the contested

[32] Case C-565/19 P, *Carvalho and Others v. Parliament and Council* (EU:C:2021:252), paras 26–95.

directive applied to all persons, both natural and legal. The EU Courts found that the applicants did not put forward any factor recognized by case law which would be capable of distinguishing them individually as addressees. Furthermore, it was noted that the applicants themselves had acknowledged that the protection and regulation of the environment is something that affects 'everyone in both current and future generations', a statement which was considered to militate against the notion of individual concern. Accordingly, even assuming that the contested directive did have a negative impact as regards forests and the operation of power plants, the applicants were not—the EU Courts held—in a situation that was different from that of the indeterminate and indeterminable body of EU citizens, which prevented the contested directive from being of individual concern to them. Finally, the EU Courts found that that assessment was not called into question by the applicants' argument that such an interpretation of the concept of 'individual concern' would be incompatible with Article 9 of the Aarhus Convention: acts adopted by the EU institutions acting in a legislative capacity are excluded from the scope of Article 9(3) of the Convention.[33]

The adoption of the Aarhus Regulation has, on the one hand, allowed private applicants to acquire more easily standing before the EU Courts in certain situations. However, given the limited scope of the action that could be brought under the Regulation, the substantive assessment of the EU acts which are considered problematic by the applicants (the acts for which internal review is requested) remains largely outside the scope of judicial review, which is essentially limited to the institutions' negative decisions adopted in reply to the review requests (i.e. requests considered inadmissible or dismissed).

In *ClientEarth*—a case which concerned the interaction between the review procedure under the Aarhus Regulation and the authorization procedure under the REACH Regulation[34]—the General Court dismissed an action for annulment directed against a Commission decision which had rejected a request for an internal review of an implementing decision granting an authorization for uses of a substance under the REACH Regulation, and against the authorization decision itself. The action was declared manifestly inadmissible insofar as the appellant sought annulment of the authorization decision, and partly unfounded and partly inadmissible as regards the review decision. On appeal, the Court broadly agreed with the General Court. Inter alia, it

[33] Case T-141/19, *Sabo and Others v. Parliament and Council* (EU:T:2020:179), and Case C-297/20 P, *Sabo and Others v. Parliament and Council* (EU:C:2021:24).

[34] Regulation (EC) No. 1907/2006, OJ 2006 L 396/1.

confirmed that, in the context of an action relating to the Commission's decision on the request for an internal review, only pleas seeking to demonstrate that that decision was vitiated by errors of law or errors of assessment, and not pleas concerning the application for authorization, are admissible.[35]

In *Mellifera*, the applicant (an NGO) sought the annulment of a Commission decision rejecting the request for internal review, based on then Article 10 of the Aarhus Regulation—a provision that has now been amended—as regards the extension of the approval period of the active substance 'glyphosate'. In its decision, the Commission had held that the request for internal review to be inadmissible on the ground that the contested regulation did not constitute an administrative act (a measure of individual scope) but an act of general application (its provisions were applicable to all operators manufacturing or placing on the market plant protection products containing glyphosate). The General Court upheld the Commission's findings in that regard. It held that the approval of an active substance:

> not only entails legal effects for the person who has applied for such approval, but also for any operator whose activities require such approval ... and for any competent public authority ... in charge of authorising those products. ... Therefore, first, so far as producers of plant protection products are concerned, they may, once the active substance has been approved, apply to the competent national authorities for authorisation of a plant protection product containing that active substance, without the need for them to have taken part in the procedure for approval of that active substance. Secondly, so far as the competent authorities of Member States are concerned, ... the approval of an active substance has the legal consequence of enabling them ... to authorise the placing on the market of plant protection products containing that active substance, if a request to that effect is made.

The General Court also refused to interpret the concept of 'administrative act' in the light of Article 2(g) of the Aarhus Convention. An appeal against that judgment was then rejected as unfounded by the Court.[36]

In *TestBioTech*, two associations challenged the Commission's decision concerning the review of a Commission Implementing Decision authorizing the placing on the market of products containing, consisting of, or produced from

[35] Case T-108/17, *ClientEarth v. Commission* (EU:T:2019:215), paras 18–47, and Case C-458/19 P, *ClientEarth v. Commission* (EU:C:2021:802), paras 20–42.

[36] Case T-12/17, *Mellifera v. Commission* (EU:T:2018:616), paras 40 ff, and Case C-784/18 P, *Mellifera v. Commission* (EU:C:2020:630), paras 35–90.

certain genetically modified organisms (GMOs). The applicants requested the Commission to carry out an internal review of the authorization decision, pursuant to Article 10 of Aarhus Regulation, arguing, in particular, that the assessment of the GMOs in question was flawed for various reasons. By the challenged decision, the Commission informed the applicants that it did not accept any of the allegations invoked to substantiate the request for internal review. In its judgment, the General Court acknowledged that, contrary to the Commission's assertions, an applicant cannot be required to prove that the authorization decision is in breach of the relevant EU regulation. Indeed, the applicant is only required to 'provide a set of material raising serious doubts as to the lawfulness of the authorisation decision'. However, it then rejected the applicants' pleas as unfounded (manifest error of assessment of the Commission was not adequately proven) or inadmissible (errors allegedly made by the Commission not clearly specified or not raised in the context of the administrative procedure). On appeal, the Court essentially confirmed the first instance findings. The Court stated that a request for internal review of an administrative act is 'intended to establish that, as alleged, the act in question is unlawful or that it is not well founded'. The party making the request may then bring the matter before the EU judicature by instituting proceedings against the decision rejecting the request for internal review as unfounded. Subsequent judicial proceedings cannot, however, 'be founded on new grounds or on evidence not appearing in the request for review, as otherwise the requirement ... relating to the statement of grounds for such a request would be made redundant and the object of the procedure initiated by the request would be altered'.[37]

Two Opinions are particularly interesting in this context, since they attempt to provide guidance to the parties concerning the nature, scope, and conditions of actions for annulment based on the Aarhus Regulation. AG Kokott in *ClientEarth v. EIB* focused, in particular, on the interaction between the standing requirements set out in Article 263 TFEU and individuals' ability to seek judicial review of an institution's decision taking a position on a request for review.[38] In turn, AG Szpunar's Opinion in *TestBioTech* sought to clarify, inter alia, the burden of proof placed upon the applicants: 'the applicants for review should be able to base their argument on any ground and/or evidence that would raise serious doubts as to the aforementioned presumption. Comprehensive proof is never needed. Speculation, on the other hand,

[37] Case T-177/13, *TestBioTech and Others v. Commission* (EU:T:2016:736), paras 34 ff, and Case C-82/17 P, *TestBioTech and Others v. Commission* (EU:C:2019:719), paras 30 ff.

[38] Opinion of AG Kokott in Joined Cases C-212/21 P and C-223/21 P, *EIB and Commission v. ClientEarth* (EU:C:2022:1003), paras 42–83.

would not be sufficient either.' He then went on to emphasize the margin of manoeuvre enjoyed by the institution in question: they enjoy broad discretion with regard to the outcome of the review—it may: (i) come to the conclusion that the review does not require review of the authorization; (ii) reopen the authorization procedure; (iii) take any other measure it deems appropriate to amend the authorization decision, including amendment, suspension, or repeal of an authorization; and (iv) in case of a clearly unsubstantiated request for internal review, it may reject the request as clearly being unsubstantiated. In his view, the exercise of that discretion depends on the quality of the arguments presented by the party requesting review: the more the arguments are substantiated, the more the institution in question must proceed in the direction of review of the authorization procedure. Finally, concerning the intensity of judicial review of an institution's review decision, that review is limited—AG Szpunar stated—when that decision entails a complex assessment of facts and, therefore, involves broad discretion of the authority making the decision. In such cases, the EU judicature must restrict itself to examining the accuracy of the findings of fact and law made by the institution concerned and to verifying, in particular, that the action taken by that institution is not vitiated by a manifest error or a misuse of powers and that it did not clearly exceed the bounds of its discretion.[39]

The above decisions appear—taken together—consistent with earlier case law, in which the EU Courts had a rather restrictive approach with regard to standing of non-privileged applicants in actions for annulment[40] and their ability to rely on Article 9 of the Aarhus Convention in order to interpret 'more flexibly' the requirements of Article 263(4) TFEU.[41]

2. Standing: Regional and Local Authorities

It is well established that the status of 'privileged' applicants given to Member States under Article 263 TFEU is confined to actions in which they are represented by their (central) government. Provided it enjoys legal personality

[39] Opinion of AG Szpunar in Case C-82/17 P, *TestBioTech and Others v. Commission* (EU:C:2018:837), paras 24–56.

[40] See especially Case C-321/95 P, *Greenpeace and Others v. Commission* (EU:C:1998:153), paras 27–35, dismissing as inadmissible for lack of standing Greenpeace's challenge to the Commission's decision to disburse to Spain financial assistance for the construction of two power stations in the Canary Islands; and Case C-355/08 P, *WWF-UK v. Council* (EU:C:2009:286), paras 39–50, dismissing as inadmissible WWF's challenge to certain provisions of a Council regulation setting total allowable catches in respect of the fishing of cod.

[41] See, in particular, Joined Cases C-401/12 P to C-403/12 P, *Council and Others v. Vereniging Milieudefensie and Stichting Stop Luchtverontreiniging Utrecht* (EU:C:2015:4), paras 52–62, and Joined Cases C-404/12 P and C-405/12 P, *Council and Commission v. Stichting Natuur en Milieu and Pesticide Action Network Europe* (EU:C:2015:5), paras 44–54.

under national law, any other public authority can also bring proceedings before the CJEU but, for the action to be admissible, the standing requirements set out in the fourth paragraph of Article 263 TFEU would have to be met. Although the case law is by no means clear or consistent,[42] a numerically significant line of case law suggests—as noted by AG Bobek in *Région de Bruxelles-Capitale*—that a regional or local entity is concerned by an EU act when it is entrusted with powers that are exercised autonomously within the limits of the national constitutional system of the Member State concerned and the EU act prevents that entity from exercising those powers as it sees fit. That said, the mere fact that an entity has some competence—as a body competent for economic, social, or environmental matters in its territory—with regard to the matter regulated by an EU measure cannot, of itself, be sufficient for that entity to be regarded as 'concerned' within the meaning of Article 263 TFEU. Territorial entities are precluded from taking action against EU acts which affect their interests in a general manner. Something more than that is required: a direct restriction in the exercise of a specific power attributed to the region at the constitutional level in the Member State. Interestingly, AG Bobek noted that the EU Courts seem to have used this test ('the *Vlaams Gewest* test'[43]) to determine both direct and individual concern for regions and other local entities.[44]

That notwithstanding, the validity of that test appears to be called into question in *Région de Bruxelles-Capitale*. In that case, the General Court came to the conclusion that such a region was not directly concerned by the Commission's 2017 Implementing Regulation renewing the approval of the active substance 'glyphosate', insofar as that Regulation required some national implementing measure to deploy its effects vis-à-vis the region.[45] On appeal, AG Bobek advised the Court to set aside the judgment under appeal, consider the action admissible, and refer the case back to the General Court. In his view, by denying standing to the region, the General Court erred in law, misinterpreting the fourth paragraph of Article 263 TFEU as well as a number of provisions of applicable secondary law. Indeed, he considered that the contested regulation produced legal effects which altered the legal position of the region in at least four regards.

[42] See e.g. Turmo, 'Paris-Bruxelles, ou l'Impossible Droit d'Áccès au Juge des Collectivités Territoriales dans l'Union Européenne', *Revue des Affaires Européennes* (2022) 641.

[43] Case T-214/95, *Vlaams Gewest v. Commission* (EU:T:1998:77), para. 29.

[44] Opinion of AG Bobek in Case C-352/19 P, *Région de Bruxelles-Capitale v. Commission* (EU:C:2020:588), paras 58–63.

[45] Case T-178/18, *Région de Bruxelles-Capitale v. Commission* (EU:T:2019:130), paras 27 ff.

First, the region could not exercise, in the manner it saw fit, its autonomous powers (recognized at constitutional level) to regulate the use of plant protection products in its territory. Second, the contested regulation required the Belgian authorities, including the region, to preserve the validity of existing authorizations for the entirety of the time required to complete the procedures for the renewal of those authorizations. Third, the contested regulation triggered, at national level, a national procedure in which the region was required to participate, and in which it could neither *de jure* nor *de facto* make use of the prerogatives granted to it under the Belgian constitution. Fourth, the contested regulation also required the region to recognize, under the mutual recognition system, any authorization granted by a Member State belonging to the same zone. Despite the region's doubts about the harmful nature of glyphosate in general, it was not entitled to refuse recognition, unless it acted in disregard of its EU law obligations.

Importantly, all those effects were imputable—AG Bobek stated—to the contested regulation. There was no 'intermediate' measure of implementation which, in his view, could break the causal link between the contested regulation and the alteration of the legal position of the region. The Advocate General then went on to complete the examination with regard to the region's standing. He took the view that the region was also 'individually concerned' within the meaning of Article 263 TFEU. That was not all: in his opinion, the contested measure was also a 'regulatory act' that did not entail any implementing measure.[46] However, the Court did not share the Advocate General's analysis. In a particularly short judgment, the Court held the various arguments put forward by the region against the General Court's finding on lack of direct concern to be either unfounded or ineffective. In addition, unlike AG Bobek, it did not consider it necessary to check whether the contested measure could be considered a 'regulatory act' that did not entail any implementing measure. The appeal was thus rejected.[47]

In *Ville de Paris*—one of the cases following 'diesel-gate'—the Court came to similar conclusions, this time disagreeing not only with the Advocate General but also with the General Court. By their actions, the applicants (the cities of Paris, Brussels, and Madrid) had sought the annulment of the 2016 Commission Regulation which amended the 2008 Regulation as regards

[46] Opinion of AG Bobek in Case C-352/19 P, *Région de Bruxelles-Capitale v. Commission* (EU:C:2020:588), paras 46–107 and 148–177.

[47] Case C-352/19 P, *Région de Bruxelles-Capitale v. Commission* (EU:C:2020:978), paras 30–67. For criticism, Turmo (n. 42). See also Anrò, 'L'intervento delle Regioni nei Giudizi di Fronte alla Corte di Giustizia dell'Unione Europea: una Proposta de Jure Condendo', 20 *Federalismi* (2022) 498.

emissions from light passenger and commercial vehicles (Euro 6), in particular with regard to the application of the 'pollutant conformity factors' to be applied to the pollutant emission limits laid down for the Euro 6 standard. In their view, the Commission was de facto amending the emission limits set out in a Council Regulation, something which it lacked the power to do. The General Court considered the action admissible on the ground that the regulation was a regulatory act that was of direct concern to the applicants and did not entail implementing measures. The finding of direct concern was based on the reading of a provision of the contested regulation according to which the cities could not, in certain circumstances, limit the circulation of Euro 6 vehicles. That Court also found the substantive arguments put forward by the applicants convincing and thus annulled part of the contested regulation.[48]

On appeal, the Commission contested, inter alia, the General Court's findings concerning the standing of the applicants. In that respect, AG Bobek did find the General Court to have erred about the reasons for which it had established direct concern of the applicants. Indeed, the provision in question did not restrict the cities' power to lay down traffic regulations, including those affecting Euro 6 vehicles. However, he took the view that the applicants were, actually, directly concerned on another ground: the contested regulation had an impact on the way the cities were able to lawfully exercise their specific powers in the area of environmental protection and the protection of public health when tackling pollution and ensuring the appropriate standards of air quality, in accordance with national and EU laws. Indeed, if the EU institutions do not strive to ensure compliance with the limits set out in 'their own' legislation regarding polluting emissions from vehicles, the burden to adopt measures to ensure air quality logically shifts—the Advocate General argued—onto the authorities of the Member States. That is especially true with regard to national authorities responsible for the regulation of traffic.

To that end, national authorities such as the applicants were therefore required to adopt certain measures that, had the Union prohibited the registration and sale of vehicles failing to meet its own emission standards, would most likely have been less restrictive or perhaps even unnecessary. In those circumstances, to suggest that the position of the local entities is affected by the contested regulation only in fact and not in law was considered by AG Bobek as extremely formalistic, if not outright cynical. He thus suggested the Court

[48] Joined Cases T-339/16, T-352/16 and T-391/16, *Ville de Paris, Ville de Bruxelles and Ayuntamiento de Madrid v. Commission* (EU:T:2018:927), paras 34–159.

uphold the judgments under appeal.[49] For its part, the Court agreed with the Advocate General regarding the error of law made by the General Court in interpreting the provisions of the contested regulation. However, the Court's analysis of the applicants' standing ended there and the alternative arguments that the applicants had made at first instance and which the Advocate General found well-founded were not examined. On that basis, the Court set aside the judgment under appeal and dismissed the actions for annulment as inadmissible for lack of standing.[50]

The restrictive approach of those decisions finds a precedent in the Court's order of 2009 in which the appeal brought by the Azore Region against the judgment of the General Court declaring inadmissible its action for annulment against certain provisions of a Council regulation concerning fishing activities was dismissed by way of an order. The region had argued that it was individually concerned by those provisions because, as an outermost region, it was entitled to specific protection under Article 349 TFEU, and because of the harmful effects of the regulation on the specific marine environment of the Azores and, consequently, also on the economy of the Azores region. The Court agreed with the General Court that those arguments were inadequate to prove that the region was individually concerned by the contested regulation.[51] On the other hand, however, several rulings of the General Court (un-appealed, or upheld on appeal by the Court) appeared to adopt a less formalistic approach with regard to this matter, as pointed out by AG Bobek in the already-mentioned Opinion in *Région de Bruxelles-Capitale*.

B. Actions for Failure to Act

This form of action, provided for in Article 265 TFEU, enables the lawfulness of EU institutions' *failures to act* to be reviewed by the EU judiciary and is thus complementary to the action for annulment. The institution in question can be brought before the Court when it has failed to address the applicant an act which has legal effects. This means that the institution was under a duty to act. Such an action may be brought only after the institution concerned has been called on to act by the applicant. If, within two months of being so called

[49] Opinion of AG Bobek in Joined Cases C-177/19 P to C-179/19 P, *Germany—Ville de Paris and Others v. Commission* (EU:C:2021:476), paras 36–110.

[50] Joined Cases C-177/19 P to C-179/19 P, *Germany—Ville de Paris and Others v. Commission* (EU:C:2022:10), paras 69 ff.

[51] Case C-444/08 P, *Região autónoma dos Açores v. Council* (EU:C:2009:733), paras 36–41 and 44–48.

upon, the institution concerned has not defined its position, the action may be brought within a further period of two months. Where the failure to act is held to be unlawful, it is for the institution concerned to put an end to the failure by appropriate measures.[52]

This form of action is not very frequently used, including in the context of environmental litigation. Cases are rare and of relative importance. The Court's database records only 11 cases of actions for failure to act closed, to date, with 'environment' as the subject matter.[53] Most of those cases were, moreover, withdrawn by the applicant or declared moot by the Court. Indeed, it is a frequent occurrence that, during the procedure, the institution being requested to act takes a formal position on the request of the applicant, thus depriving the judicial proceedings of their object.[54] Interestingly, none of those 11 cases was heard by the Court (either on appeal from the General Court or directly in the first and only instance).

In addition, the admissibility of the action has also been an issue in a number of cases. According to settled case law, Articles 263 and 265 TFEU merely prescribe one and the same method of recourse. It follows that, just as the fourth paragraph of Article 263 TFEU allows individuals to bring an action for annulment against a measure of an institution which is not addressed to them, provided that the measure is of direct and individual concern to them, the third paragraph of Article 265 TFEU must be interpreted as also entitling them to bring an action for failure to act against an institution which they claim has failed to adopt a measure which would have concerned them in the same way.[55] Similarly, the Court has consistently held that natural and legal persons may rely on Article 265 TFEU 'only for the purpose of obtaining a declaration that, in infringement of the TFEU, [an] institution has failed to adopt acts, other than recommendations or opinions, the legality of which they would also be entitled to challenge by means of the action for annulment referred to in the fourth paragraph of Article 263 TFEU'.[56]

For example, in *Federcaccia*, two Italian associations promoting hunting brought proceedings against the Commission, alleging that that institution had failed to take into account certain data communicated to it by the Italian government in the context of an ongoing infringement procedure and, by way

[52] More generally, on this form of action, with references to the case law, see Barents (n. 17) ch. 8.

[53] Database checked by the author in December 2023.

[54] See e.g. Case T-623/19, *ArcelorMittal Bremen v. Commission* (EU:T:2020:173), paras 22–25. For a case in which the applicant was successful, see Case T-164/10, *Pioneer Hi-Bred International v. Commission* (EU:T:2013:503), paras 23 ff.

[55] See, to that effect, Case C-68/95, *T. Port* (EU:C:1996:452), para. 59.

[56] See, recently, Case C-221/23 P, *NO v. Commission* (EU:C:2023:754), para. 20 and the case law cited.

of a consequence, failed to adopt the appropriate measure. The General Court declared the action inadmissible since the measure which the applicants had requested the Commission to adopt was not an act with binding legal effects and, in any event, the applicants were neither individually nor directly concerned by that measure.[57] Those findings appear consistent with earlier case law. For instance, in *Scientific and Technological Committee*, the General Court was seized of a case brought by a number of legal persons, who argued that, despite their letters to several Commissioners drawing their attention to certain environmental problems, the institution had failed to: (i) adopt a position concerning the risks for the population of the European Union from the subterranean storage of carbon dioxide and its escape from geological formations towards the earth's surface and (ii) take effective measures for the protection of the population and the environment. The General Court found that not only did the applicants lack standing but also that the Commission was under no obligation to adopt the measure requested (regardless of whether that measure could be regarded as producing binding legal effects), and thus declared the action inadmissible.[58]

C. Preliminary Ruling Procedure

The reference for a preliminary ruling is designed to ensure the uniform interpretation and application of EU law within the European Union by offering the national courts a means of bringing before the CJEU questions concerning the *interpretation* of EU law or the *validity* of acts adopted by the EU institutions and bodies.[59] A request for a preliminary ruling is admissible when, inter alia, the Court's answer to the questions referred is necessary to enable the referring court to give judgment. It is, in principle, for that court to determine, in the light of the particular circumstances of each case, the need for a request for a preliminary ruling, and the questions that must be addressed to the Court. However, where a question is raised in the context of a case that is pending before a national court of last instance, that court is required to make a reference

[57] Case T-570/15, *Federcaccia della Regione Liguria and Others v. Commission* (EU:T:2017:767), paras 52–95.

[58] Case T-125/07, *Scientific and Technological Committee of AGH and Others v. Commission* (EU:T:2009:82), paras 19–30.

[59] At present, all references are heard by the Court. However, in December 2022, the CJEU submitted a request for amendment of Protocol No. 3 on the Statute of the CJEU, in order to transfer the competence to hear and determine questions referred for a preliminary in some specific areas to the General Court.

unless the correct interpretation of the rule in question admits of no reasonable doubt (*acte clair*) or there is already well-established case law on the point (*acte éclairé*). In addition, national courts do not have the power to declare EU acts invalid and, consequently, when they entertain doubts on the validity of such an act, they must refer the matter to the Court under Article 267 TFEU. National litigation is suspended until the Court has given its decision. In deciding the dispute before it, the referring court is bound by the interpretation given in the judgment of the Court. That judgment also binds other national courts before which the same problem is raised.[60]

In essence, the preliminary ruling on *validity* permits the CJEU to check, directly, the validity of an EU act when a national court entertains doubts in that respect. On the other hand, the preliminary ruling on *interpretation* permits the checking, indirectly, of whether national measures comply with EU law. Although the CJEU does not have jurisdiction within that framework to rule directly on whether national legislation is compatible with EU law, it does have the authority to provide national courts with rulings on the interpretation of EU law so as to enable those courts to determine for themselves whether such compatibility exists in order to resolve the disputes brought before them. In practice, this means that, where a national court refers a question as to whether national legislation complies with EU law, the Court will rarely withhold its jurisdiction but will typically reformulate the question to focus on the interpretation of EU law. This allows the Court simultaneously to assist the referring court in applying EU rules while at the same time respecting the formal allocation of jurisdiction between them. Indeed, the Court gives an interpretation of the relevant EU rules which is formulated in abstract terms but is, in reality, close to a direct application of those rules to the case at hand. Therefore, preliminary ruling proceedings on interpretation may also be regarded, as then Judge Pescatore famously stated, as 'the infringement procedure of the European citizens'.[61] In addition, the preliminary ruling *on interpretation* may also lead to both a direct and indirect check of validity of the EU measures at stake. The Court may, on the one hand, raise issues of validity of the EU measures invoked *ex officio*[62] and, on the other hand, give an interpretation of the

[60] More generally, on this procedure, with references to the case law, see M. Broberg and N. Fenger, *Broberg and Fenger on Preliminary References to the European Court of Justice* (3rd edn, 2021).

[61] Pescatore, '*Van Gend en Loos*, 3 February 1963—A View from Within', in M. Maduro and L. Azoulai (eds), *The Past and Future of EU Law: The Classics of EU Law Revisited on the 50th Anniversary of the Rome Treaty* (2010) 7.

[62] See e.g. Case C-362/14, *Schrems* (EU:C:2015:650), para. 67.

relevant EU rules in the light of superior rules of law (such as the Treaties or the Charter) in order to ensure their lawfulness.[63]

One procedural issue that regularly arises in procedures under Article 267 TFEU is the *admissibility* of the reference, in particular as regards the relevance/necessity requirement. In that regard, the well-established case law is that questions relating to EU law 'enjoy a presumption of relevance'. The Court may thus refuse to give a ruling only where it is 'quite obvious' that the interpretation, or the determination of validity, of a rule of EU law that is sought bears no relation to the actual facts of the main action or its purpose, where the problem is hypothetical, or where the Court does not have before it the factual or legal material necessary to give a useful answer to the questions submitted to it.[64]

In that regard, the *Blaise* case is of particular interest. The case originated from a reference by a French criminal court hearing a trial against a number of environmental activists on charges of defacing or damaging the property of another, by having entered shops and damaged cans of weedkiller containing glyphosate, as well as glass display cases. In their defence, those activists argued that the products in question presented an unacceptable potential risk to human health and the environment and that the EU approval process for glyphosate was defective and, therefore, unlawful. On that basis, the referring court posed four questions to the Court concerning the validity of the regulation concerning the placing of plant protection products on the market. The European Parliament and the Commission contested the admissibility of the reference. They argued, in particular, that the Court's reply to the questions referred could have no effect on the outcome of the criminal prosecutions brought before the referring court. However, the Court disagreed with that view. It referred to the presumption of relevance and then went on to point out that it was apparent 'from the order for reference and from the response of the referring court to a request for clarification that, according to that court, a declaration that [the regulation in question] is invalid might, pursuant to the rules of French criminal law, lead it to hold that the legal element that is a constituent of the crime that the accused are alleged to have committed is nullified, taking into consideration that the plant protection products at issue are harmful to human health'. The reference was thus held admissible and, after examining the issues raised by the referring court, the Court came to the conclusion that

[63] See e.g. Case C-401/19, *Poland v. Parliament and Council* (EU:C:2022:297), para. 70.

[64] See, inter alia, Case C-100/21, *Mercedes-Benz Group (Liability of manufacturers of vehicles fitted with defeat devices)* (EU:C:2023:229), para. 53 and the case law cited.

the examination of the questions referred for a preliminary ruling had revealed nothing capable of affecting the validity of the relevant regulation.[65]

Other recent cases of environmental litigation confirm this generous approach to admissibility. Indeed, it is not an infrequent occurrence that one of the parties having submitted observations (e.g. the government of the Member State concerned or the Commission) expresses doubts as to whether an answer from the Court to the questions referred by the national court is actually necessary for that court to solve the dispute pending before it. However, in the vast majority of cases, the Court dismisses the objections on the grounds that the elements invoked by the parties in question are not sufficient to rebut the presumption of relevance.[66]

Another issue which has been raised, often in legal scholarship, is whether preliminary rulings on validity are actually an effective alternative to actions for annulment.[67] The case law is not particularly large in that regard. Apart from the already-mentioned *Blaise* case, the *Vereniging Hoekschewaards Landschap* case is of interest. It originated from a reference by a Dutch court which inquired about the validity of a Commission decision adopting an update of the list of sites of 'Community importance' for the Atlantic biogeographical region. The request was made in proceedings between an environmental association and the State Secretary concerning the legality of a decision to reduce the size of a special area of conservation (SCI). By its question, the referring court asked, in essence, whether the reduction in the size of one site, by excluding one specific area on the ground that the initial inclusion of the latter in the site was the result of a scientific error, was valid. The Court ruled that, on the occasion of the update of the list of SCIs in the Atlantic biogeographical region, the Commission could not lawfully rely on the existence of an initial scientific error in order to place the site in question on that list without including the contested area. Consequently, the Court declared the Commission decision partly invalid.[68] Apart from that case, however, environmental litigation does not offer other examples, unlike other areas of law, such as data protection.

[65] Case C-616/17, *Blaise and Others* (EU:C:2019:800), paras 31–39.

[66] See, inter alia, Case C-688/21, *Confédération paysanne and Others (In vitro random mutagenesis)* (EU:C:2023:75), paras 29–37; Case C-24/21, *PH (Regional ban on the cultivation of GMOs)* (EU:C:2022:526), paras 33–38; Case C-463/20, *Namur-Est Environment* (EU:C:2022:12), paras 35–42; Case C-15/19, *Azienda Municipale Ambiente* (EU:C:2020:371), paras 23–30; and Case C-693/18, *CLCV and Others (Defeat device on diesel engines)* (EU:C:2020:1040), paras 45–58. Conversely, for a case in which the questions were held partly inadmissible, see e.g. Joined Cases C-80/18 to C-83/18, *UNESA and Others* (EU:C:2019:934), paras 27–43.

[67] Inter alia, with further references, see Winter, '*Plaumann* Withering: Standing before the EU General Court under Way from Distinctive to Substantial Concern', 15 *European Journal of Legal Studies* (2023) 85; and Hadjiyianni (n. 4).

[68] Case C-281/16, *Vereniging Hoekschewaards Landschap* (EU:C:2017:774), paras 25–41.

D. Actions for Non-Contractual Liability against the European Union

Pursuant to Article 340, second paragraph, TFEU, the European Union must, 'in accordance with the general principles common to the laws of the Member States, make good any damage caused by its institutions or by its servants in the performance of their duties'. Under Article 268 TFEU, the CJEU has sole jurisdiction to hear actions for non-contractual liability against the European Union. An action for non-contractual liability can be brought as a self-standing action or in conjunction with another action (e.g. an action for annulment). According to settled case law, EU law confers a right to reparation where three cumulative conditions are satisfied: (i) the rule of law infringed is intended to confer rights on individuals; (ii) the breach of law is sufficiently serious; and (iii) there is a direct causal link between the breach of the obligation and the damage sustained by the injured parties. Applicant bears the burden of proving that those three conditions are satisfied.[69]

An issue that often arises in cases of liability brought before the CJEU is whether the applicant succeeded in establishing, to the requisite standard, that the breach was sufficiently serious. According to settled case law, whether a breach of EU law is sufficiently serious depends on whether the EU institution concerned 'manifestly and gravely disregarded the limits on its discretion'. In particular, where that institution has only a considerably reduced, or even no, discretion, the mere infringement of EU law may be sufficient to establish the existence of a sufficiently serious breach.[70] However, for normative and quasi-normative acts, the institutions are often recognized to have a large degree of discretion, insofar as they have to operate policy choices in the general interest and/or undertake complex assessments of, for example, a scientific or economic nature.[71] As the law stands, the CJEU has not yet ruled as to whether the European Union may, in some circumstances, be called upon to compensate damage under a regime of *strict* liability—that is, also in the case of *lawful* conduct on the part of the EU institutions—for unusual or special damage suffered by a particular circle of individuals or economic operators. Whereas it ruled out that such a liability exists where the EU institutions' conduct falls

[69] On this action, in general, with references to the case law, see P. Aalto, *Public Liability in EU Law—Brasserie, Bergaderm and Beyond* (2011); and Hanf, 'EU Liability Actions', in R. Schütze and T. Tridimas (eds), *Oxford Principles of European Union Law*, Vol. 1 (2018).

[70] See e.g. Case C-301/19 P, *Commission v. Printeos* (EU:C:2021:39), para. 103 and the case law cited.

[71] See, with ample references, Opinion of AG Emiliou in Case C-389/21 P, *ECB v. Crédit lyonnais* (EU:C:2022:844), paras 41–74.

within the sphere of their legislative competence, it has not expressly excluded it where the EU institutions' conduct relates to the exercise of administrative (or other non-legislative) powers.[72]

The requirement of having to prove not only that a breach occurred—which may in itself be difficult where the action for liability is joined to an action for annulment but the latter is rejected for lack of standing—but also that the breach is 'sufficiently serious', appears to place a rather heavy burden on the applicants.

In *SGL Carbon*, the General Court dismissed actions for damages brought by a number of manufacturers of a given substance claiming to have suffered loss as a result of the erroneous classification of that substance as hazardous to the aquatic environment. Since that classification resulted from what was found, in earlier judgments, to have been a manifest error of assessment by the Commission, there was no dispute as to the unlawfulness of the act which caused the damage relied on. The case therefore raised the question of whether the breach of the obligation of the Commission to take all relevant factors into consideration when exercising its powers constituted a 'sufficiently serious' breach of a rule intended to confer rights on individuals. The General Court came to the conclusion that—given the lack of clarity and the difficulties in interpreting the relevant substantive provisions of EU law—the error committed by the Commission appeared to be excusable. In fact, the Commission's conduct appeared:

> close to that which could reasonably be expected from an administrative authority exercising ordinary care and diligence in an analogous situation, that is to say, a situation characterised by scientific complexity connected to the classification of a substance of unknown composition ... with the purpose of ensuring a high level of protection of human health and the environment.

That conduct was not equivalent—the General Court found—to a manifest and grave disregard of the limits on the Commission's discretion. On appeal, the Court confirmed the General Court's findings.[73]

In the already-mentioned *Carvalho* case, the applicants had not only requested the annulment of certain EU measures but also, in the context of non-contractual liability under Articles 268 and 340 TFEU, an injunction obliging

[72] Case T-317/12, *Holcim (Romania) v. Commission* (EU:T:2014:782), paras 234–240, confirmed on appeal in Case C-556/14 P, *Holcim (Romania) v. Commission* (EU:C:2016:207), paras 105–108.

[73] Case T-639/18, *SGL Carbon v. Commission* (EU:T:2020:628), paras 57 ff; and Joined Cases C-65/21 P and C-73/21 P to C-75/21 P, *SGL Carbon and Others v. Commission* (EU:C:2022:470), paras 25 ff.

the Parliament and Council to adopt measures 'requiring a reduction in greenhouse gas emissions by 2030 by at least 50% to 60% compared to their 1990 levels, or by such higher level of reduction as the Court shall deem appropriate'. The General Court rejected this part of the action as being inadmissible, finding that, both by their claim for annulment and by their request for an injunction, the applicants were seeking to obtain the same result, namely the replacement of the contested provisions of the legislative package at issue with new measures that will have to achieve a greater reduction in GHG emissions than was laid down in the EU measures in force. Accordingly, given that the applicants did not have *locus standi* and that, accordingly, they could not request annulment of the relevant measures, it followed—the General Court held—'that their action for compensation, which in reality seeks to achieve the same result, must also be declared inadmissible'. On appeal, the Court confirmed that approach.[74]

In *Ville de Paris*, the city of Paris sought not only the annulment of the contested EU regulation but also compensation from the Commission for the harm caused to it as a result of that regulation (in the symbolic amount of one euro). The city of Paris argued that harm was actual and certain, and consisted in the cost of the measures which it would have been required to implement in order to offset the increase in vehicular pollution, Paris' loss of appeal from the perspective of tourism, and the reduced effectiveness of its campaigns to raise awareness amongst the city's inhabitants of the risks caused by pollutant emissions. The General Court also dismissed the claim for damages. Regardless of the admissibility of the claim, which it did not find necessary to evaluate, the General Court took the view that no evidence had been produced either of the alleged damage or of the fact that such damage, assuming it was proven to exist, was the result of the adoption of the contested EU measure. In any event, the damage to image and legitimacy claimed by the city of Paris provided—according to the General Court—'a particularly good example of how symbolic and sufficient reparation can consist simply in the annulment of the provision of the contested regulation which it called into question'.[75]

Similarly, in *Abel*, several individuals acted before the General Court against the Commission, asking that court to: (i) recognize the irregularity of the Commission's conduct; (ii) acknowledge the damage caused to them by the adoption of the regulation amending the Euro 6 regulation; (iii) order

[74] Case T-330/18, *Carvalho and Others v. Parliament and Council* (EU:T:2019:324), and Case C-565/19 P, *Carvalho and Others v. Parliament and Council* (EU:C:2021:252).

[75] Joined Cases T-339/16, T-352/16 and T-391/16, *Ville de Paris, Ville de Bruxelles and Ayuntamiento de Madrid v. Commission* (EU:T:2018:927).

the Commission to pay to each of them 1,000 euros as compensation for the non-material damage caused by the adoption of that regulation and one euro as compensation for the material damage; and (iv) order the Commission to alter the compliance factors established by that regulation which allegedly permitted emissions above those set out in the relevant legislation. As far as the claim for damages was concerned, the General Court rejected it on the ground that the applicants had not proven the existence of any damage or that such damage could be compensated: the contested regulation had been in operation for a relatively short period and there was no evidence that, in such a period, it produced any (material or non-material) damage to the applicants.[76]

Previous case law, including in the environmental field, appears to confirm that establishing the existence of serious breach to the requisite standard may be quite demanding.[77] In addition, in numerous cases the applications were dismissed for lack of proof of the damage[78] and/or of a causal link between the alleged damage and the conduct of the EU institutions complained of.[79]

E. Infringement Proceedings

Infringement proceedings enable the Court to determine whether a Member State has fulfilled its obligations flowing from EU law. Actions can be brought by the Commission (usually) under Article 258 TFEU or any other Member State (more infrequent) under Article 259 TFEU. Before bringing the case before the Court, after a possible informal stage (e.g. via the EU Pilot mechanism), the Commission is to carry out a preliminary administrative procedure in which the Member State is given the opportunity to reply to the complaints alleged against it. To that end, the Commission must address to the Member State in question, first, a letter of formal notice and, subsequently, a reasoned opinion. If the Member State does not dispel the doubts expressed by the Commission or remedy the alleged failure, within the deadline set out in the reasoned opinion, an action may be brought before the Court. The ruling of the Court has a declaratory nature. If the Court finds that an obligation has not been fulfilled, the State must bring the failure to an end without delay. If, after a second set of proceedings is brought by the Commission, the Court finds that the Member State concerned has not complied with its previous judgment, it may impose a lump

[76] Case T-197/17, *Abel and Others v. Commission* (EU:T:2018:258), paras 26–36.
[77] See e.g. Case T-42/04, *Komninou and Others v. Commission* (EU:T:2006:12), paras 32–45.
[78] See e.g. Case T-198/05, *Mebrom v. Commission* (EU:T:2007:147), paras 50–73.
[79] See e.g. Case T-461/93, *An Taisce and WWF UK v. Commission* (EU:T:1994:244), para. 42.

sum and/or periodic penalty payments (Art. 260(2) TFEU). In addition, if the Member State's failure consists in non-communication of the national measures transposing a directive, the Commission can already ask for the imposition of financial penalties in the first set of proceedings (Art. 260(3) TFEU). The Commission has considerable discretion in deciding whether, when, on what grounds, and against which Member State(s) it intends to bring proceedings. Private persons can submit complaints to the Commission regarding possible breaches of EU law but have no right to require the Commission to start a procedure or challenge its action or inaction. Nor have they any right to formally intervene in the proceedings (either at the administrative stage or at the judicial stage).[80]

There is a rather significant body of case law concerning actions against breaches (or alleged breaches) of environmental legislation by the Member States. In particular, the Commission has consistently brought numerous proceedings for lack of transposition, erroneous transposition, or erroneous application of EU environmental directives throughout the years.[81] Some of those cases subsequently gave rise to a second infringement procedure in which the Commission asked the Court to impose financial penalties for alleged failures to comply with the first judgment of the Court.[82] In the vast majority of those cases, brought under both Article 258 and Article 260 TFEU, the Commission was wholly or partly successful.[83]

In addition, it was precisely in the context of actions brought for alleged failures to comply with environmental legislation that the Commission first alleged a Member State's 'general and persistent infringement' of the relevant EU provisions. In the seminal *Irish Waste* case, the Court found that:

> in principle nothing prevents the Commission from seeking in parallel a finding that provisions of a directive have not been complied with by reason of the conduct of a Member State's authorities with regard to particular specifically identified situations and a finding that those provisions have not been

[80] More generally on infringement proceedings, with references to case law, see L. Prete, *Infringement Proceedings in EU Law* (2017).

[81] See, among many, Case C-220/22, *Commission v. Portugal (Limit values—NO2)* (EU:C:2023:521), para. 1; Case C-444/21, *Commission v. Ireland (Protection of special areas of conservation)* (EU:C:2023:524), para. 1; Case C-683/20, *Commission v. Slovakia (Environmental noise)* (EU:C:2022:22), para. 1; and Case C-217/19, *Commission v. Finland (Spring hunting of male common eiders)* (EU:C:2020:291), para. 1.

[82] See e.g. Case C-261/18, *Commission v. Ireland (Derrybrien wind farm)* (EU:C:2019:955), paras 1, 126, and 135.

[83] For a rather rare case in which the action was completely dismissed: Case C-174/21, *Commission v. Bulgaria* (EU:C:2023:210), para. 32.

complied with because its authorities have adopted a general practice contrary thereto, which the particular situations illustrate where appropriate.[84]

That principle has since been confirmed in subsequent case law.[85] A claim based on a general and persistent failure by the Member State to comply with the relevant EU legislation is now regularly put forward by the Commission in cases started before the Court for alleged non-compliance with, in particular, environmental directives.[86]

F. Interim Measures

Articles 278 and 279 TFEU provide that, in the context of the proceedings before it, the CJEU may, if it considers that circumstances so require, order that the act whose validity is challenged be suspended and/or prescribe any necessary interim measures. The aim of those measures is to prevent serious and irreparable damage to a party while the proceedings are ongoing. The request by the applicant must be introduced jointly with, or subsequently to, the application in the main action (e.g. action for annulment, infringement procedure). The applicant bears the burden of proving satisfaction of three cumulative conditions: (i) *fumus boni iuris* (the case does not appear prima facie unfounded); (ii) *periculum in mora* (the need for an interlocutory order in order to avoid serious and irreparable damage to the party seeking the interim relief); and (iii) the balance of interests involved pleading in favour of granting the measures requested (the interest of the applicant in obtaining the measures requested outweighs the other interests affected by the possible order of the CJEU). The decision on the request for interim measures can be decided by the President of the Court having jurisdiction in the main action (General Court or Court)—a power which can also be delegated to the Vice-Presidents—or by the Courts themselves sitting in a collegiate formation. Procedures under

[84] Case C-494/01, *Commission v. Ireland* (EU:C:2005:250), para. 27.

[85] See, with further references, Eliantonio, 'Systemic Breaches of EU Environmental Law and Techniques of Judicial Engagement with Science: the Underused Potential of Infringement Proceedings', 24 *German Law Journal* (2023) 948. More generally on the concept of 'general and persistent infringements', see Prete, 'The Systemic Criterion in the Use of Infringement Proceedings', 24 *German Law Journal* (2023) 1011.

[86] See e.g. Case C-444/21, *Commission v. Ireland* (EU:C:2023:524), paras 107–121, and Case C-336/16, *Commission v. Poland* (EU:C:2018:94), paras 38 and 83.

Articles 278 and 279 TFEU are normally very rapid and the interim measures may, where appropriate, also be granted *inaudita altera parte*.[87]

The field of environmental protection is certainly one where recourse to interim measures has been more frequent, especially in the case of procedures brought by the Commission under Article 258 TFEU. The *Tyrol Motorway Ban* case against Austria[88] and the *Spring Hunting* case against Malta[89] are two such examples. More recently, it was precisely in an environmental case that the Court gave a particularly innovative and far-reaching decision.

In July 2017, the Commission brought infringement proceedings against Poland for breaches of the Habitats and Birds Directives due to the increase of active forest management operations authorized by the Polish government in the Białowieża Forest, a Natura 2000 site. On the same day, the Commission also lodged an application for interim measures, asking the Court to order the Polish authorities to halt those operations, pending the judgment in the main action, except where there was a threat to public safety. The Vice-President of the Court, owing to the risk of serious and irreparable damage to the integrity of the site, provisionally granted the requested measures, *inaudita altera parte*, within a few days. In the following weeks, however, the Commission took the view that the Polish authorities had deliberately ignored that order (and, at times, openly contested its legitimacy) as the logging operations continued unaffected. Thus, the question arose as to whether any means existed for the Court to enforce compliance with an order issued under Article 279 TFEU. In its order of 20 November 2017, on a request by the Commission, the Court answered that question in the affirmative. The Court emphasized that Article 279 TFEU confers on the Court the power to prescribe 'any interim measures' that it deems necessary. Although it is for the applicant to request such measures as considered appropriate, the Court must satisfy itself that the measures which it intends to order are sufficiently effective to achieve their aim. The Court enjoys broad discretion in that respect. Therefore, if deemed appropriate, the Court may also adopt, where necessary *ex officio*, any ancillary measure intended to ensure that its order is complied with. The Court found that such a measure may include the imposition of periodic penalty payments. That measure must not be regarded as a punishment but merely as a means to encourage the relevant Member State to comply with the order.

[87] More generally, on interim measures, with references to the case law, see K. Lenaerts, K. Gutman, and J. T. Nowak, *EU Procedural Law* (2nd edn, 2023) ch. 13.
[88] Case C-320/03 R, *Commission v. Austria* (EU:C:2004:231).
[89] Case C-76/08 R, *Commission v. Malta* (EU:C:2008:252).

In the case at hand, the Court found it unnecessary to establish whether the first order had not been complied with. There was enough evidence in the case file to establish doubt that Poland had complied, or that it intended to comply, with the new order. In such circumstances, the Court considered it necessary to enhance the effectiveness of the interim measures ordered by providing for a periodic penalty payment to be imposed if Poland failed to comply with them immediately and fully. Poland was thus requested to send to the Commission, within 15 days, details of all measures adopted in order to comply. If the Commission was of the view that Poland had failed to comply with the order, it could request that proceedings be resumed. The Court would then give a decision by way of a new order. If the Court found an infringement, it would order Poland to pay to the Commission 'a periodic penalty payment of at least 100,000 euros per day' from the date of notification of the new order until compliance was achieved or until the judgment in the main proceedings was delivered. Subsequent to the delivery of the latter decision, Poland ensured compliance with the measures ordered by the Court and the interim procedure was, accordingly, not resumed.[90]

In a subsequent case, the Court this time found it appropriate to impose such penalties. In 2021, the Czech Republic brought proceedings against Poland under Article 259 TFEU, for an alleged breach of the provisions of the EIA Directive, on the ground that the Polish authorities had authorized the extension of lignite extraction in the Turów Mine without, in particular, conducting an environmental impact assessment.[91] The Czech Republic also asked the Court to impose interim measures. By order of 21 May 2021, the Vice-President of the Court ordered Poland to cease lignite mining activities immediately at the Turów Mine pending delivery of the judgment closing the main proceedings. Taking the view that Poland had failed to comply with that order, on 7 June 2021 the Czech Republic lodged another application for interim measures, seeking an order requiring Poland to pay a daily penalty payment of 5,000,000 euros for its failure. In its order of 20 September 2021, the Vice-President of the Court ordered Poland to pay a penalty payment of 500,000 euros per day from the date of notification of the new order until it complied with the measures set out in the previous order. Subsequently, the

[90] Case C-441/17 R, *Commission v. Poland* (EU:C:2017:622 and EU:C:2017:877), paras 89–119. For a comment, Wennerås, 'Saving a Forest and the Rule of Law: *Commission v. Poland*', 56 *Common Market Law Review* (2019) 541; and Prete, 'Can't see the Forest for the Trees? Penalties under Article 279 TFEU' in D. Sarmiento, H. Ruiz Fabri, and B. Hess (eds), *Yearbook on Procedural Law of the Court of Justice of the European Union* (2020) 157.

[91] Case C-121/21, *Czech Republic v. Poland* (*Turow Mine*), action withdrawn by the applicant in May 2022.

two Member States found an amicable settlement of the dispute and (both the main and the interim) proceedings were terminated.[92]

4. Procedures before National Courts

As mentioned in the introduction, pursuant to Article 19(1) TEU, and in conformity with the principle of sincere cooperation, it is generally for the Member States to ensure judicial protection of individuals' rights under EU law. As AG Léger stated, national courts have an essential role in the implementation of EU law and in the protection of the rights derived from it for individuals and can thus be considered, in that regard, EU 'courts of ordinary jurisdiction'.[93] Therefore, unless a specific form of action is provided for in the EU Treaties, public and private parties can bring proceedings before national courts against other public or private parties when alleged breaches of EU law affect the rights they derive from EU law.

As a matter of principle, the protection of EU rights before national courts is governed by the principle of *procedural autonomy*: in the absence of EU rules governing the matter, it is for the domestic legal system of each Member State to designate the courts and tribunals having jurisdiction and to lay down the detailed procedural rules governing actions for safeguarding rights which individuals derive from EU law. That principle is subject to the condition that such rules are no less favourable than those governing similar domestic actions (principle of equivalence) and do not make it impossible or excessively difficult to exercise the rights conferred on individuals by EU law (principle of effectiveness).[94] In the individual cases, the effective application of the EU rules may be achieved, in particular, thanks to the operation of a tetralogy of principles: direct effect, primacy, consistent interpretation, and state liability. Depending on the factual circumstances of the dispute and the legal background thereto, national courts may, for example, interpret domestic law in the light of the letter and spirit of the relevant EU law in order to ensure compliance therewith; alternatively, they may apply the relevant EU provisions directly, setting aside any contrary provisions of national law, whether the latter predate or postdate the former; they may also award damages when the

[92] Case C-121/21 R, *Czech Republic v. Poland* (EU:C:2021:752), paras 47–51.

[93] Opinion in Case C-224/01, *Köbler* (EU:C:2003:207), para. 66. The important role played by national courts in environmental protection is emphasized by Bogojevic (n. 4).

[94] See, inter alia, Case C-71/14, *East Sussex County Council* (EU:C:2015:656), para. 52 and the case law cited.

relevant conditions are met.[95] In addition, should the national courts entertain doubts on the interpretation and, where relevant, the validity of the applicable EU rules, they have, under Article 267 TFEU, *direct access* to the supreme interpreter of EU law—the CJEU—via the preliminary ruling procedure.[96]

It is not infrequent that national courts refer questions to the Court, inquiring as to whether some national procedural rules may make it impossible or excessively difficult for the applicants to enforce their EU law-based rights. For example, in *Eco Advocacy*, an Irish court asked the Court, inter alia, whether the EU principles of primacy, sincere cooperation, and effectiveness required it to disapply, in an action started by an NGO against the public authorities, the national rules according to which (i) the parties' written pleadings must set out with clarity the specific infringements alleged and (ii) the court is precluded from examining certain grounds of challenge of its own motion. The Court, essentially following the Opinion of AG Kokott, answered that, in principle, the procedural autonomy of the Member States allows the parties to a dispute to be required to set out infringements of EU environmental law in a sufficiently clear and precise manner in their written pleadings at an early stage in those proceedings in order for such infringements to be taken into account by the national court, and does not compel the national court to raise of its own motion pleas alleging such infringements.[97]

By contrast, in various cases the Court's rulings restrict the Member States' procedural autonomy by requiring them to provide some means of redress for the applicants allegedly affected by some EU law breaches.

For example, in *Deutsche Umwelthilfe I*, a reference was made by a German court seized of a dispute between a non-governmental organization and the Free State of Bavaria ('Bavaria') concerning a decision of the Higher Administrative Court of Bavaria ordering Bavaria to amend its air quality plan by imposing a traffic ban on diesel vehicles in the city of Munich in order to comply with the nitrogen dioxide limit values prescribed by the Ambient Air Quality Directive. Bavaria had persistently and openly refused to introduce such a ban, despite an order for recurring financial penalties having been made against it. According to the referring court, the setting of fresh financial penalties, even of a higher amount, was not liable to alter Bavaria's conduct. Indeed,

[95] See, in more detail, Lenaerts and Gutiérrez-Fons, 'The General System of EU Environmental Law Enforcement', 30 *Yearbook of European Law* (2011) 380.

[96] In that regard, see Wahl and Prete, 'The Gatekeepers of Article 267 TFEU: On Jurisdiction and Admissibility of References for Preliminary Rulings', 55 *Common Market Law Review* (2018) 511.

[97] Case C-721/21, *Eco Advocacy* (EU:C:2023:477), paras 16–29, and Opinion of AG Kokott (EU:C:2023:39), paras 26–57.

the payment of a financial penalty would not have resulted in any economic loss for Bavaria as the amount paid would, in practice, go back to its budget. The referring court took the view that, in principle, it could be conceivable to ensure compliance with the judicial decision at issue by ordering the coercive detention of certain members of the government of Bavaria. However, national case law was not clear on whether such an instrument, albeit provided for by the national rules, was applicable vis-à-vis the public authorities. In those circumstances, the referring court asked the Court whether EU law empowers or even obliges the national court having jurisdiction to order the coercive detention of office-holders involved in the exercise of official authority. In its judgment, the Court emphasized that, under EU law, a national court cannot order coercive detention solely on the basis of the principle of effectiveness and of the right to effective judicial protection. Any limitation on the right to liberty must be provided for by national provisions that, in the light of their wording and substance, are sufficiently accessible, precise, and foreseeable in their application and thus enable all risk of arbitrariness to be avoided. In addition, since the ordering of coercive detention entails a deprivation of liberty, so as to respect the principle of proportionality, recourse to such an order may be had only where there is no less restrictive measure that enables the objective pursued to be attained. Nevertheless, where the two requirements of an adequate legal basis in national law and of proportionality are met, the Court ruled—in striking difference with the Opinion of AG Øe in the case—that EU law not only allows, but requires, recourse to a measure such as coercive detention.[98]

In *Mercedes-Benz Group*, a German court asked the Court whether the relevant provisions of the directive establishing a framework for the approval of motor vehicles must be interpreted as protecting the specific interests of an individual purchaser of such a vehicle. The Court answered in the affirmative. That directive, the Court found, established a direct link between the car manufacturer and the individual purchaser of a motor vehicle intended to guarantee to the latter that that vehicle complies with the relevant EU legislation. Consequently, the Court considered that the provisions of the framework directive protected, in addition to public interests, the specific interests of the individual purchaser of a motor vehicle vis-à-vis the manufacturer of that vehicle where that vehicle was equipped with a prohibited defeat device. The Member States were therefore required, the Court concluded, to ensure that

[98] Case C-752/18, *Deutsche Umwelthilfe* (EU:C:2019:1114), paras 29 ff, and Opinion of AG Øe (EU:C:2019:972), paras 33 ff.

the purchaser of such a vehicle had a right to compensation from the manufacturer of that vehicle.[99]

In *Protect Natur* and in *Wasserleitungsverband Nördliches Burgenland*, the Court emphasized that natural or legal persons directly concerned by an infringement of provisions of a directive must be in a position to require the competent authorities to observe such obligations, if necessary by pursuing their claims by judicial process. In addition, it ruled that Article 9(3) of the Aarhus Convention, read in conjunction with Article 47 of the Charter, imposes on Member States an obligation to ensure effective judicial protection of the rights conferred by EU law, in particular the provisions of environmental law. The Court added that such right to bring proceedings would be deprived of all useful effect, and even of its very substance, if, by imposing certain conditions, some categories of 'members of the public', *a fortiori* 'the public concerned', such as environmental organizations that meet the relevant legal requirements, were to be denied of any right to bring proceedings.[100]

Similarly, in *Deutsche Umwelthilfe II*, the national court asked the Court, inter alia, whether an environmental association should, on the basis of Article 9(3) of the Aarhus Convention, read in conjunction with Article 47 of the Charter, be entitled to challenge, before the national courts, an administrative decision granting EC type-approval of vehicles in the light of Article 5(2) of the Vehicle Emissions Regulation. In this case too, the Court answered in the affirmative. Although Article 9(3) of the Aarhus Convention lacks direct effect, Member States are also bound by the principles of consistent interpretation, effectiveness, and by Article 47 of the Charter. Accordingly, a national court seized of an action such as that in the main proceedings was required to interpret national law in conformity with the relevant provisions of international law and, where necessary, disapply the national provision depriving an association of standing, thereby making it impossible for the latter to challenge a decision granting or amending EC type-approval which may be contrary to the regulation in question.[101]

That trend of enforcing the powers of national courts, especially vis-à-vis the national administration, or of requiring those courts to open up remedies that were in principle not available to the parties—thereby limiting the scope

[99] Case C-100/21, *Mercedes-Benz Group (Liability of manufacturers of vehicles fitted with defeat devices)* (EU:C:2023:229), paras 68–85.

[100] Case C-664/15, *Protect Natur-, Arten- und Landschaftsschutz Umweltorganisation* (EU:C:2017:987), paras 45–46, and Case C-197/18, *Wasserleitungsverband Nördliches Burgenland and Others* (EU:C:2019:824), paras 32–34.

[101] Case C-873/19, *Deutsche Umwelthilfe (Approval of motor vehicles)* (EU:C:2022:857), paras 46–81.

of national procedural authority—can be observed in earlier decisions in environmental litigation.[102]

A. Actions for Non-Contractual Liability against the Member States

As from the well-known *Francovich* and *Brasserie du Pêcheur* cases, the Court has held that individuals must be able to bring, before national courts, an action for damages against a Member State to make good losses occasioned by that Member State's breach of EU law. The Court found that liability for loss and damage caused to individuals as a result of breaches of EU law attributable to a national public authority constitutes a principle inherent in the system of the Treaties, which gives rise to obligations on the part of the Member States. The Court has held that, under EU law, individuals harmed have a right to reparation when three conditions are met: the rule of EU law infringed by the Member State is intended to confer rights on individuals; the breach of that rule is sufficiently serious; and there is a direct causal link between the breach and the loss or damage sustained by the individuals. Fulfilment of these three conditions was held to be necessary and sufficient to found a right of individuals to obtain redress, although that does not mean that the Member State cannot incur liability under less strict conditions on the basis of national law.[103]

A recent interesting case originated from a reference made by a French court, in a dispute between JP (an individual) and the French authorities, concerning JP's applications seeking, inter alia, (i) the annulment of the implied decision of a local authority to refuse to take the necessary measures to address his health problems linked to air pollution and (ii) compensation from the state for the damage which JP attributed to that pollution. The first question posed by the national court was whether the provisions of the Ambient Air Quality Directive should be interpreted as entitling individuals, in the event of a sufficiently serious breach by an EU Member State of the obligations resulting from those rules, to claim compensation from the Member State concerned for damage to their health in cases where there is a direct and certain

[102] See e.g. Case C-240/09, *Lesoochranárske zoskupenie* (EU:C:2011:125), paras 49–50; Case C-530/11, *Commission v. United Kingdom (Access to justice)* (EU:C:2014:67), paras 33 ff; and Case C-664/15, *Protect Natur* (EU:C:2017:987), paras 34 and 44–55.

[103] Joined Cases C-6/90 and C-9/90, *Francovich and Others* (EU:C:1991:428), paras 31–46, and Joined Cases C-46/93 and C-48/93, *Brasserie du pêcheur and Factortame* (EU:C:1996:79), paras 16 ff. See, more generally, Aalto (n. 69).

causal link with the deterioration in air quality. The Court answered in the negative. It noted that:

> besides the fact that the provisions concerned of [the directive] and the directives which preceded it do not contain any express conferral of rights on individuals in that respect, it cannot be inferred from the obligations laid down in those provisions, with the general objective referred to above, that individuals or categories of individuals are, in the present case, implicitly granted, by reason of those obligations, rights the breach of which would be capable of giving rise to a Member State's liability for loss and damage caused to individuals.[104]

Interestingly, in her Opinion, AG Kokott had taken another view. The Advocate General considered that the limit values for pollutants in ambient air and the obligations to improve air quality laid down by EU directives were intended to confer rights on individuals. She went on to explain that 'a serious breach' exists where the limit values were exceeded without there having been an air quality improvement plan without manifest defects. That said, she acknowledged that proving a direct causal link between the breach of the rules on air quality and the damage to health suffered by an individual may be hard to prove, and she thus attempted to provide the national court with some guidance on how to assess that element.[105]

B. Interim Measures

As mentioned in Section 3.F, it is normally for the CJEU to order the suspension of EU acts whose validity is called into question, or any other appropriate interim measure to that effect. However, in its case law, the Court has clarified that, where the validity of an EU act is contested before a national court, a suspension measure may *also* be adopted by that court, provided that certain conditions are met. Those conditions are, in essence, as follows: (i) the national court must entertain serious doubts as to the validity of the EU measure and, if the validity of the contested measure is not already in issue before the Court, that court must itself refer the question to the Court; (ii) there must be

[104] Case C-61/21, *Ministre de la Transition écologique and Premier ministre (Liability of the State for air pollution)* (EU:C:2022:1015), paras 34–65.

[105] Opinion of AG Kokott in Case C-61/21, *Ministre de la Transition écologique and Premier ministre (Liability of the State for air pollution)* (EU:C:2022:359), paras 33 ff.

urgency, in that the interim relief must be necessary to avoid serious and irreparable damage being caused to the party seeking the relief; (iii) the national court must take due account of the interests of the European Union; and (iv) in its assessment of all those conditions, the national court must comply with any decisions of the EU Courts on the lawfulness of the EU measure or on an application for provisional measures seeking similar interim relief at EU level.[106]

As regards judicial review of the conduct of the Member States, the Court can—as mentioned earlier—order any appropriate provisional measure where that conduct is examined in the context of an infringement procedure. When, on the other hand, judicial review of national measures is carried out by national courts in the context of disputes brought before them, it is clearly for those courts to adopt the necessary interim measures, in conformity with the principle of procedural autonomy. That said, the Court made clear that the full effectiveness of EU law requires that a national court seized of a dispute governed by EU law *must* be able to grant interim relief in order to ensure the full effectiveness of the judgment to be given. A national rule which was to prevent a national court from granting interim relief, where necessary, would thus have to be set aside by that court.[107] The effectiveness of EU law would also be impaired if the authority attaching to such interim relief could be disregarded, in particular, by a public authority of the Member State in which those measures were adopted.[108]

5. A Global Assessment: Complete and/or Effective?

A. The CJEU and Environmental Protection

It is well known that the original EEC Treaty did not contain any reference to the environment.[109] Only the Single European Act, entered into force in 1987, provided the then EEC with an explicit legal basis to develop an environmental policy for the first time. However—with a move that former AG Jacobs called of 'judicial anticipation'[110]—the Court had already stated, as early as in 1985,

106 See Joined Cases C-143/88 and C-92/89, *Zuckerfabrik Süderdithmarschen and Zuckerfabrik Soest* (EU:C:1991:65), para. 33, and Case C-465/93, *Atlanta Fruchthandelsgesellschaft and Others (I)* (EU:C:1995:369), paras 32–51.

107 Case C-213/89, *Factortame and Others* (EU:C:1990:257), paras 21 and 22.

108 Case C-487/19, *W.Ż. (Chamber of Extraordinary Control and Public Affairs of the Supreme Court—Appointment)* (EU:C:2021:798), para. 142.

109 For an historical perspective, see Jans, 'The Development of EC Environmental Law', in G. Winter (ed.), *European Environmental Law—A Comparative Perspective* (1996) 271.

110 Jacobs, 'The Role of the European Court of Justice in the Protection of the Environment', 18 *Journal of Environmental Law* (2006) 187.

that environmental protection was 'one of the Community's essential objectives'.[111] Remarkably, the Court did so despite the absence of any legal basis for, and without any explanation of, that finding. In the subsequent years, the Court repeated that statement again and, in several cases, adopted a relatively benign attitude towards national measures that, on environmental grounds, restricted intra-Community trade or granted state aid.[112] The Court showed—Jacobs writes—'laudable enthusiasm ... to assess measures aiming at the protection of the environment favourably', although the legal reasoning followed to do so was, in his view, at times questionable.[113]

If we 'fast forward' 25 years, we see that, *mutatis mutandis*, the CJEU's relatively friendly approach to substantive issues of environmental protection has not changed. After all, the various amendments to the Treaties have clearly enhanced the status of environmental policy,[114] endowed the (now) European Union with a broader competence in that respect,[115] and provided it with more significant powers to carry it out effectively.[116] Many observers are in fact of the view that, when interpreting substantive provisions of EU law, the Court has, in most cases, adopted decisions that were favourable to environmental protection.[117] The case law shows, inter alia, a rather robust application of the precautionary principle, a frequent use of the principle of effectiveness (*effet utile*), and a preference for a broad interpretation of the concepts set out in the EU environmental legislation.

For example, in a number of recent references for a preliminary ruling, the Court was asked to interpret the concept of 'defeat device' within the meaning of the Vehicles Emissions Regulation to determine the extent to which such devices are unlawful and to rule on certain consequences that their use may entail for the producers and buyers of vehicles. In its judgments, the Court embraced a broad definition of 'defeat device', ruling that such concept covers software (i) that improves the performance of an emission control system during vehicle type-approval tests, even if such improvements can also exceptionally be observed under normal vehicle use conditions or (ii) that ensures compliance

[111] Case 240/83, *ADBHU* (EU:C:1985:59), para. 13. For a comment, see L. Krämer, *European Environmental Law—Casebook* (1993) 11.

[112] See, inter alia, Case 302/86, *Commission v. Denmark* (EU:C:1988:421), para. 8; Case C-389/96, *Aher-Waggon* (EU:C:1998:357), paras 14 ff; and Case C-379/98, *PreussenElektra* (EU:C:2001:160), paras 73–81.

[113] Jacobs (n. 110) 188–194.

[114] See e.g. Art. 3(2) TEU, Art. 11 TFEU, Art. 114(3) TFEU, and Art. 193 TFEU.

[115] See e.g. Art. 21(2)(d) and (f) TEU, Art. 4(2)(e) TFEU, and Arts 191 and 192 TFEU.

[116] See e.g. Art. 177 TFEU.

[117] See, inter alia, J. Setzer *et al.*, *Climate Litigation in Europe: A Summary Report for the European Union Forum of Judges for the Environment* (2022) 23–25, and Kingston, 'The Democratisation of EU Nature Governance. Making EU Nature Law Effective', *Revue Européenne du Droit* (2021) 145.

with the emission limits laid only when the outside temperature is within a certain range and altitude is below a given value. The Court also limited the scope of exceptions for their use in vehicles sold in the European Union. It then found that, since vehicles equipped with such devices were not in conformity with the law (and, possibly, with the sale contracts), and that such a lack of conformity could not be classified as 'minor', rescission of the sale contract in respect of the vehicles in question was not in principle precluded.[118]

In *Pesticide Action Network Europe*, the Court was essentially asked whether Article 53 (entitled 'Emergency situations in plant protection') of the Regulation concerning the placing of plant protection products on the market allowed a Member State to exceptionally permit the sale of plant protection products for seed treatment, where the placing on the market of those products had been expressly prohibited by an implementing regulation. The wording of the relevant provision was not entirely clear on the point. The Court, relying mainly on a contextual and teleological interpretation of that provision, answered in the negative, thus precluding, in the specific case, the Belgian authorities from relying on the temporary derogation regime to permit the placing on the market of plant protection products which contained two substances considered harmful to bees.[119] In *WertInvest Hotelbetrieb*—a case which concerned a large construction project in the Historic Centre of Vienna (a UNESCO site)—the Court held that the requirement to carry out an environmental impact assessment for an urban development project, under the EIA Directive, could not be dependent exclusively on the size of that project. Indeed, EU law precludes thresholds set at a level such that, in practice, all or almost all of the projects of a certain type would be exempt in advance from the requirement for such an assessment.[120] In addition, in *Latvijas valsts meži* the Court interpreted Article 6(3) of the Habitats Directive (which requires a prior assessment of the effects of any plan or project likely to have a significant effect on areas of conservation of Natura 2000 sites) broadly, so as to include precautionary fire protection measures in forest areas, where those activities altered the physical aspect of the site concerned, even where their implementation was required by the applicable national legislation on fire prevention. Absent a prior assessment, those activities may not be initiated or, *a fortiori*,

[118] Cases C-693/18, *CLCV and Others (Defeat device on diesel engines)* (EU:C:2020:1040), paras 59 ff; Case C-128/20, *GSMB Invest* (EU:C:2022:570), paras 26 ff; Case C-134/20, *Volkswagen* (EU:C:2022:571), paras 33 ff; and Case C-145/20, *Porsche Inter Auto and Volkswagen* (EU:C:2022:572), paras 46 ff.

[119] Case C-162/21, *Pesticide Action Network Europe and Others* (EU:C:2023:30), paras 29–54.

[120] C-575/21, *WertInvest Hotelbetrieb* (EU:C:2023:425), paras 33 ff.

continued and completed before the completion of the assessment procedure, and the Member State's authorities were required to adopt measures to remedy any significant effects on the environment of works carried out without the appropriate assessment.[121]

B. The CJEU and Environmental Proceedings

The evaluation of the CJEU's case law in environmental litigation becomes more difficult to make when one zooms in on the cases which raised issues of a procedural nature. On the one hand, it cannot be overlooked that it is precisely in the context of environmental litigation that the CJEU has delivered a number of decisions which brought about important developments with regard to some key aspects of judicial proceedings, in particular by strengthening its own powers and those of the national courts against the administrative authorities in default and by requiring national courts to make appropriate remedies available to physical and moral persons potentially affected by breaches of EU law.[122] On the other hand, however, the CJEU's interpretation and application of the EU provisions and principles governing judicial procedures have led some observers to point to the limited effectiveness of those procedures.[123]

In particular, with regard to the judicial review of EU institutions' actions—which is centralized on the *Plateau de Kirchberg*—the ability of non-privileged applicants to have *direct* access to the CJEU is often considered too restrictive and the possibility to reach the CJEU *indirectly*, via the preliminary ruling procedure, deemed to be, in some cases, an unsuitable alternative. Indeed, the requirements of standing set out in Article 263(4) TFEU have proven to be a rather high barrier, not only for individuals and associations[124] but also for local authorities,[125] when the contested act is one of general application. More specifically, as regards 'individual concern', it is often argued that the *Plaumann* test does not necessarily follow from the text of the Treaties and is, at any rate, applied formalistically and inconsistently.[126] *Mutatis mutandis*, similar

[121] Case C-434/22, *Latvijas valsts meži* (EU:C:2023:966), paras 34 ff.

[122] See e.g. the above-mentioned judgments in *Białowieża Forest*, *Irish Waste*, *Deutsche Umwelthilfe I* and *II*, and also Case C-304/02, *Commission v. France* (EU:C:2005:444), paras 80–86. Similarly, Jacobs (n. 110) 201–202.

[123] Cf. Peeters and Eliantonio, 'On Regulatory Power, Compliance, and the Role of the Court in EU Environmental Law', in Peeters and Eliantonio (n. 4) 489 ff.

[124] As regards associations, see esp. M. Eliantonio *et al.*, *Standing up for Your Right(s) in Europe—A Comparative Study on Legal Standing (Locus Standi) before the EU and Member States' Courts* (2012).

[125] See Turmo (n. 42).

[126] See, among many, Winter (n. 67); Krämer, 'The Environment before the European Court of Justice' (n. 4) 25 ff; and Hadjiyianni (n. 4) 786.

problems emerge when one turns to the conditions of 'direct concern' (after *T&L Sugars*[127]) and of 'regulatory act which does not entail any implementing measure' (starting with *Inuit*[128]).[129] In both regards, the CJEU appears to have favoured a rather narrow interpretation of those concepts. The restrictive approach to standing has had, in turn, consequences for private parties' capacity to claim damages from the European Union or its Member States for possible breaches of EU law. Leaving aside the problems of proving damage and causality to the required standard, the condition relating to the *sufficiently* serious breach of the law appears to be, more often than not, a relatively difficult obstacle to overcome. This problem is compounded by the fact that, as explained, standing for associations (such as NGOs) before the EU Courts is limited to, in essence, three main scenarios.[130] Yet, as AG Sharpston emphasized in *Djurgården-Lilla*, those entities play a key role in promoting environmental protection and, more specifically, ensuring judicial review in environmental matters.[131] One may thus wonder whether a strict application of the traditional case law may not, in certain circumstances, deprive some interested parties of a voice and penalize the effectiveness of the court proceedings by depriving the bench of valuable sources of information.

Clearly, a detailed and exhaustive assessment of the CJEU case law on standing would go beyond the scope of the present study and would require a lengthy ad hoc work. For the purposes of the present chapter, it suffices to stress a number of elements which may be relevant in that respect.

First, it must be acknowledged that the distinctiveness criterion enounced in *Plaumann* is by no means the *only* possible way of interpreting the term 'individually' set out in Article 263 TFEU.[132] Alternative interpretations have been proposed, both within the Court and in academic fora.[133] At the same time,

[127] Case C-456/13 P, *T & L Sugars and Sidul Açúcares v. Commission* (EU:C:2015:284), paras 37 and 38.

[128] See Case C-583/11 P, *Inuit Tapiriit Kanatami and Others v. Parliament and Council* (EU:C:2013:625).

[129] As regards 'direct concern', see similarly Hadjiyianni (n. 4) 788.

[130] As explained in Section 3.1.A, these three scenarios are the following: (i) where a legal provision expressly grants a series of procedural powers to associations; (ii) where the association represents the interests of its members, who would themselves be entitled to bring proceedings; and (iii) where the association is distinguished individually because its own interests as an association are affected, in particular because its negotiating position has been affected by the act in respect of which annulment is sought.

[131] Opinion of AG Sharpston in Case C-263/08, *Djurgården-Lilla Värtans Miljöskyddsförening* (EU:C:2009:421), paras 59–64.

[132] Opinion of AG Jacobs in Case C-50/00 P, *Unión de Pequeños Agricultores v. Council* ('*UPA*') (EU:C:2002:197) para. 75.

[133] E.g. AG Jacobs (in his Opinion in *UPA*) proposed to use a test based on 'a substantial adverse effect' on the applicant's interests. The General Court (in Case T-177/01, *Jégo-Quéré v. Commission* (EU:T:2002:112)) phrased the test slightly differently, referring to applicants whose legal position is affected 'in a manner which is both definite and immediate, by restricting his rights or by imposing

however, it follows quite clearly from the text and scheme of the provision that a rather restrictive interpretation is required[134] and it is undisputed that the EU constitutional legislature never—that is, neither when the Treaty of Rome was signed[135] nor when that Treaty was subsequently amended[136]—wished to introduce some form of *actio popularis* before the EU judiciary. Both the principles of democracy and of institutional balance, and the need to maintain the judicial docket at a reasonable level, strongly militate against a wide opening of the judicial floodgates.

Second, it is objectively not easy to envisage an (arguably less restrictive) alternative test that would open those gates, but 'not too much': allowing the 'deserving' actions to reach the Court while filtering out spurious, self-serving, and 'less noble' ones.[137] Any adjective which could be used to reinterpret the criterion of individual concern—such as 'substantial', 'immediate', 'personal', or 'severe'—is only as good as is the use that is made of it.[138] In other words, all those concepts are inherently imprecise and can be interpreted and applied with various degrees of stringency (or, alternatively, of moderation). Thus, I am not sure that a change of the test would *ipso facto* solve the problems of access to the EU Courts that legal scholarship complains of.

Third, it would appear that the Court is very unlikely to abandon the *Plaumann* test (or even to substantially revisit it), at least in the short to medium term. If anything, the momentum to do so would have been at the time of the mentioned *Jégo-Quéré* and *UPA* judicial proceedings. However, in those

obligations on him'. Winter has recently suggested interpreting 'individual concern' as requiring a 'personal and severe' concern. Winter (n. 67).

[134] The plain meaning of the adjective 'individual' is (according to the English Merriam-Webster dictionary): of, relating to, or distinctively associated with an individual, intended for one person, being an individual or existing as an indivisible whole, having marked individuality. Importantly, the other language versions of the Treaty include similar terms: e.g. 'individualmente' (Spanish), 'individuell' (German), 'individuellement' (French), 'individualmente' (Italian), 'individwalment' (Maltese), 'individueel' (Dutch), 'indywidualnie' (Polish), 'individualmente' (Portuguese), and 'individual' (Romanian).

[135] See Opinion of AG Lagrange in Joined Cases 16/62 and 17/62, *Confédération nationale des producteurs de fruits and légumes and Others v. Council* (EU:C:1962:40), p. 482, and the judgment of the Court in the same case (EU:C:1962:47), p. 478.

[136] See, inter alia, Final report of the discussion circle on the Court of Justice, published by the Secretariat of the European Convention in Brussels, 25 March 2003, CONV 636/03. In that regard, with further references, see van Wolferen and Eliantonio, 'Access to Justice in Environmental Matters: The EU's Difficult Road Towards Non-Compliance With the Aarhus Convention', in Peeters and Eliantonio (n. 4) 153.

[137] See, in that regard, Cheneviere-Mesdag (n. 4) 138.

[138] One may have the impression that, at times, the value of certain adjectives is overstated. This may remind the readers of the following exchange between two characters of the 1996 movie *The English Patient*. Katherine Clifton: 'I wanted to meet a man who could write such a long paper with so few adjectives.' László Almásy: 'A thing is still a thing no matter what you place in front of it. Big car, slow car, chauffeur-driven car, still a car.'

cases, the Court expressly and firmly stated that that was a task for the drafters of the Treaties, which in fact amended Article 263 TFEU with the Treaty of Lisbon by adding a third scenario of standing. Currently, there does not seem to be any appetite, at the political level, for introducing any further change to Article 263 TFEU[139] and the recent reforms concerning the judicial architecture of the Union and the allocation of jurisdiction within the CJEU would appear to exclude major structural changes within the current set-up.[140]

In light of those elements, one may wonder whether there is a real and pressing need to repeal the *Plaumann* test. Would not a pure and simple *application* of that test, in each specific case, in the light of present-day conditions suffice? By 'present-day conditions',[141] I refer, first and foremost, to those brought about by the evolution of EU law which, from 1963 (when *Plaumann* was delivered) to date, went from being mainly a body of economic laws to becoming a 360° legal system which affects almost any aspect of EU citizens' lives. That significant evolution is also reflected in the choice, made by the drafters of the Treaties, to render the Charter a legally binding source of primary law. That instrument cannot but require a *strengthened* protection of those (substantive and procedural) rights which have been deemed of such importance to be defined 'fundamental', such as the right to the integrity of the person (Art. 3) and the right to an effective remedy and to a fair trial (Art. 47). The Charter also requires the Union to *ensure* '[a] high level of environmental protection

[139] In this context, I would just add that a change to that provision would, in all evidence, also be required in order to grant, as suggested by some academics, legal personality, and thus active standing in court, to 'Nature'. See Stone, 'Should Trees Have Standing? Towards Legal Rights for Natural Objects', 45 *Southern California Law Review* (1972) 450. More recently, Epstein and Schoukens, 'A Positivist Approach to Rights of Nature in the European Union', 12 *Journal of Human Rights and the Environment* (2021) 205.

[140] That excludes, e.g., the actual feasibility of creating, pursuant to Art. 257 TFEU, a specialized court, attached to the General Court, having jurisdiction at first instance on proceedings concerned with environmental matters (for such a suggestion, see Eliantonio *et al.* (n. 124) 17). In any event, the mere creation of a specialized court would, in itself, have no bearing on the existing rules on standing, and whether the decision establishing such a specialized court could introduce a rule that derogates from Art. 263(4) TFEU is dubious. Furthermore, as Lenaerts and Gutiérrez-Fons—rightly, in my view—argued (n. 95) 395: 'in terms of enforcement, environmental law is not awarded special treatment. Nor is it treated as a "special case". Far from that, at the constitutional level, there is no difference between the enforcement of EU environmental law and the enforcement of other fields of law in which the Union enjoys (shared) competence.' Lastly, I would agree with M. Pallemaerts, *The Aarhus Convention at Ten* (2011) 312, in that 'modifying a fundamental provision of the Treaties governing the functioning of the Court of Justice to deal with a specific problem in the environmental field by creating a derogation from the general rules for a particular class of non-privileged claimants ... may be considered discriminatory and politically difficult to justify by many governments'.

[141] That is a term commonly used by the ECtHR with reference to the ECHR, and also by the Court with reference to the Charter (see e.g. Judgment of 17 December 2020, Case C-336/19, *Centraal Israëlitisch Consistorie van België and Others* (EU:C:2020:1031), para. 77. For an interpretation of Treaty provisions on CJEU procedures in the light of 'present-day conditions', see e.g. Opinion of AG Wahl in Joined Cases C-58/13 and C-59/13, *Torresi* (EU:C:2014:265), para. 26.

and the improvement of the quality of the environment' (Art. 33) and 'a high level of human health protection' (Art. 35).[142] The latter provisions, arguably, laid down an obligation for the European Union to take adequate measures to pursue those objectives, thereby giving individuals a corresponding 'right', at least in the 'Hohfeldian' sense.[143] It is true that, as the Court stated again in *Carvalho*, a claim that EU acts 'infringe fundamental rights is not sufficient *in itself* to establish that the action brought by an individual is admissible, without running the risk of rendering the requirements of the fourth paragraph of Article 263 TFEU meaningless'.[144] However, that does not exclude that such a claim may be among the elements which the Court could take into account when applying the *Plaumann* test to the specific circumstances of the case.

The CJEU's case law on standing in the field of antitrust, state aids, and anti-dumping shows quite clearly that (i) the fulfilment of the *distinctive* criterion is not a black-or-white situation but rather a matter of degree and (ii) the applicant need not be in a *unique* position, since other persons may also be in a position that is distinctive enough. If that is so, it may be reasonable to consider that, when severe interference with the fundamental rights of individuals is at stake, the degree of distinctiveness required of the applicant's situation to satisfy the *Plaumann* test should not be set at the highest level. In addition, the fact that a measure may affect, to different extents, a variety of persons does not exclude 'individual concern' for those who can positively establish the very peculiar nature of their situation. A certain *souplesse* in appreciating whether the distinctive criterion is fulfilled would also address the environment paradox: despite their vital importance, issues of environmental protection, because of their general and collective nature,[145] do not easily find their way to a courtroom, unlike disputes concerning private economic interests,

[142] Generally, on this topic, de Sadeleer, 'Enforcing EUCHR Principles and Fundamental Rights in Environmental Cases', 81 *Nordic Journal of International Law* (2012) 39.

[143] See, in that regard, W. N. Hohfeld, *Fundamental Legal Conceptions as Applied in Judicial Reasoning and Other Legal Essays* (1919).

[144] Case C-565/19 P, *Carvalho and Others v. Parliament and Council* (EU:C:2021:252), para. 48. Emphasis added.

[145] See Opinion of AG Cosmas in Case C-321/95 P, *Greenpeace Council and Others v. Commission* (EU:C:1997:421), para. 102: '[E]nvironmental protection is indeed a matter of general interest. Conservation of the environment is a legal interest theoretically shared by all natural persons; it thus has a communal dimension. Furthermore, the more significant is the intervention in or impingement on the environment, the greater is the number of persons affected thereby.' See also Opinion of AG Kokott in Case C-260/11, *Edwards* (EU:C:2012:645), paras 40 and 42: 'Legal protection in environmental matters ... generally serves not only the individual interests of claimants, but also, or even exclusively, the public. ... Recognition of the public interest in environmental protection is especially important since there may be many cases where the legally protected interests of particular individuals are not affected or are affected only peripherally. However, the environment cannot defend itself before a court, but needs to be represented, for example by active citizens or non-governmental organisations.'

including very trivial ones. The more environmental harm is significant and widespread, the less likely it is that an applicant can challenge the EU measures allegedly responsible for such harm before the EU Courts.

In addition, as far as environmental protection is concerned, the 'access to justice' requirements flowing from the Aarhus Convention are not anodyne. Admittedly, the Union's participation in an international agreement does not permit the CJEU to interpret the Treaties *contra legem*. Its reluctance to reverse long-standing case law on concepts enshrined in EU primary law, such as the conditions for standing set out in Article 263 TFEU, is thus understandable. However, it is by no means clear why it should not be possible to take the rules of that agreement into account when it comes to (yet again) applying the *Plaumann* test in a specific case, in particular when an action is brought by an association and the CJEU is to check whether it falls in one of the three scenarios where standing is recognized.[146] If national courts should strive to apply their procedural laws in a manner which ensures compliance with the Aarhus Convention, it is difficult to understand why the Court could not; that would amount to an inexplicable double standard.[147] In that regard, one has to agree with AGs Jääskinen and Bobek who stressed the need for a consistent approach on this matter: 'what is required of the national courts must also be required of the EU Courts'.[148]

On the basis of the above, I wonder (just to give a few examples): would the local authorities (or the local association of fishermen) of an island affected by a fishing measure that concerns only the waters near that island not be in a situation which is sufficiently peculiar or differentiated from that of other individuals to consider that they are individually concerned by the measure? Similarly, should not an association which has as its statutory mission the protection of a specific geographic area or animal species, or to combat a certain type of environmental pollution, be considered to be peculiarly or distinctively affected by an EU measure which concerns that specific area, animal species, or type of environmental pollution? Likewise, would it not be reasonable to consider that the local (regional or municipal) authorities tasked with the responsibility and the powers to regulate certain public activities be in a distinctive situation

[146] On this issue, see Danthinne, Eliantonio, and Peeters, 'Justifying a Presumed Standing for Environmental NGOs: A Legal Assessment of Article 9(3) of the Aarhus Convention', 31 *Review of European Community and International Environmental Law* (2022) 411.

[147] See e.g. Schoukens (n. 4) 111; and Krämer, 'Access to Environmental Justice: the Double Standards of the ECJ', 14 *Journal for European Environmental and Planning Law* (2017) 159.

[148] Opinion of AG Bobek in Case C-352/19 P, *Région de Bruxelles-Capitale v. Commission* (EU:C:2020:588), para. 117, with reference to the Opinion of AG Jääskinen in Joined Cases C-401/12 P to C-403/12 P, *Vereniging Milieudefensie and Stichting Stop Luchtverontreiniging Utrecht* (EU:C:2014:310), para. 132.

when an EU act has immediate and significant repercussions on the manner in which they can (and by all means should) exercise their powers in those areas?

In my view, finding the applicants in the above-mentioned hypothetical scenarios to be individually concerned would not require any overruling of the *Plaumann* test and would not be inconsistent with the letter and spirit of Article 263(4) TFEU. In this context, I observe that, recently, there have been (i) a number of notable judgments in which the Grand Chamber of the Court reversed an overly restrictive application of the standing requirements, including that of 'individual concern', made by the General Court (*Montessori*, *Nord Stream 2*, and *Venezuela*[149]) and (ii) several Opinions from some Advocates General whose analyses of the concepts of 'direct concern' (AG Bobek[150]) and of 'regulatory act which does not entail any implementing measure' (AG Wathelet[151]), despite not having been followed by the Court, may have laid the groundwork for future developments on those matters.[152] Such a (relatively limited) relaxation of the standing requirements under Article 263(4) TFEU would also have, for the reasons explained earlier, a direct repercussion on the admissibility and likelihood of success of actions for failure to act and actions for non-contractual liability against the European Union.[153]

That notwithstanding, it can be safely said that, at present, the 'preferred way' for non-privileged applicants to challenge measures of general application should remain to act before the national courts against the domestic measures of transposition or implementation and then attempt to trigger a reference for a preliminary ruling on the validity of the original EU measure. Indeed, preliminary rulings offer—at least in theory—an alternative to direct

[149] Joined Cases C-622/16 P to C-624/16 P, *Scuola Elementare Maria Montessori v. Commission* (EU:C:2018:873) paras 19–68; Case C-348/20 P, *Nord Stream 2 v. Parliament and Council* (EU:C:2022:548), paras 42–115 and 151–166; and Case C-872/19 P, *Venezuela v. Council* (EU:C:2021:507), paras 61–94.

[150] Opinion of AG Bobek in Case C-352/19 P, *Région de Bruxelles-Capitale v. Commission* (EU:C:2020:588) and Opinion of AG Bobek in Joined Cases C-177/19 P to C-179/19 P, *Germany—Ville de Paris and Others v. Commission* (EU:C:2021:476).

[151] See the Opinions in Case C-132/12 P, *Stichting Woonpunt and Others* (EU:C:2013:324), paras 48–79; Case C-244/16 P, *Industrias Químicas del Vallés* (EU:C:2017:635), paras 37–58; and Case C-384/16 P, *European Union Copper Task Force* (EU:C:2017:634), paras 44–65. On the concept of a 'regulatory act that does not entail implementing measures', see also the Opinion of AG Bobek in Case C-352/19 P, *Région de Bruxelles-Capitale v. Commission* (EU:C:2020:588), paras 159–176.

[152] By contrast, a number of recent rulings from the General Court in environmental matters appear to make a rather restrictive application of the standing requirements: see inter alia, Case T-321/20, *enercity v. Commission* (EU:T:2023:253), paras 25 ff, and Case T-628/22, *Repasi v. Commission* (EU:T:2023:353), paras 23–38. In both cases, an appeal before the Court is currently pending.

[153] The latter aspect is also likely to have, in turn, a favourable repercussion on individuals' ability to bring actions for non-contractual liability against the Member States, since the two forms of action for liability are governed by the same principles.

actions before the CJEU. Yet this judicial route, too, suffers from a number of limitations.

First, their effectiveness depends on the national courts' willingness and ability to refer questions. Nevertheless, that problem should not be overemphasized, given that (i) questions regarding the validity of EU acts must, in principle, be referred and (ii) national courts of last instance must, in principle, also refer questions of interpretation. In addition, both the CJEU and the ECtHR have found that, if national courts of last instance decide not to refer, despite the parties' invitation to do so, they are under an obligation to explain to them the reasons for that.[154]

Second, the overall procedure (national court → CJEU → national court) is obviously more cumbersome, time-consuming, and (quite possibly) costly than one before only one court. That said, it is also true that direct actions by non-privileged applicants before the CJEU would also be dealt with by (up to) two levels of adjudication: first instance before the General Court, followed by a possible appeal before the Court. Third, where at the heart of the dispute are the choices made at the EU level, and not by the central/local government when transposing or implementing the related EU act, most of the proceedings take place before the *least* well-placed court.[155] That appears to go against the principle of the *sedes materiae* (i.e. the seat of the matter),[156] something that is *a fortiori* puzzling after the reform of the EU judicial architecture, which doubled the size of the General Court, giving it the resources to review more and potentially more complex disputes.[157]

As far as review of Member States' conduct is concerned, we have seen that such a review is based on two complementary pillars. On the one hand, there

[154] See, respectively, Court of Justice, Case C-561/19, *Consorzio Italian Management* (EU:C:2021:799), para. 51, and ECtHR, *Dhahbi v. Italy*, Appl. no. 17120/09, Judgment of 8 April 2014, para. 33. All ECtHR decisions are available at http://hudoc.echr.coe.int/. See also Opinion of AG Emiliou in Case C-144/23, *Kubera* (EU:C:2024:522), paras 122–133.

[155] See also Opinion of AG Jacobs in Case C-50/00 P, *Unión de Pequeños Agricultores v. Council* ('*UPA*') (EU:C:2002:197) para. 41: 'In a case concerning the validity of a Community measure, the competence of the national court is limited to assessing whether the applicant's arguments raise sufficient doubts about the validity of the impugned measure to justify a request for a preliminary ruling from the Court of Justice. It seems to me, therefore, artificial to argue that the national courts are the correct forum for such cases. The strictly limited competence of national courts in cases concerning the validity of Community measures may be contrasted with the important role which they play in cases concerning the interpretation, application and enforcement of Community law. In such cases, the national courts may ... be described as the ordinary courts of Community law. That description is, however, not appropriate for cases which do not involve questions of interpretation, but raise only issues of the validity of Community measures, since in such cases the national courts do not have power to decide what is at issue.'

[156] See Winter (nn. 4 and 67).

[157] See Opinion of AG Bobek in Case C-352/19 P, *Région de Bruxelles-Capitale v. Commission* (EU:C:2020:588), paras 142–146.

is a centralized system of judicial review which has, at its heart, infringement proceedings under Articles 258 to 260 TFEU. On the other hand, there is a system of review that is of a diffuse nature and mainly guided by the pursuit of private interests. That is carried out by the national courts that are seized of disputes in which the compatibility with EU law of some national measure is called into question by the parties. Those procedures are generally governed by national law, in accordance with the principle of procedural autonomy.

Infringement proceedings appear to be rather effective (also thanks to the financial penalties[158] that can now be imposed on Member States in default even during the interim stage) but they depend on the goodwill of, and resources available to, the Commission (and, indirectly, of the complainants). That said, it is also true that ensuring Member States' compliance with EU environmental legislation has always been a priority for the Commission and the sheer number of cases opened, investigated, and ultimately brought before the Court in that field on a yearly basis confirms that.[159] The downsides of this procedure are, mainly, that there is a limited role for private parties and the average time taken by the procedure(s) is significant.

In turn, the effectiveness of the proceedings before the national courts is hard to assess. It is safe to assume that it will also vary from Member State to Member State, in the light of their different rules on judicial proceedings. That is why, back in 2003, the Commission proposed a directive of the European Parliament and of the Council on access to justice in environmental matters, with the dual objective of implementing the Aarhus Convention and of 'fulfil[ing] some shortcomings in controlling the application of environmental law'.[160] However, the proposal was withdrawn as obsolete in 2014[161] and the Commission went on to publish an interpretative notice on that matter in 2017[162] and announce new initiatives in a communication of 2020.[163]

[158] On the effectiveness of penalties, see e.g. UK House of Lords, 'Brexit: environment and climate change', Report published on 14 February 2017, ch. 4, para. 70.

[159] On this matter, see extensively Smith, 'Enforcing Environmental Law through Infringements and Sanctioning: Steering not Rowing', in Peeters and Eliantonio (n. 4) 213.

[160] COM/2003/0624 final.

[161] For a comment, published shortly before the withdrawal, see J.-F. Brakeland, 'Access to Justice in Environmental Matters—Developments at EU Level', 5 *Gyoseiho-kenkyu* (2014). For another comment, published shortly after the withdrawal, see Eliantonio, 'The Proceduralisation of EU Environmental Legislation: International Pressures, Some Victories and Some Way to Go', 8 *Review of European Administrative Law* (2015) 99.

[162] Commission Notice on access to justice in environmental matters (2017/C 275/01).

[163] Commission Communication, Improving access to justice in environmental matters in the EU and its Member States (COM/2020/643 final), see esp. paras 28 ff.

6. Conclusions

The research question explored in this chapter was whether, with regard to EU environmental law, the system of legal remedies set up in the EU Treaties is actually complete and generally effective. It seems to me that there is no simple 'yes or no' answer to that question. In fact, a certain subjectivity in the evaluation appears almost inevitable and, consequently, the answer would depend, to some extent, on the observer's perspective. For example, certain features of the judicial proceedings examined in this chapter could be regarded by a constitutional or public international lawyer as normal and almost inevitable characteristics of procedures taking place before a supranational court. At the same time, an environmental lawyer could take the view that those features create, de facto, nearly insurmountable obstacles for individuals, associations, and local authorities to challenge measures that may be harmful for the environment, rendering effective judicial protection in this area to some extent illusory. From a legitimacy perspective, therefore, whilst the appropriate constitutional process values may be enhanced, the environmental outcomes may suffer. The balance between the integrity of governance processes in general and the relationship this has with the specific challenges of environmental decision-making are brought to the fore.

In this context, it would seem that, to date, the amendment of Article 263 TFEU made by the Treaty of Lisbon, the entry into force of the Aarhus Convention, and the adoption of the Aarhus Regulation have not significantly altered the situation as regards standing of private applicants, and in particular of environmental associations.[164] Admittedly, the modification of the Aarhus Regulation—mainly prompted by negative 'Findings and Recommendations' of the Aarhus Convention Compliance Committee (ACCC), issued in two parts in 2011 and 2017[165]—appears to some extent promising[166] but it is too recent to permit any final assessment in that respect. In addition, the measures which the Union envisages to adopt in the next few years, in the context of

[164] See, Eliantonio, 'Towards an Ever Dirtier Europe? The Restrictive Standing of Environmental NGOs before the European Courts and the Aarhus Convention', 7 *Croation Yearbook of European Law and Policy* (2012) 69, at 81–82; Eliantonio, 'The Role of NGOs in Environmental Implementation Conflicts: "Stuck in the Middle" between Infringement Proceedings and Preliminary Rulings?', 40 *Journal of European Integration* (2018) 753; Hadjianni (n. 4) 786–787 and 797; and Schouckens (n. 4) 85 ff.

[165] See documents ACCC/C/2008/32 (Part I) of 14 April 2011 and ACCC/C/2008/32 (Part II) of 17 March 2017. In that regard, see extensively Hedemann-Robinson, 'Access to Environmental Justice and European Union Institutional Compliance with the Aarhus Convention: A Rather Longer and More Winding Road than Anticipated', 31 *European Energy and Environmental Law Review* (2022) 175.

[166] See Hedemann-Robinson (n. 165).

the Green Deal[167]—should they be challenged in court—could provide further opportunities to develop the case law,[168] also in respect of procedural issues which may have remained relatively unexplored to date.[169]

That said, it seems to me that, regardless of the perspective adopted by the observer, any reasonable evaluation of the system cannot overlook the fact that certain elements thereof must be taken as 'given'. First, one must accept that, as in most other legal systems, an *actio popularis* against legislative acts does not exist.[170] Second, given that the European Union is not a nation state, the system of judicial remedies must be considered as being composed of proceedings before both the CJEU and the national courts. Third, environmental protection is, under Article 4(2)(e) TFEU, a shared competence of the Union and the Member States.[171] Not only: several provisions of the Treaties give Member States some leeway in introducing higher standards of protection that those agreed at EU level.[172] It is thus not surprising that, in this field, most EU legislation is adopted in the form of directives, an act that—under Article 288 TFEU—is 'binding, as to the result to be achieved ... but [leaves] to the national authorities the choice of form and methods'.[173] Fourth, as regards EU measures which embody choices made by institutions which enjoyed policy and/or technical discretion, the standard of review applied by the EU judiciary—in accordance with the principles of separation of powers and institutional balance—consists of verifying whether the rules on procedure and on the statement of reasons have been complied with, whether the facts have been accurately stated, and whether there has been any manifest error of assessment of the facts or misuse of powers.[174] Fifth, there are some structural limits, flowing from the very text of the Treaties' provisions, when it comes to the Court's jurisdiction and powers: an EU act may be set aside (actions for annulment) or declared invalid (preliminary rulings on validity), an EU institution

[167] Commission, The European Green Deal, COM/2019/640 final.

[168] Setzer *et al.* (n. 117) 27.

[169] Including lines of arguments (e.g. on standing) which have not, so far, been put forward (or, at least, fully developed) before the EU Courts. Cf. Pagano, 'Overcoming Plaumann in EU Environmental Litigation—An Analysis of ENGOs Legal Arguments in Actions for Annulment', *Diritto e Processo* (2019) 311, at 357–360.

[170] That feature is compatible with the ECHR. As the ECtHR has consistently held, 'Article 6 does not guarantee a right of access to a court with power to invalidate or override a law enacted by the legislature'. See e.g. ECtHR, *Posti and Rahko v. Finland*, Appl. no. 27824/95, Judgment of 3 September 2002, para. 52.

[171] See, extensively, L. Krämer, *EU Environmental Law* (7th edn, 2011) ch. 7.

[172] Arts 144(4) and (5) and 191(2) TFEU.

[173] Similarly, K. Lenaerts, 'Climate Change as a Challenge for Constitutional Law and Constitutional Courts', speech, Berlin, 4/5 May 2023.

[174] See, with further references, Opinion of AG Emiliou in *ECB v. Crédit Lyonnais* (n. 71) paras 54 and 55.

may be declared in breach of its obligations for having failed to adopt an act (actions for failure to act) or ordered to make good the damage caused (actions for liability), and a Member State may be declared in breach of EU law directly (infringement proceedings) or by implication (preliminary rulings on interpretation). However, it is then for the competent EU or national authorities to draw all the appropriate consequences from the CJEU's rulings: the CJEU can issue injunctions or other similar measures and impose financial penalties only in the context of some specific procedures.

In conclusion, the overall system of judicial remedies is, currently, one of 'bits and pieces'. Admittedly, it may not be easy for private parties to identify the competent (national or EU) court with regard to a given matter, which may force them to start parallel proceedings in several fora, only 'to be on the safe side'. Also, it is not clear that, in all cases, the parties are actually able to bring before the CJEU, directly or indirectly, a dispute that turns on the validity and/or interpretation of EU law. As previously mentioned, that situation of fragmentation and, possibly, lack of legal certainty entails costs and delays for the applicants. It goes without saying that, in environmental matters, time is often of the essence.

The CJEU is obviously not unaware of the special characteristics of environmental law and the importance and urgency of the subject matter of the disputes brought before it.[175] Yet, there are certain structural and systemic aspects of EU procedural laws which limit the effectiveness of the system of judicial review in that field and over which the CJEU has limited or no control. Moreover, there is no 'silver bullet' to tackle all the issues relating to access to justice in environmental matters.[176] That said, a less rigid application of the criteria set out in Article 263(4) TFEU for the standing of non-privileged applicants—in line with the suggestions made by several Advocates General—would probably go a long way towards achieving a more balanced approach in that regard. The key question in that respect is how far could (or should) the CJEU go in re-examining and clarifying its well-established case law on certain general principles of EU law and the procedural provisions set out in the Treaties in order to take into account the special characteristics and the importance and urgency of disputes raising major issues of environmental protection. From a legitimacy standpoint, it is in this trade-off that we can see the ways in which

[175] See e.g. Opinion of AG Ćapeta in Case C-116/22, *Commission v. Germany* (EU:C:2023:317), para. 1, citing Sir D. Attenborough.

[176] See Kingston, 'Mind the Gap: Difficulties in Enforcement and the Continuing Unfulfilled Promise of EU Environmental Law', in S. Kingston (ed.), *European Perspectives on Environmental Law and Governance* (2013) 175.

the criteria for legitimacy in the governance of environmental problems can pull in two directions. As we have seen in other chapters, however, who decides how this balance is struck is of as much importance as the balance itself. In the context of remedies, the strong judicial reliance on the text of the Treaties emphasizes that these rules are of relevance far beyond the environmental context and are interpreted in a way which reflects that.

8

Conclusions

Mariolina Eliantonio and Emma Lees

1. Introduction

Throughout this volume we have witnessed two important phenomena relating to the contribution of judicial decisions and processes (in particular those of the European courts) to the legitimacy of EU environmental governance as a whole. These concluding comments draw out some of the consequences of these two phenomena, not only for the courts but for the EU political system in general.

First, it is clear that the courts' contributions to the governance frameworks on which they adjudicate are not monolithic—the ways in which those contributions are modulated through specific contexts are critical to an understanding of EU environmental governance as a whole. There are myriad examples within our authors' contributions of the enormous importance of paying attention to the specific legal context within which questions of environmental protection are asked. Of course, it is possible to take questions of contingency too far, such that we would be precluded from drawing any useful conclusions, but the primary lesson of focusing on context—that legal questions do not arise in isolation from legal culture—is hugely important in assessing the relationship between courts and legitimacy.

For that reason, broad generalizations about the judicial role, such as that a court is 'pro-environment', are unhelpful. Rather, as we have seen through our authors' contributions, it is in the detail of the courts' approaches that we find the nuance in the courts' roles and therefore the value in analysis.

Second, in assessing the courts' contributions to the legitimacy of the governance system as a whole, we have needed not only to look at environmental contributions but to wider questions relating to their proper judicial role and how that role interacts with the pressing concerns of environmental degradation. In other words, consideration of the relationship between the European courts and the legitimacy of EU environmental governance not only requires

Mariolina Eliantonio and Emma Lees, *Conclusions* In: *The Legitimacy of EU Environmental Governance and the Role of the European Courts*. Edited by: Mariolina Eliantonio and Emma Lees, Oxford University Press.
 DOI: 10.1093/oso/9780198972808.003.0008

us to examine what the courts have done and how, but also to examine more deeply what we understand legitimate governance to be in an era of pressing environmental concerns.

In concluding this volume, we therefore seek to bring together the assessments of our authors through the lens of these two issues. First, in what ways does context appear to modulate the courts' apparent understanding of the proper judicial role and, second, how does the environment per se seem to be influencing this understanding.

2. The Relevance of Legal Context

In this volume, we have striven to ensure that our approach is one which appreciates the critical importance of legal context. De Sadeleer's comments in Chapter 4 that 'the relationship between the free market and environmental protection is not always resolved either with the same balance struck or by reference to the same legal techniques'[1] rings true in sentiment for the totality of our contributions. Discussions of the role of environmental principles cannot be convincing unless those discussions also recognize the broader constitutional questions surrounding the allocation of power between court and administrative authority. Evaluation of the rules on standing requires appreciation not only of the desire of environmental actors to bring cases before judicial organs, but of how the EU governance system divides responsibility for adjudicating on issues of concern between national and European actors. Considerations of environmental restrictions on trade demand a deep understanding of the rules relating to the free market more generally and how they, too, are nuanced and specific. Similar comments could be made in relation to all questions this volume has asked.

Elsewhere, one of us has described the processes of environmental adjudication as involving the insertion of a 'green' filter onto courts' reasoning, in the manner of a theatrical light.[2] The filter does not change the direction or power of the light, but it changes its character. That is equally what we see when we consider the environmental adjudication occurring in the European context. Depending on what other choices are made, however, the impact of that green filter can be decidedly weak or it can create fundamental revolutions in approach. Thus, the power of the filter is affected by the precise legal context

[1] See Chapter 1, Section 1.

[2] E. Lees and O. W. Pedersen, *Environmental Adjudication* (2022) ch. 2.

within which the court is operating; and the insertion of that filter into judicial processes is not a 'given' but rather challenges our preconceptions about, for example, the contribution which a *policy-neutral* judiciary makes to the legitimacy of a political system. Nevertheless, whilst monolithic conclusions are unhelpful, some commonalities are visible in how and when legal context seems to diminish the power of environmental concerns in shaping the courts' response.

First, and perhaps unsurprisingly, as Winter's example in Chapter 5 shows, the CJEU appears to be rather unwilling to innovate or adapt its jurisprudence or process in cases of fundamental constitutional balance, be that in the case of constitutional allocations of power between decision-makers or in the process of shaping EU fundamental rights in an environmentally-friendly fashion, or in the constitutional principles of the EU itself in terms, for example, of market freedom or energy sovereignty. In legitimacy terms, if one approaches the question from the angle that courts are primarily mandated to uphold rule-of-law values, then this relatively uncompromising approach would be entirely appropriate. The consequence of this, however, is that 'legitimate' environmental governance, as modulated through the courts, may also be environmentally harmful. Legitimacy in this sense is not always equated to environmental protection.

A useful example of this can also be found in Chapter 3, where Lees shows that the CJEU was particularly unwilling to interfere in the question of nuclear power because a subtle balance between the pro- and anti-nuclear Member States had already been ensured in the foundation of the European Union through the principle of energy sovereignty. Given the different approaches to nuclear power (and its relevance for the low-carbon transition), the Court did not use a 'pro environment' approach to challenge an existing settlement between the Union's Member States. As Lees argues, the relatively hands-off approach there, 'tells us something about the interaction between the precautionary principle and known risk, and the balance of democratic values, in contrast to the role this principle plays in handling unknowns and uncertainty, where it weighs in to read the evidence in such a way as to transform doubt into proof of risk'.[3] In other words, in matters of constitutional balance, democratic values and individual state sovereignty weight heavily in the courts' reasoning.

[3] See Chapter 3, Section 3.C.

This can be seen, too, in how Prete assesses the role of the courts. In Chapter 7, he argues that:

> [C]ertain features of the judicial proceedings examined in this chapter could be regarded by a constitutional or public international lawyer as normal and almost inevitable characteristics of procedures taking place before a supranational court. At the same time, an environmental lawyer could take the view that those features create, de facto, nearly insurmountable obstacles for individuals, associations, and local authorities to challenge measures that may be harmful for the environment, rendering effective judicial protection in this area to some extent illusory.[4]

This highlights that the constitutional lawyer, who is assessing not environmental protection but the balance of power between state actors, is more concerned with how a judicial decision affects that power than they are with the substance of the outcome. When faced with decisions which can profoundly affect that balance of power, courts, too, tend to be more focused on the systemic consequences of the decisions they reach than with the environmental outcome which thereby emerges.

This is not to say, of course, that the environmental consequences of such a decision are not important. De Sadeleer shows that, 'the Court's role in allocating power between the Member States and the Union has important consequences in that it allows or precludes a higher level of environmental protection than the harmonized EU standards'.[5] Thus, the resolution of constitutional law balances is not without environmental consequences, even where that is not the primary focus of the court's logic. Furthermore, as de Sadeleer's chapter discusses, these environmental consequences are not irrelevant to the court's reasoning and indeed motivate much of the jurisprudence cited in this volume.

The courts—both European and national—are, however, more willing to use the environmental context as relevant to their decision when they are being asked not to adjust the proper judicial role but, rather, to demand more or better information, to enhance the quality of decision-making processes, or to reconceptualize the kinds of protection which are available to citizens within the EU. This is demonstrated with great precision by Iordachescu and Krajewski in Chapter 6 when considering the legal techniques employed to

[4] See Chapter 7, Section 6.
[5] See Chapter 4, Section 1.

handle scientific uncertainties. In particular, when considering how the courts and other adjudicative fora overcome a lack of knowledge in relation to serious risks, the authors demonstrate that the use of environmental principles actually provides a robust and legitimate way to overcome such uncertainty. Here, the courts are operating in their traditional role—that of overseers of the use of state power—but do so recognizing the responsibilities of the state in terms of environmental preservation. Similarly, Eliantonio and Petropoulou Ionescu in Chapter 2 show that the EU Courts do use soft law, despite its non-binding nature, to overcome the lack of knowledge and scientific expertise in-house, something which, they argue 'contribute[s] to a better understanding of environmental problems by national authorities and courts alike, thereby ultimately leading to more legitimate environmental governance'.[6]

How much the pressure emerging from environmental questions changes judicial attitudes, the techniques the courts will employ, or their own assessment of the limits of their power, however, is not homogenous as Winter's chapter amply reveals. In comparing the German, Norwegian, English, and European courts, Winter shows that a court 'will ... look at the circumstances on a case-by-case basis and will be heavily influenced by the legal culture in which it is based, and also by the personal attitudes and political affiliations of the judges'.[7] These matters of culture are not to be taken lightly.

In the context of fundamental rights, the courts are specifically faced with a double challenge—fundamental rights jurisprudence has an enormous impact on the power of the state but the upholding of such rights is absolutely central to the proper judicial role. Thus, the courts are specifically tasked with managing the boundaries of such constitutional imperatives and, as such, perhaps feel more able to reshape such rights to reflect contemporary concerns. Similarly, when it comes to the use of soft law instruments, courts are in a delicate constitutional situation, which is specific to the peculiar (and, from a legal point of view, uncertain) status of soft law in the EU legal order. As Eliantonio and Petropoulou Ionescu argue, the CJEU can be '"damned' if it does engage with soft law by endowing it with an "epistemic force" which it was arguably not supposed to have and equally "damned" if it disregards relevant scientific knowledge and only relies on its non-specialist background'.[8]

[6] Chapter 2, Section 1.
[7] Chapter 5, Section 7.A.
[8] Chapter 2, Section 5.

3. Environmental Concern and Legitimacy

As mentioned, however, it is important not to take questions of contingency too far. Although it is more than clear that specificity is important when considering the relationship between the courts and the legitimacy of governance, it is nevertheless possible to conclude that there is a very profound relationship between that legitimacy and the environment itself.

Indeed, perhaps the most important conclusion that we have drawn in the writing of this volume, and the analysis of our authors' contributions, is that environmental concerns are, without doubt, having a profound influence on how we understand 'good governance' and the judicial role in it. Concerns of long-standing, particularly those relating to the rule of law—legal certainty, clarity, and non-retroactivity are now being considered alongside much more recent ideas relating to the preservation and enhancement of the natural environment as essential criteria for successful governance and for legitimate judicial action. Departures from the strictures of certainty are justified and permitted by the reality of the environmental situation as the role of the environmental principles amply demonstrates. Similarly, the sacrosanct primacy given to the free market is also challenged by environmental concerns in a way which is barely permitted to many other pressing societal pressures.

We can see this profound challenge about what constitutes legitimacy in the use of state power in the contributions of our authors. For example, Winter's chapter demonstrates very clearly that the boundaries of the responsibility of the courts are being deeply affected by the impact that environmental harm will have on the citizenry of Europe. Courts are required to address such impact head-on. In doing so, the courts have to address the tensions in their role, and in the legitimacy of that role, to accept that they have environmental responsibilities. This responsibility adds to their existing responsibilities in important ways. As Winter concludes, 'judicial self-restraint has its place in the weighing up of the interference with preponderant public interests and in the choosing of mitigation measures. However, this should not amount to fundamentally denying the judiciary from assuming its proper role as the guardian of fundamental rights.'[9] This 'proper role' is one deeply impacted by the real-world consequences of climate change and biodiversity loss, amongst others.

Having said this, as Chapter 3 concerning environmental principles also shows, an attitude of environmental protection not only challenges existing standards of legitimacy in a conflictual way. Rather, the two can also work

[9] Chapter 5, Section 8.

together. Here, where courts are challenged by uncertain or inconsistent evidence, and the limits of their own capacity, the environmental principles as much as soft law instruments help render decisions in the face of uncertainty more consistent, clear, and predictable. In doing so, as Lees argues in Chapter 3, it is important to ensure that such uncertainties are not swept under the carpet.[10] The capacity of 'tools of environmental governance' to support courts in fulfilling the proper judicial role of scrutiny, supervision, and upholding of the values of rule of law, by necessity, supports the contribution of the courts to the legitimacy of the political system as a whole.

Iordachescu and Krajewski reach a similar conclusion—emphasizing that too much deference on the part of the courts not only risks environmental protection but can also tend to undermine effective judicial oversight of the use of state power. Thus, 'When courts shy away from delving into complex and uncertain empirical assessments linked to legal issues, despite such assessments appearing significant for the outcome of the disputes, the goals of judicial proceedings, such as upholding the rule of law or effective judicial protection, seem to be at risk.'[11] At the same time, as Eliantonio and Petropoulou Ionescu warn, when soft law is at stake, an increase in the scientific and administrative capacity of courts through the use of soft law instruments, while increasing the epistemic legitimacy of judicial decisions, might bring about risks for the political legitimacy of those very decisions.[12]

By bringing together a framework for legitimacy that embraces not only rule-of-law values, such as transparency, consistency, predictability, and accessibility, but also environmental outcomes, this volume has brought these potential dilemmas for courts and their proper function in the governance framework to the fore.

4. Final Word

In editing and contributing to this work, we struggled to conceptualize legitimacy and to set up a framework against which we can test the actions of courts. But as the previous comments show, this should not be a surprise. Not only is such a nebulous concept hard to define, and sometimes internally inconsistent, but, more profoundly, its content is moulded by the context in which

[10] Chapter 3, Section 3.
[11] Chapter 6, Section 1.
[12] Chapter 2, Section 5.

the question is being asked. That context is a subtle one, built up not only of environmental concerns but of a myriad of legal rules and principles, old and new, which interact together when a court is required to answer the legal question before it.

If we do not delve into the nuances which those rules and principles bring, and instead attempt a monolithic answer to what role the courts play in enhancing the legitimacy of EU environmental governance, we fail to appreciate the subtleties of the judicial role. However, even more importantly, by acknowledging the power of context and of detail, we can also see the ways in which environmental degradation is shifting how the courts, and how we, assess what legitimate governance actually consists of. In our definition of legitimacy, we cannot but include environmental protection as part of the balance. The role of the court, therefore, is not only to enhance the legitimacy of governance but to enhance the very conception of what legitimate governance is.

Index

For the benefit of digital users, indexed terms that span two pages (e.g., 52–53) may, on occasion, appear on only one of those pages.